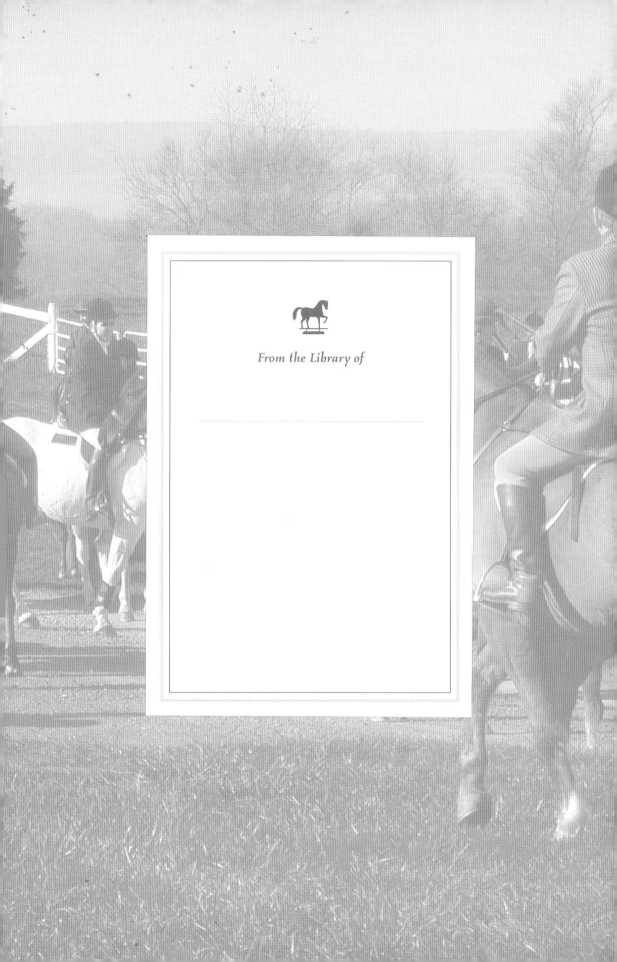

From the Library of

# A COMMUNITY OF THE HORSE

## Partnerships

*Bruce Smart*

**Bruce Smart**

# DEDICATION

This book is dedicated to

Edith Merrill Smart

and

Her Horses

For the Love, Companionship, and Inspiration

without which

This journey could not have been undertaken.

A COMMUNITY OF THE HORSE – Partnerships
by Bruce Smart

Published by Lost Mountain Graphics, a division of Novascope, Inc.
200 Stonewall Avenue, P.O. Box 1590, Middleburg, Virginia 20118
www.lostmtn.com

Library of Congress Cataloging-in-Publication Data
Smart, Bruce
A Community Of The Horse – Partnerships / by Bruce Smart
First Edition
Non-fiction

ISBN 0-9745424-0-7


Designed at Lost Mountain Graphics, Middleburg, Virginia
Printed at Mid-Atlantic Printing Company, Alta Vista, Virginia

Printed in the United States of America
October, 2003
First Edition

# ACKNOWLEDGEMENTS

*This book is the product of many people; after all, it is the story of a community. Recognizing by name every one who contributed, directly or indirectly, is manifestly impossible. Collectively, though we thank all who helped — by thought, word, deed or graven image — to develop this picture of our Community of the Horse, an association that we all share and treasure. More specific recognition, however, is due certain essential participants, most of whose names accompany their contributions appearing in the pages that follow. The author is especially grateful to:*

The many patient souls who welcomed him to their homes and stables, introduced him to their horses and submitted graciously to interviews.

The experts who read pieces of the text for completeness and accuracy, and made many helpful suggestions. Any errors that remain are the author's.

Those who took the time to prepare significant written pieces specifically for this book.

Those whose writings for other audiences have contributed to our understanding of the horse history and horse sports of the Virginia Piedmont, hopefully with appropriate recognition when they have been quoted directly.

The research facilities — The Middleburg Library, The Museum of Hounds and Hunting, *The Chronicle of the Horse*, the Meadow Outdoors Foundation and especially The National Sporting Library and their staffs. The hours spent with them are among the most pleasant memories of this endeavor.

The photographers — amateur and professional — who have allowed the use of their artistry and their archives to add visual depth to the written words. They are in every sense co-authors. If you admire a specific picture, please take the time to note who provided it.

The members of the Trappe Hill Farm team — Betsy and Jerry Crenshaw, Jeremy Denson, Leslie and Wayne VanSant — who have been gracious in supporting the author in this work, forgiving his occasional neglect of farm needs. They are family, and we refer to them often using only their first names.

Finally, the staff of Lost Mountain Graphics, whose enthusiasm sustained the project in its early stages, and whose editorial and design skills later brought it to maturity.

Working with all of you to tell our collective story has been one of life's great pleasures. Thank you.

# FOREWORD

By John Strassburger, Editor, *The Chronicle of the Horse*

Though it's been more than 20 years since I was an American Studies major at Dickinson College in Carlisle, Pa., I can still remember my indoctrination into the method that forms the basis for that branch of study. It's called ethnography, an anthropological term for a text or journal describing a particular culture or subculture at a certain point in time. The ethnography's purpose is to determine, describe and analyze the social, political, economic, familial, historic and other factors that give a culture its personality and its sense of community.

This is essentially what Bruce Smart has done in this, his first of three volumes on the equestrian community of the Northern Virginia Piedmont.

Bruce writes in the Preface that his goal is to tell the community's story primarily through the words of the people that live and work there. And he does just that through thousands of personal observations and experiences and through both brief and in depth interviews with what seems like hundreds of people. He's sought many of them out expressly for the purpose of this work, but many more are simply people he and his wife, Edie, have met through the normal course of their lives within the equestrian community.

Indeed, through Bruce's efforts, even long-time residents will learn about people they have only met at a race meet, out hunting or at a party. And "out-of-towners" will feel as if they too have lived here for 20 or 30 years.

The area surrounding the towns of Middleburg, Upperville, Berryville, The Plains and Warrenton is home to an unusual but not entirely unique equestrian community. While growing up, and then as editor of *The Chronicle of the Horse* since 1986, I've spent a fair amount of time in what I call the "equestrian ghettoes" of this country, places like Bedminster / Peapack in New Jersey, Unionville in Pennsylvania, Southern Pines and Tryon in North Carolina, Aiken and Camden in South Carolina, South Hamilton in Massachusetts, Millbrook in New York, Wayne in Illinois, and Lexington in Kentucky.

Each of these lovely places has a similarity in that you can walk into the Safeway or the Post Office in breeches and boots without a sense of embarrassment, you regularly see horse trailers parked in the street, and words like "fetlock," "furlong," and "martingale" knowingly pepper conversations in restaurants and bars. But each of these towns has dissimilarities in climate, flora, geography and – often consequently – in the horse sports they favor.

I think , though, that the northern Virginia Piedmont has a broader diversity of equine participants than any of these others - as Bruce demonstrates. I've always been amazed at how little some participants in one horse sport know about their neighbors who participate in another. Horse people often develop such tunnel vision that they never realize that one or more people who have legendary status or influence in another sport live in the same community, perhaps even just down the road.

I'd bet that many, perhaps even a majority of the steeplechasing set have no idea that the area has been the eventing capital of the United States for almost the entire last decade  — or that all four members of the 2000 Olympic eventing team live here (including gold medalist David O'Connor.). And I'd bet that most of the eventers who live or migrate here to train have no idea of the influence the area's residents – many of them interviewed by Bruce – have on the worlds of foxhunting and steeplechasing.

In a way, Bruce Smart has written a time capsule that should help bring a sense of communal history to the people who live here, a place that is devoted to the horse and, I hope, will always stay that way.

John Strassburger
August, 2003

# PREFACE

Preface

The seeds of this book lie in an earlier effort, a personal memoir entitled *Indian Summer*. In writing that book it became apparent that in rural northern Virginia and adjacent areas horses play an unique role in bringing people together, creating what we are calling *A Community of the Horse*. And so, with some outside encouragement and considerable internal enthusiasm, we set about exploring the relationships that result in this "Community."

To do so it seemed best to let members of the Community tell its story as they see and have experienced it, in their own words wherever possible. However, as Community members ourselves, it has been tempting, and easy, and perhaps even necessary to include personal experiences. Hopefully the reader will understand and forgive these autobiographical insertions.

Unfortunately, it is impossible to include every individual and activity that is a part of our Community's fabric. Almost every discussion of the subject identified several more people and events that deserved to be covered. The author hopes he will be forgiven for his inability to follow up on all of these suggestions, and that those who are quoted or pictured herein adequately represent the many more who are not.

Like its predecessor, *Indian Summer*, this book is compiled from a collection of writings – essays, interviews and descriptions of events – made over the period of years adjacent to the advent of the new century. These pieces have now been arranged in what is hoped to be a logical development of the subject. Inevitably this sequencing has led to inconsistencies in chronology, with recent happenings often appearing in the text ahead of earlier occurrences.

And, during the years the picture has been developing, some players – horses, people, institutions – have changed or moved on, while others have newly appeared. So we present neither a snapshot of an instant in time, nor a chronological moving picture. Instead we describe a sampling of the personalities, experience, opinions and events encountered, the observations made, and the memories retained during a random walk of several years through the horse country of the Virginia Piedmont.

The writer hopes the reader will enjoy following along this path, savoring both the familiar and the less well known aspects of our time and place. For himself, he knows that his journey has confirmed and strengthened his respect, gratitude and affection for his neighbors and the horses that connect us to one another.

*Bruce Smart*

# INTRODUCTION

*The author's father and Freelance winning the Master's Plate,*
*Fairfield and Westchester Hounds Hunter Trials, c. 1930*

H orses have lurked in the periphery of my whole life. My father rode hunters and show jumpers in amateur classes in the 1920's, and hunted with the Fairfield and Westchester Hounds until the unpleasantness that followed the crash of 1929 put an end to those pastimes for him.

As his business fortunes revived somewhat he was determined to supply my two sisters and me with a modest horse apiece, which we cared for, rode around the Bedford, New York, countryside, and exhibited in local shows. Inevitably, as my sisters proved more competent as riders, I drifted away to strictly masculine teenage sports, and in due course World War II interrupted our family's horse ownership.

Some years later I became aware that my future wife Edie had a long standing and competing love affair with a bevy of equines: her old pony Buster, her father's ex-hunter Charlie, her neighbors the Kuhns' Ladybird, and a series of classy Thoroughbred hunters that she rode and showed for older Bedford ladies. One soft spring evening we visited some of these (the show hunters, not the older ladies) in their stable. There, in the dusk and warmth of their home, I found them beautiful, intriguing, and very cuddly – perhaps because those were also my feelings for the girl I was with.

Gentle inquiry disclosed that owning one of those animals – in fact any horse – was then economically far beyond our reach. I resolved then that some day I would make it possible for Edie to have such a horse of her own. And, more selfishly, I thought I might also enjoy its company.

A fall wedding was followed by the intermingling of children, army recall, and several job-related moves. Eventually we found ourselves living in suburban Chicago, with a horse-addicted young daughter among our four children. Riding lessons led to ownership of a small show hunter, which we boarded further out in the country.

A move to Connectcut expanded the horse opportunity, and eventually a succession of horses led to having two living at home, stabled in what was once a garage so that the cars could enjoy the outdoor weather. In due course our by now two horse-inclined daughters abandonned equines for college and the company of young gentlemen (at least we hoped they were gentlemen), and their mother inherited the horses and discovered foxhunting in the Connecticut wilds.

A government job led to a move to Virginia, escalating Edie's hunting fever. Following government service, Upperville, Virginia, became our permanent home. In order avoid the perils of chasing foxes across uneven country at high speed, I took up breeding horses as a means of establishing contact with our horse-centered community. Soon thereafter, in the midnight presence of a tired broodmare and the foal she and we had just delivered, there was an epiphany – I became hooked on horses too.

For years I had thought of the human – horse relationship as that of master – servant, or perhaps, wise human – dumb animal. But over the last few years here in Virginia it has become clear that the connection is a lot more balanced and complex than that. In trying to understand that relationship lie the seeds of this book, for those are very special bonds that connect the horseman to his horse, and horse people to each other.

These interconnections tie much of our Northern Virginia Piedmont community into a web of love, respect, and interdependence, adding depth and meaning to our lives, and a living as well as a way of life for many of our friends and neighbors. This book is therefore an exploration into why people honor, revere, and love horses, how horses bring people together, how they permeate our culture and our economy, and a celebration of that special quality the horse lends to our existence.

One day a friend from Washington, an inhabitant of another world, was visiting us at the Orange County Point-to-Point. We stood on the hill by the announcer's stand, watching the preliminary hunt team relay races, a melange of horses, ponies, kids, pink coats, small jumps and spectators against a backdrop of spring meadows falling away to the Blue Ridge. Our friend Wendy said, almost in awe:

*"It's just like a painting!"*

And she was right. Art, it seems to me, is an effort to capture a moment so that it may be remembered, savored perhaps, for many years after its time is past. In the kaleidescope of history nothing lasts forever. Our community of the horse will be no exception; in due course it will be assigned to its place on a shelf in the library of human memory.

So this is also a small effort to record some of the many dimensions of that community while it is still vibrant. Wherever possible we have tried to describe it through the actions and words of representative horses and horse people, though inevitably there is a considerable autobiographical element as well. It is our hope that the reader will enjoy the picture now, and that through it our successors can with pleasure revisit the community and the country we love long after we are gone.

*Afternoon on a shoulder of the Blue Ridge*

EDITORIAL NOTE:

This work has been over four years in the making. As we assembled and arranged its elements, piece by piece, it eventually became apparent that the subject we were exploring was too diverse and extensive to fit comfortably within the covers of one reasonably sized book. And so we decided to produce it in three volumes:

**Volume One**, which you are now reading, describes many of the ways in which the horse has been and is now man's partner here in the Virginia Piedmont.

**Volume Two**, for which the draft manuscript is well along, will follow those relationships as they permeate the area's economy, covering the many support professions on which the horse depends.

**Volume Three**, will describe the institutions, art and literature that celebrate him; the threats that a changing world presents to our Community of the Horse; and the defenses that can preserve the best of what we have and love.

# WHAT IS IT ABOUT HORSES?

PHOTO BY THE AUTHOR

*Edie Smart on Romeo and Malcom Cook on Bonica*

*"The Horse; The noblest of the animal creation ever rendered subject to
the hand of man, his most valuable, best and bravest servant, dauntless in danger,
enduring in extremity, uncomplaining in distress."*

– Frank Forester, from the dedication of his book *The Horse of America*, 1857

---

*"There is something about the outside of a horse that is good for the inside of a man."*
– Attributed to Sir Winston Churchill, among many others.

Our Community of the Horse is tied together by the bonds that develop between horse and horseman, and among horsemen because of their shared respect and affection for their equine partners. In this chapter we explore how these bonds develop and manifest themselves to the benefit of both species.

## – Building a Relationship –

Bonica is a Thoroughbred yearling hunter prospect. Since coming to Trappe Hill Farm she has had three hour-long sessions with her "breaker," Malcolm Cook.

In the first Malcolm taught her to move about the round pen as directed. In the second he saddled her and rode her back and forth in the stable yard, lead shanks attached to the halter serving as reins. In the third, fully tacked up, they soloed on a 45-minute trail ride. Today she and Romeo will go out together. Malcolm has prepared her by holding her loosely by a lead shank, letting her rest her face on his chest while he stroked her, reinforcing the relationship that has evolved during the prior sessions.

During the hour-long ride that follows this picture Bonica will handle two frightening and unfamiliar situations – fording a small running stream and con-fronting a large black bull. Malcolm, who grew up in Argentina raising, breaking and training polo ponies, is matter-of-fact about handling young horses.

*"It's a process of gaining their trust, and building their confidence in themselves and in you. Your job is to make sure that every new experience ends up a happy one. Horses expect justice. If they don't do what you want because they don't understand, you must explain, not get mad. Only if they know what they did was wrong is it permissible to reprimand them."*

As for the bull… *"In Argentina, when horses learn that cattle are afraid of them, not vice versa, they get a great kick out of chasing them."*

———

One evening we started talking to our houseguest, Dr. Lisa Newton, Professor of Philosophy at Fairfield (CT) University, about the human-horse relationship. Lisa is not a "horse person", but here is what she said:

> *"There are philosophers who talk about a social contract between people and animals. Animals have modified their behavior – allowed us to use them, and we have modified our behavior to accommodate their needs and adjust to their feelings. That bond of affection improves the functioning of both the human and the animal as they associate with each other."*

She went on to describe experiments that showed that when a person stroked a horse the blood pressure of both went down as a result of the physical interaction.

The best horsemen (and women)* seem to exude an aura of affection and confidence that even the most wary horses recognize, welcome and recipro-cate. Last fall we had four weanling colts, one of whom was much more stand-offish than the other three. As Debbie Easter (manager of Albemarle Stud), Dr. Reynolds Cowles (a noted veterinarian) and I were visiting them in their paddock the non-social member sought out Dr. Cowles, wishing to be petted by him as much as the other three were eager for attention from Debbie and me. Somehow that shy creature recognized something special in this horseman, and wished to be associated with it.

One spring we visited our two-year-old Cozzene colt on the day he was to be sold at Keeneland. He had been in Florida for five months, training for the sale, following recovery from earlier colic surgery. The horse had a very good pre-sale work, 10⅕ seconds for a furlong, and we were there to wish him well. At the trainer's request a groom, who did not know who we were, led the big roan from his stall and out into the courtyard for our inspection. As I laid my hand on his warm shoulder I felt a strange feeling of peaceful comfort, while the colt turned to look over at Edie. Suddenly I wondered why we were selling this beautiful animal. Then the groom looked toward Edie and said…

   *"He knows you."*

Later on, as the colt was being walked around prior to his turn in the auction

---

*[Ed. note] Henceforth for simplicity we will use the term **horseman** to apply to an individual of either gender and all ages, unless there is a specific reason to do otherwise. We believe few ladies will object. At least we have found none yet who would prefer the title "Mistress of Foxhounds" to that of "Master."

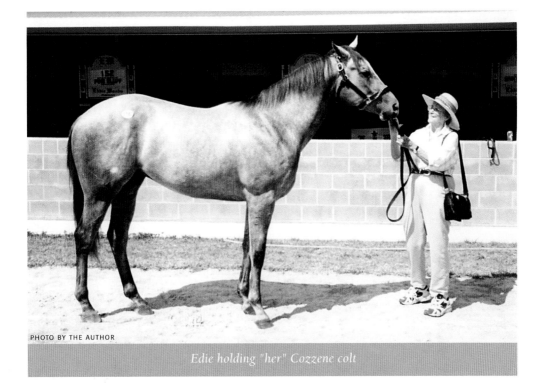

*Edie holding "her" Cozzene colt*

ring, we saw him act up, standing on his hind legs and waving his feet at his handler. As he was brought under control and started walking again he looked over at us and rolled his eyes, as if pleading to...

*"Get me out of here."* But it is our business to breed for the market, and we need to sell the best to cover our costs. So now the roan colt has gone to Japan, leaving many millions of Yen as recompense. But we have not forgotten our parting, wondering still if we should have kept him.

Some believe there can be a mind-to-mind connection between horse and owner. Peggy Carter, a veteran horsewoman from Tryon, NC, is convinced she has communicated with one of her horses by mental telepathy. She first suspected it one day, riding at a walk. She thought...

*"Let's trot,"* and without any physical signal from Peggy the horse started trotting.

At first she decided that her body had given some inadvertent sign to the horse, so to check out that possibility she saddled another horse and ponied the sensitive one along side, again at a walk. When there was no physical contact between the horses, and a slack lead line, she again said silently to herself...

*"Let's trot."* The horse on the lead line immediately broke into a trot, to the surprise of the animal Peggy was riding, who had received no command to do so. She repeated the experiment four times with the same result.

———

Winkie Mackay-Smith tells of a family experience. They were given a tough Thoroughbred by fellow distance rider Denny Emerson, but the horse proved too unreliable to take across country. Winkie got on with him, but everyone else had trouble – the horse acted mean on purpose. When they tried to get rid of him no one would take him. So Winkie put the horse in cross ties, sat down in front of him, and started thinking:

> *"This is your last chance. There's a little girl coming, a good rider. If you don't work out for her I'm going to have to put a bullet in you."*

Then, after a few minutes she stood up, loaded the horse in the trailer (which he hated) and drove to a neighbor's ring. There the girl got on, and the horse went around the ring to perfection. Winkie concludes:

> *"They took the horse, but as the little kid led him to the trailer he stopped at the ramp and looked back at me. I thought 'oh-oh, here we go again.' Then he turned his head back and got happily on the trailer. His look meant 'we made a deal.' It was a fabulous match, and the girl went on to be a great horsewoman."*

Winkie's husband Matthew, a noted veterinarian, is less certain of equine ESP:

> *"It's impossible to have a thought that does not impact your body. Horses are very sensitive to body language. They too cannot separate mind from body, so they read your whole being the only way they know."*

But he doesn't have an explanation for Peggy Carter's experience.

The relationship goes two ways. John Heckler was hunting, galloping his favorite horse Blue, when the horse stepped in a concealed hole and fell. John was pitched into the ground in a fall that left him permanently paralyzed from the waist down. John gave the horse to Mount Vernon, where he became the mount for "George Washington" in the many re-enactments at the plantation. At the end of one re-enactment, as John was watching from his wheel chair on the mansion's veranda, "George Washington" dismounted, leaving Blue unattended. The horse saw John, and came over to him, putting his head on John's shoulder, as if to say *"I'm sorry, I miss you."* John Heckler was a tough optimist, but this time he cried.

## – What Do We See in Horses? –

Pursuing this person-with-horse relationship, I asked a random group of horse people, out of the blue, *"What is it about a horse that attracts you?"*

Here are some answers:

**Lindsay van Melle Kamp**, budding equestrienne, age 11:

*"I like horses because they have a nice way of being. They have body language, similar to cats, and use their body language to talk to you."*

**Florence Hillman**, endurance rider, foxhunter and owner of driving horses:

*"They represent individual freedom for me. It's to be able to climb on their back and go!"*

**Peter Winants**, horseman, photographer, scholar, historian, and builder of equine institutions:

*"My day begins with riding. Riding once was physical – getting in shape to hunt. Now it is an intellectual exercise – training a horse, developing a rapport with him, loving how he keeps me in touch with the countryside."*

**Linda Devan**, foxhunter and whipper-in:

*"The physical beauty and grace appeals to the artist in me. I've loved horses ever since I read* The Black Stallion *as a little girl. They are noble, adrenaline-raising animals. I feel cool riding them."*

PHOTO BY DOUGLAS LEES
*Donna Rogers*

**Donna Rogers**, horsewoman and environmental activist:

*"I never tried to put it into words. From my earliest memories I was in love with horses. I manipulated my entire life so I could be with them."*

**Lily Calvert**, five year-old emerging equestrienne, who also owns and manages a stable of fifty toy horses:

*"I like them because I can ride them and take care of them."*

**Cari Furze**, Grand Prix rider:

*"I love horses for the companion-ship, and working together with them to achieve something."*

PHOTO BY THE AUTHOR
*Cari Furze and Geneva*

**Patty Recklett**, a former New York banker now beginning a new career as a veterinarian:

> *"Horses have tied me to all of my best friends, and are responsible for the relationships that grew from those friendships."*

**Sean Clancy**, retired steeplechase jockey and writer on horse subjects:

> *"It's the generosity of the horse, the pureness of them. They are peaceful, and people gravitate to them. They're honest. Any bad habits are usually man-made."* Then, almost wistfully, *"It's so sad – so many human relationships are based on what someone wants. Not so with the horse."*

**Winkie Mackay-Smith**, distance rider:

> *"Because they like me. Been crazy about them since I was a little kid. I like judging, riding, being with them – their soft noses and sweet breath."*

**Michael Motion**, retired bloodstock agent (after a long pause):

> *"I find them – I suppose – I find them animals that respond greatly to the human touch, willingly. Kipling wrote* Thy Servant, the Dog. *Horses are not servants, it's a partnership, they reciprocate. I derive enormous pleasure from being around them."*

PHOTO BY STEEPLECHASE TIMES

*Sean Clancy*

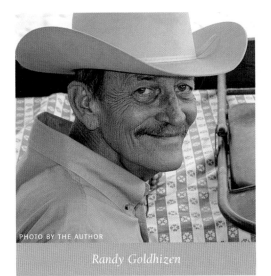

*Randy Goldhizen*

*Ken Tomlinson*

*Tippy Payne*

**Randy Goldhizen**, retired police officer, recovering diabetic and lifetime western rider and roper:

> *"I've been infatuated since boyhood. My father was a herdsman, horses mesmerized him. We have 15 out at the house now, love 'em, walk in the tack room, smell the leather. They make me high on life."*

**Teresa Harp**, of Manassas, VA, owner of six pleasure horses:

> *"They're kind and generous. They don't talk back. It's the generous spirit."*

**Ken Tomlinson**, President of the National Sporting Library:

> *"For those who ride, going over jumps approaches a Bombay Martini. For those of us into breeding and racing, it is one of the great intellectual pursuits; we think we can bring our power of reasoning to figure it all out."*

**Belinda Hyde**, staff member, *The Chronicle of the Horse*:

> *"I haven't seen my horse in three weeks, so I take him in and take the blankets off of him, and start to groom him. He's nickering, and I'm in seventh heaven. It's a love connection, working with him."* [Then, referring to her job at The Chronicle]… *"I get to live my passion."*

**Tippy Payne**, Riding Instructor and Secretary of the Piedmont Foxhounds:

> *"Because they are generous, and give the best they have to an owner or rider."*

**Matthew Klein**, New York photographer and Virginia foxhunter:

*"Foxhunting is the edge between nature and culture. At work I'm surrounded by things that represent something – symbols and signs. But on a horse none of that means anything – it's a deep thing, almost religious."*

**Kim Hurst**, mother of two young horsewomen:

*"I love 'em because they teach my kids to be responsible, which I never could."*

**Rusty Cline**, ski, auto, and motorboat racer:

*"A girl friend introduced me to riding. After the second ride I was hooked. Today was my first hunt. It was an adrenaline rush beyond any I've ever had."*

PHOTO BY THE AUTHOR

*Jill Garity*

**Jill Garity**, Foxhunter:

*"They make me feel good. They bring out the nobility in people."* [Then, after being pressed on whether there is a gender difference]… *"I think lots of men think of horses as sports equipment."*

**Vilda Royer**, foxhunter:

*"I loved horses since before I could walk. As a child my horse was my best friend. Their beauty, movement, expression, and temperament make me happy. They are regal creatures that condescend to please us."*

**Randy Rouse**, MFH, commenting at 84:

*"I quit race riding at 71. Cinzano won our next to last race over timber by 30 seconds. I miss it – and him,"*

—said as he inspects a photograph of Cinzano crossing the finish line with the competition barely visible in the distance, a couple of fences behind.

**Jacob Puleo**, high school senior, winner of the Theo Randolph scholarship for young horsemen, and whipper-in for the Fairfax Hunt:

*"I loved horses since I was a baby. There is a photo of me falling asleep with a book with pictures of cowboys and horses. My horse is my friend, and I like to be outdoors with him. Now my brothers and sisters ride too."*

**Joseph Keusch**, one of the Fairfax Joint Masters, adds:

*"When Jacob started whipping-in his 'Tally Ho' was a little, squeaky thing,*

Randy Rouse

*you could hardly hear it. Now he sounds like someone has just shot a moose."*

**Michelle Rouse**, steeplechase jockey:

*"I like the seasoned old campaigner, because he can be the brains of the outfit, and let me be the co-pilot."*

**Jonathan Thomas**, 20-year-old steeplechase jockey:

*"Horses are my best friends. They are always there for you. Unlike people, they can't hide who they really are. They can't lie; they're so honest. It makes the relationship so much easier."*

Michelle Rouse

*Wendy Ying and her Irish Draught gelding*

**Wendy Ying**, Veterinarian, foxhunter, and devotee of combined driving:

*"I really like the challenge of getting the best out of each horse – figuring out their personalities. The straight forward horse is too boring."*

**Billy Wilbur**, retired MFH and competitive distance rider:

*"Because of the surroundings, and the people that are interested in them, and the sport."* [Then, after a pause]… *" I love everything that goes with them, and working with them."*

**Danielle Kuper**, South African-born equestrienne:

*"The feeling of beauty and power. The horse connects you to the instinctive part of your*

*Anita Baarns*

*being and lets it blossom. They've been part of my life since I was six."*

**Anita Baarns**, artist, dressage rider and foxhunter:

*"They're beautiful, elegant, powerful, sensitive to people. They obey, always do their best for you. It's a relationship of trust, a balance of trust. There's something special about the strength of this big animal. If I bend over, my horse massages the back of my neck with his muzzle. It gives me goose bumps."*

**Pam Wooley**, Director of Marketing, Westmoreland Davis Foundation and a horse person since childhood:

*"I swear to God horses listen, they know what you have coming up. Horses can teach you an awful lot – and they can also make you humble."*

**Tim Weed**, Veterinarian:

*"I like them because they are aesthetically pleasing, with a fragile, athletic beauty. They are complex animals that have evolved to a point where their desire to perform can be detrimental to their health, a potentially tragic characteristic. I enjoy trying to help them."*

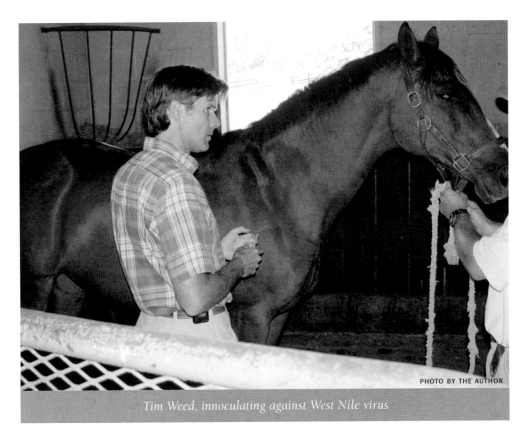

*Tim Weed, innoculating against West Nile virus*

PHOTO BY THE AUTHOR

*Susan Bishop*

PHOTO BY THE AUTHOR

*Heidi Stirrup*

**Paul Mellon**, hunting and racing enthusiast, distance rider, and art collector. [taken from his book *Reflections in a Silver Spoon*]:

> *"It is the color, the movement, the speed, the excitement, the competition, the skill of riding, the cleverness of the horses, and the primitive element of luck... but it is mostly the love of the horse, the well-kept, well-trained, beautifully moving horse, the horse as an object of art."*

**Susan Bishop**, foxhunter:

> *"They're sensual. You can relate to them."*

**Adrienne Hewitt**, endurance rider and foxhunter:

> *"They bring me where I want to be, both outdoors and spiritually. They carry me there. I do not see God in cities, in concrete canyons. I see Him in the fox, and the rocks, and the light."*

**Heidi Stirrup** [yes, that is her last name], policy staffer to the Majority Leader, U. S. House of Representatives.

> *"It's the magnificance and beauty of the animal, and the love and appreciation it engenders. There is great gratification in caring for it, as well as the fun of riding. I love grooming them, the sweet smell of hay, listening to them munch, even mucking stalls. Some people get it, and some just don't."*

These friends have provided a summary answer to the question: What is it about a horse that appeals to humans?

Collectively, they tell us: *"It's a beautiful, powerful, trusting, generous, honest, sensual, even spiritual partner, in a relationship that lifts your soul, flatters your ego, and adds a dimension to life that otherwise would not be there."*

And, as Heidi says:

*"Some people get it, and some just don't."*

In the following chapters we will see how these relationships are played out between horses and people, and among horse people, in the horse-loving community in which we live.

*A veteran horse, interested in the people across the fence of his "backyard" paddock*

# III

# THE HORSE IN HISTORY

*"How the horse dominated the mind of early races… You were a lord if you had a horse. Far, far back in our dark soul the horse prances… The horse, the horse! the symbol of surging potency and power of movement, of action, in man."*

—D.H. Lawrence. "Apocalypse". 1931

Human fascination with horses has ancient roots, both historical and mythological. Stone Age men saw wild horses as a source of food, and perhaps as religious objects as well. European cave paintings of horses date as far back as 20,000 years.

By the Bronze Age horses were being domesticated. In about 3000 BC, as people in the Caucasus turned to cultivating grain, the horse became a source of power, pulling carts and then chariots. Later on he was ridden, at first bareback. He had become a military asset as well as an economic one.

NSL BLOODGOOD PAPERS

*Cave painting of a horse in Lascaux Cave, France*

In China, India and Persia horses attained a spiritual level of respect, perhaps inspired by the qualities they gave to mounted warriors, the combination of man and horse becoming a terrifying centaur-like creature that dominated dismounted opponents.

In ancient Greece the Golden Horses of the Sun were thought to pull Apollo's chariot across the sky each day. The legendary flying Pegasus inspired poets for centuries, even now re-emerging in the name selected by a Japanese for a celebrated modern Thoroughbred stallion, Fusaichi Pegasus. Bucephalus was a heroic figure as the warhorse of Alexander the Great. The Roman emperor Caligula was so enamored of his horse that he appointed him a Consul, the highest Roman rank next to that of Emperor.

Over the centuries the various roles assigned to horses led to the breeding of specialized strains, the development of tack and horse-drawn vehicles, and the evolution of horse-based military tactics.

An early development, the light chariot, made possible by trained horses, was key to the military control of important areas of the Middle East by the kingdoms of the Mitanni and Hittites. From there domesticated horses

spread across North Africa and Europe, reaching the Atlantic coast by 1000 B.C. These horses and their riders brought Arab domination to many of the lands surrounding the Mediterranean. Later, mounted knights in armor controlled the battlefields of medieval Europe. For almost three thousand years horses have played a pivotal role in the economic, military, and cultural history of civilization. No other animal has had such a large part in developing the society of which we are today the heirs.

## – Horses in the American Colonies –

Though Horses and their predecessor species, starting with the tiny Eohippus, inhabited North America in prehistoric times, by around 7000 B.C, they had died out on that continent.

Horses returned to the New World around the end of the fifteenth century, as Columbus and his successors transported them, first to the islands of the Caribbean, where breeding operations were set up, and later to the mainland to provide mounts for the Conquistadors. Over time, as the Spaniards conquered large areas of Mexico, Central America, and what is now the southwestern United States, horses passed into the possession of the Indians, and became important to their mode of living and fighting. By the early eighteenth century escaped horses had also founded wild bands that roamed the grasslands of the southwest, providing a reservoir of animals for both Indian and settler.

Following the defeat of the Spanish Armada and Spain's lessening grip on the sea lanes, the English and French began colonizing the Atlantic coast of North America. Horses came to the Virginia Colony as early as 1608, though in small numbers, as cattle were more valuable as sources of food and hides, and oxen the draft animals of choice. The census of 1649 reported only 200 horses for 15,000 humans.

As the Virginia Colony grew, life there called for a comfortable saddle horse for travel, and some speed for war - or racing. The "Irish Hobbie" proved ideal. Named for the progenitor sire, the racehorse "Hobbie," this breed was a favorite both in Ireland and England. Its intermediate gait – "amble" or "rack" [now called "pace"] – was lateral (front and rear leg on one side moving at the same time), and thus very comfortable.

The number of horses in Virginia grew rapidly, through both breeding and import, to support a growing population and the widening frontier. Some were imported from Spanish breeding farms in the West Indies, though others, especially stallions, were from England. Some think that the feral horses on Assateague and Chincoteague Islands off the Virginia coast are descendants of horses shipwrecked there during this trade. And some horses, descended from the stock brought to America by the Spaniards, were sold by the Indians to settlers in the southern colonies.

The development of "post" roads made faster travel possible, and new breeds brought the diagonal "trot" more common in today's riding horses. By the mid-eighteenth century, "post" boys developed the technique of "posting" to ride to this less comfortable gait.

In their fondness for horses Virginians were true children of country England. In the stables of wealthy planters specimens of the finest breeds were soon to be found, and interest in racing was universal. It is reported that the first shipment of books, other than religious, to Virginia was of a two-title volume, the first described as:

> "...containing the whole art of riding great Horses in a very short time, with the breeding, dyeting and ordring [training] of them, and of running, hunting and ambling horses, with the manner of how to use them in their travell."

The second title was about:

> "...the English Huswife : Containing the inward and outward vertues which ought to be in a compleat Woman."

---

First things first.

## – Early Horse Sports –

American horse racing originated as sprints over short distances; since open land was scarce, tracks had to be cleared in the forest. The British actor, John Bernard, wrote in his autobiographical *Retrospections of America* that it was:

> "... called quarter racing, which was a match between a pair of horses to run a quarter of a mile in a straight direction. This feat usually took place near some tavern, in a field where a path was hedged in, about ten feet wide, for the competitors, the sides of which were generally lined by a motly multitude of negroes, Dutchmen, Yankee pedlers, and backwoodsmen, among whom, with long whips in their hands to clear the ground, moved the proprietors and bettors, riding or leading their horses."

Many leading Virginians came from English landed gentry families, supporters of the King and the Church of England in the English Civil War, and thus "Cavaliers." By flocking to Virginia in the1650s to escape from Cromwell, they increased the population of the colony from 15,000 to 40,000 in less than two decades. Racing was both popular and contentious in Virginia. A court order issued in Williamsburg in 1674 is instructive:

> "James Bullocke, a Taylor, having made a race for his mare to runn w'th a horse belonging to Mr Matthew Slader for twoe thousand pounds of tobacco and caske, it being contrary to Law for a Labourer to make a race, being a sport only for Gentlemen, is fined for the same one hundred pounds of tobacco and caske.

> "Whereas Mr Matthew Slader & James Bullocke, by condition under the hand and seal of the said Slader, that his horse should runn out of the way that Bullock's mare might win, w'ch is an apparent cheate is ordered to be putt in the stocks and there sitt the space of one houre."

The court order sent two clear messages. The sport of horse racing was reserved for the gentry, and fixing races would not be tolerated.

New Englanders, on the other hand, made little use of horses in this way. In religion many were Puritans; in vocation they tended to be craftsmen, artisans, seamen, and of yeoman parentage, small farmers or city-dwellers, and political supporters of Cromwell. Horse racing and pleasure riding were frowned upon by the Puritans, who generally took a dim view of the pastimes of the English countryside. Their disapproval, however, was not so great as to deter them from setting up horse breeding farms to supply stock – at a profit, of course - to the southern colonies and the West Indies. And New England eventually made an exception for trotting races, since light harness horses provided utility as well as sport.

Each side brought to America some of the biases and politics of their forebears in the parent country. It is easy to see how these differences were reflected in their approach to horse racing and to social structure, and one can detect a faint reflection of them in the seeds of the American Civil War 200 years later.

The colonial-era "Quarter Horse" is perpetuated in the modern breed of the same name, and in the Tennessee Walking Horse and the American Standardbred. By the eighteenth century Hugh Jones tells us in his *Present State of Virginia*, published in 1724, that the Virginians,

> "…are such lovers of riding that almost every ordinary person keeps a horse; and I have known some spend the morning in ranging several miles in the woods to find and catch their horses, only to ride two or three miles to church, to the court-house, or to a horse race."

As the Virginia countryside was cleared, longer race courses became practicable, and new strains were introduced to develop horses attuned to greater distances. By the mid-eighteenth century there was breeding from imported English Thoroughbreds, crossing them with local mares. The first of these Thoroughbred sires was Bulle Rock, son of the Darley Arabian, one of the three progenitor sires of the modern Thoroughbred. Bulle Rock arrived in Virginia in 1730, followed in 1752 by perhaps the most influential import, the famous Janus, a grandson of the Godolphin Arabian, another of the three cornerstones of the Thoroughbred breed.

Since the Virginians were excellent horsemen, it was natural that they should enjoy hunting on horseback. No sport was more dear to them than chasing the fox. In *Legends of Loudoun* Harrison Williams credits tidewater Virginia planters, who moved inland to the Piedmont around 1740, with bringing,

> "…the love of social intercourse, the ardour for outdoor sports, particularly the devotion to horses, dogs and foxhunting, all of which so definitely distinguish it [Loudoun County] today and contribute to the outstanding and well-recognized charm of its life."

In 1745 Thomas, the sixth Lord Fairfax, arrived in Virginia to take possession of the lands his mother had received as a dowry from her father, Lord Culpeper. He established his home at Greenway Court, southeast of what is now Winchester, and engaged George Washington to survey his lands, thus launching that young man on his remarkable career. Archdeacon Burnaby, on a visit to America (1759-60), wrote of Lord Fairfax that his,

*Lord Fairfax and George Washington*

*"…chief if not sole amusement was hunting; and in pursuit of this exercise he frequently carried his hounds to distant parts of the country; and entertained any gentleman of good character and decent appearance, who attended him in the field, at the inn or ordinary, where he took up his residence for the hunting season."* [From *Legends of Loudoun*]

George Washington also delighted in foxhunting with Lord Fairfax in what is now the Blue Ridge Hunt territory near Berryville, an area that Washington was surveying. In all, there are over 200 entries regarding foxhunting in Washington's diaries, according to author / historian Kitty Slater, whose exhaustively researched book *The Hunt Country of America* is an invaluable source for those interested in pursuing this history.

Kitty Slater later reports, in a 1984 article in *Middleburg Life* that *"'Pioneer Style' racing took place as early as 1760 on Garrett's Race Paths, now the site of the annual Piedmont Point-to-Point."*

During the Revolution American horses were extensively used for transport and farm work, but cavalry was limited in most cases to scouting, random raids, and forays. Samuel Carter's *The Last Cavaliers* calls the Colonial horsemen…

> "…land-roving privateers, an accidental breed compared to the disciplined [British] cavalry of General Banastre Tarleton."

In addition to the guerrilla exploits of Francis Marion, "The Swamp Fox", in the Carolinas, there were two Virginians who were successful cavalry commanders. In 1779 Major Henry Lee, to be known thereafter as "Light Horse Harry," was sent by Washington to raid a British fort at Paulus Hook, New Jersey, to worry General Sir Henry Clinton, who was threatening West Point. With a combination of audacity and good luck, Lee's force of 300 men took the fort, garrisoned by 500. As the British ships offshore started to retaliate, Lee withdrew with 159 prisoners, at the cost of only two Americans killed.

Later, as the war's focus shifted south, Lee and Lt. Colonel William Washington, a cousin of the commander-in-chief, joined General Greene in the Carolinas. Greene had an appreciation for the tactical use of cavalry, and a campaign of constant movement ensued. Greene divided his forces, and forced General Cornwallis to divide his as well. One British command, under General Tarleton, was lured by the American General Daniel Morgan to attack the Americans at Cowpens on January 17, 1781. With higher ground and superior marksmanship, the Americans delivered withering fire on the enemy, and completed the rout with a double envelopment of the British, the most spectacular element of which was a cavalry charge by Washington's troopers. Morgan and his cavalry had scored the greatest tactical success of the war.

Two months later, at the battle of Guilford in North Carolina, Cornwallis was again struck hard by Greene, aided by Lee and Washington. The British withdrew after a series of engagements to Yorktown, where Cornwallis surrendered his entire force to the Americans on October 17, 1781, thus ending the war.

## – Between Wars –

After the war Diomed, the English Derby winner of 1780, was brought to Virginia, as was a mare in foal to him named Castianara. The offspring was Sir Archy, owned jointly by Colonel John Tayloe and Colonel Archibald Randolph, family names that persist to this day in Virginia.

Sold to Colonel William Johnson (known as the Napoleon of the Turf for winning 61 of 63 races in 1807 and 1808), Sir Archy went on to a great race career and equal success at stud, charging $50 per mare bred. Sir Archy's grandson Boston – named for a card game, and Virginia bred – together with Boston's son Lexington were dominant American stallions in the mid-nineteenth century.

Their blood continues on in more recent star sires such as Man O'War, Blue Larkspur, Northern Dancer and Mr. Prospector.

COURTESY OF MRS. WALTER M. JACOBS

*Sir Archy, from a painting by E. Troye*

COURTESY OF THE JOCKEY CLUB

*Lexington, 1850, by E. Troye.*

Diomed also shows up in the history of a young and impetuous Tennessee horseman named Andrew Jackson. Jackson, always near bankruptcy, had lost a race in 1805 to a horse named Greyhound, who had also beaten Truxton, a Virginia-bred by Diomed. Believing Truxton well bred but not properly conditioned, Jackson bought him for $1,500 by assuming the owner's debts. After some training, Truxton ran again against Greyhound, winning a bet of $5,000 for his new owner.

Truxton's stud fees became a stream of income for Jackson, and an annoyance to the owner of Ploughboy, the reigning sire in Tennessee. A match was arranged, with each owner betting thousands on his horse. Ploughboy's owner, sure of victory, withdrew his horse from stud until after the race, advising mare owners to wait for Ploughboy rather than seek a lesser alternative. Though lame, Truxton won again. Jackson was not a gracious winner, as this notice signed by him suggests:

*"...And lastly to crown the much-debated speed of Truxton with his opponents, he beat, on only two sound legs, on the 3rd of April, 1806, the celebrated horse Ploughboy, who was never before beaten, over the Clover Bottom Turf, and beating him without the assistance of whip or spur... and his [Truxton's] colts are not inferior to any on the continent."*

COURTESY OF THE HERMITAGE, HOME OF ANDREW JACKSON

*Andrew Jackson mounted on Sam Patch. From a portrait by Ralph Earl*

Circumstances surrounding this race led to hard feelings between the two owners and their supporters, insults were exchanged, aspersions made on the character of Jackson's wife, and challenges to a duel followed. This altercation was fought first in the newspapers, and then with pistols. Jackson was seriously wounded, his opponent killed. Despite the outcry, Jackson went on to earn a huge place in American history. But that is another story.

Racing was not limited to the rugged and quarrelsome frontier people of Tennessee. As told in *Legends of Loudoun*, an advertisement in the October 14, 1817 issue of the newspaper *Genius of Liberty* appeared, announcing:

*"Leesburg Jockey Club. RACES will be run for on Wednesday the 15th October, over a handsome course near the town. A Purse of 200 dollars three miles and repeat, and on Thursday, two miles and repeat a Purse of $100 Dollars, and on Friday the 17th and repeat, a Towne's Purse of at least $150 and on Saturday the 18th an elegant SADDLE, BRIDDLE and MARTINGALE, worth at least FIFTY DOLLARS. P.SAUNDERS, sec'y & treas'r. "*

Parallel with Virginians' interest in race horses was their continuing passion for foxhunting. Many plantation owners had private packs of hounds, which they hunted in the company of friends and neighbors, and without the ceremony and formality now accepted as part of the sport.

Improving the breed was not restricted to producing faster animals. There was increasing demand for easier and faster travel, and for better means to transport goods from farm to city, and from factory to consumer. As settlement moved inland, improved roads followed, leading to demand for heavier draft animals to pull carts, wagons, and coaches along them.

The Upperville Colt and Horse Show, now the longest running horse show in America, started in 1853 with two classes, one for colts and one for fillies, vying for silver trophies crafted by Tiffany. A local planter, Richard H. Dulany, conceived of the show to focus attention on improving the breeding and care of young horses. As a show site he selected a grove of tall oak trees on one of his farms, now called Heronwood, on the turnpike (now Route 50) two miles east of Upperville.

Dulany also improved the local stock by importing the Morgan stallion Black Hawk from New England, and the Cleveland Bay stallion Scrivington from England. Both sires were made available without stud fee to local mares. The Morgan line, suitable for both draft and riding, appealed to farmers whose resources limited them to one or two animals. Admirers of American folk art will recognize Black Hawk as the model for a line of famous weathervanes crafted for barn roof tops in the nineteenth century, and now highly prized by twenty first century collectors of Americana.

By 1857 the show, now sponsored by the Upperville Union Club, had three divisions, Riding Stock, Quick Drafts, and Heavy Drafts, representing the equine categories critical to the local economy. Two years later the show had grown to about 80 entries, with Black Hawk *the getter of more fine colts than any other on exhibition.*

A few years later the Civil War put a temporary end to such activities.

## - Horses in the Civil War -

*"For a flash of time it seemed chivalry and romance rode*
*to battle in the 1860's – never to return."*
—Samuel Carter, in *The Last Cavaliers*

Horses played an immense role in the Civil War, especially in the fighting in the Piedmont region of Virginia. At the start of the war the South had an enormous edge in skilled horseman, the result of its plantation economy and its Cavalier heritage. Once Virginia decided to secede, area horsemen joined Confederate cavalry units in great numbers.

An early nucleus to which aspiring mounted soldiers flocked was the company formed by Captain Turner Ashby of Fauquier County. Following this

*Col. Richard H. Dulany – painting by T.C. Corner*

example 20 other companies were rapidly formed. This unwieldy group of units was soon reorganized into what was later called the Laurel Brigade, consisting of the 7th and 12th Virginia Cavalry regiments (ten companies each) and the 17th Virginia Cavalry Battalion. The 7th Virginia Cavalry Regiment, to which many area men belonged, was soon commanded by now-Colonel Ashby, and after his death was eventually led by Colonel Richard H. Dulany of Upperville Horse Show fame.

The Union General William T. Sherman is quoted in *The Last Cavaliers*, describing the Confederate horsemen as,

> *"... the young bloods of the South, sons of planters, lawyers about town, good billiard players and sportsmen, who never did work and who never will. War suits them, and the rascals are brave and bold to rashness... They hate Yankees per se, and don't bother their brains about the past, present, or future... They are splendid riders, first-rate shots, and utterly reckless... the most dangerous set of men this war has turned loose on the world."*

It took the Union at least two years to train men from factories, offices, and farms to approach their Southern counterparts in horsemanship. Perhaps because of this difference, Northern cavalry was used at first mostly as an adjunct to the infantry – scouts for intelligence, and dragoons who moved by horse, but fought dismounted as infantry. Southern cavalry was more often used as an independent strike force.

The greater visibility and elan of the Southern horsemen, embodied in the person of their commander, General J.E.B. Stuart, added glamour to the Southern cause. As Sherman suggests, though, these free spirits were sometimes hard to discipline, a shortcoming that was to cost the South dearly as the Northern forces gained equality and wore down the South's supply of fine horses and bold, daring riders.

In June of 1863 a large body of Union cavalry surprised Stuart near Brandy Station, about 20 miles south of Warrenton. After a day's hard fighting, with perhaps 20,000 thousand horsemen engaged in the largest cavalry battle of the war, the Northerners fought Stuart on equal terms for the first time. The South's cavalry advantage was evaporating.

Hard on the heels of Brandy Station came the battles of Aldie, Middleburg, and Upperville, bloody preludes to the Battle of Gettysburg destined to take place two weeks later, and towards which both armies were already moving north. Ida (Mrs. Henry G.) Dulany watched the battle of Upperville from her porch on the second floor of her home at Oakley, just south of the turnpike (now Rte. 50), as it flowed from Green Garden Road west through the village of Upperville to Trappe Road. She described it as follows:

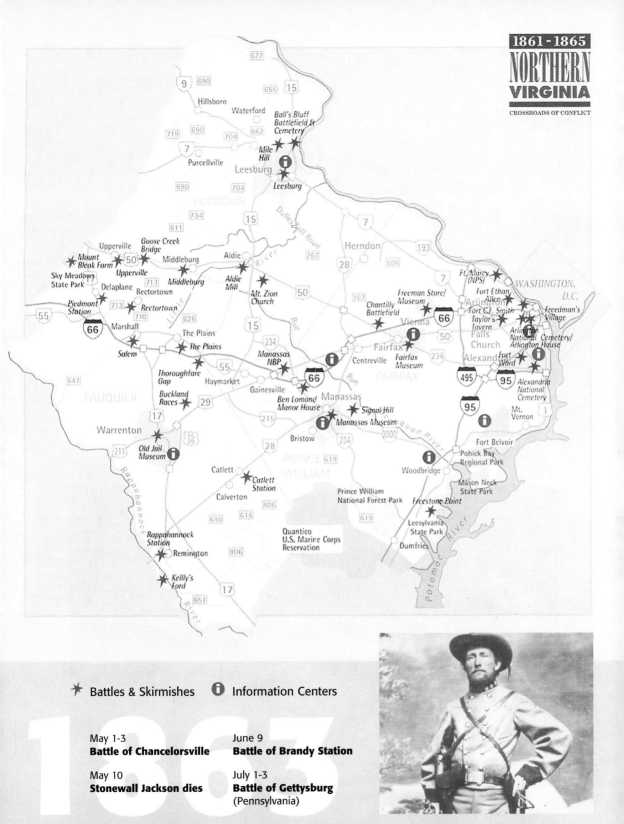

**1863**

★ Battles & Skirmishes    ⓘ Information Centers

May 1-3
**Battle of Chancelorsville**

May 10
**Stonewall Jackson dies**

June 9
**Battle of Brandy Station**

July 1-3
**Battle of Gettysburg**
(Pennsylvania)

COURTESY OF VIRGINIA TRAILS ASSOCIATION

*A map delineating Mosby's Confederacy and location of Civil War actions therein*

———

31

*"The artillery on both sides kept up a continuous roaring, while reports of the small arms, the shouts of the men, the cries of the wounded, and the flash of the firing made a scene terrible to me, and every now and then a horse with an empty saddle ran terrified by the house, telling the sad tale of his rider's fall. Once my blood ran cold seeing one gallop by, dragging a dead man under him."*

–from *Cavalry Battles of Aldie, Middleburg, and Upperville*, by Robert F. O'Neill; published by H.E. Howard, 1993

No doubt some of the Colt and Horse Show's former adherents, by then in uniform, wistfully recognized the old show grounds as they swept through the area during the battle. While Stuart achieved his strategic purpose, screening Lee's movements in the Shenandoah Valley by holding the Union forces east of the Blue Ridge, he was steadily driven back towards those heights by Gen. Pleasonton's horsemen in what was a tactical setback for the Confederates.

Some historians conjecture that Brandy Station and Upperville impelled Stuart to try to repair his reputation by some dramatic exploit. Lee's orders after Upperville gave Stuart discretion as to route and raiding, but emphasized the primary need to screen the right flank of the Army of Northern Virginia as it moved north. Stuart chose a route many miles east of Lee's, raiding as he went. On July 1st he was in Carlisle, Pennsylvania, 33 miles

PHOTO BY JANET HITCHEN

*Re-enactors depicting a Confederate scouting party crossing Goose Creek*

north of Lee who was by then already fighting at Gettysburg. For a week prior to Gettysburg Lee was thus without Stuart to serve as his Army's eyes. Whatever the motivation, by losing contact with Lee's army in the days immediately preceding Gettysburg, Stuart's cavalry failed in its primary mission and missed most of the battle, a critical mistake that contributed to the Confederate defeat. [For further details on Stuart and Gettysburg see *Bold Dragoon: The Life of J.E.B.Stuart* by Emory M. Thomas.]

Following Gettysburg, as the Confederate forces fell back, there remained one more dramatic war-time role for Virginia Piedmont horsemen. Guerrilla bands of "partisans" had been a factor for both sides throughout the war.

*Historical marker describing Mosby's command joining the army*

*Clinton Caleb Rector's house in Atoka in which Mosby's command was formed*

Some, like Elijah V. White's "Comanches," officially known as the 35th Virginia Cavalry Battalion, drawn from men living around Leesburg, coordinated pretty well with the regulars, though they enjoyed their initial freedom of operation and the absence of camp discipline. Relatively early in the war, though, they were integrated into regular service and eventually became a component of the Laurel Brigade.

Other bands were magnets that drew young men away from the regular Confederate Army, where they were badly needed, to join the more exciting and free-wheeling mounted irregulars. Some groups were little more than brigands intent on plunder and booty, with no concern for which side they attacked. To bring order to this situation, all but one of the guerrilla units were inducted into the regular army. The exception, made at Lee's request, was Major (later Colonel) John Singleton Mosby's Rangers. They would become the 43rd Battalion, Virginia Cavalry, but continue to operate independently. Stuart is quoted as saying that

Mosby's command was, *"the only efficient band of Rangers I know."*

The History of the 43rd Virginia Cavalry lists at least two men whose namesake descendents appear elsewhere in this volume:

- Pvt. Samuel E. Rogers, Co. A. enlisted June 16, 1863 (previous enlistment Sept. 3, 1861). Captured April 10, 1865 in fight near Arundel's Tavern, in Fairfax County. Sent to old Capitol Prison in Washington and thence to Elmira, NY. At the war's end, after signing his oath of allegiance he walked home to Hamilton, VA. Grandfather of Samuel and Dr. Joseph Rogers.

- George M. Slater. One of the first fifteen men enlisted by Mosby carried mortally wounded General J.E.B. Stuart from the field at Yellow Tavern. Purchased "Mt. Bleak" near Paris after the War. Died Jan. 2, 1923. Buried in Ivy Hill Cemetery, Upperville. Great grandfather of George N. (Nick) Slater, who says that

*"my ancestor was picked by Mosby, not because he was a fine rider – which he was – but because of the capability of his horse for guerrilla operations."*

Mosby's irregulars had been operating in northern Virginia for some years, collecting intelligence and making raids to capture or destroy Union supplies. Mosby described his purpose as follows:

*"To weaken the armies invading Virginia by harassing their rear – to destroy supply trains, to break up the means of conveying intelligence, and thus isolating an army away from its base, …to confuse their plans by capturing despatches, are the objects of partisan war. I endeavoured… to diminish the aggressive power of the army of the Potomac, by compelling it to keep a large force on the defensive."*

PHOTO BY THE AUTHOR

*Gravestone of G.M.Slater*

He usually operated at night, dispersing his men at daybreak. He had no discernable base camp, but was able to assemble his troops from their hiding places on short notice. He was of course supported by the local population. As *Legends of Loudoun* quotes Mosby,

*"They would scatter for safety, and gather at my call, like the Children of the Mist."*

Mosby's area of operations was bounded by the Potomac on the north and east, extended into the Shenandoah Valley on the west, and to below Warrenton on the south, a region known as "Mosby's Confederacy," that coincides quite closely with that now central to our Community of the Horse. By 1864 Mosby's Rangers had become such a problem that General Grant issued the following order to General Sheridan:

> *"If you can possibly spare a division of Cavalry, send them through Loudoun County to destroy and carry off the crops, animals, negroes and all men under 50 years of age capable of bearing arms. In this way you will get many of Mosby's men." In passing this order down the chain of command Sheridan added,*

> *"…burn all barns and mills and their contents, …bearing in mind, however, that no dwellings are to be burned…"*

The winter of 1864-5 was hard indeed in the Virginia Piedmont. In the spring came Lee's surrender at Appomattox. Mosby and his men refused to surrender, but disbanded, and their exploits – and those of their horses – became Virginia legends.

*Confederate war horse bronze at NSL. Sculpture by Tessa Pullan. Gift of Paul Mellon*

We are sitting in the front room of Dr. Joe and Donna Rogers' eighteenth century stone farmhouse, located on a country road a mile south of the village of Hamilton, Virginia, and talking with its owners.

I am enthralled by Joe's recitation of the history of the house and the area, told in a soft voice with a faraway look in his eyes – how the place has belonged to a Rogers for over 200 years, and before that to the family of maternal ancestors. Joe himself is president of the Loudoun Historical Society. He has been researching the Battle of Hamilton, which took place in March, 1865, very near where we are sitting, an engagement between Mosby's Rangers and a Federal force. According to Joe, a newspaper of the time reported that *"the widow Rogers* [his great grandmother] *rescued a horse from the battlefield."*

Her son Samuel rode with Mosby. The Union commander, brevet Lt. Colonel Marcus Reno*, devised a "Trojan Horse" strategy, filling covered wagons with concealed infantry who were to emerge from hiding when Federal riders decoyed the more lightly armed Mosby forces to them. Apparently the ruse

PHOTO BY THE AUTHOR

*Rogers home near Hamilton*

---

\* As Major, **Marcus Reno** later played a controversial role under Custer at the Battle of the Little Bighorn.

———

*Ebeneezer Church today*

didn't work, and Mosby in turn ambushed the Federals in a deep cut on the Sillcott Springs Road, where 16 were killed by Confederates positioned on the banks rising on each side of the road.

Donna hands me a photograph of a painting of Mosby's men presenting the mare "Coquette" to their commander. Some unidentifiable soldier in the ranks watching the proceedings is Joe's grandfather Samuel, and Joe proceeds to tell the story of Coquette and the Greenback Raid.

On a foray into West Virginia one October night the Mosby force wrecked a Baltimore and Ohio train carrying two Union paymasters and a large amount of money. Being partisan irregulars, no army regulation prevented them from appropriating the booty for their own use. According to Joe,

> *"They took the loot back to the Ebeneezer Church – near where you live – and divided it up. Each man received about $2,000, but as was his custom Mosby declined taking any."*

So the soldiers quietly took up a collection, a "purse" which they gave to Mosby's wife. When the Colonel heard of it he returned the money to the men, but the donors were not to be outdone. They knew that Mosby greatly admired a mare owned by the Carters at nearby Oatlands Plantation, and they went and bought the horse and gave her to Mosby at the ceremony the painting illustrates, and he accepted. Joe continues:

COURTESY OF VIRGINIA HISTORICAL SOCIETY

*Presentation of Coquette to Mosby. Painting by John J. Porter, one of Mosby's men. Given to Mosby and handed down in Mosby family until given to the Virginia Historical Society.*

*"Mosby loved horses and he raced them after the war… but I haven't been able to find out if any were descended from Coquette. It's hard, because they didn't start keeping good stud book records until later."*

## – Re-enactors –

One evening we were having dinner with our neighbors and friends, the Royers. Our host, Gar Royer, mentioned a recent incident on his farm. One afternoon he was out near his stable, tending to his horses, when he noticed a group of riders approaching. What caught his eye first were the huge, furry hats they were wearing. As the detachment of twelve riders drew closer he could see their pommel holsters, and that each was in the colorful uniform of the 7th regiment of Napoleon's Hussars, once a noted French army unit serving under Marshall Ney. As the horsemen pulled up the leader asked, in very bad French, for *"L'eau pour notre chevaux"* – water for our horses.

As he drew the water, Gar asked, also in French,

*"Where are you going?"*

*"Jena,"* the leader replied, pulling out his map, which Gar recognized as a section of Germany. *"Can you direct us?"*

*"Why are you going there?"*

*"We go to defeat the Prussians."*

With that Gar pointed south, towards the nearest cavalry battlefield he could think of, that of Upperville. Their horses watered, the Hussars rode off happily to the south, little caring that Jena took place 57 years earlier than Upperville, and was located some 4000 miles to the east. Time and place meant nothing to them. After all, three had recently helped re-enact the Battle of Waterloo, and some of them had served as Revolutionary War soldiers in the movie *The Patriot.*

G. ROYER ARCHIVES

*Gar Royer(R) as a Union staff officer at Gettysburg*

For Dr. Gar Royer, a PhD in biochemistry, the sudden appearance of military re-enactors is not unusual. Some years ago, when living on a farm near Gettysburg, Gar discovered that he had an ancestor who had fought there in 1863. He researched the life of then Corporal, later Sergeant David Royer of the 5th US Cavalry. Corporal Royer is listed on the Pennsylvania monument on the Gettysburg battlefield. Sergeant Royer was wounded and captured in the action around Gordonsville, VA., near the end of the war. The entry in his unit's muster roll lists him as "Present" one day, "Absent" the next, and "Died in the Hands of the Enemy" on the third, Christmas Day, 1864. Dr. Royer comments as follows:

*"Thinking about the life of my ancestor reminds me of the strong feelings evoked by the research. My discovery of Sergeant Royer's death through the muster roll* [unearthed from the National Archives by a consultant] *was a very emotional moment for me. It was unlike anything I have ever felt before or since. 'Present' was written with perfect penmanship day after day, and then 'Absent.' It was very sad, but a relief in that I had the true story."*

———

Shortly after this research the present day Royer offered his Pennsylvania farm to the movie company filming *Gettysburg*, based on the book *The Killer Angels*. The offer was accepted, and Dr. Royer became not only the movie's host but also a paid extra as a staff officer to General John Reynolds, the Union leader killed during the first day of the battle.

Gar Royer's imagination has been stirred by the role of the Cavalry in the war, leading him to become a better rider, take up foxhunting, and eventually

PHOTO BY PAT MACVEAGH

*Re-enactors as Civil War cavalry*

move to Virginia. He and his horse, Hartford, served as models in a famous painting of Stonewall Jackson, titled "Jackson in the Valley" (by Dale Gallon). An officer mounted on Hartford awaits Jackson's orders, while Massanutten Mountain, a topographical feature of immense tactical importance in the Shenandoah Valley campaigns, looms as a blue shadow in the background.

Today Gar Royer, the newly minted Virginian, pursues his work-a-day dream of creating a successful business based on an exciting medical discovery he has made. The moments he sets aside for play find him remodeling his horse barn, foxhunting, or serving as a Union Cavalry officer in the reenactments of Civil War engagements that show tourists the difficulties and horrors that Sergeant Royer, his Union colleagues, and his Confederate opponents underwent 140 years ago.

One senses that the real Sergeant Royer's spirit returns to Virginia at those moments, promoted again, for a few days each year, and reincarnated in the body of his descendant as a Captain in the Union Cavalry.

Many ghosts still ride about today in the Virginia horse country, be they Yankees, Rebels, – or even Frenchmen.

## – The Reconstruction Period –

The years following Appomattox were difficult ones for the states of the former Confederacy, both economically and socially. Mosby's Confederacy had been ruined economically by Sheridan's forays. As Mosby himself said many years later in his memoirs, published just after his death in 1916, that area *"was the Flanders of the war."* [Flanders was the section of Belgium most devastated in World War I.]

Except for their land and houses people were essentially destitute, barns burned, livestock expropriated. A new social and economic order involving impoverished former masters and newly freed slaves was unsettling to both groups.

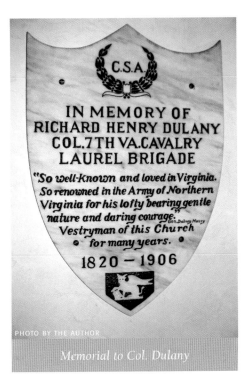

The 1870 census found 447 people living in Middleburg. In that same year the public schools for white children reopened, (though private schools had been operating for some time), and colored schools were being built. But the war had left a void of several years in the education of the young.

Despite these setbacks the horse persevered in Virginia. Soon after the war ended the Upperville Colt and Horse Show was back in business, sponsored by the same organization as before, though with the new name of Upperville Colt Club. The word "Union" had gone out of fashion in Virginia. The reborn show was to be led by Colonel Richard Dulany for

PHOTO BY THE AUTHOR

*Memorial to Col. Dulany*

about 40 more years, and is still held today under the same grove of old oaks that he selected as its site in 1853.

Slowly, working the land allowed a return towards normal. Raising of horses for sale and sport continued as an important area activity. Squibs from Scheel's *History of Middleburg* are illustrative:

- Prosperity was tied to the countryside – 20 bushels of corn per acre, 10 bushels of wheat. Clydesdales and Percherons were eventually favored as draft animals.

- Northerners came down to buy fine horses from Colonel Dulany.

- Camp meetings – gatherings of old Confederate soldiers that kept alive the cavalry spirit.

One form of entertainment was jousting, riding at speed with a lance to spear small suspended rings. Tournaments involved young men, named and often costumed as knights, as contestants. At the end of the morning's event the winner crowned the lady of his choice "The Queen of Love." A picnic ensued, followed by dancing. There was also the occasional informal horse race. And the Southerners remained tough horsemen: in 1869, at the age of 99, William Benton was killed in the hamlet of Pot House by a fall from a colt he was breaking.

By the end of the century there was a brisk business selling draft horses for $75 each to pull city street cars. A fine pair of carriage horses might bring $1,000, and recreational horse activities re-emerged in full force. In 1895 a steeplechase meet was held by the Deep Run Hunt at Curles Neck Farm. It later moved to Strawberry Hill, near Richmond, and is now held annually at the Colonial Downs race track. By 1898 Thoroughbreds, saddle horses, ponies, carriage classes and heavy draft animals were on the Upperville Horse Show program, as was a high jump event. In turn-of-the-century Virginia the general sentiment seemed to be:

*"Now it's time to have some fun."*

In nearby St. Louis, Virginia – called by some the "Black Middleburg" – 1898 saw the beginning of the "St. Louis Colored Colt Show" whose charter explained that its purpose was to…

*"…hold exhibitions of horses and colts and to manage and conduct contests of speed and jumping… but no gambling of any sort shall be allowed."*

Apparently there were still limits in some circles on "having fun." The role of the horse in American life had begun shifting inexorably from work, war and transport to recreation.

*"In the last decade of the nineteenth century a notable inflow of new residents, new money, new determination… of which the most significant result was the vigorous growth of the horse and sport-loving community around Middleburg."*
—Harrison Williams in *Legends of Loudoun*

*" I was the first outsider from the north… I saw the future of this area as a great hunting country and spoke to a number of friends. …The Foxhound Match took place in 1905… The Match and its publicity made Virginia."*
—Harry Worcester Smith, as quoted from *Fortune* magazine by Kitty Slater in her book *The Hunt Country of America*

COURTESY OF NSL

*Harry Worcester Smith*

By the early part of the 20th century the industrial cities of the north were spreading out, suburbs replacing farms, with horse sports such as foxhunting pushed increasingly far from urban centers. The tractor and the larger machines it could pull began to supplant horse-power in agriculture, giving competitive advantage to the wide, flat, machine-friendly farms of the middle west. The results were higher suburban land prices in the north, and non-competitive farms, and hence low land prices, in Virginia. For Virginia landowners, stripped by the Civil War of any other wealth, the turn-of-the-century agricultural trends did little to help restore prosperity.

Loss of open spaces at home on one hand, and the warmer Virginia climate, beautiful scenery, and cheap land on the other, combined to lure northern horse-lovers to the Commonwealth, first to foxhunt, and soon thereafter to settle, build or buy homes, and in some cases breed race horses. This second "Yankee Invasion" - Kitty Slater calls it "The Northern Avalanche" - was more kindly received than the first, for it brought money, and soon jobs to the local economy. For the most part, the newcomers were good citizens and friendly neighbors; some have had significant impact on the Virginia Piedmont, and their contributions are worth noting. To understand this better I turned to Tom diZerega.

Tom is a native Virginian with a lawyer's mind, a sharp eye, and a good sense for people. His wife, Mary Howe, is also a multi-generation Virginian. Tom breeds and runs race horses. So he seemed an excellent prospect to explain the local reaction to the northern immigrants who infiltrated the Piedmont country, starting a generation or more after their soldier forebears went home from their four year stay in Virginia. Tom points out,

> "…that if your wealth is in land you can have a good standard of living, but it doesn't bring in enough cash to maintain several children at that same standard. Land here was cheap, $50 per acre in the 1940's, and only $500 in the 1960's.

> "Everyone rode, it was ingrained in the area, and people had time to foxhunt. Attracted by the hunting, the northerners came down as their hunting country became built up. The first big influx was the Orange County Hunt. They would park their private railroad cars at The Plains. They built a club house, and eventually started to buy land. You should look at Kitty Slater's book."

The book's first chapter begins:

> "The flag of the Hunt Country was first unfurled in 1905 by the American - English Foxhound Match in the rolling hills, valleys, and woodlands near the historic Virginia villages of Middleburg and Upperville."
> —Kitty Slater, *The Hunt Country of America*

Contemporaneous with the Foxhound Match, the Orange County Hunt dacamped from its Goshen, New York, base and started to hunt regularly in Virginia. As they spread their operations – and their land ownership – over country that locals had hunted with private packs for generations, there was understandable friction. Rozier Dulany of the Piedmont Hunt, and nephew of Colonel Richard Dulany, is quoted as having said:

> "Welcome the damn Yankees – let 'em come – but, by Gawd, if they stay, let's make sure it's on the other side of Goose Creek."

| | Winner | Place | Show |
|---|---|---|---|
| E STRATFORD-ON-AVON | 9 | 8 | 13 |
| E ROUGE DRAGON | 2 | 5 | 1 |
| BRYCE WING M...L | | | 7 |
| E VIRGINIA GO... | | | |
| ERT C.WIN... | | | |
| THOR...BRE | | | |

*Paul Mellon, jockey Paddy Neilson, and trainer Ridgley White*

Jealousies between native and newcomer, between rich people and those less fortunate, are nothing new. Apparently they were for the most part well handled in Virginia. The Orange County Hunt soon had a native Virginian, William Skinker, as Field Master, and hunting territories were formalized to avoid competing over land. Tom sums it up:

*"Most newcomers were friendly,"* and of course, they provided an influx of money that the economy badly needed.

We fall to talking about specific newcomers. Tom reminisces rapidly; here are some names, with Tom's comments italicized, that I put down, followed by what – in summary – appears about them in other sources.

**Paul Mellon –** *"had the biggest impact."* See the references to him elsewhere in this book and its sequel.

**Daniel and Edith Sands –** *"from New York, active in the horse world (her money). Gave Glenwood Park land. Mrs. Sands was killed in an auto wreck near 1763 House Restaurant."* Daniel Sands was MFH of the Middleburg and

*Miss Charlotte Noland and Mr. Daniel Sands, Masters of the Middleburg Hunt.*
*Painting by Edward L. Chase*

Piedmont hunts. He learned to ride after he came to Virginia. He bred fox-hounds and founded the American Foxhounds Association and founded and ran both the Middleburg Race Meet and the Middleburg Bank. He helped many local not-for-profit organizations, and was considered by many to be Middleburg's number one citizen.

**Charlotte Noland** – A native Virginian, widely known as "Miss Charlotte," she founded the Foxcroft School in 1914, and was for 14 years Joint Master of the Middleburg Hunt.

**Alexander Mackay-Smith** – Mackay-Smith was a prolific author on horse subjects and editor of The Chronicle of the Horse. His life will be covered in more detail in a subsequent volume.

**Admiral Cary Grayson** – *"maintained a racing stable."* Rear Admiral Cary T. Grayson was personal physician to President Wilson. A native Virginian (born in Culpeper County), he founded Blue Ridge Farm, now managed by his grandson, George Grayson, following many years in the hands of his sons Gordon and Cary.

**Joseph B. Thomas** – *"man that owned Huntland,"* a native of Boston, built a replica of an early American manor house on the Pot House Farm near

Middleburg. He assembled a fine pack of hounds for Piedmont, of which he became MFH. His book *Hounds and Hunting Through the Ages* was considered the first comprehensive American book on the subject. Later owned by the Brown family of Texas, Huntland was occasional host to then-Senator Lyndon Johnson and Speaker of the House Sam Rayburn.

**Harry Worcester Smith** – Kitty Slater writes, *"If self-effacement was not one of (his) most notable characteristics, nevertheless (he) must be credited with sounding the reverberating Tally-Ho that heralded the founding in 1905 of the Hunt Country Era and the Renaissance of foxhunting in America."*

Em Hutchison

**Em Hutchison** – *"Her father ran the local Stuyvesant School."* Em was a horsewoman, and raced steeplechasers until her recent death. Her passing represents a changing of the guard, leaving it to a younger generation to embrace her love of sport and countryside, and do their best to protect it.

**Theo Randolph** – *"She was what she was. I didn't know her well, but I thought well of her because she thought well of me."*

Mrs. Archibald C. Randolph, the former Theodora Ayer of Boston (and once married to a Winthrop), was the niece of General George Patton and the wife if Dr. Archibold C. Randolph, whom she succeeded as Master of Piedmont, a position she held until her death in 1996. She bred and raced Bon Nouvel, Steeplechase Horse of the Year three times.

**Liz Altemus Whitney** – *"Her effect is a matter of opinion. She was a smart, tough person. Threw some of the wildest parties that were thrown."* In her youth she was a beautiful woman. She was also a superb rider, a polo player, a noted owner of show horses and hunters, and breeder of race horses. A widely diverse list of guests shared her hospitality at Llangollen Farm, a wedding present from her first of four husbands, Jock Whitney.

Jerry Crenshaw adds a more recent bit to the Liz Whitney (by then Mrs. Tippett) legend. In 1985, near the end of her life, he and Tommy Stokes, who lived across the road at Ayrshire, were invited to come by one afternoon to sell her a bull. As Jerry tells it:

*"We arrived for our appointment at four, and after a bit guests started*

*Liz Whitney as a young woman*

*arriving, from Washington and everywhere, and she asked us to stay. She was by then old and heavy, and hadn't bothered to dress. Instead she lay in her bed in the center of the living room while the party swirled around her, the guests drinking wine and champagne and eating cheese and crackers.*

*"Every so often she'd call out 'Cookie, more champagne' and hold up her glass. Cookie was the maid. Sometime in the evening Colonel Tippett came down to join in, wearing a pair of fuzzy old slippers. When we left at midnight the party was still going. …And we never did sell her the bull."*

**Marion duPont Scott** – Master of the Montpelier (VA) Hunt for 61 years, a great supporter of breeding and racing Thoroughbreds – steeplechase and flat – and the "angel" of the Marion duPont Scott Equine Medical Center in Leesburg. In 1915 she was the first woman to ride astride at the National Horse Show. She bred Neji, Steeplechase Horse of the Year three times. Her horse Battleship won the English Grand National in 1938. She was the last private owner of Montpelier, originally President Madison's home, where she grew up. Montpelier is now the property of the National Trust for Historic Preservation, and open to the public. It is also the site of the Montpelier Race Meet, founded by Mrs. Scott in 1934.

**Taylor Hardin** – *"Local."* With his wife Tateen he managed his Newstead Farm to become one of the most successful Thoroughbred breeding operations in America. After his death the dispersal sale set a record for average price per head which still stands. Newstead is now owned by Bert and Diana Firestone, whose mare, Genuine Risk, was one of only three fillies ever to win the Kentucky Derby.

**Russell Arundel** – *"New York money."* Russell Arundel was MFH of the Warrenton Hunt for nineteen years and an owner of steeplechase horses. His son Arthur "Nick" Arundel, himself a horseman, was the leader in acquiring the land at Great Meadow where the Virginia Gold Cup and other equine events are staged. He still manages activities there through the Meadow Outdoors Foundation.

Jimmy Young, Master of the Orange County Hunt (as was his father before him), is currently writing a book on the history of foxhunting in North America, and his observations add depth to Tom's overview. As Jimmy sees it, it is the "larger-than-life" figures that have, with their forceful personalities, created the present day community of the horse in Northern Virginia. Here are some of his observations.

NSL PHOTO
*Jimmy Young (right) with the author*

> *"There was a certain stiff-neckedness among the old timers when confronted with the idea that northerners had to teach southerners about foxhunting.*

> *"Piedmont was the old Virginia hunt, dating back to the 1840s. Actually it was the Dulanys' hunt, their recreation. There was no formal organization until after the Civil War, and the hunting was far less formal than the traditional style inherited from England. Harry Worcester Smith observed that there were 'no velvet caps,' and the only huntsman was a black man, a dare-devil rider, who made sure to stay with the hounds."*

Piedmont's territory was huge, bounded by the Bull Runs and Blue Ridge east and west, the Potomac on the north, extending south almost to the Rappahannock. Blue Ridge, Warrenton and Deep Run Hunts were all founded before Orange County. Smith was one of those larger-than-life figures. Jimmy comments:

> *"Harry Smith met Rozier Dulany through their shared interest in horse shows, and was Dulany's guest when hunting in Virginia. The great hound match brought a world spotlight to bear. Smith's drive to have this area declared the Foxhunting Country of America changed the fabric of a community still reeling from the aftermath of the Civil War. Smith hunted about 250 days a year, and was a prolific writer. I don't know when he had time to eat."*

Other significant individuals he mentions include A. Henry Higginson (like Smith he was from Massachusetts); John Townsend and Fletcher Harper, Masters of Orange County, and Daniel Sands. Jimmy says, *"The Dulanys were very giving, and tolerated a lot of night hunters in the Piedmont territory,"* but as Orange County started to expand its country at Piedmont's expense the results were squabbles between Smith on the one hand, and Harper and Townsend on the other. Out of these altercations the Master of Foxhounds Association emerged to referee territorial disputes. Jimmy continues:

> *"For years after there was edginess between Piedmont and Orange County. Theo Randolph (by then MFH of Piedmont) was partly responsible. She asked me to be a patrol judge at the races, and so I was invited to the post-race parties. There she sat in a big chair, with a footstool beside it where guests could 'make their manners' at her feet.*
>
> *"I had learned from an old newspaper that she had once been a member of Orange County, and decided to one-up her with my discovery. So I sat on the footstool and congratulated her on the races, then added,*
>
> *'Is it possible you were once a member of Orange County?' She looked down at me.*
>
> *'You're absolutely right. I was. That was when I was a Winthrop, before I knew how to ride.' "*

Jimmy considers her another larger-than-life figure. He adds:

PHOTO BY DOUGLAS LEES

*Mrs. Randolph (left) presenting the Rokeby Bowl to rider Willie McCormick and winning owner Katherine Turner*

*"They are the anchors of a sport and a culture, a gentle curb chain on those that would like to change things too quickly."*

Tom's list and Jimmy's comments surely are not complete, but they give a feel for the people drawn to the area by the horse. Mostly, the early ones that made a dent had money – and some lived to excess. Those years were not known as the "Roaring Twenties" for nothing. A Fortune article described the Middleburg society of that era as:

> *"The Valhalla of the young married Valkyries, who drink, dance, and over-bid from dinner table to next morning's Meet… completely exonerated from all affectation about work. "*

Kitty Slater's comment in response is briskly acid:

> *"If ever existing to truly bear out Fortune's version, this super jet set was undoubtedly submerged – hopefully drowned – in the Wall Street Crash of 1929. And if the Crash didn't do it, the Depression and WWII surely tried, despite occasional media efforts to paint the area today as it perhaps once seemed to paint itself, long ago."*

Jimmy Hatcher, who first knew Middleburg in 1947 and moved there in 1966 because of his love of horses, feels Kitty's denial may be a bit too sweeping. After filling me in on the tangled genealogy of a few locals he points to the experience, perhaps apocryphal, of the young lady who came to work in the office at Foxcroft.

> *"She was at a party, and had a bit too much to drink. A friend found her alone and sobbing. 'What's the matter?' asked the friend. The unhappy answer: 'Everyone told me to come to Middleburg to find a rich husband. They didn't tell me that first you had to have one to trade in.'"*

In affluent communities – as in others – life between the sexes can be complicated, but it usually gets more notice if the names are well known. Of course most of those who came were good neighbors, good sportsmen, and good citizens. Many have left the area a better place. Their descendents are working hard, with long-time Virginians, to keep the beauty of the Piedmont intact for future generations to enjoy.

## – Musings of a Virginia-born Horseman –

Unlike the immigrants of the Northern Avalanche, Dr. Joe Rogers and his forebears have lived on a farm in Loudoun County *"forever."* Horses have always been part of his farm and his life – he was born with them.

> *"I went away to Med School, but as soon as I was a resident and had some time I started riding again. I could live and practice where I wanted. I never wanted to live anywhere but here. When I was young the farm was still worked by horses. When my father died we counted 60 on the place. Older horses that had done well were respected and cared for."*

As he moved up in the horse world the young Joe Rogers added the Initials MFH to go with his MD, eventually becoming one of the grand old men of

PHOTO BY DOUGLAS LEES

*Joe Rogers being awarded the Gold Cup in 1972
by Mrs. Harcourt Lees*

local horsedom. As he tells the story one's eyes wander to the silver plates on the mantel, the photographs of young Dr. Rogers riding steeplechasers over intimidating fences, and the handsome bronzes of horses in the windows. Despite these mementos of a notable equine career the home is unostentatious, comfortable, and well worn. It is a house for living in, for memories, for friends, but certainly not for public display.

At one point in our discussion Donna Rogers has to leave for a meeting. Before she does, she says,

> *"You ought to get in touch with Nancy Lee in Middleburg. She was a power at* The Chronicle. *She knows all about the Northern invasion of foxhunting."*

Then, going out the door, she suggests Joe and I adjourn to a drink. Passing through the dining room, on the way to the kitchen with Joe, I note more horse pictures and trophies, especially admiring a large engraved silver bowl in the center of the table.

*"That's the Rokeby Bowl,"* says Joe. The Rokeby Bowl is Piedmont's most prestigious race, and probably the most coveted win on the Virginia Point-to-Point circuit. Joe won it eight times (over a 42 year span) as owner, and four times as rider, and in the process retired the "permanent" trophy. On the sideboard is a large gold urn.

> *"That's the Gold Cup over there."*

Joe's third Virginia Gold Cup win as an owner retired that iteration of the trophy in 1984. After several people retired it with three wins, the last being Joe, the sponsors got tired of buying new Gold Cups and raised the possession barrier to five. The replacement remained unclaimed until Saluter won it for the fifth time in 1998.

In the kitchen we pour ourselves a drink. We sip slowly, lulled by the pleasure of a budding friendship brought about by the horse. When it is time to leave Joe goes with me out the door, walking a bit carefully because of a recent illness. I look out across the small valley at a pretty dark bay animal on the far slope, commenting,

*"That's a beautiful horse there."* As if on cue the colt canters towards us, across a small stream and up the hill to the barn.

*"Yes, he's a yearling by El Prado."*

*"I've always wanted to breed to El Prado, but..."* Joe finishes my sentence for me,

*"... he's getting too expensive. They keep raising his fee. Nothing but greed."*

Over the sins of commercial Kentucky stallion owners we part in fond agreement.

## – Memory Cards –

Donna Rogers was right when she said *"You ought to get in touch with Nancy Lee."*

Mrs. Lee is a charming lady, and a raconteur par excellence. After we got acquainted she apologized for her occasional lapses of memory. She said a friend had once told her,

PHOTO BY THE AUTHOR

*Nancy Lee reminiscing*

> *"The memory is like a file of cards in a box. As life goes along you add cards to the box, and pull them out as you need them. Eventually the box gets so full you have to tug at the crowded cards to pry one out, and sometimes that one brings others spilling out with it, and you get distracted. [Pauses then adds] ...And sometimes when I do get a memory card out I forget why I was looking for it."*

Despite these demurrers Mrs. Lee has a pretty clear picture of the village that was Middleburg before it became a tourist destination, overlaid with the skim of celebrity that conceals the work-a-day realities of life here. Nancy Lee was raised in Middleburg, where her father, Arthur Gartrell, was postmaster, and a partner in the local grocery store with his brother Donald. Customers would telephone in their orders, and the store would deliver them, toting up charge accounts they hoped would be paid promptly. As a child she grew up with horses.

*"I had my first pony when I was about four. Next door to our house Dorothy Lee [her future mother-in-law, and a noted show rider and trainer] had a place full of horses, we used to go through the fence and just watch 'em. I don't know when I didn't like 'em. There were still farmers driving four-horse teams with wagons, and the sporting element drove four-in-hands with coaches. Horses have been just a part of my life – a very important part.*

*"The street on the south side, where the bank and post office are now, was called Vinegar Hill. There was a paddock and a barn and people that came into town on horseback could leave their horse there, no charge or anything. We used to set up sawhorses between the barn and Route 50, and school our ponies over them, showing off to the people who drove out from Washington for the weekend. That must have been in the 1920's. This was a fun place to grow up.*

*"In the past the Upperville Show had classes for draft horses. In the early 1960's George Robert Slater asked me and my office to take over managing the show, which we did for 16 or 17 years. George Robert wanted to re-institute the work horse division. Well, Miss Charlotte at Foxcroft had two horses, Brookmeade had two, and someone had a team of four with bells on the harness and all that. With only one team of four they got a blue ribbon, but the bells scared the show hunters and they had to give them up before entering the ring."* [The current president of the Upperville Horse Show is Nick Slater, George Robert's son, and the third generation of Slaters in that position].

Nancy graduated from Middleburg High School in 1934, one of six members of the school's last class, of which she was valedictorian. One classmate was David Lee, whom she married in 1939 – they're still together.

*"For a year and a half after graduation I got to stay in Middleburg. Mrs. Lee owned Shy Acres, the property where the Community Center is now. She had show horses and what we called 'hunting hunters' which I exercised six days a week.*

*"Both my parents were college graduates. The Depression was in full swing, and finally my mother said, 'I refuse to raise a daughter with a hoof pick in one hand, and a rub rag in the other!' Dad found out about Strayer Business College in Washington. Because my work correcting papers would offset my tuition it was possible for me to go there."*

Without her saying so, these were not easy years for the family. The grocery store was done in by the Depression and the advent of the chain store, one factor being the reluctance of some customers – even the better off – to settle up on their charge accounts. On finishing Strayer Nancy turned down a job in Washington – she wanted to foxhunt. Back home, she held a variety of business-related jobs, eventually as Harry Tiffany's secretary at the old Loudoun National Bank in Leesburg. The Loudoun Hunt had been disbanded…

> "…but Hunton Atwell [one of its Masters] *still had hounds and he asked some of us to join him if we wanted.*"

Then came the war, with the men called away in the service. *The Middleburg Chronicle* – later called *The Chronicle of the Horse* – had been founded in 1937. Now Stacy B. Lloyd, its publisher, and Gerald B. Webb, Jr., its managing editor, were both leaving for the service, and they asked Nancy to take over as managing editor, which she did for over a decade, as will be described in a subsequent volume. After the war Stacy decided to sell *The Chronicle* because his wife was ill and they had to move to a different climate. The asking price was $100,000. Nancy wanted to buy it, but…

> "…one hundred thousand was like three million to me, I couldn't do it, though a friend lined up a syndicate."

*The Chronicle* was sold in 1952 to George Ohrstrom, Sr., who brought in Alexander MacKay-Smith to run it. Nancy continued for a while as managing editor, but as often happens, the new management style later became uncomfortable for her, and she resigned. Writing for the *Morning Telegraph* on Virginia Thoroughbred breeding was followed by several years as a partner in a local advertising business, which led to her founding the Lee Advertising Agency, Inc. She continues to be active, going to the office every day, but, she notes, *"doing as little as possible."* Lee Advertising was…

> "…started in 1961 in the basement of my house. The Thoroughbred Record *wrote us up as the first agency established just to do horse-oriented advertising. We helped advertise the sales of weanlings, yearlings, brood-mares, stallion shares and similar horse-related assets. In the evenings I proof-read Fasig-Tipton sales catalogs.*"

Another line of business was registering Thoroughbred foals, a process that involved visiting the farms, photographing the foals, filling out application forms, and submitting it all to the Jockey Club. Nancy reflects on the coming change from blood samples to hair as a source of a horse's DNA identification.

> *"We did 400 foals one year. Can you imagine going to farms and pulling hairs out of the manes of 400 foals?"* [Foal registry is no longer a Lee product line.] *We moved out of the basement to a large log building on the Eglinton farm, and eventually had nine people on the payroll.*"

I comment to the effect that that sounds like a lot of work. Her reply is quite definite:

---

*"This is the USA, and I'm one of the most bull-headed women in it!"*

I attempt to leave, but Nancy is having too good a time pulling cards out of her memory file. She is high on the impact Paul Mellon has had on the community and its horses, and shows me a Givenchy silk scarf given her by Mr. Mellon, which she has framed.

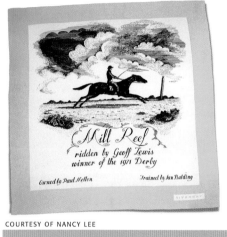

COURTESY OF NANCY LEE

*Scarf commemorating Mill Reef's 1971 Derby win in England*

Then, as a counterpoint,

*"One day a well-known man [she uses his name] called me, he wanted to advertise his prize yearling colt. I asked 'You mean the one by Assyrian?'* [The real name of the sire is NOT Assyrian]

*"Yes , that's the one.*

*"How are his front legs?"* Nancy knows that Assyrian is apt to pass on his crooked front legs to his offspring, but his few correct horses run like the wind.

*" 'Nothing wrong with mine, my agent said so.' "*

The caller decided to advertise his colt in the *Wall Street Journal*, which Nancy arranged, though she felt it was an unconventional venue for selling horses. She adds:

*"The cost of that ad would take all the fillings out of your teeth. And he didn't get a single reply to it. Then he took the horse to the Saratoga yearling sales in August. The bids didn't reach the reserve, so he had to bring him home unsold. The legs were crooked."*

We talk about people who have moved to the Middleburg area.

*"General Patton (he was a Colonel then) kept horses for himself and Mrs. Patton at Mrs. Lee's. He had been made Master of the Cobbler Mountain Hunt, and would stay at Shy Acres until his new quarters were ready."*

I note to myself that Nancy refers to her mother-in-law in the old fashioned, respectful way, as she has done several times so far in our conversation. She continues,

*"General Patton was Theo Randolph's uncle. George Bland, a colored man, named Theo 'The Kingfish' and it stuck. She never held it against him."*

My own acquaintance with the legendary Mrs. Randolph was minuscule, but from what I have learned of her dominant style of management I suspect she took pleasure in her nickname.

Months later, at a Point-to-Point, I am talking to Mildred (Bucky) Slater, then the newly appointed Master of the Piedmont Foxhounds. Bucky often hides her steel-trap lawyer's mind under a wardrobe of beautiful hats, but now she is moving vigorously into her new assignment. As the first female in charge since Theo Randolph she is working hard to make a few changes. Her husband Nick comments on how she is getting on…

*"Some of them are starting to call her the Queenfish!!"*

PHOTO BY ANITA BAARNS

*Mildred "Bucky" Slater, MFH*

# THE STABLE TOUR

*At Blue Ridge Farm tour-goers meet and "talk to" a miniature mare and her foal.*

*"The Trinity Stable Tour?… It's a wonderful outing for everyone. Working together, the parishioners get to know each other better. The tour-goers have a great day in the country, visiting farms and learning about horses. Through Trinity's outreach programs their money goes to help less fortunate people. When I'm taking tickets at Rokeby, every car that comes in says 'Thank you for having us,' and we say 'Thank you for coming.' Without the fellowship you couldn't have a Stable Tour."*

—Betsy Crenshaw, Trinity Church's "utility infielder," and a veteran of fifteen tours

———

For over forty years Trinity Church of Upperville has arranged a Memorial Day weekend tour of local horse facilities, an opportunity to sample our Community of the Horse. Trinity members plan the event, arrange for the farms to be visited, and serve as stewards and guides at the farms. The tour introduces the visitor – or in this case the reader – to a variety of horse related activities that flourish in northern Virginia.

Tour attendance is typically three to four thousand people. While no one discounts the appeal of the beautiful spring countryside, or the chance to peek behind private gates, it is the horse, in all his local manifestations, that holds the principal appeal for the visitors, and is the cohesive force that brings Trinity's parishioners and friends together in a community effort.

## – Volunteers –

PHOTO BY THE AUTHOR

*Betsy Crenshaw*

To manage the event 100 volunteers must be recruited for each day, and assigned to spots they will enjoy. Hunt Country Stable Tour polo shirts, recently given for stable tour volunteer service, have become a smash hit.

This year Cissy Bunn, a charming gray-haired lady of uncertain age, is Trinity's Coordinator of Volunteers. On the Thursday morning before the tour, she has found 23 phone messages on her answering machine, and the phone keeps ringing off the hook. Cissy is not yet through with her callbacks when I arrive at the Tour office at two o'clock.

Trinity's Rector, Robert Davenport, phones in. A senior parishioner is disappointed that he has not been called to serve – *"he does it every year."* A spot is quickly found for him, but someone points out that he missed the last two years, and so fell off the list. Probably he has seen the polo shirts and wants to earn his Varsity letter.

The phone rings again. Cissy answers:

*"Hunt Country Stable Tour."*

A pause ensues as she listens, then the silence is broken:

*"Ten to five, both days, except at the training track. They only work the horses on Saturday, seven to ten. They have Sunday off...[Another pause] Tickets at the Church or any of the tour sites. Look for the blue signs."*

Cissy hangs up. The phone rings again:

*"Stable Tour... [pause] Where are you calling from? Come eight miles west of Middleburg on Route 50. It's a big stone church on the right. Can't miss it."*

Another caller, a steward, wants an extra one of "Don's Johns" for his site. Cissy is firm:.

*"No, the Don's Johns truck came yesterday, and is all through. You're out of luck."*

I wonder about the visitor who may later find him or herself "out of luck."

A replay from the answering machine says, testily:

*"This is the third time I have called. Please call me back!"*

As in the past two occasions he gives his name but not his number, and he is unlisted in any local directory. Cissy's frustration is palpable:

*"Damn fool is mad we don't call him back, and he doesn't leave his number!"*

Then Cissy is talking to an unidentified caller, a steward (presumably a woman) who says:

*"We need a really strong girl to handle traffic and parking at Rock Ridge. No, not a kid. They just walk all over kids. Yes, I'll take a man."*

A volunteer calls to ask when she can get her polo shirt. She wants to wear it while on duty. Perhaps she wants her letter before playing in the game. But her heart is in the right place. Cissy groans:

*"It's a zoo."*

She sighs as the phone rings again. Cissy listens, then says:

*"Hi, Linda, it's Cissy Bunn. How can I help you?... [She listens some more] ...Oh, how neat."*

A long silence, occasionally broken by "...uh-huh." Then she laughs. More listening. My curiosity grows intense. Cissy is usually crisp and direct, not chatty.

---

*Rokeby is a long-standing draw on the Stable Tour*

> *"OK, Linda. You need to just come here and get some 'comp' tickets and take off following the map."*

Cissy gives detailed directions and hangs up. I ask, *"Who's Linda?"*

> *"She's with a firm hired by the Loudoun County tourism people to do a film on the area."*

No wonder Cissy schmoozed her a bit. She calls another one of the numbers left on her answering machine. What I hear is:

> *"Twelve and under are free. You can pick up the tickets at the 'will call'. You'll owe me thirty bucks. Give us your address so we can send you a brochure next year."*

She writes the information down, then adds:

> *"Tours of the Church are at 10,12, 2 and 4. See you Saturday."*

Cissy hangs up, grabs an envelope, stuffs two tickets in it, muttering to herself as she puts her pen to the envelope:

> *"Hope I'm spelling your name right, lady. But you'll get in, I'm sure."*

The phone rings again as I thank Cissy and retreat for home. As I leave I hear her say to herself, *"Oh, hush up!"* Then she answers the ring:

> *"Hunt Country Stable Tour... [pause] Do you know how to get to*

*Middleburg? Eight miles west of Middleburg…"*

Cissy is right. It's a zoo in there.

At Saturday breakfast Edie is wearing her stable tour polo shirt from last year, as she is on her way to spell Cissy on the phones. The schedule calls for me to go first to the training track. Half way there a goldfinch flashes across ahead of the car, his yellow and black breeding plumage assuring us that it is spring despite the damp morning.

## – *Taking The Tour* –

At the **Middleburg Training Center** horses are already working.

Arch Randolph is Stable Tour steward-in-charge, assisted by Cathy Zimmerman. They check tickets and offer coffee and sweet rolls to all comers. Two grooms of Hispanic origin go by us, leading two racehorses that have finished their morning work. The grooms turn their charges loose in a nearby paddock, and we watch the horses race off, bucking, kicking, and squealing for the pure joy of being young and fit and free. A country training track offers them a horse-friendly environment, impossible at a city track with its regimen of tedious confinement in a shed row stall.

Tanya Perez, from Skagit County north of Seattle, and her Aunt Maria, from Washington, DC. are taking the tour. Tanya is starting a business of breeding and training quarter horses, and this trip east is her birthday present. She is especially interested in barn designs. Maria is quiet, obviously proud of her niece, but insecure in English herself.

A teenage tour-goer, Lisa from Alexandria, appears. She allows as how she rides Molly, a Percheron cross. We observe, *"Pretty wide for you, isn't she?"*

   *"Yes,* [says her father] *…she's bowlegged when she gets off."*

Right now Lisa's interest is in photographing the barns as a backdrop for the "virtual" web site she is designing.

Walking toward the track I overtake a lady in a motorized wheelchair who, with the help of her husband, is attempting to navigate the deep sand of the approach. Finally, with a determined effort, she makes it to the grassy road-side, where she bounces along up to the rail. It turns out that the lady, Kim Buseman, is suffering from multiple sclerosis, and that her escape from the confines of her illness is a program of therapeutic riding. Her program at "Lift Me Up" near Chantilly…

   *"…gives me strength, balance, endurance, and keeps my spirits up. I love it."*

———

PHOTO BY THE AUTHOR

*Misty morning at the Training Center*

PHOTO BY THE AUTHOR

*A Middleburg Training Center barn*

The **Equine Swim Center** is near the track. Originally built by Piedmont MFH Randy Waterman, the facility is now owned and run by Roger Collins, its amenities including a 12-foot deep pool with entering ramp for horses, and a horse jacuzzi which Roger uses mostly to train his Labrador Retrievers. Also included are two barns with a total of 34 stalls. The lack of spit and polish suggests that Roger is running this as a business – $12 for one swim, $10 each for a book of 10 tickets, $8 for twenty, hold the maintenance to a minimum.

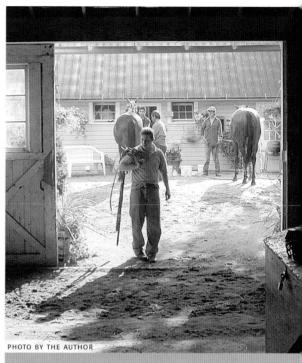

PHOTO BY THE AUTHOR

*Training Center barn and wash area*

Donny Yovanovich and his big trailer appear and begin unloading the day's first swimmers. Trainer Donny tells us he swims his active horses every day. It keeps them fit but leaves their legs unstressed, so he has horses running while some of their competitors are nursing their hurts.

**Paper Chase.**\* Here we are greeted by Trinity stewards Don Musch and Dan Haney, who report that the program will start at 11. Meanwhile, tour the facility.

Paper Chase is a boarding and training operation for riders wanting to improve their skills for showing and foxhunting. On Route 50, east of Middleburg, it is convenient to those who live nearer Washington, where open spaces are disappearing under black top and housing developments.

In the stable I find a lady grooming a Dutch Warmblood. She lives down in Old Dominion Hunt country, but keeps her horse at Paper Chase so that she can ride it on her way home from work. Nearby, Laura Baltus, a young woman from Fairfax, is zipping up her saddle in a Black Watch plaid carrying bag. Her enthusiasm and pink cheeks confirm her comment:

> *"I've been coming out here for four years. Like a bunch of us, I come because I like getting out into the country and riding on all the trails."*

Walking by the indoor arena one comes to stall #14, the home of Southern

---

\*[Ed. Note:] **Paper Chase** has recently been sold by its former co-owners, Joseph Keusch and his wife Jan Neuharth. Now called **Fox Chase**, it continues on the stable tour.

———

*Paper Chase – instruction in the indoor riding ring*

Comfort (nicknamed SoCo), according to the brass plaque outside the stall. Stall #15 is similarly adorned - its horse is named Baron. As I pause to read the plaque, Baron sticks his nose out between the bars to be petted. On stall #17 hangs a blue, red, and yellow championship ribbon, the property of the inhabitant Lucky Charm and his owner Erin Mistele. Elsewhere, riders of all ages are tending to their horses and their tack.

Outside, a gazebo opens onto the outdoor ring with its assortment of show jumps. It has begun to rain, and the traffic on Route 50 produces the wet whispering sound of tires on damp pavement. Horses are warming up in the ring for the coming program. Three stylish young ladies appear, riding side-saddle and dressed in identical dark blue riding habits, with black top hats and veils to protect their complexions from the sun (if any). The scene takes one back to the gay nineties, of which many have heard but no one here has experienced.

The crowd builds to about 100, replete with foul weather jackets, and cameras. Announcer Rick Isner warms up his microphone, warning people about the newly painted fence...

> *"Don't bump it. And, by the way, don't open or wave your umbrellas near the horses, they scare easily."*

As co-owner Joseph Kuesch enters the ring, clad in his "Pink" hunting coat, accompanied by two ladies in traditional black hunting jackets, Rick begins the program.

*"Paper Chase teaches English riding. We'll start with foxhunting. Actually fox chasing is a more descriptive term. I've hunted for thirty years, and never caught a fox; that suits me just fine. "*

PHOTO BY THE AUTHOR

*Paper Chase – cleaning tack*

As Joseph and his ladies canter slowly around the ring and over some jumps Rick describes the sport, its traditions and the reason Joseph's scarlet coat is referred to as "Pink" – the English originator of this type of coat was a Mr. Pink. At the last jump one of the ladies' horses refuses and she almost falls off. Hunting horses obviously aren't used to taking unnaturally painted jumps at such a slow pace.

The program will go on through a menu of equine disciplines, but it is time for us to move on, and the rain has subsided.

**Sporting Life Stables**, the home of pro football's Hall of Famer Sam Huff, is a small jewel of an operation for mares, foals, and young horses.

In his post-football years Sam has become a successful breeder of Thorough-breds, a radio announcer who applies his football broadcast talents to calling Point-to-Points over the air, and the guiding spirit behind the renaissance of horse racing in his native West Virginia. The layout of the farm reflects his many talents.

An unostentatious barn, immaculately maintained, sits in the center of 23 acres divided into several paddocks, each served by an automatic waterer, and accessible from the barn by aisleways between paddock fences. Maximum use has been made of its land. All grass is kept cut low, discouraging weeds but allowing horses access to both grass and the clover underneath.

Mares, foals, and yearlings all come up to "talk to" the tour visitors – evidence that they have become used to handling and enjoy people. This early relation-ship with humans will produce a positive attitude towards the vigorous

PHOTO BY DAVID L. SALLY

*Sam Huff talking to tour-goers*

training that lies ahead. Inside the barn a horse cooler\* is displayed. As it hangs, the white letters on its green background say:

COLONIAL DOWNS
THE ALL ALONG STAKES - GRADE III
OCTOBER 3, 1998

Under the cooler is a tack box, its top covered by publications referring to the stable's runners. The best of these, Bursting Forth, won four graded stakes in her career and earned $525,000 in addition to the cooler. Down the sand aisle of the stable is a neat tack room. Sam is temporarily away, leaving Carol Holden in charge, sitting by a TV monitor on which you can watch Bursting Forth's races. We see the mare run her race often – winning every time. (Horse owners seldom preserve film records of their losses.)

We chat about the Sporting Life horses. Carol reports:

> *"My Big Talkin' Man won an allowance race the other day at Keeneland. So now I have a cup to go with Sam's."* Then she adds:

> *"Bursting Forth set a new course record once. Every time there is a filly race at that track and distance Sam watches, hoping that 'his' course record will not be broken."*

Like leopards, fierce competitors never lose their spots.

---

\*A **cooler** is a light horse blanket, often used after a horse has been bathed and is cooling off. Coolers are popular awards for winning horses.

---

**The Goose Creek Bridge**
gives tour attendees a
glimpse into the area's
equine past. Nearby,
Union and Confederate
forces fought for control of
the area in local engage-
ments such as that at the
Bridge in June of 1863.
Re-enactors add realism to
the on-site descriptions of
cavalry tactics and soldiers
employed in that engage-
ment, a part of the battles
leading up to Gettysburg
in early July.

PHOTO BY PAT MACVEAGH

*The Goose Creak Bridge, still as it was when Stuart
and Pleasonton fought for it.*

**Blue Ridge Farm** is perhaps the most popular stop on the tour. It has been
in the Grayson family for a century, and for most of that time has been a
breeding farm.

The layout is attractive but unimposing, many acres of rolling fields inter-
spersed with copses of woods. Along with a small ante-bellum manor house
on a hill are two large, well worn white wooden barns of indefinite vintage,
dirt floors, and generous stalls in which are mares with foals, and mares
waiting to be bred to one of the farm's six stallions. Visiting the barns, one is
engulfed in the pleasant, gentle odor of hay, horse, and unpainted old pine
boards, a deep feeling of "yesterday" in the atmosphere.

Around those buildings lie a series of paddocks, occupied by several mares
with foals at side, grazing, nursing, or napping in the sun. Most are
Thoroughbreds, but Blue Ridge also stands a Connemara stallion, and in one
enclosure are two miniature horses, a mare and her tiny foal, a special
attraction for small children.

The stallions themselves are kept in a series of smaller structures scattered
about the farm. Each little stable has its own stall and private paddock for its
inhabitant, since stallions, if housed together, are likely to find combat
preferable to amity, especially during the breeding season.

A recent addition to Blue Ridge is Pleasant Colony. This great horse, born in
Virginia, won the Kentucky Derby and the Preakness, finished third in the
Belmont, and was three-year-old champion in 1981. As a sire he has produced
73 stakes winners, of which three have been champions.

Now Pleasant Colony has been retired to Blue Ridge to live out his days in the serene quiet of this lovely old farm. As I write this I reflect on the horse's name – Pleasant Colony – and how it so aptly describes the Virginia of 250 years ago, a heritage evident in the relaxed ambiance of the present day Blue Ridge.

Stable tour days at Blue Ridge, however, are an anomaly, bustling with activity – a sequence of arriving cars, ticket takers, car parkers, families with small children, interaction with horses by both naive and knowledgeable admirers, questions and answers, and – the highlight for some – the occasional covering* of a mare by a stallion down in the breeding shed.

Over all of this Bunny Nesbit holds sway. Bunny is a short, solid lady, endowed with a strong command presence, and a great love for children, her Church, her community, and its history. Managing the tour at this farm has been her responsibility for years, and she is not about to let anything go wrong now, as she leads a crowd of perhaps 25 curious people to the breeding shed.

Inside the shed is a mare, tail wrapped, held by handlers. Her demeanor suggests both eagerness and apprehension; probably her hormones are telling her what is in the offing. Quickly Bunny takes charge:

*"Stand back, over there against the wall."*

---

\**Cover* is the industry term for the act of equine procreation.

PHOTO BY THE AUTHOR

*A Blue Ridge Farm stable*

*Pleasant Colony*

The crowd congeals along the wall, mesmerized if not quite cowed by its temporary commander. Bunny adds, loudly:

"*Stallion's coming!*"

And so he is, prancing at the end of his lead shank. Seeing the mare, he lets out a loud whinny. He approaches her, sniffs her. She is quiet, signaling that she accepts him. Quickly the coupling occurs, lasts a few seconds, and is over. One realizes that these are large, physical animals with which it would be unwise to interfere at this moment in their lives. Then the stallion is led calmly away, his excitement drained. The mare follows, and the crowd is released by Bunny. As they disperse she turns to me and says, *soto voce*:

"*So much for foreplay.*"

**Rokeby**. We leave Bunny's domain to go to nearby Rokeby. Here one feels an air of wistful sadness. Paul Mellon, owner of Rokeby, a leading local citizen and an international figure in the worlds of horse breeding, racing, art and philanthropy, died in 1999. Much of his stable of renowned horses has been sold. What is left here is their former home, intact and immaculate, but occupied by only a residual handful of the horses that made up what was one of America's great breed-to-race operations.

We proceed up a manicured driveway, admiring the fields and vistas of the lovely farm, to the three-sided mare and foal barn, its stalls opening on a grassy courtyard in the center of which is a bronze statue of Mill Reef, winner of the Prix de l'Arc de Triomphe and the English Derby, Europe's two greatest races. Tour visitors seem to be hushed, peering in through stall screens at napping broodmares and their foals, or quietly inspecting the simple elegance of the building and its grounds, without any of the bustle that permeates other tour stops.

Ernie Bugg, for many years the manager of the Rokeby stable

PHOTO BY THE AUTHOR

*Mill Reef memorial*

PHOTO BY M.E. SMITH

*Rokeby mare barn courtyard*

operation, is there to answer questions. Another old-timer, Earl Loughborough, senior spirit of the periodical *In and Around Horse Country*, eyes the crowd from his seat next to the stall in which Jackie (Kennedy) Onassis' favorite gray hunter is munching hay.

We have been to this tour stop many times, but today we leave with a feeling of nostalgia for two icons of the Virginia Piedmont horse community – Paul Mellon and "Jackie O" – who have now passed into memory and legend.

**Rock Ridge** provides a sharp contrast to Rokeby. Snowden Clarke runs an active horse training operation, located in a little valley on a back road. Riders can board their horses, take lessons, and find help buying and selling horses. The clientele includes those interested in either hunting or showing, at levels ranging from beginner to expert rider. As a final touch, Snowden stands a noted Welsh Pony stallion, Houdini, who stamps his offspring with both jumping ability and the quiet temperament so desirable in animals that will teach eager youngsters to become skilled horsemen.

Entering Rock Ridge one passes up a sloping dirt lane to the top of a small rise on which is located a large wooden barn and an adjacent ring with several jumps. Inside the barn a sizable crowd of adults and children are mingling with stable workers, and making friends with horses in stalls on both sides of a long aisle. Here there is none of the "horses bite, don't touch" attitude that pervades many stables. The interaction between children and horses is great tonic for both, and both seem to be enjoying it without benefit of legal counsel. Rock Ridge is all about having horses for companionship and fun, which after all is why most horse people treasure them.

The features for the tour visitors are the jumping lessons and exhibitions scheduled for 1:30 and 3:00pm each day. Unfortunately we are on another schedule, and so miss that part of the program.

**The Middleburg Agricultural Research and Extension (M.A.R.E.) Center** is our next stop. On 400 acres donated by Mr. Mellon, Drs. Wendell Cooper and David Kronfeld preside over an extension of Virginia Tech's veterinary education and research program.

Their specialty is nutrition of broodmares and young horses, with attention to the role of pasture grasses and food supplements in the development of young animals. Donors have provided the MARE Center with about 40 mares and two or three stallions for their experimental work, the studies being conducted by post-graduate students.

In addition to a general introduction to the facility's work, and visits to its animals, tour-goers are able to observe ultrasound inspections of in-utero

---

*Mares and foals at the MARE Center*

fetuses, examinations helpful in determining pregnancy and the effect of various elements in a mare's diet on her coming baby. The Center also tests horses exercising on its treadmill to determine effects of nutritional additives on endurance. In the fall of each year the subjects of past studies, now yearlings, are auctioned off to become racehorses, hunters, show horses or pleasant riding companions.

*Working the treadmill*

In 2002 the Center had a very rare experience – the birth of healthy twin Thoroughbred foals, which were auctioned as weanlings that fall.

The Center is also researching pasture management techniques to reduce the runoff of nitrogen and phosphorous, "non-point source" pollutants that are having serious adverse effects on the nation's surface waters.

**Salamander Farm**, owned by Robert and Sheila Johnson, is not far to the west of Rock Ridge. The Johnsons are the founders of Black Entertainment Television, and bought Salamander in 1996 from Bill Ylvisaker, a noted former polo player. Its unusual name comes from an earlier owner – Bruce Sundlun – who was saved during World War II by the use of the code word "Salamander." Mr. Sundlun left Virginia to become Governor of Rhode Island, a juxtaposition of geography and politics the explanation of which lies beyond the scope of this writer's research.

The Johnson family includes a teen-aged daughter, Paige, already an accomplished show rider. They have added a 14-stall stable and large indoor riding arena to the property, and stocked it with sev-

PHOTO BY RON AIRA

*Sheila Johnson*

eral beautiful show hunters. Sheila Johnson drifts among the admiring guests with great ease, emanating friendship, grace and humility – traits sure to overpower any incipient feeling of envy in the mind of a visitor.

One is taken with the attractive design of the new structures and the detailed attention to quality. Along the side of the indoor arena are two or three rooms with large picture windows facing the riding area. One of these is a well-appointed small sitting room, located adjacent to a pantry and wet bar.

Here I find my friend George Beavers, watching a baseball game on the television. George is a Trinity steward detailed to Salamander, and has the job of preventing untoward behavior in the entertainment and bar area. I am forced to comment, *"Isn't this like asking the fox to guard the hen house?"* George only smiles, though I assume that what he is drinking is Stable Tour Coca Cola.

One suspects that Salamander will soon surpass Rokeby as the leading attraction for Trinity stewards. And one day, when Paige Johnson makes the US Olympic team… but that is for many years hence.

**Newstead Farm** is the home of Bert and Diana Firestone, and the prior home of one of Virginia's legendary Thoroughbred breeders, Taylor Hardin. Since those days the center of gravity of Thoroughbred breeding has shifted to Kentucky, and with the death of Paul Mellon Virginia breeding is centered on a few quality but smaller operations such as Newstead.

The Firestones wear two equine hats - breeding to race in both Europe and North America, and showing, now mostly through the efforts of their daughter, Alison, a rising star on the International Grand Prix circuit.

PHOTO BY THE AUTHOR

*Diana and Bert Firestone with Genuine Risk*

A graceful manor house - not on the tour - is surrounded by broodmares, foals and well-kept stables. Here the center of tour attraction is Genuine Risk, one of only three fillies ever to win the Kentucky Derby. To understand what a special horse she is, consider that 18,000 Thoroughbred fillies are now born each year; she is one of only two females in the last 85 years to win America's most coveted race.

Born in 1977, the old lady poses as the quiet *grande dame* she has become. Her knees show the effects of hard racing, but she consents to be petted and admired, and she has kept her figure very well, thank you. Her life since her days on the track has been in a way disappointing, for she has proved very hard to get in foal. In 14 years of trying, her total offspring number two, both colts that have never raced.

But few people have had the privilege of owning a horse that started 15 races, won ten, and was second or third in the other five, including seconds in the Preakness and Belmont to go with a Derby win, let alone done it with a filly. During the 1970s the Firestones also bred and raced Honest Pleasure – six Grade I stakes wins, and a second in the 1976 Kentucky Derby – and General Assembly, another Grade I winner and also second in the 1979 Kentucky Derby. Then came 1980, and Genuine Risk's blanket of roses – icing on the cake.

As at Rokeby, the mood around Genuine Risk is pleasant nostalgia, mixed with a feeling of longing for times when Virginia was at the center of American Thoroughbred breeding, an era that now seems to be passing quietly into history, along with the genes of Genuine Risk.

PHOTO BY PAT MACVEAGH

*Peace and Plenty broodmare in stall*

**Peace and Plenty**, Rose Marie Bogley's farm near Upperville reaches even further back into local history. Like all the area around, it was part of the original crown grant to Lord Fairfax. In the nineteenth century it was a peach orchard, with a cannery to process the fruit and other area produce. Later the land was for a time part of the large holdings of Bedford Glascock. Its 17 stone buildings have been carefully preserved by the present owner.

Artifacts – photographs, paintings, trophies and bronzes – in the barn's tack room testify to the Bogley family love of horses and horse sports. In a smaller barn next door two gravid broodmares alternately nibble on their hay and peer at the crowd, patiently awaiting the imminent arrival of the equine stork.

But the owner's present cause is the reclamation of abandoned animals. At the entrance to the farm yard are tables with literature on ways to assist animal rescue organizations. There also is a cage with kittens available for adoption, and a pen with a black Schipperke bitch with six pups of the same color, but with the other half of their pedigree uncertain.

Other animals include a three-legged goat and 37 horses, most of them rescued and retired to the fields of Peace and Plenty. One senses from the reaction of the tour goers that they relish the quiet of the place as well.

PHOTO BY PAT MACVEAGH

*Casanova - the pride of Coachman Farms*

**Coachman Farms**. While Jay Fetner's farm is home to a variety of breeds its collection of huge Belgian Draft Horses is special. The largest, Casanova, a roan stallion, stands almost 19 hands and weighs about 2300 pounds.

Their home is a trim dark green barn, built into a hillside so the hay and other supplies can be driven easily onto the floor above the horses. And with one wall of the horse floor cut into the hill there is a natural moderating effect on the temperature - cooler in summer and warmer in winter than the outside air.

A visitor, Marie Ripley, calls me shortly after the tour to find out where to write a "thank you" letter. She adds:

> *"Coachman Farms is my favorite, it's so well put together. The house is up the hill, almost out of view, but they can look out from it and see every-*

thing, horses and all. And the barn is perfect, done with such good taste. He did it all stick by stick."

She is also much taken with the tack room. The pictures, trophies and ribbons there confirm that these are among the best Belgians – horses, that is – in the world. Like most draft horses there is little call these days for Belgians, and so the breed depends on farms like Coachman to preserve the genetic line of these beautiful and gentle animals. Marie closes our telephone visit:

"It's so good of all these people to open their farms, and for the volunteers to put in the work required. Thank you."

## – What the Stable Tour Means –

On this particular year Trinity's Stable Tour Sunday service is conducted by Assistant Rector Blair Pogue, Robert being away at his daughter Penelope's graduation. Blair is new to Trinity. Here is how she reflects on the Tour in her sermon:

"I am hard pressed to come up with a better example of Christian witness. Over the years I have been part of many different congregations, the majority of them having more than eight hundred members. Yet rarely have I seen an event of this magnitude… I am astounded that a Church of less than two hundred regular communicants can pull off a Stable Tour.

"Yesterday I visited all the teams at farms, selling tickets, giving tours at the Church, cooking and serving the lunch. A Stable Tour cannot happen with one person. It cannot happen even with a handful of people working together. Only when many, many people join together, to work for a larger purpose and vision, can a Stable Tour happen.

"The money we raise will help people, perhaps change their lives in some small way. But our lives are changed too. We catch up with old friends, we make new friends, and we are privileged to participate in something much larger than ourselves. And perhaps, yesterday and today, we had a glimpse of God's love and purpose.

"Is the Stable Tour just another charity event? If not, what makes it different?

"…While the Stable Tour raises money for many worthy causes, our motivation should not be just raising money or helping others… Rather, our purpose is to make God known through our love for one another and for those men, women, and children who receive our humble offerings. The Stable Tour is an act of thanksgiving, for what we are and what we have. For we know that without God we are nothing."

Blair is not (yet?) a horse person, but very perceptive. As experience expands her horizon she may also realize – perhaps she does already – that God's efforts at ecumenical community building are supported by numerous horses worldwide. As the Koran instructs:

> *"When God created the horse He said to the magnificent creature: 'I have made thee as no other. All the treasures of the earth lie between thine eyes. Thou shalt carry my friends upon thy back. Thy saddle shall be the seat of prayers to me. And thou fly without wings, and conquer without any sword. Oh, horse.'"*

Horses support His work in elevating people's understanding of self, their love for fellow beings – human and animal, and their commitment to community, and to each other, whether in Upperville or Islam. In doing so they become true agents of His grace.

*Mare nursing twin foals at the M.A.R.E. Center*

# HORSE AS HEALER

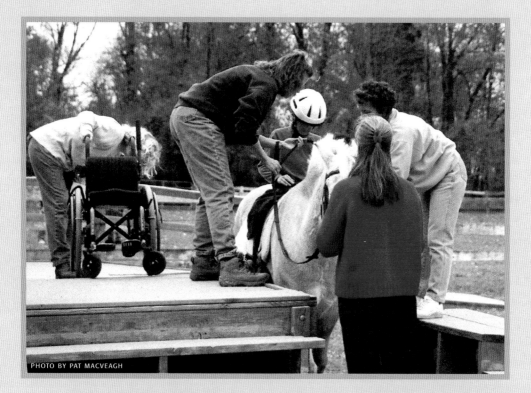

PHOTO BY PAT MACVEAGH

*Lift Me Up! staff members help a physically challenged child onto a pony.*

– From the book *Horse Sense and the Human Heart* –
© Health Communications, Inc.

*"This book is about how horses take us on another deeper journey, to the realms of healing, awareness, and soul growth. ...[They] teach us to look deeper into nature and our interconnectedness with all life, and as a result, deeper into our own hearts.*

*"Horses seem to know what people really need. They ignore the outward form, and respond instead to the person's inner substance... They embody living, breathing desire, and hold the key to the door of eternal passion... When we give up control, and let the horse be our guide, we can rediscover our souls."*

—Doctors Adele and Marlena McCormick

———

*"My emotional safe haven was a horse. My geographic safe haven was Sunnybank Farm in Middleburg. I was going through a period of economic and emotional depression, and I had a safe haven when I could ride every afternoon. My horse Topeador was a big part of that. Our relationship led to races – winning races – which gave me antibodies I would not otherwise have had to deal with my problems."*

—Henry Wood, Atlanta businessman, and seven time
Virginia champion owner-rider over fences.

The Doctors McCormick, mother and daughter, have worked for many years with handicapped people, seeking to find non-traditional ways to free them from their psychoses and set them on the path towards a normal life. After some almost random experiences connecting horses with patients, they developed methods of therapy using relationships with horses to engage their patients' minds, to build their confidence and feeling of self-worth, and from that beginning to liberate them from their isolation from other humans, taking them out of concentration on self and reintroducing them to normal relations with others. While their work has centered on mental problems their conclusions are just as applicable to those with physical challenges.

*Horse Sense and the Human Heart* is a presentation of their findings, conclusions

Racing at Blue Ridge. Henry Wood and Topeador (left)

PHOTO BY DOUGLAS LEES

that should come as no surprise after the many horsemen's quotes in our preceding chapters. The examples of the McCormicks' success are both dramatic and heartwarming. We quote below a few extracts from what they have to tell us:

> "Our work has taught us that the horses were skilled guides, divine messengers in a sense, who can show us who we are, and point us in the direction we need to go. They act as larger-than-life-size mirrors, reflecting back to us the totality of who we are, complete with light and shadows.

> "Branching out [to horses] prevents us from becoming species-specific, thus increasing our empathy with the greater universe. ...Working with horses... has taught us to be more open, more malleable, and to approach life with a sense of adventure. ...[H]orses bring people together, cementing relationships in a very profound way."

The authors point out that people in urban areas, particularly, can be helped by horses to connect with the wider world that their rural forebears took for granted, and of which much of our society is now unaware.

What the McCormicks have discovered as professionals, many caring horse people are now applying to help those in physical or mental need. Often these efforts are called "Therapeutic Riding," though some programs substitute horse care for actual riding. The North American Riding for the Handicapped Association reports there are now 700 therapeutic riding centers, where 32,000 volunteers help a like number of riders. There are about 20 such programs in Virginia, including Kim Buseman's Lift Me Up! in Great Falls.

## – Lift Me Up! –

Lift Me Up! was founded in 1975 by Colleen Zanin, a lifelong rider and an Occupational Therapist with the Fairfax County School system. The organization's web site describes its activities as follows:

> "By combining the unique and special presence of the horse and the skill and caring of our registered instructors, we have been able to help hundreds of people gain confidence, patience, and invaluable self esteem."

Its brochure goes on to say:

> "Hippotherapy [hippo is the Greek word for horse] uses the natural three-dimensional movement provided by the walking horse. This movement stimulates the client to develop balance and muscular control. The rhythmic, continuous motion of the horse provides a multitude of sensations

*Lift Me Up! kid on horseback*

*to promote relaxation, stretching, and mobility. The therapist capitalizes on this natural movement and skillfully combines it with traditional neuro-developmental and sensory integrative techniques."*

Having wandered too far into medical jargon the brochure catches itself, and concludes with:

*"…the best, and most obvious benefit of therapeutic riding is that it is just plain FUN."*

Lift Me Up! operates during the spring, summer, and fall (winter weather is too severe for its activities) on a back yard farm in Great Falls, a tract of land that has been withheld from development by the family that has owned it for over 100 years. There a staff of about eight — most having Physical or Occupational Therapy training, jobs in the school system, and a love for horses - tends to the needs of about 40 riders suffering from some form of debilitating affliction.

Beyond its professional staff, volunteers serve to prepare the program's four horses, lead them when ridden, and serve as "side walkers" to steady those riders who are too insecure in the saddle to ride unaided. Several of these volunteers are high school students interested in discharging their community service obligations in this manner, thus gaining insight into both horses and the lives of the less fortunate.

Quality of horses is a major concern for Lift Me Up!, given the nature of their riders. They must be able, as the web site says...

> "...to safely and gently carry a handicapped rider whose balance is frequently fragile and muscles unfit. A LMU horse must be kind and steady – absolutely unflappable... Our mounts are experienced veterans from many careers. Many are wise senior citizens enjoying a productive golden age."

Colleen is especially pleased with a new hydraulic lift. She explains:

PHOTO COURTESY OF LIFT ME UP!

*Child being mounted with assist from the lift.*

*"It picks up the rider under the rib cage and the thighs, lifts her (or him) slowly and places him (or her) gently, slowly and precisely in the saddle."*

Obviously this is a more comfortable and dignified process than being manhandled aloft by a couple of muscular humans. I ask Colleen about her staff and her concerns for the future...

*"We're lucky that Fairfax County is the largest employer of therapists in the state. But we still have an applicant list of about 30 prospective riders, and a wait of two years, because of the capacity of our arena and size of staff. And we are careful about the quality of our program.*

*We've kept the lessons individual, hands-on hippotherapy, rather than semi-private or in groups. But we may have to reconsider, in view of the waiting list."*

*"How about finances."*

*"Well, I'm a volunteer, but we do pay the therapists modestly. Then there is horse board, and vet bills are horrendous..."*

*"Why is that?"*

*"Maybe bad luck. Our best pony is over 30, still going strong, but on a lot of medication. The fabulous new Fjord that we just bought is anemic - more medication. And maybe we care too much and over-use the vets. Plus, there's the farrier, administrative costs and insurance."*

*"How about revenues?"*

*"We charge $30 per session, each rider comes once a week, unless we get rained out. We have fundraisers, and some generous donors. The Great Falls Newcomers Club has been very helpful with annual grants - those people know how to raise money."*

*"What else do you worry about?"*

*"Recently the Great Falls Horse Center nearby has closed, as has Bay Ridge in Centreville. That's a thousand riding lessons a week unfulfilled, all because of development. We're working with Fairfax for Horses, a grass roots organization, hoping to get a public equestrian facility on park land somewhere in Fairfax county. We'd have therapeutic riding there, too, sort of like soccer moms."*

*"That makes sense. The soccer leagues use public fields."*

From her tone of voice Colleen is justifiably proud of what she has done, but it still is a tough management job.

———

## – Kim –

We have run into Kim Buseman and her husband Bill on several occasions since meeting them on the Stable Tour. Kim is often in a wheel chair as a result of multiple sclerosis (MS). Nonetheless she is a horseman. When we first met she said that her therapeutic riding program at Lift Me Up! in Great Falls…

> "…gives me strength, balance, endurance, and keeps my spirits up. I love it."

Here she is at the Glenwood Park paddock, where she had her first Point-to-Point winner, Noble Testamony. I asked if she had ever had a fall…

PHOTO BY THE AUTHOR

*Kim and Bill Buseman*

> "Yes, I was trail riding with Andrea Weyer. When I fell off – the horse was stung by a bee and bolted – she went to get help but her Labrador, Tucker, stayed with me, and drove off the bees that were now aggressively curious about a fallen human!"

Despite the fall and the bees she is still riding.

A few days ago we received a note from Kim, whom we had not seen since the yearling auction at the MARE Center in October, where Edie bought Bonica. Here's what she wrote:

> "I include some pictures to show you what I have been doing. I continue my therapeutic riding and did dressage for the first time. We went to the TRAV (the Therapeutic Riding Association of Virginia Horse Show in Lexington) at the Virginia Horse Center, in October and I won first place in dressage. What a thrill and what a beautiful facility in Lexington. Have you been there? [Answer: Yes.]

> "Then in November, Lift Me Up! (the therapeutic riding association in

*Great Falls where I ride), had another horse show and I won another blue ribbon. This is fun !! The pony that I ride at Lift Me Up!, 'Sir Ector', is in his mid 30s – what a trooper.*

*"We still have Noble Testamony but she is now boarded at Cooney Racing Stables at Llangollen on Trappe Road – I think that's near you. It is so beautiful out there and she is happy with Susan Cooney as her trainer. She is racing at Charles Town from there."*

That led to a discussion of her experiences with Lift Me Up! and therapeutic riding. Here is what she had to say:

*"I'm originally from Pennsylvania, came down here after college, 26 years ago. I just liked the area. I wasn't horsey as a girl, though there is a picture of me on a pony.*

*"MS tells you what to do – I've had it 26 years. You could sit in a chair all day, but I stay as fit as I can. Some are bed-bound in six months, so I'm thankful for every day. I work at it, go religiously to the gym; it's made a tremendous amount of difference.*

*"I started riding six years ago. I met a friend who had a daughter in a riding program. Andrea Weyer – you know her? – taught at Lift Me Up! and she got me in the program. She had her own horses, so some-*

BUSEMAN FAMILY PHOTO

*Kim with blue ribbon*

*times I went out there in the winter when LMU was closed.*

*"Physically, riding has been a tremendous help to me – stability, balance. Mentally, I don't know what I'd do without horses."*

I ask her about Lift Me Up! After confirming most of what Colleen told me, she adds:

*"It serves adults and children. Most of the adult women have MS. Some children are autistic, others have mental problems.*

*"My instructor does dressage, so I am trying it. She went to upstate New York to learn judging for the Paralympics, and came back saying 'we're doing everything right. If you were 20 years younger you could do it,' so I said, 'Why not?' Maybe next year."*

I learn that Kim is a nurse, still working part time – on the phone – with care management and medical insurance matters. And she can drive a car, which gives her a feeling of independence. Then she adds:

*"From when I was introduced to therapeutic riding it has grown to become 50 percent of my life – the friends I've met, the activities, the projects I've worked on. It's meant everything to me."*

*"You see the little ones. Autistic children almost never change their solemn, vacant expressions – but, on a horse, there are ear-to-ear grins. It's amazing. The little ones are the FUN."*

"FUN." Come to think of it, that's what the Lift Me Up! brochure said, too.

*Rider on "The fabulous new Fjord" placing a ring where it's supposed to go.*

PHOTO BY PAT MACVEACH

Another program, called "Life Horse," is located at Stonelea Farm near Aldie, Virginia, following the success of its prototype, Margaret Hadley's Covenant Farm in Frederick County, Maryland. Life Horse is unique in that it works only with children, either those who are mentally challenged or those who have life-threatening ailments such as leukemia or sickle cell anemia.

The executive director of Virginia's Life Horse is Elizabeth Beller, a second grade teacher and a mother of small children. Elizabeth came to riding as a result of the accidental death of a very small adopted daughter, Hannah, with whom she had dreamed of horses and riding. In her period of grief, when conventional counseling proved of little value, she took up riding. Here's how she tells it:

> *"My childhood dream of learning to ride resurfaced in a flood of energy, and I remembered my promise to Hannah. We would ride horses together. Her spirit would ride with me."*

She describes the difficulties and eventual triumph of her first lesson, concluding:

> *"My grief, my rage, my broken heart dissolved that afternoon as Spec [an Appaloosa] spoke to my soul, carrying me on his back through space and time."*

A second tragedy interrupted her recovery, but then the prospect of another adopted child brought hope, and…

> *"I started riding again in the spring, just prior to bringing Briana home. Slowly, sporadically at first, but before too long I began to feel again that mystical connection between horse and rider… Riding calmed me, renewed my strength and rekindled my passion for living. It has never been a sport for me; rather it is a source of solace."*

To give something back for the help riding had been, she volunteered to help with a local therapeutic riding program.

> *"I saw children with a myriad of disabilities, [initially] too shy to speak, revel in their newfound skills as they progressed through their lessons… by the end of a session they were chattering happily, hugging and stroking their new furry friend who had taken such good care of them. To watch these children transform… validated the therapeutic benefits of horseback riding for anyone who is in pain."*

During this time Elizabeth Beller learned of the "Life Horse" program in Maryland. She describes her reactions on visiting Covenant Farm:

*"Margaret, a very religious person, had single-handedly created a country sanctuary for children and their families, a place where they could feel whole again. Horses, once again, came to the rescue for children who needed a chance to live in 'real time,' absorbed in a completely sensory experience. And perhaps the most powerful aspect of the Life Horse program at Covenant Farm was the camaraderie that was built between these children."*

Out of these experiences Virginia's Life Horse program at Stonelea Farm was born.

Elizabeth explains that so far they have survived on individual contributions, the support of about 20 volunteers, the availability of Stonelea Farm, and the moral support of US Senators John Warner and Jim Jeffords. They hope to get foundation support, but do not yet have it. And, because of the 9-11 terrorist attack their "grand opening" has been postponed to next spring, because *"Senator Warner has too much on his plate just now."*

When I arrive at Stonelea Farm this cold October evening I am not prepared for what is there. In many "named" horse farms in the Middleburg area one enters through stone gate posts, and follows a long driveway, passing through green paddocks to an elaborate stable or comfortable manor house. Stonelea, located on the Washington side of Aldie, is instead a modest-sized part of a casual sub-division, consisting of a home of unremarkable design, two dirt riding rings, an inexpensively built stable, and a mostly bare paddock of perhaps two or three acres. Populating this spread are three horse trailers, several cars, a tractor, about ten assorted horses and ponies, the proprietress Lucia Livermore, and at this particular moment four or five children, a parent for each, and the "staff" of Life Horse, Elizabeth Beller and several volunteer assistants.

As I park along the driveway three girls, ages five to eight, are forking piles of manure from the surface of the front riding ring into a wheelbarrow, obviously an introductory lesson in horse care. Walking around the house and the trailers I find the larger back ring and the stable. Elizabeth, a bundle of youthful enthusiasm topped by a mop of bright red hair, greets me as if I were a long-lost friend. Quickly I am introduced all around to a remarkable group of people, most of them engaged in tacking up four equines for the first of the two evening sessions.

Lucia, the hostess to Life Horse, was once a real estate broker. She comments:

*"I got most of my clients and leads from the people where I boarded*

[actually, where her horse boarded]. *So horses were instrumental in how I made a living. Then I switched to school teaching. Now I combine the two things I most love doing, horses and teaching, by giving riding lessons."*

With that she has explained the eclectic collection of veteran horses and ponies in the large paddock I can see behind the stable. The youth of the children surprises me – they range from about five to eight. In the area in front of the stable the evening's mounts are being prepared. One child, about six, is struggling to lift pony Patty's hind foot so she can clean it with a hoof pick. The struggle is partially successful, helped by an adult volunteer. Another is riding Kyrie for the first time, promoted to the eminence of a 16.1 hand 23 year old somewhat sway-backed Thoroughbred mare. Already in the ring are Mushroom, a dun colored small pony, and Montreal, a 27 year old dark brown quarter horse type, each with a young rider.

Soon Patty and Kyrie join them, walking or trotting around the ring as the skill of the rider permits. Each horse/rider combination is accompanied by one or usually two adults, one to lead, and one to support the rider as needed. One has to remember that these small children all have debilitating chronic life-threatening diseases. Having lived with those conditions they are far less self-confident and physically strong than their healthy contemporaries. The hope of Life Horse is that through association with and affection for the large animal under them each can progress towards enjoying a normal childhood.

The first 45-minute session soon ends, and the new – and it seems slightly older and more skilled – pupils for the second session arrive. One girl in this group has advanced to where she "solos" at a walk, trot, and canter, with an instructor helping her to get her horse on its correct lead.

Outside the ring I meet Mitchell, father of Joshua who is afflicted with sickle cell anemia. I ask, *"Is it curable?"*

*"No, not really. It's genetic."*

Mitchell explains the disease to me about as follows:

*"The sickle cell condition evolved in Africa as a defense of the body against malaria. Both my wife and I have a sickle cell trait, inherited from one parent, enough to make us immune to malaria, but not otherwise significant. Some people inherit the trait from both parents, leading to sickle cell anemia. That's what Joshua has."*

Mitchell continues:

*"I could tell that Joshua hurt a lot today, but he didn't say anything because he didn't want to miss riding."*

In the eyes of this tall, athletic-looking man, a professional computer programmer, you can see the sadness that his little boy would miss so much of what he, and I, and other boys enjoyed on the road to becoming grown men. I ask Mitchell how he heard about the program…

*"My good friend Sheldon Hutchinson told me about it."*

Then he adds:

*"I couldn't put a price on what the volunteers give."*

Sheldon, a retiring man, and his daughter Shenrye, were two I had met during the first session, as were Gail Schaller, a nurse, and her seven-year-old son Christopher, who has leukemia. Gail says she learned about the program from a patient of her office whose child was in the program. At Stonelea one is reminded of the great baseball movie *Field of Dreams*, which also has the theme of rehabilitation (though moral rather than physical), and is based on the theory that…

*"If you build it, they will come."*

Margarita, the wife of a Chilean diplomat, is there with her daughter Isadora, and a friend, Guido, who has a camcorder along to record the event. Isadora, another leukemia sufferer, has had a bone marrow transplant. Margarita tells me, as best she can in English:

*"Before we know about program, Isadora want to work with horses. Now she can't swim – danger of virus – so she's attached to horses. Animals all have a speech. Horses have high communication with people."*

Margarita's English is far better than my Spanish, and her thoughts are crystal clear. She gives me a cookie baked in the shape of a horse, then adds:

*"And Isadora has made drawings of horses."*

Ellen, one of Elizabeth's assistants, is especially helpful in filling me in on Life Horse. I comment, *"None of these kids seem to have any fear of the animals."*

*"No, they don't. When they first come they are assigned to paint 'glitter' on a horse's legs. That way they have to go all the way around the horse, touch it. The volunteer just eases them into it. It's a technique that Life Horse teaches the staff."*

By now the second session is almost over, I'm almost frozen, and I use the cold as an excuse to say good-bye. Mitchell comments:

*"I don't blame you. If I didn't have a kid out there I'd be leaving too."*

———

Since writing this piece, Life Horse at Stonelea has ceased operation, the victim of the difficulties of recruiting volunteers and financing the program. Fortunately a number of other similar programs exist in the area. Elizabeth Beller comments on the reasons, no doubt typical of the obstacles such volunteer-intensive organizations face:

> "Since 9/11 a lot of monetary and volunteer support seems to have been re-directed... Therapeutic riding needs a cadre of a special kind of volunteers. And there is always a difficulty finding a host facility that is available for the right reasons, not just to rent out space and animals. We were not alone in having to close. Madcap Farm in The Plains shut down after ten years, despite having a star-studded board of directors.

> "Then there is an on-going concern over the risk, the inherent problem of especially fragile children being near large, unpredictable horses. We had insurance, of course, but that didn't overcome the worry. The horse is wonderful, if you have the right ones, but the risk is greater than using dogs for therapy."

As she talks, there is a feeling of deep regret in her voice.

> "It was traumatic, quitting it. The program was to be a memorial to the daughter that I lost. But the experience wasn't a total loss. I learned a lot about the nature of people... and I was able to refer each of the kids to another reputable program."

Elizabeth is now deeply engrossed in her career as a teacher at Wakefield School, and planning to move her home closer to the school so that her family can be a fuller part of that community. In doing so she will also be moving nearer to horse country, and, someday, perhaps, a chance to begin Life Horse II.

# VI
## AS THE TWIG IS BENT

*Tacking her up - Lisa White, Pamela and Chessie*

——

*"Tis education forms the common mind: Just as the twig is bent, the tree's inclined."*
—Alexander Pope, essayist, 1688-1744

Horsemen do not appear out of thin air. They become infected with a love of the animal, most frequently at an early age; for many the commitment proves to be life long. One summer day, some years ago, we became reacquainted with the world of the horse-addicted young.

## - Lindsay -

We met Lindsay van Melle Kamp at a friend's house on the coast of Maine, where she was visiting with her mother and uncle. Lindsay is a bright, articulate eleven year old, an only child, born in New York, and raised first in South Africa, her father's home. She lives at present in Paris with her now divorced artist mother.*

In addition to painting, Lindsay's mother, Olivia, is a past dressage and three-day event rider, still active as a trainer. By the time Lindsay was three Olivia had introduced her to horses, both as animate creatures to be ridden, and as subjects for Lindsay's early drawing lessons. Lindsay says of Olivia:

> *"She's a great mom to have. She gets me to my riding lessons, teaches me to draw, and helps me with my 'levels.' "*

She explains that in France young riders are classified by skill levels, ranging from 1 to 9, and advance by passing tests. Now at level 4, her goal is to reach level 9.

Getting Lindsay to riding lessons in France is not easy, for the stable is two and a half hours outside of Paris. The horses she rides most are called "double ponies", apparently large ponies around 14 hands, quite suitable for a slender girl of average height. At summer riding camp Lindsay had complete charge of caring for a horse. Next year she hopes to begin showing, including dres-

---

* Subsequent to this meeting Lindsay and her mother have relocated to Connecticut. We suspect some day soon we will see Lindsay in Virginia.

sage and jumping, but is a bit skeptical of competition…

> *"I take horse riding as a sport, a thing you like to do all the time. I'm not sure about competition – there can be a lot of fraud in it."*

I ask, *"What do you want to do when you grow up?"*

> *"I want to own my own horse, and live where I can have more than one, and maybe raise and train them."*

She also wants to be a lawyer, an ambition so far not connected with her dislike of fraud…

> *"I like the law, it's very interesting. I like to know about everybody's problems, stick my nose in them, so I can help people. I want to be a workaholic, work during the week, take care of horses on weekends. I like going around the world. I'm always between France, America, and South Africa. I'll probably live in America, but I might study law in France, and practice internationally."*

It is time to refocus the discussion back to horses so I ask, *"Why do you like horses?"*

> *"I like horses because they have a nice way of being. They have body language, similar to cats, and use their body language to talk to you. You can talk to them, tell them to slow down, and they do. They have a beautiful body build, they have feelings, they are a gift to humans. Horses are not 'intelligent', they don't reason, but they are sensitive. They can tell when they're liked. They are really special animals. I talk to horses. It works better than getting mad at them."*

Then Lindsay turns to the horse - rider relationship…

> *"You can't expect to be a good rider if you are not 'one with your horse.' It's impossible if you don't think the same way he does. 'Being one with your horse' means thinking for both of you. You must show the horse that you are in command, but also give him a chance to do his own thing. It is a challenge to 'turn a horse around' by helping him get over a stubborn streak. With a new, young horse you need to show him exactly what you are doing, don't hide anything."*

Lindsay's life with horses has not consisted entirely of mutual affection, physical attraction, and equine psychoanalysis. She has also seen the rough side and the danger in the horse – human interaction. At five her leg was broken in a carriage accident caused by a frightened run-away horse. Then,

> *"Recently I had a very bad accident. I was riding 'Reglisse' – that's French*

---

*for sugar cane – a three year old double pony who had just arrived. Another horse that doesn't like newcomers kicked him and he ran away. I screamed and he slowed down. I bent forward to pat him. Just then he took off again, with me too far forward, then stopped quickly at a door and I went off. I was unconscious for a minute but didn't break anything. I had a bad cut on my chin and hurt my finger so I couldn't write. I was astonished that he reacted to my voice by slowing down."*

That takes us back to communicating with horses. I ask, *"How does a horse communicate with you?"*

*"He communicates by listening, and responds by body language, especially the ears and tail. I was riding Popcorn in South Africa, I ride her every day there. Usually I talk to a horse before I get on it. This day I was late and didn't have time to talk, and after I got on Popcorn she wouldn't jump, which she usually loves to do."*

Lindsay concludes that the change in routine had upset Popcorn. Then it is time for us to leave, and I ask Lindsay to sum up in one sentence why she likes horses.

*"I like horses because they are wonderful with humans if humans are gentle with them, they have wonderful body language, they respond well and are very attractive, not like pigs, which smell."*

*"That's a pretty long sentence, Lindsay."* I say.

*"I like long sentences."*

Her uncle comments on the greater intelligence of pigs. Lindsay concurs:

*"It's true that pigs are smarter than horses."*

[Uncle] *"Then why do they smell so bad?"*

*"Well, Einstain had crazy hair, he was still a ginius!"* [sic]

Gotcha!!

Lindsay carefully writes down the above exchange so I will not misquote her (or spell it wrong!). As we say good-bye I notice she has painted her fingernails a garish electric blue color.

*"I don't wear them that way riding, they scare the horses."*

Lindsay will go a long way with horses, two days a week. Silently, I pity the opponents who will meet her in court on the other five. And will she outgrow blue fingernails? With girls like Lindsay, you never know.

*Parent volunteers running a PC rally*

## – The United States Pony Clubs –

The first US Pony Club was founded in 1954, taking its inspiration from the Pony Clubs of Great Britain, founded in 1928. Their web site describes US Pony Club as follows:

> "Pony Club is one of the leading junior equestrian organizations in the world, represented throughout 30 countries. The United States has over 600 individual clubs throughout 48 states and the Virgin Islands, with more than 12,000 members.

> "Pony Club provides opportunities for instruction and competition in English riding, horse sports and horse management for children and young adults up to 21 years of age. The term "pony' refers to the age of the members, not the size of the mount… Parents play an important role in Pony Club… such as Club leader, chaperone, jump judge, or assist in activity events and fundraisers."

*"The land will always be open to a polite child."*
—Eve Fout, Founder of the Middleburg-Orange County Pony Club and the MOC Beagles.

Northern Virginia is a hotbed for the perpetuation of addiction to horses. The Middleburg Orange County (MOC) Pony Club, founded in 1959, is one of the oldest in the US. Like MOC, the early ones usually were associated with hunts, but now many are not. Pat Leins, its District Commissioner (DC), describes the Pony Club philosophy this way:

*"Pony Club encourages independence. It forges a relationship with a horse and with one's peers. Kids learn responsibility for each other. After a stint in a Pony Club a child will know how to organize the world. The Pony Club sets up guidelines by age and level of experience, and teaches riding. On the horse management side it also has guidelines: clean water, clean stall, and so forth. Kids have to be a team to get this done. No one does it for them. This process forms bonds with their horses and with each other.*

PHOTO BY THE AUTHOR

*Elliott Heapes, MOC Pony Club*

*"There is a Pony Club camp each summer, and after it some parents complain that the kids come home wanting to do everything for themselves, they have grown up so much. The patterns of responsibility and behavior and thoughtful emotion that they learn in Pony Club stick with them for life."*

There are now about 50 members in the MOC Pony Club, most of whom have ponies and horses that they keep at home.

Pat suggests I go to a rally, involving teams from several Virginia Clubs, to be held shortly at Frying Pan Park. We will cover this experience later in the chapter.

## – Old Rag Mountain Pony Club –

The Old Dominion Hunt's Point-to-Point at Ben Venue is a favorite. It has all the elements that make amateur steeplechasing so appealing – pony races, novice rider events, owner-rider races, and lady riders over timber. And, because all the "big" jockeys are in Southern Pines for the sanctioned races, even the two "open" races are filled with amateur riders.

The setting is superb, a rolling course visible almost in its entirety from a hillside covered with parked cars and tailgate parties. Above, on a rocky ledge, is a huge hospitality tent, from which the view of the mountains to the southwest provides a spectacular backdrop. Behind the tent is a patch of woods where children play at being Indians, as our grandson Sam did years ago. And when a rider is dislodged his horse can find solace by escaping into the woods on the far side of the course, as one did this past Saturday.

Passing through the gap in the fence that leads from tailgates to paddock there is a table on which are a number of items of pottery to be raffled off. In front of the table is a hand lettered sign – a crude poster – announcing that this is the booth of the O.R.M.P.C. – the Old Rag Mountain Pony Club, "Old Rag" being a dominating local terrain feature. Tending the table is a smiling blonde girl of 11 named Abigail Smith, whom I engage in conversation.

*"You belong to the Pony Club?* I ask.

*"Yes, sir."*

*"How many members are there?"*

*"About 20. We meet every week, we hope. We like this club because it's small."*

*"What level are you?"*

*"C-1, sir."*

*"That's pretty good for 11."* She comes back, with some pride…

*"You have to be 13 before you can go to C-2."*

*"Do you have a horse?"*

*"Yes sir, a Quarter Horse / Welsh. She's 14.2½."*

*"Just the right size – and she's a horse, not a pony."* Then I add, *"You ought to be in public relations."* Abigail smiles at me, and I suddenly realize that she already is.

———

*Timber race at Old Dominion*

*"Why did you join the Pony Club?"*

*"Me and my sister wanted to learn more about horses. She's 14.*

*"What level is she?"*

*"She's C-1 too, sir. C-1 is the highest in our club."*

I haven't been "sirred" like this since I was in the army. *"Does your sister get jealous that you are both at the same level, and you're younger?"*

*"No, she helps me and I help her. It works out pretty good."*

After telling her that this "interview" is for a book, I learn that Abigail has done some jumping and dressage, and a bit of foxhunting. She plans to take up eventing this summer, and she is excited at the prospect. About then her parents Glen and Dawn Smith appear. I learn that the Pony Club and its supporters do a lot of work for the Point-to-Point, selling tickets, parking cars, selling programs. According to Glen:

*"We make maybe three grand, it pays for the summer camp for 20 kids each year. And Old Dominion lets the kids hunt without paying any cap fees."*

*"Our older daughter, Emma, grooms for Nina Fout. She's going to go with*

*her to Rolex\* in Kentucky later in April. I like eventing better than hunter-jumper. In eventing you know when your round is going to be. In hunter-jumper shows you have to be there at eight, and you may not go 'til late in the afternoon."*

I can see how that would bust a parent's weekend.

I ask Abigail, *"Why do you like horses?"*

*"I don't know, I've always liked them since my sister got into them."*

Glen adds, *"She's been riding since she was two."* Abigail continues:

*"Our Pony Club meets at Mr. Kummlie's farm, Windsor Lodge. Our District Commissioner is Abigail Gillie."*

*"Another Abigail?"* I ask.

*"Yes, sir."*

I tell her I'll give her a chance to edit what I write, so she gives me her address, being careful to tell me how to spell her street…

*"B-U-E-N-A V-I-S-T-A… and don't forget to say that I'm starting eventing next summer!"*

## – A Pony Club Horse Show –

The local newspaper steers me one sunny day in August to Glenwood Park, near Middleburg, where an MOC Pony Club schooling show has been re-scheduled for 9:00am., following two previous rain-outs.

Entering the grounds I find a small collection of trailers, trucks, parents and Pony Clubbers grooming and tacking up their horses under the shade of a grove of trees near the gate that leads from the race course paddock to the course itself. In the shade, beside an SUV-drawn trailer, are a mother, a boy and girl, and two ponies. Introductions disclose that they are, respectively, Susan Farah, her children Jeffrey and Jessica, and Eclipse and Popeye.com. Susan comments, referring to her children:

*"They're triplets. The third – Jeremy – doesn't ride, he plays baseball and football. And I have a younger one who rides, too."*

I ask Jeffrey about Pony Club. He is quite concise:

*"In winter we learn about the pieces of tack, and how to take care of horses.*

---

\* The Rolex\*\*\*\* (four star) three day event is the premier one of its kind in America.

---

*In summer we have riding lessons, and Pony Club camp for a week. The horses live at home and we take care of them."*

"And your mother helps some?" As expected, it turns out that she does. At that moment a loudspeaker from over the ridge by the racecourse finish line announces the results of the class just ended. Now Jeffrey and Jessica start urging their mother:

*"It's time to go. Can we ride over?"*

Susan, who also has to go as she is scheduled to be in charge of the gate to the ring, is firm.

*"No, lead the horses. You don't want them to get tired."*

And I wish them luck.

Over at the ring I find grandmother Nancy Dillon and father Graham Alcock

*Jessica and Jeffrey Farah with Eclipse and Popeye.com*

watching four-year-old Haley Alcock who is showing a very small white pony. As the small class ends Haley hands her blue ribbon to a friend, as she is also riding in the next class. Nancy confides

> *"That was walk-trot. She likes it better when they canter."*

Before her part of the show ends Haley will add two red ribbons and a yellow to her collection. The consensus of her family is that Haley will be very pleased with the reds as *"she doesn't have one of those."* Graham comments:

> *"A few years ago it was hard to find shows like this. Now there are several each weekend, and some on weekday evenings."*

PHOTO BY THE AUTHOR

Haley Alcock

Over by the gate, where Susan Farah is letting horses in and out of the ring, there is a cluster of horses, riders, and fans with cameras.

One striking-looking horse – white with a few light lemon-brown splotches, is standing quietly, waiting his turn. His rider, Brianne Casey, tells me about what I silently think of as the "butterscotch paint."

> *"He's only three, and this is his first show, He's the quietest horse I've ever had. We call him 'Starky' – his real name is Stark Naked."*

At this point Starky starts to nibble at my camera, and Brianne adds...

> *"When he's bored he chews on his reins."*

Apparently Starky is now bored. I ask her about how she came to Pony Club.

> *"I joined when we moved here from north Florida when I was eleven. My dad's a horse vet – there weren't many horses there – here there are more and the schools are better. He specializes in acupuncture and lameness."*

Next to Brianne a girl named Caroline is sitting on a beautiful dark brown and white paint horse named Velvet. Brianne reports that she bred Velvet and sold him to Caroline. I do not inquire into her father's role in the process of breeding Velvet, but instead ask, *"Where do you go to school?"*

*"Notre Dame Academy. ...I love it. Next year I'll be a senior. It's a wonderful school."*

*"How about college?"*

*"Well, we're starting to think about that. Maybe James Madison or George Mason – I want to be nearby so I can ride."*

Back from the ring, a shaded table serves as the show's office, manned (if that expression's still appropriate) by two ladies – Ellen Mouri and Kim Bodoh, both Pony Club alums. I learn that the MOC Pony Club is one of about twelve in the Virginia Region, a territory stretching from Richmond north (there are other PC Regions in Virginia as well) to the Maryland border. Ellen is Regional Vice-Supervisor for education, which includes testing for advancement through the nine grades of Pony Club proficiency. Both are huge enthusiasts over the influence of Pony Club on their kids. Kim says:

*"Pony Club is mostly girls – maybe 75-80 percent – but my son loves the camaraderie. In MOC, hunting and the Beagles are a big thing, and that attracts more boys than in other clubs. And now that he's 14 he sees some advantages in being in a minority."*

It also turns out that young Bodoh won the National Junior (Ages 12-14) Pony Club Tetrathon (Riding, Cross-country Running, Shooting, and Swimming) last year, though some girls were pretty competitive too. Ellen:

*"My daughter Sarah thrives on horse management. She's one of those cleaning kids – though you wouldn't know it by looking at her room!"*

In 2001 Sarah was horse manager for the MOC team that won the National Gold Medals in both the overall competition and in horse management. Ellen adds:

*"I never heard of any other team that got zero points off for horse management."*

## – Combined Training Rally –

Following Pat Leins' suggestion, I find myself one hot Friday afternoon at Frying Pan Park, where a Combined Training Rally* of eleven pony Club teams is just getting under way.

---

\* A **Combined Training Rally** includes dressage, cross country and show jumping, the Pony Club equivalent of a Three-Day Event-type horse trial with a horse management element thrown in.

Arriving at 3:25 PM I look for the MOC Pony Club team, and immediately find two of its members, Shannon Casey and Elliott Heapes, complete with wheelbarrow and a chestnut horse. Their team is setting up their tack room in a stall assigned to them for that purpose. Both girls hope eventually to qualify for the Olympics, Shannon in eventing and Elliott in dressage. But that's many years away, if ever, and the tack room needs fixing right now. I follow them into the barn to learn about it.

Each team consists of four riding members, and a fifth non-riding (for the moment) Pony Clubber, often younger, who serves as horse manager – in charge of the tack room among other duties.

PHOTO BY THE AUTHOR

*Elliott Heapes and Shannon Casey*

One of the MOC team members is a "scramble" member, someone from another Club. The Pony Club has fairly definite guidelines for setting up the tack rooms and team-prepared stalls. My guides explain that the MOC Pony Club is strong on horse management, including *"sicknesses, how to treat them, how to take care of your horse."*

Elliott, a Foxcroft student, has been in Pony Club…

> *"…four or five years. I was in Dominion Valley – it's headquartered at Foxcroft – but I transferred to MOC. MOC has clinics more than riding lessons."*

Both sides of the aisle are active as teams are setting up four stalls for horses, and a fifth as a tack room. Parents, little brothers and hangers-on are to be out of the barn by 3:30 p.m. The adult horse-manager-in-charge, Brian Smith, politely suggests I finish my interviewing and leave.

Outside the barn is a table with several ladies sitting behind it, papers in front of them. Lisa Marfurt, the rally organizer, and Marilyn Sinderbrand, its secretary, cheerfully help me with a program and some information. Each summer there are several rallies, each concentrating on one of the Pony Club disciplines. For a team to compete they must offer up at least three adult volunteers to serve as judges, officials, staff, and chaperones. When you add in parents and other connections there are probably as many adults in attendance as Pony Club members. Despite its volunteer nature, the event is going very smoothly. The kids will be busy up to closing at 8:00 p.m., but there is not much for an outsider to see or do.

PHOTO BY THE AUTHOR
*Studying the tack room set-up*

Before 10:00 a.m. Saturday morning I am back. The dressage is in progress. Outside the building in which the ring is located Caroline Chipman, one of the chaperones, tells me:

> *"This is really a horse trials. Next year they may change the name of the rally to 'eventing'."*

In the outdoor ring next to the dressage building "on deck" riders and horses are warming up. One of them, Kristen Elliot, wearing #126, is riding Uncanny. I ask her, *"Why do you do Pony Club?"*

> *"It's good for me. I used to do it for the competition."*

Now she seems more interested in the associations with others.

> *"You go a lot of different places, meet a lot of people. They're always willing to help you out. Pony Club made us band together."*

*"Where do you go to school?"*

*"I'm going to George Mason in the fall... I like the Business School, and I've found a stable nearby for the horse. Lots of people want to buy him, but I'm taking him with me."*

*"I can see why; he's a very pretty animal."*

Inside the dressage building there are perhaps 20 spectators, watching silently, or talking in hushed voices. One lady even leans down into the trash barrel to place her empty soda can silently on the previous discards. There is something about this whole event that is quietly reassuring – that sportsmanship, civility and concern for others are still to be found in America.

PHOTO BY THE AUTHOR

*Kristen Elliot and potential PC recruits*

But now it is time to walk the cross country course laid out behind the arena building and running for just over a mile through the woods and fields of the Park. The Pre-Novice course has 12 jumps, none to exceed 2'7"; the Novice course consists of 17 jumps, limited to 2'11". Each division has about 20 entries. Near the start box is a ring in which horses can warm up. After walking most of the course I select obstacles 7, 8, and 9 as the places to be to take pictures. The light and background are good there, and at 8 and 9 there is water. Horses splashing through water are photogenic.

Near the Start Box I run into Clint Bennett, the Rally organizer for cross country. He's from the Difficult Run Pony Club (DRPC). Our conversation goes about as follows: I ask, *"How did you get into this thing?"*

*"My daughter!... The Pony Club focuses on horsemanship, sportsmanship, total horse management. It's a good thing.* [Then, apprehensively] *Some of her classmates are getting into boys."*

I remember having the same fatherly concerns. Clint continues:

*"Dues finance instruction. In winter there are unmounted lessons, ground school, clinics. 'Know down' is a quiz, an unmounted competition based on*

*Jumping the wall into the woods*

*Jumping out of the water*

horse knowledge. We have about 50 kids. Dues varies by club — I think ours is $120 per year."

"That sounds like a bargain?"

"The horse is where the expense comes in. We keep him at a stable three miles from home. In this rally DRPC is managing the cross country, others are doing dressage and show jumping. We run regular horse trials here each year in May and August as fund raisers. The money goes back into the course. This hard footing is a problem. We rented an aerator and ran over the whole course, but it's open to the public and gets lots of use."

As I set myself near jump 7, "The Stone Wall," where horses will jump out of the field onto a woods road, the public address comes alive announcing the start of Novice Cross Country. Then over the loudspeaker:

"The Novice run is about four and a half minutes. Medical science advises that this is too long to hold your breath. Please remember to breathe while your little darling is on the course."

As the event progresses this announcer has mostly good news:

"Taylor Stephens is clear at number ten, Abby Price has just cleared number two."

Only rarely does he report a "stop," (a refusal) and only once is there a minor hold up as a horse goes lame and his rider has to lead him off the course and to the vet.

Back near the Start Box the finishers are cooling off their horses and lounging in the shade, visiting. One lady observes:

"So hard, no rain."

Perhaps it was her child's horse that went lame. Then a younger voice:

"Did you go clean, Katie?"

"Yes."

"Good job!"

Again, the loudspeaker:

"The word for today is Hydrate. H-Y-D-R-A-T-E. Keep your fluid levels up. Water for your horse, Gatorade for you. You can also drink water, but your horse shouldn't drink Gatorade. Keep tuned to this channel."

As I leave I thank Elliott, who is nearby with her horse. I ask, "How did he go?"

---

*"Pretty well."*

*"I hope you win."*

She smiles. One suspects there is still some good old competitive spirit riding along with the civility and the sportsmanship. And there will be no future shortage of event riders.

PHOTO BY THE AUTHOR

*Taking a break*

## – *Youthful Bonding* –

Nancy Dillon is a legend in the equine community of the young – and those who used to be. She is best known for training children in all aspects of horsemanship, and for ferrying trailer loads of ponies and their riders to meets of the MOC Beagles and the Piedmont Foxhounds, there to initiate them in the fine points of foxhunting and its thrills.

I arrive at her farm at 8:30 one hot, humid June morning. Back at the stable older kids – "older" being from 11 up and with some experience – have already caught designated ponies in the paddocks, and are busy tacking them up for the younger students who will arrive for their lessons starting at 9:00.

*Nancy Dillon and friends*

Nancy greets me. As we are standing there a lady appears, carrying a painted turtle and attached to a small boy. She is Caroline Fitzgerald, accompanied by her son William, who seems to be about six, and is in his second week of lessons. I look at her quizzically, as she says:

> *"We found him in the road* [she means the turtle, not William] *and we plan to take him home."*

Meanwhile, William is swept off by his teenaged helper, Kaleigh, to meet his pony, who today will be Farnley Canticle. Caroline adds

> *"I also have a three year old who wants to start riding."*

Quickly I meet a number of the older girls. A gray pony, Violet, is being groomed by Emily Eldredge for her sister Charlotte, the child scheduled to ride her. The older girls help the younger ones in the morning; then, after the lessons, they clean up the horses and barn. At noon they may swim in the pool and eat the lunches they have brought. In the afternoon it is their turn for riding and lessons. They do this every day of the week, all day during the summer. In the winter several come every afternoon, after school . Some own their own horses, but most ride Nancy's, working on the green ones –

Nancy breaks all her own – and putting mileage on boarders that are at the farm for that purpose. I ask one of the girls why she does it so regularly.

*"It's fun, and you can do a lot with a horse. I like to swim the ponies in the pond, and I like foxhunting and showing. We do extra work after the little kids leave."*

Next we are confronted with a huge blue riding helmet under which is two year old Nancy Alcock, being helped to get ready to ride by two slightly older girls. Young Nancy is shy. In response to a question she tips the helmet forward and hides her face behind it. Someone says, by way of explanation:

*"She's just learned to talk."*

But then, she's big Nancy's granddaughter. First things first. Her four year old sister Haley comes up, dragging a girth, announcing:

*"This pony's too fat."*

Her mother Daphne Alcock goes off to check on the problem. No doubt Haley is right, and a larger girth is needed. The ponies all seem pretty well fed.

Brooke McLeary is nearby, and I ask, *"What's your pony's name?"*

*"It's Candy. Her whole name is Rock Ridge Candy."*

The farm name is a giveaway. I ask if she is by Houdini, and Brooke confirms that she is indeed.

PHOTO BY THE AUTHOR

*Dillon ponies*

Kristin Dillon appears, carrying an assortment of horse care items – soap, sponge, bit, rub rag and fly mask. They will be playing a game later and every beginner will be assigned an item and challenged to find it, while on horseback, somewhere in the upper ring. Kristin and Emily were in charge of hiding the items yesterday.

Then we all head to the ring, following the now-tacked-up ponies and riders. Soon, a dozen horses are circling under Nancy's eye, some attended by older kids on foot. Canticle joins us in the center of the ring, bearing William. A voice of authority intrudes:

*"Kick him, William, and make him go back out into the circle."*

William kicks. Nothing happens. William lectures Canticle loudly. Again, nothing happens. Someone comes and leads Canticle away. Canticle prefers idleness to work, and we will see him twice more before long in the center of the ring. I ask about another older girl riding among the smaller students.

*"That's Allegra Lee – her mother Susan works at The Chronicle. She's riding Peanut, just broke last fall, to put mileage on him."*

It's now 9:30 and the day is getting hot and humid. Nancy has all the 13 young ones line up in a single rank, as they would at a horse show, so that the older girls can give each a cup of water, while two other older ones continue to canter around the ring. Then Nancy asks each child to do "around the world," which involves taking feet out of stirrups and pivoting 360 degrees around in the saddle. I think I hear the two year-old announce…

*"I kicked Mouse in the back."*

Her talking is coming along about on a par with her riding. Then there is a commotion: Canticle has shaken himself, causing William to do an involuntary dismount. William gets back on, hands his crop to the accompanying junior coach, and does his "around the world."

*"Good job,"* says the coach.

Nancy then has them put their hands on their hats, and post on their motionless ponies. Next it's "fly like a bird" – reins dropped, arms extended and flapping. Then they take their feet out of the stirrups, and Nancy orders:

*"Put them back in fast without looking."*

Next is a session covering the various colorations of the ponies present: roan, gray, bay, dun, paint, chestnut,

PHOTO BY THE AUTHOR

*Helpers*

PHOTO BY DAPHNE ALCOCK

*Nancy Dillon's foxhunting youngsters*

dark brown. Nancy explains how you tell dark brown from black (look at the muzzle). She moves on to anatomy:

*"How many knees does a horse have? How many hocks? How many frogs? How many necks?"*

The answers come in a chorus. Then she asks:

*"What is the barrel? What are the withers?"*

The kids point to the mentioned areas. Finally:

*"What is the rump?"*

A small boyish voice is enthusiastic:

*"That's where you hit 'em!"*

It is unclear whether the respondent is William or Findlay Ohrstrom, a late arrival. Then it's off to the upper ring for the search, each to look for her or his assigned item. *"If you see someone else's item, keep quiet, don't tell,"* Nancy instructs. *"Find your own."*

With the little ones searching, and a covey of older ones headed out to a far field, Nancy has time to talk. She clearly is dedicated to foxhunting, her first love (along with children), and she wants her pupils to love it too, but…

*"I don't believe in the game of 'hang on.' You need to ride well to hunt. We*

*take the green ponies to shows so they can learn to hunt. Once you've hunted you've got the disease. Hunting is just fun."*

A nearby youngster agrees:

*"It's fun because there's so much terrain and stuff.*

Nancy continues:

*"We take the more dedicated kids and the green ponies trail riding. Dot*

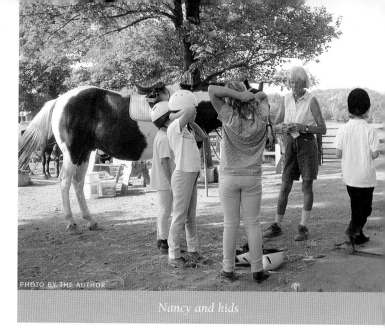

PHOTO BY THE AUTHOR

*Nancy and kids*

*Smithwick is so nice, and lets us use her place. Mary Braga and Dickie and Sallie Rogers, too. We can't do it right around here now, it's too built up.*

*"All children are involved in things they learned growing up."*

As she describes her own she proves her point:

*"Neal Dillon, my youngest, team ropes in competitions, and buys and sells horses and cattle. He lives in Berryville, but gets horses from places like Oklahoma. His two year old daughter Gracie rides English and western, and his wife Rebecca keeps my books. Daphne is married to Graham Alcock. She's here every day, normally all day long, and instructs the older, more serious students. Dale works as the farm manager for Robert Duval at Burnley [in the Plains]. Dale married one of my students. Buck works for Hazel, but does farming on the side, including making my hay."*

Back at the barn we again find William. He is curious and asks me:

*"Are you just visiting?"*

*"Yes, I'm too old to join the program. Wouldn't I look silly on a pony?"* William looks me over, and says, *"Yes,"* then snickers at the thought.

Just up the line Haley is sponging off her pony using liberal amounts of water. Since she can reach only to the middle of the animal's shoulder the job is being shared with an older girl. Tiffany Dillon, Kristin's older sister, is standing with her back to her horse Eddy, who is rubbing his hot, itchy face against her to the pleasure of both. Tiffany explains that Eddy…

*"…was bred in South Carolina. He's a trail ride and hunt horse, he loves cross country. My uncle Neal bought him in Maryland."*

———

Further up the line there is a very low saddle rack on which rests a tiny saddle. Two year old Nancy is busy sponging it off, overseen by her grandmother. Now it's time for me to leave, but first I ask Nancy why she does it.

*"Probably because I'm crazy."*

But then she adds:

*"My father and mother were horsemen, and I never got away from it. And I really like the younger children. Dr. Joe Rogers took me on my first hunt — that was the start. And it's great discipline for the kids. In cubbing season they have to be here at 4:00 a.m. if they want to go. We've started some pretty good horsemen. When people like Jimmy Wofford ask you to teach their kids it makes you feel pretty good."*

PHOTO BY THE AUTHOR

*Nancy Dillon's barnyard*

# VII
## OUT OF THE FRYING PAN

PHOTO BY THE AUTHOR

*Auction at Frying Pan Park*

*Out of the Frying Pan into the Fire  (De calcaria in carbonarium.)*
—Quintus Septimius Tertullianus c. 160 - 240

---

So you have decided to acquire a horse? Relax, you are one of many who do so, every day. And it may be one of the best moves you ever make. But where do you get one? If your objective is a child's "starter" pony or a pleasure horse, a horse auction is an important source to consider.

Frying Pan Park is an equestrian oasis lying just east of Dulles Airport, north of the suburban neighborhood of Floris Downs, and south of the dense urbanization – high rise office buildings, condominium apartments, and town houses – that has sprung up along the Washington-Dulles Toll Road. Perhaps the Park is a last vestige of what was the original country of the Fairfax Hunt.

Three times a year the Park is the site of a horse auction – The Virginia Hunter and Bloodstock Sale. On this Saturday in late September  we arrive and park among well over 100 cars, and join a crowd of buyers, sellers, tire kickers, and plain spectators gathered for the showing and subsequent auction of the 135 horses and ponies entered in the sale.

The Frying Pan crowd is young, innocent, middle income, and interested in horses as soul mates. It is a crowd in blue jeans and T-shirts, occasionally

PHOTO BY THE AUTHOR

*Section of the auction crowd*

upgraded to riding pants and hunt caps for those who will show or try out the merchandise. Ages range from infants to octogenarians, the latter few and far between. The median age seems about 30, and the crowd predominantly female. Most consignors are amateur – only about 20 percent identify themselves as "agent," and 70 percent are selling just one animal.

*Entrance to Frying Pan Park*

At 10:00am., the show ring, near several wooden stables and an indoor arena, is occupied by a group of horses and ponies, trotting, cantering and jumping. The riders in the ring – a few professionals, but mostly young owners – are under the guidance of an announcer who identifies the horses by hip number (a number pasted on each horse's hip for identification) and outlines their fine points as presented in the sale catalogue. Defects are minimally reported – "caveat emptor" being the watchwords at horse auctions. The showing will continue until the actual auction begins about noon.

From the arena building I obtain a catalog and a listing of stable locations for the horses. A lady and her 12 year old daughter Katlin are there because, as Katlin says:

> "I've outgrown my pony and he's arthritic, so we're looking for a horse."

Her mother interjects:

> "We're not horse people, we really don't know much about it, we don't know how to pick one, so we're just looking."

I ask Katlin, "What kind of a horse are you looking for?"

> "Maybe 15 to 16 hands that can jump, I'd like to be able to show."

I'm cautious: "I wish my wife was here. She knows much more than I do."

Obviously these people need a coach to help them.

In the ring several small hunters are jumping. Hip # 183 is a beautiful five-year-old Thoroughbred gray mare, 15.2 hands, perhaps the prettiest horse in the sale, and a polished jumper, possibly a bit light boned. The catalog says, in part:

> "She has excellent bloodlines, tracing back to Native Dancer and Nasrullah. She is a fancy small hunter show horse, …winning ribbons in the VHSA… 2'6" and 2'9" divisions… shown by a junior rider as well as an adult."

―――

This horse is so nice I start thinking *"Edie's new hunter."* As she leaves the ring I ask her owner, *"Have you ever hunted her?"*

*"Yes, [pause] …but she got antsy, she really didn't like it. You can see how quiet she is here, even with the crowd and the noise. But she just didn't like hunting."*

I pet the horse. *"My, she's pretty. What do you hope to get for her?"*

*"Well, we don't know. The appraiser said she was worth ten thousand."*

Frying Pan Park is not the place to sell $10,000 horses, and we are not going into the show hunter business. But she is a beautiful mare.

Nearby is #190, a three-year-old thoroughbred gelding, property of Teresa Harp of Manassas. She has six horses, and bought this one, by Balls Bluff, at the MARE Center auction. I ask, *"Why do you have them?"*

*"My husband asks me that too. It was my father who encouraged me. He said 'Horses are better than boys!' So he sent me to an all girls college. Now I have four kids and a baby granddaughter. Two daughters ride. I keep a baseball bat to fend off boys. My older son goes to horse shows to meet girls."*

Ah, the thrills of bringing up teenagers.

Kathryn Southard's brother-in-law, Richard Butts, trains at Charles Town. Her sister-in-law gallops for Katy Voss. Kathryn herself breeds ponies. Her system seems creative:

PHOTO BY THE AUTHOR
*Horses warming up in the ring*

PHOTO BY THE AUTHOR
*Showing her pony to buyers*

*"I buy, claim, whatever, small Thoroughbred mares, 15.2 or below. They have to be structurally correct, not necessarily pretty, but not 'butt ugly'. Then I breed them to an 11.2 stallion."*

I'm curious. I ask, *"Natural or A.I.?"*

*"A.I, of course. For natural he'd need a big hill."*

*"What do you do with them, sell them?"*

*"We show them on the line in conformation classes. I sold one once for eighteen hundred."*

I gather that may be the only sale she's made. She continues:

*"I'm bringing home two new ones. Our family has a lot of horses. We have 15 acres, and are leasing six more. My husband has put me on 'pony probation'."*

Then it's time for the auction, ponies first. The auctioneer runs through the sales conditions, concluding with…

*"It's my job to help determine the price. It is your job to decide whether to bid, and on which horse. You should do your homework before you bid. Assume nothing. But remember, to get a good horse you have to bid on it."*

*Cams Misty Gold, a career broodmare just started under tack*

The first horse in the ring is Ace of Spades, a ten hand Shetland pony, jet black except for a patch of white at the back of his rump, and some white hairs at the tail head. He looks smashing, but he goes for $450, a disappointing price. Prior to the sale his agent, Sheryl Jordan, told me he had cost the owner $1,200, and that…

*"These tiny ponies can be ridden by small children, but mostly it's adults who drive them or show them. I'm selling them here as a favor to a client."*

Sheryl, formerly a whipper-in for the Warrenton Hunt, now manages the Nemacolin Woodlands Resort and Spa, whose tantalizing description is "West Coast Attitude, East Coast Latitude." If you are interested the resort is located in Farmington, Pa, southeast of Pittsburgh.

As the sale progresses prices seem low and buy backs are over 35 percent. September 11th, the Day of Terror less than three weeks past, has sewed up a lot of horse lovers' pockets.

Hip # 13, "Chessie," a 15-year-old chestnut mare, 13.1 hands, catches my eye. She is led into the ring by a 14-year-old girl in a red shirt, with a nine year old as rider, holding a two year old in front of her. Then the leader releases the horse and the two riders trot around. Next, the two year old is off-loaded, and the nine year old remounts, facing backwards, and trots around the ring again. With Chessie's skills underlined by this marketing program she goes for $1,600, and I follow her out of the ring. Debbie Fishback, the adult in charge of Chessie, tells me:

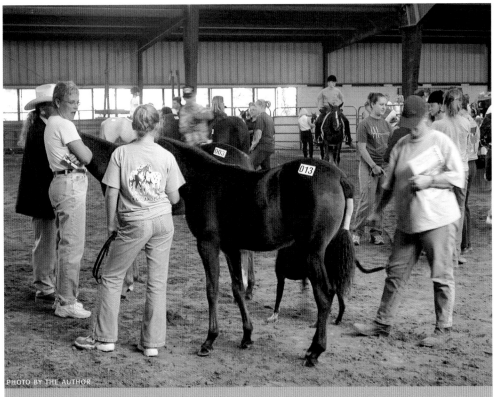

PHOTO BY THE AUTHOR

*Checking the hind leg's conformation*

*"She's automatic, bomb proof. You say 'trot', she trots. Say 'canter', she canters. She's been in a summer camp and lesson program at Picturesque Farm near Warrenton. It's time for her to go to a family. I just hope she gets a good home."*

The buyer comes up, a slim young lady with two small blond girls trailing behind. Debbie and the buyer know each other. Turning to me, Debbie comments:

*"She's getting a good home."*

The buyer is Lisa White, daughter of our friends Hank and Betty Long, and daughter-in-law of Middleburg barn and fence builder George White. As we chat the two little girls, five and three, slip into Chessie's stall, where the pony is munching hay spread on the ground. Pretty soon they are crouched around her nose, talking to her and patting her as she eats. As I leave the five year-old has climbed aboard and is lying stretched out on Chessie's back, face up. Bombproof Chessie is spreading happiness all around.

Back at the auction they are just through the ponies and starting to sell the horses. The first is a Quarter Horse. The program says he was born in 1984, and then comments:

*"[He] is started over fences. He is willing but still green."*

Is his birth date – 1984 – a typo, or is he just a slow learner? In any event, the bidding stops at $2,300 and the auctioneer reports:

*"No sale."*

Later the owner says:

*"I'd of let him go for $4,000."*

His friend adds:

*"Yeah. One like him sold for $12K."*

But that was before September 11th, and some horses at auction have a higher value in the eyes of the owner than anyone else. As the sale progresses we see prices like $1,050 (No sale), $850, $1700, $400, $350 (for a weanling filly). Then there is some excitement.

Hip #109 is in the ring, an Anglo/Arab mare. The catalog says she is in foal to the Paint stallion Definite Class, but the auctioneer reports she is not pregnant; a breeding right to Definite Class will be included in the deal. Suddenly the mare rears up and heads for the exit, dragging her handler out of the ring with her. Then she escapes him and leaves the building at a gallop, but is

*Chessie and new owners*

quickly caught. The auctioneer becomes safety instructor:

> *"Now, that's why we ask you to keep your children away from the horses, and out of the area where horses are coming to or going from the ring."*

The horse re-enters, and the bidding starts. Someone says $500. The mare takes offense – one can hardly blame her – and departs the premises once more. Again she is caught and brought back into the arena building. Turning and looking at her, the auctioneer says:

> *"Keep her back there. We don't want to do that again."*

Then he resumes his auctioneer's spiel, to no avail. The price stays glued at $500.

#110 is led in by a serious and professional looking lady. The catalog identifies him as a 1996 bay Arabian gelding named BFA Kubla Khan, and goes on to say, in part, that he's…

> *"…the horse owner's dream… an absolute gentleman to handle; his trail, endurance or show career is assured."*

After the commotion with #109, and perhaps with other Arab memories fresh in people's minds, Arab horses are out of fashion, and the bidding stops at $300 – No Sale for Kubla Khan.

———

Now it's time to leave and feed our own portfolio of animals. I drive home thinking of the two little blond girls playing in the stall with their new big sister, Chessie.

We revisit Frying Pan Park a year later. The stock market may be down, but pony prices have firmed, and the crowd is even larger than a year ago. Here our favorite is Puzzle Mouse, an 11.1 hand Pinto three-year-old gelding, ridden by eight-year-old Denya Leake, and superintended by her mother Caroline.

Puzzle Mouse faces the problem of all small ponies – he has not sprouted to keep up with Denya, so, sadly, he is here to find another home. If he suspects this – and his expression says he well may – he doesn't seem very happy about it, nor for that matter does Denya.

Caroline is a former event rider and the step daughter of Dr. Matthew Mackay-Smith. She was injured in 1974 when her event horse fell attempting a jump with a six-foot drop on the far side, and she has a badly distorted

*Caroline and Denya Leake with Puzzle Mouse*

collar bone to show for it. Discreetly displaying her injury, she explains:

> *"I remounted, but I couldn't use my broken shoulder, so I just held that
> wrist and the reins in the other hand. The horse seemed to say 'just show
> me where to go and I can do it.' We jumped 10 more fences, including the
> notorious Trout Hatchery, and finished the course. Then a teammate said,
> "Thank God you were hurt. If you'd tried to ride over the Trout Hatchery,
> instead of letting the horse do it, you'd never have made it!"'*

Is Caroline getting Denya a bigger horse to prepare her for the Trout Hatchery?

## – Chessie –

Several months after her purchase we pay a visit to Chessie in her new home.
Lisa White opens the door, and we enter a comfortable living room. Two
saddles and saddle pads are riding on the banister, and several horse pictures
are in evidence. Three little girls join us, and Lisa introduces them, adding:

> *"Allie is now almost six, and Pamela is about to be four. Lily here is Allie's
> friend."*

I ask why they bought Chessie. The girls smile and Lisa answers:

> *"Allie had been riding my old horse, and she learned some basics on him. But
> she wanted to go out with the Beagles, so we were looking for a mix of kind-
> ness and safety, the right pony to be their next best friend and baby sitter.*
>
> *"Riding is my sport. I bought her as a starter pony so we could do it all
> together – family rides, foxhunting. If they take to it they can keep going. If
> not, that's OK. But I wanted them to have a really safe start.*
>
> *"I was about Allie's age when I started. My sister and I fell in love with it at
> an early age. Dad didn't want to buy a lot of ponies, so he bought one that
> was too big."*

I interject, *"Like buying kid's shoes?"*

> *"Yes. His theory was 'ride her together, grow into her.'*
>
> *"I started with local shows and riding out of the back yard, took some lessons.
> Eventually I did the big show circuit."*

*"Did you ever think of going pro?"*

> *"I did give some lessons, and ran a boarding stable. But it's a hard way to
> make a living. I decided to make money elsewhere to support my habit, and
> keep the horses for fun."*

*Pamela and Allie White with Chessie*

About this time Lisa's husband Chip appears, getting ready to go to his real estate office. Chip grew up in Middleburg, and did Pony Club as a boy. I ask him: *"Do you still ride?"*

*"I did when we were dating – had to."*

Lisa interjects:

*"As soon as we were married he quit."*

Before we go out to interview Chessie Lisa shows me a picture of Allie in the lead line class at the 1999 Upperville show.

*"She's on Susie, the pony I won with in 1979 at the Washington International Horse Show. Susie's about 36 now."*

I ask, *"How did she do?"*

*"She got a green ribbon – sixth – like all those who weren't in the first five. I don't know how they judge those classes. But the main purpose was to have fun and earn a lollipop, and to be able to say we both showed the same pony."*

Pamela soloing on Chessie

We leave the house and head outside. Down the hill behind the house is a rough, hilly "ring" strewn with rails and jump standards, alongside of which is a small stable and a woodsy paddock – clearly a do-it-yourself-at-home operation. The rails on the ground simulate jumps for the girls.

Lisa gives a progress report:

*"Allie did Pony Club camp this summer, and will start with Pony Club lessons this fall when she will also start Kindergarten. She's also been out with the Beagles a couple of times. Pamela is learning to solo; when she goes on trail rides without a lead shank I walk along with her for safety."*

We proceed through the inspection and petting of Chessie, tacking her up, watching Pamela take her into the ring and mount her. Pamela needs a little help remembering which stirrup for which foot as she climbs on board unaided, but she is soon soloing around the ring.

Chessie? *" She's been way above and beyond our expectations,"* concludes Lisa.

Allie has disappeared to play elsewhere with Lily.

# VIII
# TRAIL AND ENDURANCE RIDING

PHOTO BY THE AUTHOR

*A fall ride along a country lane – Franny and Walter Kansteiner*

*"In distance riding you discover how much deeper your resources are than you believed."*
—Matthew Mackay-Smith, veterinarian, endurance rider, historian, and amateur philosopher

## – Just Going Riding –

I n earlier times most people began to ride by going out with a horse across farm or ranch land, along bridle trails, or on country lanes, perhaps after only a lesson or two from a parent or friend. For many this form of pleasure riding, with their horse as a companion, is all they want from the relationship.

As a child I rode around neighboring properties, occasionally with family or friends, often alone. An informal organization called the Private Lanes Association (PLA) maintained many miles of trails through the large estates and farms that typified the Bedford of those days. Those rides were treasured for the chance to see the natural side of the country, and perhaps also to think quietly, and alone, as is often necessary when confronted with the quandaries of adolescence. No one questioned a rider's right to pass over the PLA trails, and no one worried about liability if some child fell off and was injured. Such an accident was the child's fault, not the landowner's. Next case.

We had a special fondness for a nearby pine thicket, perhaps 100 acres in extent, called Piney Woods. Here we galloped along the PLA trail, or skulked in the underbrush to ambush the good guys, recreating the scenes that the Lone Ranger and Tonto brought us every Friday evening on the radio. We were free of adult supervision, on our own to learn the ways of the animals and the woods. And the horses loved it, too. Hi-yo, Silver!

Piney Woods had a sand bank of some height, the residue of a glacial moraine. The face was exposed, pure sand inclined at its natural angle of repose. Edie's father taught her – and her horse – how to slide down the bank, the horse on its rump, back feet tucked up behind, front feet forward, with the rider in the saddle, just as you see in the westerns. My mother, however, was haunted by images of children smothered in landslides in such banks, and so our father never divulged this practice to us, if he even was aware of it.

By the time our daughters took up riding, my job dictated that we live in a Chicago suburb. We were lucky to have a half-acre lot, and our horse, Mischief, lived 15 miles away, in a stable with a riding ring. The end goal was horse shows; the only chance to ride free was a stretch of state-owned park land along a waterway nearby. Edie did on occasion try to reconstruct her youth there, riding Mischief with the hum of traffic on Eden's Expressway in her ears, and the Lone Ranger's "Hi-yo, Silver" a distant echo far back in the past.

Today most people work in a big city and fewer live in true country, as our fathers did when we were young. So, most people start their riding in a ring, at a stable. The opportunity to take a horse beyond that circumscribed environment, and bond with him in the big outdoors, is treasured once a rider experiences it. Also lost for many is the chance to take responsibility for the care of a horse, whether on a farm or in a stable or shed out behind the house.

As a result, recreational trail riding has taken on forms that are organized far more than the catch-as-catch-can riding of our youth. In addition to just "going riding," as those of us living in the country can still do, there are organized group trail rides, Competitive Distance Rides, and Endurance Rides of up to 100 miles.

## – A Fall Trail Ride –

Carole Stadfield is a "social" member of the Fairfax Hunt, and a recent escapee from the clutches of leukemia. Though not a horse person, with her affliction in remission, and her career in real estate back on track she was anxious to do something for the people that saved her. She had heard of the Fairfax Hunt spring trail rides emanating from Trappe Hill Farm, and she came up with the idea that a fall ride, with proceeds dedicated to the Leukemia and Lymphoma Society, might be a good way to say "thank you." We agreed, carried along by Carole's enthusiasm. Edie describes Carole as:...

> "...feeling strong, well, and most grateful."

Trail rides are normally group efforts to extend the camaraderie of a foxhunting season just past, or to "leg up" horses in anticipation of a season just ahead. As such they are usually sponsored by one hunt or another, and appeal to active foxhunters. They usually proceed over typical hunting country for a couple of hours, at speeds appropriate to their off-season status, followed by a picnic lunch.

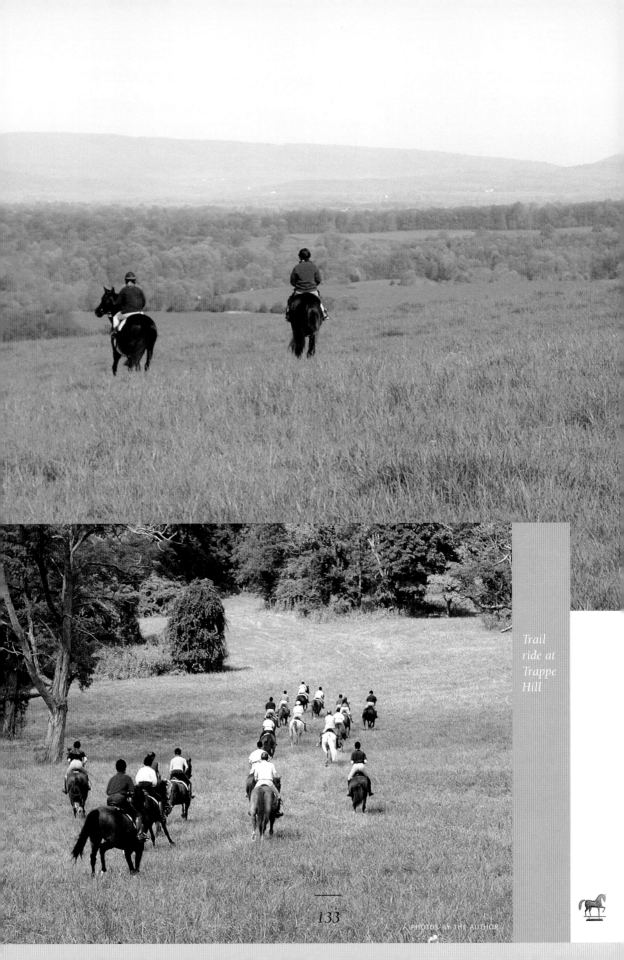

*Trail ride at Trappe Hill*

*Prepping the horses*

While Carole's proved to be different in detail, reflecting its sponsor, it conformed to the general format.

One does not put on a trail ride lightly. One must plan the route, get permission from landowners, arrange for food and beverages, and dragoon friends into helping with details. And of course prospective attendees must be invited, and an estimate of participation established to guide food procurement and parking plans. Ideally, one also instructs the Deity on the weather desired.

This ride was planned for Labor Day. Carole had been in touch, it seemed daily, since we had returned from Maine the prior week. By Friday we had a general plan: Edie would lead the "fast" group, Betsy the less adventurous riders, and I would conduct a "nature walk" for non-riders, ending up with a visit to the broodmares, foals and yearlings.

Our woodland trail – we call it the "riding" – was to be used by both riders and walkers. It had not been bush hogged this year, and so with Jerry's expert help on Sunday afternoon we rigged up the six-foot bush hog and tractor for trail clearing. All was going reasonably well until the tractor was confronted with the carcass of a 20-inch diameter Tulip Poplar, blown down in a recent storm and now lying across the entire width of the lower section of the riding.

Now Carole's trail ride became a contest of chainsaw vs. darkness, aging muscle vs. 200 pound segments of freshly cut tree trunk, estimates of how much to cut away vs. width of tractor and bush hog so they might pass though the aperture being created in order to clear the trail beyond. Safe to say, the good guys won, but by a narrow margin, and I was late returning to the house. A normally tolerant wife was heard to say:

——

*Assembling for a trail ride*

*"What in Heaven took you so long?"*

Answer: *"Wait 'til you see the tree that used to be lying across your riding."*

Meanwhile, Carole has delivered many supplies, and settled in for the night, saying, as we have a nightcap…

*"I'm so excited!"*

She also seems so full of life, after the scare she has survived. But no one yet has the slightest idea of how many people might come. Carole has invited all the Fairfax Hunt, many friends in her church, and who knows whomever else. As the ride is a benefit, those who do not want to part with $35 have probably demurred, without explicitly saying *"No."* And so the parking of an unknown quantity cars and trailers weighs heavily on the mind.

We set the alarm for 6:15, unpleasantly early for a holiday. Unfortunately, the clock functions properly, and I roll out of bed on schedule. Edie, up at 5:15, has already fed the dogs and started breakfast. The weather promises to be clear and cool for early September. God has cooperated with Carole again.

Reflections while sleeping have resulted in a parking plan: big rigs on the lower lawn, smaller trailers in the hunter paddock by the house, trailerless cars against the fence outside the paddock, no cars, horses, or trailers anywhere near the mares and foals. Signs – "P" for parking, arrows, "P" with a line through it for "NO PARKING", are created. The ride is set for 9:30. As I am installing the last sign at 8:35 a huge rig appears in the driveway, driven by a woman and followed by a car with two young ladies. The guests are forthright:

*"We're always early."*

I agree with their policy, and note with approval the expert way in which they back their big trailer into exactly the position suggested. But there is no time to retreat to the house. Duty calls: Direct traffic, collect checks, get riders to sign releases (we live in a litigious society).

Business picks up slowly. Suzanne Rouland appears to take over the check collection duty, sitting at a little table by the driveway to rest her injured back. By 9:45 Edie is mobilizing perhaps 20 riders on the lower lawn, and after some milling about they head up the hill towards the "riding." After waiting for stragglers we collect a dozen walkers. As we cross the hunter paddock towards the woods someone points out the distant riders at the top of the "ruins" field, a half mile away, looking south over the valley towards the twin peaks of The Cobblers.

We follow the track of the horses into the riding, being careful to avoid stepping into what, in deer hunting, some might refer to as "sign." We then circle through cattle pastures, eventually to reach the mares and foals. As we do, enthusiasm mounts from level 6 (having a good time in the country) to level 9 (this is great!). There is something about mares with foals at side that stirs people – even non-horse people – in some basic way. Eager foals stick their noses over the fence to be petted. Intelligent questions are asked on breeding, management, training and the economics of Thoroughbreds. Answers are hopefully enlightening.

In the run-in shed used by three foal-less mares a crowd gathers around Forest Treasure, the self-appointed boss mare, who loves attention. Among those petting her is a lady clutching a plastic water bottle. Forest Treasure is curious. She pushes her nose towards the water bottle, then starts to take it in her teeth. The lady jumps back, pulling the bottle away. The sudden movement startles the mare. Backing off about three feet, she glowers at the crowd. One guest says:

*"See, you hurt her feelings."*

Another adds:

*"She's crying!"*

I explain that horses, being flight animals, react unpredictably to sudden movement, and one must move slowly in their presence. Stroking returns Forest Treasure to her usual calmness and regal posture; she accepts the gentle handling as an apology for the assault by the water bottle on her dignity.

Lesson learned, we start back towards the house and the terrace picnic.

Frankly, I am concerned that the turnout is modest, perhaps an inadequate reward for Carole's efforts. But when we reach the terrace by the house my fears vanish. There we find a fine crowd, mostly of unfamiliar faces, drawn by association with horses and horse people, if not by personal participation in equine doings. I especially admire Jim Wray, a man verging on my own level of geezerhood, who climbs on foot to the top of our mountain field to earn the view of the Loudoun Valley that some of the rest of us, including Jim's wife Carol, soon enjoy effortlessly, courtesy of a four wheel drive truck.

*Relaxing after the ride*

From our vantage point at the top of the mountain field we can look out over all of the valley – northeast to the Catoctin Hills, east across to the Bull Run Mountains, and south to

*Autumn view of Loudoun Valley from the mountain field*

Thoroughfare Gap, the twin Cobblers, and beyond. Within our view is land that was surveyed by the young George Washington, most of the territory that was known in 1864 as "Mosby's Confederacy", the heart of the present Virginia hunt country, the sites of the 1863 battles of Aldie, Middleburg, and Upperville, and the place at which Disney recently tried unsuccessfully to build a theme park. The landscape lies before us, ridge on ridge, green dissolving into misty blue, much as it did in those past times, and today still held in that state of suspended animation by protective landowners enthralled by and committed to the happy mix of horse and countryside. Roger Rutti, our new Trappe Road neighbor, is specific.

> *"The view from your terrace is great. But this is tremendous. It's as if you are in an airplane."*

We drink in the fresh openness, and then we see, far below, the riders returning. It is time to go down and join them. On descending we are not surprised to learn that they have had a happy experience. Edie later writes it up as follows:

> *"All ages were represented. Susie Speer brought her daughter on her first such event away from home grounds. The Beers came with two of the three very accomplished young riders in their family. And then there were the seniors! One showed up with a horse she had owned for just four days; all seemed to go smoothly for her. A friend of Chips Chester's was riding Chips' new 17.3 hand mare, pending the owner's recovery from damaged ribs. There were many others representing 'tween' ages, and I was thrilled to have Gay Estin and Mary Swift [foxhunting friends of long standing] join our ranks.*

> *"I had planned a two hour loop behind Cleremont, then through Newstead, Corotoman and home as there are some very nice walls and coops [to jump] on that route, only to be thwarted by a sticky gate and new fence separating the Royer's hayfield from Newstead. So we changed the route to the lovely fields behind the old ladies' farm at the corner of Route 719 and Trappe Road.*

> *"Our ride was rewarded by a bumper crop of wildflowers, including Cardinal Flowers in the moist areas, Black-eyed Susans, Queen Anne's Lace, Joe Pye Weed, wild Ageratum, and many delicate Asters in the uplands, all responding resplendantly to the summer's rains that have left our fields unusually green for this time of year.*

> *"In our group, Leslie [VanSant] and Rosie brought up the rear, to help close gates and encourage stragglers."*

At this point in Edie's narrative I have a vision of a gentle cavalry commander controlling her troop precisely in accordance with proper military practice.

Edie continues:

*"Romeo is always delighted to be the leader. He took exception when I asked Leslie to go ahead and open the last farm gate as we came home. He does not feel that his job description ever includes being passed by Rosie, and he let me know it. Rosie, on the other hand, is calm anywhere."*

Romeo is a Thoroughbred, by the way; Rosie is not. Edie concludes:

*"Betsy and Marguerite [Walsh] led a slower ride which seemed to have just as nice a time as ours did.*

PHOTO BY THE AUTHOR

*Coming out of the woods at a canter*

*"On returning we visited with the hikers and terrace-sitters to enjoy the bountiful lunch provided by Carole and her young friend Yvonne."*

On the terrace some riders who have not been to Trappe Hill before leave names and addresses so that they might be invited again. The combination of nice horses and beautiful country is once again addictive. But that is not news to those who live here with such animals.

The luncheon that Carole has organized – beer, wine, soft drinks, ham, salad, ice cream – is followed by some nice remarks by her thanking the Leukemia people for a miracle, a drawing for door prizes, and general good humor and fellowship. By three o'clock the crowd has thinned to almost nothing, the wine is gone, the remaining food put away, and Carole is free to eat lunch, and then be driven by Edie to the top of the mountain field, where she has never been, so that she too may see why this valley is so treasured.

Was the event a success? How do you measure success?

Carole has helped those who work to conquer the disease that almost felled her, both by raising $3,000 in support of their efforts, and by making sixty of her friends more aware of leukemia's

PHOTO BY THE AUTHOR

*Carol Stadfield (left) and friend*

deadly threat, and the promise of a cure if the research that has helped her is supported.

The riders have started the fall early, in the manner they love best, enjoying their horses and each other's company amid the charms of the countryside.

Non-riders have had a beautiful day outdoors, some of them learning more about horses in the process.

All of us have enjoyed the company of old friends and met new ones.

As for the work involved, it was satisfying and fun – as work should be. More important, it has been a chance for the participants to do something worthwhile for their less fortunate fellow human beings.

And the catalyst for all these good things is the horse.

EPILOGUE:

The next fall there was a similar trail ride over the same countryside, with Carol Stadfield among the 80 or so riders, her ailment absent, as was her riding experience. As she signed the required waiver, someone was heard to remark:

*"We hope it won't be needed."*

And it wasn't. She had a marvelous time, but commented afterwards:

*"My saddle was crooked, one stirrup was longer than the other, I had a cramp*

*in my right knee and both toes were numb. I was a mess. So I decided to walk the rest of the way."*

Edie was not totally sympathetic.

*"That's why you have to get lessons."*

*"I know. I will. I've already talked to Malcolm Winter [of J.R. Field Hunters]."*

## – Competitive Distance Rides –

One off-shoot of trail riding is the sport of competitive distance riding, conducted hereabouts under the supervision of the Virginia Trail Riders Association. These are serious contests, calling for very fit horses and riders, and bear little resemblance to the casual trail rides just described. In many ways they are throwbacks to the times when the horse was vital to rapid and sustained transportation in Virginia.

Almost since the end of WW II there have been annual 50 mile and 100 mile rides held each spring at Hot Springs, VA. Each ride covers three days, the 100 mile event broken into daily segments of 40 miles, 40 miles, and 20 miles across varying and usually mountainous terrain. Classes within each

*Checking his feet during a distance ride*

event are lightweight, middleweight, and heavy weight – allowing riders of all sizes to participate on an equal footing. Held in April, the ride was conceived so foxhunters could use their fit horses in another way before putting them out to pasture for the summer.

According to one informant:

*"Any fit foxhunter can do the 50."*

The 100 is a different matter, as is the weather. In the Virginia mountains April holds a spring lottery – equal odds on rain, snow, or balmy weather with wild flowers at trailside.

The contests are taken seriously, with weighing–in each day for rider and tack, and strict rules governing the management of horses before and after the day's ride. Parties the night before the first race segment and the evening after the last do not detract from the competitive instincts of the riders.

Although the time limit is quite demanding the ride is not a race. The contest is really over fitness, and veterinary judges are stiff markers when it comes to out-of-shape conditions such as excess sweating, high pulse rate, or damaged hooves. Horses are inspected frequently by a veterinarian, both on course and at the end of each day, and penalized for any evidence of lack of condition, or even removed from competition if serious irregularities appear.

To have a chance of finishing within the time limit there can be very little walking except in the most difficult spots, with trot or canter chosen according to the nature of the trail at the moment, the condition of the horse and rider, and perhaps tactics vis-à-vis the other competitors.

Assuming no physical problems disqualify it, the horse that completes the prescribed distance within the allotted window of time, and with the fewest demerits, is the winner. There are no similar inspections of the rider, whose only requirement is to remain connected to his horse.

Today we are sitting in the home of Billy Wilbur, who rode in many of these events in the 1970's on a horse borrowed from Paul Mellon. Billy shows me a picture of two very successful ex-steeplechasers, Christmas Goose and Mongogo, as he describes how he and Mellon approached the sport:

*"To get ready we had to ride two and a half hours a day, three or four times a week, conditioning ourselves and our horses. Paul never delegated the conditioning to anyone else, did it all himself.*

*"Then we'd go down to The Homestead Hotel in Hot Springs and do the 100 Mile ride. One year (1976) Paul put me on Christmas Goose, and he took Mongogo. Paul had won occasionally in the past, but this year Christmas*

*Billy Wilbur reminiscing over a picture of
Christmas Goose and Mongogo*

*Goose and I won the middle-
weight, and Paul and Mongogo
got nothing.*

*"Next year (1977) Paul decided
we should switch horses – they
were of course both his horses
– and he and Christmas Goose
won the Grand Championship,
which they did again in 1978,
a year in which Mongogo and
I got Reserve."*

In his book *Reflections in a Silver
Spoon* Paul Mellon remembers
the results a bit differently:

*"My own scores were almost
consistently 99 or 98, while
Billy would turn in a score of 98 or 97, earning him and the horse the
reserve championship rather than the championship."*

As Billy puts the picture back on its hook, his face beams with the recollection
of a very happy day in a long friendship. No doubt he has forgiven Paul his
interpretation.

*Distance
riding
enthusiasts
Billy
Wilbur
and Paul
Mellon on
fit fox-
hunters*

# – Endurance Riding –

Endurance riding began as a cavalry exercise, in part to evaluate different breeds – Thoroughbreds were faster, Arabians the most durable, and Morgans in between.

Adrienne Hewitt is one of the world's most enthusiastic people, and she saves her special superlatives for this sport. She loves the Homestead 100 Mile Ride – it was her introduction to distance riding, and her mother won it in the 1960's – but for her endurance riding is a cut above anything else.

*A vet check on the first ever Old Dominion 100, which was won by Blackberry and Winkie MacKay-Smith, #21*

Unlike competitive distance riding, endurance rides are races, with divisions varying from "limited distances" of 20-35 miles, to endurance races of 50 or 100 miles. At each of two or three check points along the course, your "in" time is taken as you reach it. To this is added the time it takes your horse's pulse to slow down to a predetermined rate. The sum becomes your time for that leg. You also have from 30 minutes to one hour uncharged "hold" time (same amount for all contestants) from your "in" time, to feed and water your horse and yourself before setting out on the next leg, assuming a veterinary check, covering various metabolic and physical conditions, shows your horse to be "fit to continue."

A final veterinary check after finishing must show your horse still to be "fit to continue" for you to qualify as a finisher. And the final "pulse down" time is taken to complete your score. The winner is the team of horse and rider with the lowest total time. There is also a "Best Condition" prize for the horse finishing among the top ten that is deemed in the best condition at the end of the ride. Anyone who finishes within 24 hours (for a 100 mile ride) including hold time is deemed a finisher.

The managers of The Old Dominion, Virginia's premier endurance race and the second oldest in the country, have this to say about the sport:

> *"It is basic to our philosophy that to complete an endurance ride is to win. This conviction stems from the belief that your only real adversary is the trail. You should be directing all your efforts toward getting your horse and yourself over a given trail in a time and condition which is best for you and your horse, and which is only secondarily related to the pace and progress of the other participants. – The primary reason for [the Old Dominion's]*

*existence is to give you, the rider, an opportunity to study your horse more closely under demanding conditions; this will make you more understanding and more effective as a horseman, trainer, and participant in future endurance events."*

They should have added, *"and you will also know yourself better as a person."*

Adrienne describes one of her favorite races, an Old Dominion 50 miler.

*"At the first check my horse pulsed down two minutes faster than the next*

PHOTO COURTESY OF WINKIE MACKAY-SMITH

*horse, and when we started off again there was this mountain ahead and he just ran up it and we built a 15 minute lead by the next check point. We won by 45 minutes and got "best conditioned, too. That was cool!"*

Typically the Old Dominion 100 takes 12 to 14 hours to complete, exclusive of the "hold" times. Thus some of it must be done at night.

Adrienne is skeptical of those who refer to the "long, hard, training rides" needed to prepare:

*"If they were long and hard I wouldn't be doing it. It's a joy for me. Seeing a fox, or a bear, or a bald eagle – and I've seen all three on training rides – is just the icing on the cake."*

The Old Dominion used to start at Leesburg and cross the Blue Ridge at our Trappe Hill Farm. But now the country to the east is too built up, and so the ride starts south of Front Royal, passing along country trails to McCoy's Ford on the Shenandoah, across the river and along the crest of Massanutten Mountain down to Camp Roosevelt at the south end of Fort Valley, then

———

145

*Adrienne, Carey (behind Adrienne) and kids crossing the Shenandoah*

making a big circle back across McCoy's again and back to "Go." Adrienne describes a night crossing:

*"The ford was marked with two lines of milk jugs anchored in the water, with glow sticks in them, looking just like lanterns. It was beautiful."*

She loves the sport on two levels:

*"First, just to be out there with the horse, a horse you love – mine's half Dutch Warmblood, half Arabian. When you're ahead you are alone with your friend – your horse, a horse you really trust, and he wants to do it too. It's joyful because you both want to do it. Then, we do it as a family sport too."*

Adrienne's proud that her husband Carey Beer finished 20th in the 50 mile event. She and their children Alexander and Adrianna did the 25 mile version and all finished, despite a huge thunderstorm. Now, three years later, Alexander has completed the spring, summer, and fall races in each of three consecutive years; Adrienne adds:

*"They gave him a 'Triple Triple Crown prize'."*

Apparently the endurance riding virus is catching. Flora Hillman gave us her write-up of a recent Old Dominion 50 miler, and here is a Readers Digest-type condensation of the narrative that appeared on her web site:

*"Our final ride this spring was the Old Dominion 50 mile endurance ride in the Shenandoah National Park and the George Washington National Forest.*

*"The ride set off at 6:00 am., the first two miles leading up a narrow mountain path towards Skyline Drive. My Welsh / Arab 'Itch' was full of himself and ready to roll.*

*"By the time we crested the top, and crossed the Drive, the trail opened to a glorious gravel path four horses wide. My pony came into his element then, and took off down the one mile slope like a slalom skier. Nobody can keep up with him when he's cruising down hill. I sat as quietly as possible and just let him go.*

*"In no time we had flown the 12 miles across the valley, and were soon fording the Shenandoah River. My game plan was to ride the OD only to complete it – not place – and to continue learning our respective limitations / strengths / weaknesses. So, when we reached the first hold at the Shenandoah I took my time, just making sure my pony had ample food and plenty of time to relax.*

*"As a result, we left the first hold about 10 minutes past our initial out*

---

147

*Flora Hillman and Itch crossing the Shenandoah*

*Vet check – Flora*

time, following the trail markers as they headed towards Massanutten Mountain. The climb was steep and grueling – the trail deteriorating as it ascended until it was nothing except loose shale and rock. I got off and let my pony tow me up with his tail, looking over my shoulder from time to time at the breathtaking views as we climbed high above the valley. I was sweating and breathing heavily by the time we reached the top, but my pony was fine, happy to carry me again as we walked and trotted along the rocky crest of the mountain. It wasn't until we wound our way down to the valley on the other side that the path leveled out, allowing us to move along at a quicker pace.

"The second vet check was in a lovely grass field, next to a deep creek. After vetting, lunch, and some time to relax during the mandatory hold, Itch and I set out, following the trail as it led across the bottom of the valley before it began to rise again, this time taking us over the mountain through the rocky pass of the infamous "Little Crease." I had explored this pass with my friend Adrienne a few weeks prior, and knew just how far I could ride before I had to get off and walk. The woods were cool and comfortable, so it was no effort to walk behind as the trail ascended. We actually passed several other horses picking their way through the rocks on tiptoe as they struggled to balance themselves and their riders. I kept thinking that all those weeks

Hillman and Itch

PHOTO BY FLORA HILLMAN

Kitty Newman on Massanutten Mountain trail

of my walking 4-5 miles a day were paying off.

"Several miles later the path finally crested the mountain and the trees opened to give a spectacular view of the valley below, and the Shenandoah River looping back and forth upon itself in shimmering ribbons of water.

"The trail proceeded down the other side of the mountain, a nightmare of rocks and boulders, and more narrow than before. Several times it hovered on the edge of a cliff that dropped straight down – far too steep for comfort! Itch never missed a beat, and walking behind him afforded me a unique view of how his aluminum shoes – reinforced with steel wear plates in front and steel set-screws in the heel – grabbed and gripped the rocks, never sliding or slipping even a fraction of an inch.

"Midway through the descent the trail markers directed us to another path that would take us down the remaining slope. I mounted and when Itch and I reached the gravel road at the bottom we went into a canter heading towards the third hold next to the Shenandoah River. Once there, I sponged my pony off, waiting for his respiration to reach parameters. He came down quickly and we vetted through with flying colors. He was getting really hungry, so it was fortunate that the field we were in was full of lush green grass. While he grazed I arranged a clean saddle pad and drank some human

*View from Massanutten Mountain*

*electrolytes with my lunch.*

*"We were only 12.5 miles from the finish when we left McCoy's Ford, crossed the river, and headed towards the final hold at Liberty Hall. We were pretty much alone on this stretch. It was nice to open up into a canter at times, enjoying the cool woods and less trying footing of dirt paths and gravel roads. We reached Liberty Hall, Itch's pulse immediately dropping to parameters. The vet gave me a huge smile, I could tell he was more than happy. All around us vets were quietly talking in concerned voices to attentive riders, and more than once I heard the words 'marginal' and 'it would be wise to take it slower.'*

*"While I was pleased that my pony was physically doing exceptionally well. I could also tell he was becoming mentally tired. It was now the hottest part of the day, and the sun was blistering out in the open. Since the mind drives the body, we left the hold at a walk for about a half mile before moving into a trot. The trail was uphill for two miles. Itch dropped into a slow jog trot, conserving energy. About a quarter of a mile from the top we slowed to a walk. I got off and walked beside him just as five riders came trotting up the slope. As they passed us Itch pricked up his ears. Their horses were*

*Justin MacKay-Smith on Massanutten trail*

breathing heavily. I watched as they slowed to a walk at the very top. 'OK, Itch,' I said as I mounted. 'We're rested enough. Let's go.'

"We broke into a trot, reaching the other riders as they crossed Skyline Drive. The lead horse in the group hesitated at the log step-downs on the opposite side, giving Itch just enough time to zip in front. It was all we needed. Refreshed and ready to go, he flew into his downhill mode, leaving the others far behind as he cruised down the hill at a flying trot.

"I could feel his enthusiasm returning, and by the time we reached the bottom he was back in focus, his trot strong and ground-covering, his ears pricked towards home.

"I knew at that moment that my plan had worked to perfection. I had kept all the stress points to a minimum, and still had plenty of pony left under me. For the first time I felt a surge of excitement… we were going to complete the Old Dominion, and do it in terrific style.

"The ground flew under our feet as we rounded the last turn, entered the woods that lead to the finish line, and crested the final hill above the camp. I asked Itch for a canter, and he replied with a hand gallop as the path exited the woods at the top of base camp. I could see a crowd of people at the finish line, and as we turned up the speed to a gallop up the final slope, I could hear the cheers and applause. It was the most memorable moment of my life as Itch galloped, strong and happy, across the finish line.

"Itch passed the final vetting with flying colors. For all our extra time relaxing at holds, and not bothering to worry about going out on time, we still ended up finishing 31st out of 74 horses. We'd accomplished what we set out to do – which was to learn all about the ins and outs of endurance riding… and have fun.

---

151

*Flora Hillman celebrating. It's over!*

## – Past, Present and Future –

Two of the most experienced local distance riders are Winkie and Matthew Mackay-Smith. As Matthew tells it one evening in his living room, recreational endurance riding evolved from cavalry exercises intended to evaluate horse breeds for cavalry service, and the three day 100 milers are patterned after this.

The first long distance competitive endurance ride, 100 miles in 24 hours, grew out of a logging rivalry in the west. Apparently a lumber baron named Wendell Robie was beating his competition in bidding for government timber. When asked about it he said:

> *"I cruise timber on horseback. I load up my horse in the trailer, ride Saturday and Sunday, making notes, then back to the office Monday."*

*"How many horses do you use?,"* he was asked.

> *"Just one."*

The friend was incredulous, so Wendell said:

> *"Meet me in Carson City before daybreak."*

Though the friend folded after 60 miles of riding, he had fun. He said, *"Let's do it next year."* And so the ride known as the Tevis Cup began.

In 1961 the Mackay-Smiths bought a mare, Black Maria, from a friend who had got her at an auction of horses used in the Pentathlon. According to Winkie:

*"She was a difficult mare, and I thought distance riding might rehabilitate her. I conditioned her in the summer of '62 and entered her in the Vermont 100 mile three-day ride. She came in fourth in her division, and I was hooked."*

Winkie, in due course, won everything in the East with Maria.

Matthew interjects:

*"She was born to ride. It could be the death of her because she doesn't come off."*

He goes on to explain her natural "seat" and her riding skills generally. Winkie breaks up this family mutual admiration society meeting by telling about her toughest ride:

*"Marge Moyle invited me to fly out to Reno and join her to ride in the 102 Ranch Bonanza Ox-trail Ride, a 100 mile endurance ride starting at Nick Mansfield's 102 Ranch in Sparks, Nevada…"*

Matthew: *"If you're going to ranch at the 102 you've got to be optimistic. "* (The country is all desert.) Winkie continues:

*"I accepted the invitation and flew out to Reno two days before to meet Marge who was bringing the horses.*

*"I had a terrible cold – took some penicillin the day before, but it didn't have any immediate effect.*

*"The ride started at 8 PM and we were told 'ride that way – to Virginia City.' There were a few ribbons tied to an occasional sage bush, but basically it was desert, rocky footing, no visible markers, and soon it was very dark. We followed a group of local riders and got into Virginia City, where they all scattered like quail. We finally joined up with two girls on a railroad grade who assured us they knew where the trail went. This got us up out of town, but we were stymied by a chain link fence around some sort of reservoir.*

*"After dealing with that we rode on in the dark, and finally topped a rise from which we could see some lights in the distance, which the girls said was Reno, our destination. Having just been in Reno, it didn't look like the right layout but we went down anyhow, only to find that it was Carson City, and we had made a 15 mile error, so we retraced our steps."*

The sailor in me asks, *"Didn't you have a compass?"*

*"Unfortunately, no. The next vet check was at Mt. Rose, a ski resort, and getting there was a nightmare. Soon it was dawn, and we spent six hours*

*Don Moyle and Matthew Mackay-Smith passing a snow bank in the high country – Tevis Cup, 1964*

*Winkie and Carol Hannum near a ski lift on a Tevis Cup ride. Winkie was pregnant at the time.*

*thrashing over the shoulders of mountains, stumbling over rocks, and pray-ing we could get to the vet check and withdraw from the race."*

Matthew: *"They went up into the Sierras – a gruesome mountain goat trail, just a deer path through the chaparral. A ranger stopped them at the wilderness area and made them fill out a form – NAME; PLACE OF BIRTH; NEXT OF KIN…"*
Winkie continues…

*"At Mt. Rose we were told we couldn't pull out, we were running fourth and fifth, there were only a very few left in the race, and our horses were in*

*Emily Mackay-Smith winning the Old Dominion 50. The adult rider is in the 100.*

*great shape. So we went back down into the valley, no water and the heat over 100 degrees. We were trotting along the Loma Linda road at about 4 pm. when a jeep pulled up and the vets jumped out, telling us we were the last of the four or five left in the ride, and that Nick Mansfield and his buddies were the ones ahead. They pulled off a hub cap and poured some water in it so the horses could get a drink.*

*"The trail back to Sparks was bare, moun-tainous and rocky, the heat intense. I was falling asleep in my saddle when we spied the Truckee River. It was about 7:30 pm., and we could hear voices on the other side where the riders were camped. On our side was a chain link fence with the gate locked. The ride master had gone through and locked it, not realizing we were out there.*

*I had no voice, but Marge put up a pretty good racket. With 15 minutes left in our 24 hour time limit someone heard her, came and opened the gate, and we finished. For about 23 and three-quarters hours the horses' performance was so generous and extraordinary that it made our ordeal seem trivial by comparison."*

At the awards ceremony they were two of four finishers. The "winner" – the ride master – declined the winner's buckle because of his official position, and tried to give it to his companion, who had finished second. Winkie cleans up that old westerner's comment:

*"I'll be God damned if I'll take the award for finishin' second. You can take it and shove it \*@##!!\*!!! The only way I can see you behavin' as you did is so*

*you could win it. If it ain't good enough for you, it ain't good enough for me."*

And he threw the buckle on the floor.

Winkie says, *"Margie and I figured later we had covered an added 22 miles."*

Some years later, Winkie went west again for a Tevis Cup ride, did a lot of galloping, and managed to finish in the top ten. She continues:

> *"Coming home on the plane from that one I just sat all the way, I was pregnant with Emily. When it was time to get off I couldn't walk down the ramp, I had to back down. My quads had blown as a result of all that galloping with Emily aboard."*

Thirteen years later Emily herself won the Old Dominion 50.

Matthew: *"In distance riding you discover how much deeper your resources are than you believed."*

Matthew has left most of the evening's heroics to Winkie, but he has some great horse credentials of his own:

- With his horse Fred, winning both The Old Dominion 100 Mile Ride in Virginia and the 100 Mile Tevis Cup in California in the same year.

- Past President of the American Endurance Riding Conference (AERC).

- Member if the AERC and Veterinary Halls of Fame.

- 25 or so years – and counting – as Medical Editor of *Equus* Magazine.

But above all he is a philosopher, no doubt honing that skill on horseback. He finds endurance riding… *"a powerfully enabling activity."*

He feels that endurance riding was, and should be, a…

> *"…demonstration that you have a hell of a horse. Racing to be fastest may be unfair to the horse. Racers should remember that their duty is first to their horse. Duty to one's ego is fourth or fifth among the obligations a rider has.*
>
> *"It's the nature of humans to be arrogant. Peer pressure was once enough* [to suppress arrogance], *but international endurance riding has been almost all bad news. It escalates pressure to make the horse perform up to his maximum – international prestige is on the line…I hope to tweak it* [the sport] *back towards where it was."*

It is getting late, and our evening drifts away from horses. I tell Matthew about a meeting on climate change that I am to co-chair. This provokes a final burst of philosophy from our host:

———

*"Obsessive Naiveté – the American belief that nothing bad is ever going to happen.*

*"The human race will eventually become a different thing than it is today. You should have a meeting on genetic drift in the human race: where we started, where we are, where we must go if we are to survive as a species.*

*"We must go from being individualistic – the circle of good used to stop at the end of the fire light – to being communal, and we've made some progress. But we have a long way to go.*

*"Keep in mind that the total body mass of [the planet's] termites is equal to the total mass of human beings."*

You can see a very long way from the back of an endurance horse.

*Hacking home*

# IX

# FOXHUNTING

PHOTO BY ANITA BAARNS

*D'ye ken John Peel, with his coat so gray\*?*
*D'ye ken John Peel at the break of the day?*
*D'ye ken John Peel when he's far, far away,*
*With his hounds and his horn in the morning?*

*'Twas the sound of his horn called me from my bed,*
*And the cry of his hounds, which he oft times led;*
*For Peel's view-halloo would 'waken the dead*
*Or a fox from his lair in the morning.*

First two verses of "D'ye ken John Peel," words by John Woodcock Graves c.1829. Peel (1777 - 1854) lived in the County of Cumberland in northwest England.

---

\*No doubt the "Pink" coat had not become fashionable as yet in Peel's hunt. When it did the word "gray" might better be "gay."

---

*"Creatures can open up a world to you, can connect you to other people. Foxhunters — can you imagine such a diverse group getting together under any other circumstances? Hunting is the oldest thing we do together as a species."*
—Rita Mae Brown, MFH, huntsman, author and amateur philosopher

Galloping after hounds as they search for and pursue foxes has been a favorite pastime of Virginians for centuries. Though the sport has fewer devotees than horse shows it is probably the most visibly representative of the many equine sports in the Virginia Piedmont, often referred to as Virginia's "Hunt Country."

Centered on Middleburg, Warrenton, and Charlottesville, this area consists of gently rolling land, a mixture of farms and large estates, and it is sprinkled with small streams, ravines, patches of woodland and the occasional small town. It teems with foxes. No one disputes its ranking as the premier fox-

PHOTO BY DOUGLAS LEES

*Warrenton Hunt led by Huntsman Jim Atkins*

*Loudoun Hunt Huntsman Joe Cassidy, Whipper-in Perri Green, and MFH Anita White*

hunting area in America. Only a few die-hard Brits would argue that it is not now the best in the world.

As a result it is home to 15 of Virginia's 25 "recognized" hunts (there are a total of about 175 in North America), and several informal "farmer's packs" as well. And there is the "farm team" of embryo foxhunters, the M.O.C. Beagles, the pack organized to teach young people the principles, traditions and enjoyment of hunting behind hounds.

This hunting country has attracted many people for whom foxhunting is life's greatest enjoyment, in some cases verging on religious fanaticism. So, too, is it with horses. Foxhunter Gar Royer observes:

> *"Horses love to gallop in open country. It is very rare to find a healthy horse that does not like foxhunting. To gallop with the herd is what they like best."*

After all, horses were once wild, herd-oriented animals. Hunting takes them back to their ancestral roots.

Fox hunting needs stretches of undeveloped countryside for fox habitat and long runs following hounds. Without open country and sympathetic landowners the sport is impossible. It also requires foxes – the objective in

*Jim Simon is owner of Little Brook Farm, a frequent site of Loudoun Hunt meets. The Simons moved recently from Connecticut, and Jim's wife Carol has joined the Loudoun Hunt. Foxhunting depends on supportive landowners like the Simons for its existence.*

America today being to chase them, not kill them. A hunt may run two or three foxes in a day's outing, but not have a kill in several years. Foxes that have "gone to ground" are left undisturbed. To ensure good hunting, foxhunters are ardent protectors of the natural habitat on which the fox depends, and frown on any shooting, trapping or poisoning of foxes.

Hunts vary greatly in their style – some being autocratic, others democratically cosmopolitan, others social, still others extremely challenging in the size of their fences and the pace at which they pursue their sport – but they all conform to the traditions and etiquette of foxhunting as it developed over the centuries in England.

The leader of the hunt is the Master of Foxhounds – "MFH" or "Master" for short – who leads the "field" of riders and generally directs the action. He or she is usually supported by one or more "Joint Masters" – also called "Master" and entitled to the designation "MFH" – who share in the tasks of hunt management, landowner relations, admissions to membership, oversight of the professional staff, and ancillary activities such as trail rides, hunt balls, and Point-to-Point races. The title of MFH may seem to be a desirable honorific, but to do the Master's job well calls for long hours of unseen hard work and oceans of tact. A few moments

*Old Dominion Masters Gus Forbush and Douglas Hytla*

in the spotlight are visible, the hours of careful preparation that underpin the hunt's success usually are not.

To control the hunt the Master must ride at the head of the field. Protocol dictates that the more senior members ride up front near him, and the more junior stay to the rear. A distinguished visitor, perhaps the Master of another hunt, may be invited by the Master to ride with him.

Care must be paid by riders not to interfere with hounds. Letting your horse step on a hound or kick it is considered extremely bad form. So is crossing the line of the fox, thus interfering with the scent and the ability of the pursuing hounds to follow it. Owners of horses with a propensity to kick when crowded are expected to braid a red ribbon or a piece of red wool into the horse's tail as a warning of this danger.

Equal in importance to the Master(s) is the other critical player, the Huntsman,

*Piedmont entering a wood*

usually a professional employee who trains the hounds and directs and controls them during the action, using both voice and horn to do so. He (or she) is aided in the field by two or more "Whippers-In", riders who patrol the flanks of the hunt's progress in order to deflect hounds who may stray out of the hunting territory, or get too near hazards such as roads or forbidden areas. "Whips" may be either paid professional "Hunt Servants" or experienced hunt members, an honor for the latter so chosen.

The Virginia Piedmont has been the nursery for generations of legendary huntsmen, many of whom have emigrated to build other hunts and packs of hounds with the skills learned here in childhood. Of the current local crop, the Poe brothers, Melvin (82 years old in 2002) and Albert stand at the pinnacle.

———

Melvin Poe

One Sunday afternoon in February Peter Winants drew on a biography he has written to give some insights into the life of Melvin Poe. The site of Peter's talk was the Trinity Church parish house, and the SRO crowd assembled would be the Sunday envy of any clergyman. As the tale unfolded it was easy to see what it takes to be a good huntsman. Here are some notes taken from Peter's remarks:

*"What prompts people to become huntsmen? Melvin says it all revolves around the land, and an understanding of animals and nature… When Melvin was a boy the Poes were real farmers, living near Hume, not 'recreational farmers' like some of us in this room.*

*"There were ten Poe children. For them the horse was all important for transport. It was before the days of yellow buses, and they'd ride to school, sometimes three on a single horse.*

*"Hounds were important – the Poes kept six or eight. Turn-out hunts – bring your own hounds – were big social events in those days.*

*"In this country environment Melvin was close to the land, animals, nature. In fact, in his Boy Scout troop he was called 'nature boy'… Later on, grown up and back from the army, Melvin started at $90 per month with Old Dominion. They had 13 hounds then, and Melvin could outrun 10 of them."*

He built up that pack, and served as huntsman at Old Dominion for 16 years. Eventually he went on to be huntsman at Orange County for 27 years. After retiring at 70, George Ohrstrom invited him to start up a new hunt in Bath County, where he is still active. Meanwhile Albert, 11 years younger, was serving as Huntsman over 39 years for a succession of local hunts – Fairfax, Middleburg and Piedmont

John Coles, Joint Master of Orange County, particularly remembers Melvin's impact as a woodsman, *"A man of the land, of forest and fishing."*

PHOTO BY DOUGLAS LEES

*Albert Poe*

This background, added to a love of people and a colorful and charismatic personality, has led Melvin to a great career in the sport he loves. Working with his wife Peggy there have been side projects as well, including a bed and breakfast for weekend fox-hunters, a stud farm breeding miniature horses, and some home-brew wine making. Of the latter Edie well remembers being introduced to "Chateau Poe" after one of her first hunts with Orange County. (Thoughtfully, we have decided not to ask for her analysis of the vintage.)

At the end of the parish hall gathering, Melvin and Albert were asked, *"Which of you is the better rider?"* The Poe brothers demured, so Peter answered:

*"Albert is a great rider, one of the best. He sits on a galloping horse and his body hardly moves at all. Now, on the other hand, Melvin has his own style!"*

A week later Melvin confided to me:

*"They asked the wrong question. They should have asked: Who was the better huntsman?! "*

You don't have to be a great rider to be a great huntsman, but you better know and love the ways of the fox, the hounds, and the people around you. And the stimulus of a bit of sibling rivalry doesn't hurt.

Though they are not the same, there is a close relationship between the MOC Pony Club and the MOC Beagles, another Eve Fout innovation which she still runs as Master of Beagles, aided by huntsman Hubert Davy who has replaced Hank Woolman, now retired. The purpose of the Beagles is to introduce children to the thrills and customs of foxhunting using the smaller, slower breed of hounds. Eve describes the MOC Beagles this way:

> *"We started the Beagles with kids. We never had any problem with 'lock the door and do your homework.' Instead it was 'get out, ride your pony, do something outside.' You absorb the country by riding through it.*
>
> *"Kids need a responsibility, not just riding in the back [of the hunt]. With the Beagles we assign children to the duties of whippers-in and field master, so they may learn by doing what is involved in conducting a hunt. We hunt Sundays, going to various hunts' territories. Dot [Smithwick] allows us to use her land with the beagles. On a typical big day we may get 50 kids… Nancy Dillon may bring 15-18 with their ponies."*

The Beagles meet on Sundays at 1:00 PM, and on school holidays. Elders are usually allowed to "ride to the beagles" only if they have brought a child along.

PHOTO BY THE AUTHOR

*Prospective MOC Beagles Hunt Servent*

The management of the Beagles is separate from the Pony Club, but the Pony Club sponsors trail rides in support of the Beagles, and kids put in time early in the season walking and helping train the pack. Though originally bred to chase rabbits, the MOC Beagle pack works on pursuing the faster foxes, assuring both longer runs for the field and safety for the quarry.

On this particular day, the Sunday before Thanksgiving, a large crowd of participants and spectators has assembled at Glenwood Park, the site of many steeplechases, whose land backs up to Dot Smithwick's. Family groups congeal into a mass of ponies, children, adults and hunt horses that dwarf the tiny Beagles that mill about the green-coated huntsman's feet .

PHOTO BY THE AUTHOR

*Huntsman assigning tasks*

Calling the field to order the huntsman designates certain experienced youngsters – usually wearing red shirts and green armbands – as field masters and whippers-in. Then he moves off with his beagles and newly-appointed hunt staff along the edge of the race course to the woods beyond.

Following them is a huge field of perhaps 80 riders, who will soon disappear into the far reaches of Dot's fields. We tried circling to intercept them, by way of Polecat Road, but found only two beagling adults, also disconnected from the main body. As we snapped their picture one said

*"At least we're modeling for you."* We do not expect to receive a bill for their services. And we never do catch up with the action. We are quite certain the participants did not miss us.

## – *Scarlet if Convenient* –

When we first moved to Washington, Edie hunted with Fairfax, Middleburg and Piedmont, and I learned more about hunting traditions.

In almost all hunts it is traditional for the Masters and Huntsman (and often Whippers-in) to wear scarlet-colored coats ( called "Pink" after the man who invented them) and white breeches so that they can be readily identified by the field, consisting of anywhere from a dozen to (on rare occasions) a hundred riders. In many hunts it is customary for those male members who have been awarded their "colors" (the foxhunting equivalent of a Varsity letter) to also wear "Pink".

Ladies (except lady Masters and hunt servants) and men without their colors wear black jackets and tan britches. White shirts, white Ascot stocks, and

*Casanova Hunt Huntsman Tommy Lee Jones*

*Ratcatcher*

canary (yellow) vests are standard for all. For those with their colors the wool or velvet collar of the jacket is in the color of the hunt. In cold weather white gloves go with "pink," others wear black. Those responsible for the behavior of hounds carry hunting whips. Others, whose only concern is their horse, are generally restricted to riding crops. A black velvet-covered hunt cap, derby or top hat crowns the sartorial arrangement.

Details of dress, down to each hunt's proprietary design of jacket buttons, and the brown leather tops on black boots for men with their colors (all others wear plain black) are rigorously adhered to during the "formal" hunting season, starting in October. For the early fall weeks during cubbing season dress is informal – tweed jacket and tie – and referred to as "ratcatcher."

At formal evening affairs, such as hunt balls, gentlemen with their colors wear scarlet tail coats, a vivid approximation of military officers' dress uniforms. Ladies usually wear only black or white, or a combination thereof. Hangers-on such as myself are expected to be inconspicuous in our tuxedos, coincidentally conforming to the color scheme prescribed for ladies. In fact, in our area some dinner parties and most formal charity events specify the dress code as "Scarlet if Convenient," an encouragement to male foxhunters to enliven the optical drama of the evening.

At this point it may have occurred to certain readers that foxhunting demands an adherence to protocol and dress matched only by the most prestigious European embassies, ancient British Guards Regiments, and the New York Yacht Club. In this assumption they are correct. The pageantry of a hunt on a fall day is beautiful beyond words, in part because of these traditions.

SMART FAMILY PHOTO

*Mary Swift, the author, and Mike Kearny at a hunt ball*

But something much more basic than protocol and formality lies firmly beneath all the trappings and traditions of foxhunting . What truly excites the blood of the foxhunter is the relationship between animals, hunter and hunted, the beauty of the countryside, the thrill of the chase, the shared danger of possible falls at high speed, and the intimate connection between rider and horse. Given the dedication to foxhunting in the South of the mid-nineteenth century it is no surprise that Confederate cavalry gave Yankee horsemen a very hard time. And surely there are still some in today's hunt fields who imagine themselves galloping over our historic countryside as later-day incarnations of JEB Stuart's or John Mosby's riders.

## – Catching the Bug –

Matthew Klein came to foxhunting almost by accident, late in life as those things go.

We met Matthew recently, at a casual small dinner party. He's a pleasant, unathletic-looking, middle-aged man, a photographer and designer from New York. For escape he has been "into" bull terriers, through which avocation he met fellow terrier fancier Winkie

PHOTO BY CAROLINE LEAKE

*Opening Meet at Blue Ridge*

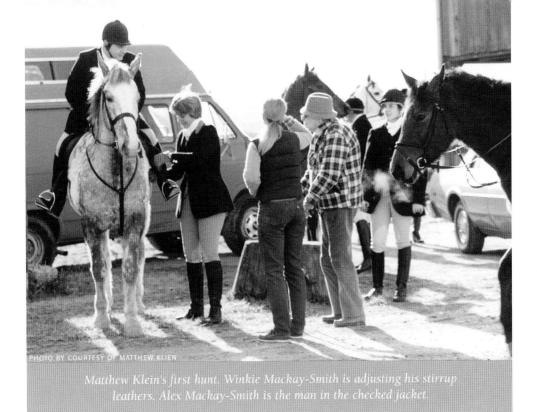

*Matthew Klein's first hunt. Winkie Mackay-Smith is adjusting his stirrup leathers. Alex Mackay-Smith is the man in the checked jacket.*

Mackay-Smith. One thing led to another, and he came down to Virginia, saw a fall Blue Ridge Hunt meet, and was intrigued.

On that weekend the Mackay-Smiths said to him:

> *"There's a big meet on New Years Day, do come on back for it."*

> [Klein]: *"But I've never ridden, and I don't have a horse."*

Matthew Mackay-Smith countered:

> *"Not a problem. We have a horse so good the only way you're going to fall off is if you stand on the saddle and run like hell."*

So Matthew Klein said, *"...gulp. I'll be there."* And he started taking lessons. To us he later added:

> *"My coach is half Israeli, half French, and he doesn't think much of foxhunting. He told me 'they only jump jumps they wouldn't jump if they were sober.' He gave me three lessons in an hour the first day I went to him, and I fell off when we went outside at the end of it. But foxhunting is about tenacity, so by December I was ready."*

Alexander Mackay-Smith, an ex-Blue Ridge MFH and by then an old man, came out to the New Years meet. Matthew Klein remembers:

> *"He came over to me, walking with the help of two silver headed canes,*

*looked me over, and said, 'Either you won't care for it… or it will change your life.'*

"*Alex was right. My life has changed. At work I'm surrounded by things that represent something. But on a horse none of that means anything. There I found a way of communicating that is not all symbols and signs — it's a deep, personal thing, almost religious.*

"*Foxhunting is at the edge between nature and culture, a totally consuming world. It takes a society of people who develop a check list of skills — know about horses, tack, driving a trailer in the mud, tenacity. You can't go hunting if you're not tenacious.*"

So now Matthew has joined the Blue Ridge Hunt.

The outsider may be forgiven if he still wonders how a person is drawn to this sport, or madness as Mr. Klein's coach sees it. Here, in her own words, is Edie's Odyssey as a rider, from her start as a passenger on a child's balky pony to her present role as Joint- MFH of the Fairfax Hunt, a position she has held for 11 years.

## – *The Making of a Foxhunter* –

*by Edith M. Smart*

My riding began when I was about five, and my grandfather gave me a pony named Buster. Buster was a Fjord who had spent a good many years teaching other children. He had learned all manner of ways of displacing the unwary small rider. He was adept at making quick right or left hand turns and brushing me off on the corner of the barn, and he seemed to know which apple trees had branches under which he could safely pass but I would not fit.

My parents retained a lovely Englishman named Jarvis to help my horsemanship along. I really enjoyed my outings with Jarvis, as the pony's behavior was exemplary with Jarvis around.

Father thought I would develop a better seat if I learned without a saddle. For several years I rode with a blanket and surcingle and no stirrups. My excitement was high when I was finally allowed a saddle. It was then that I determined to learn how to jump. The pony saw little point in going over an obstacle if there was a perfectly open way around it. Jumping took a bit of learning about keeping a leg on the animal, and sometimes encouragement from a crop.

Later on I inherited a small chestnut mare, Ladybird, about 14 ½ hands, that had been outgrown by our neighbors. She had a horse mentality (rather than a pony's) which meant that she jumped the fence she was pointed at, rather than ducking out.

I was now hooked on jumping, but I was a senior in high school before I went on my first hunt, a "drag*", encouraged to do so by an older family friend, Jean Chambers. The horse I rode was a man's hunt horse named Charlie. Charlie had been bought in Virginia by my totally unhorsey grand-mother for her daughter Priscilla. As horse after horse was paraded before Granny, she finally chose Charlie because she thought he looked sorry for her. He was totally unsuitable for a girl to be hunting, but no one told that to him or me. The horse loved it, but I spent most of the time being run away with.

*Edie showing a neighbor's horse*

Mrs. Chambers did much to help me improve my riding over fences. And she let me show one of her "made" hunters, Truckman. My job was to pilot, keep my leg on him, and not hit him in the mouth [by pulling too sharply on the reins]. We got a third place ribbon in our first show, in the pouring rain. It was my introduction to an oxer and a roll-top, but Truckman never stopped or pulled a rail.

---

*In a **"drag"** hunt a bag of strongly scented anise seed is drawn along a previously determined course for the hounds to follow. This simulation of a hunt involving wild foxes is used in confined or fox-free areas.

Then, a neighbor across the road asked me to show her mare in a local hunter trials. I said I would, without knowing that the mare had not been schooled for it. This mare refused every fence at least once. She finally jumped into a box in-and-out, but couldn't be persuaded to jump out. I was mortified. To this day I'm not sure exactly how we got out, though perhaps a Good Samaritan lowered a side rail so we could walk free.

At Smith College I rode a bit, but I discovered team sports, especially volleyball, and also had some fine instruction in tennis and squash, which I loved. At home, Charlie, though aging, was still there for me to ride on the trails during vacations.

Half way through college Bruce persuaded me to marry him. My riding took a break which lasted for 14 years, across several geographic relocations brought on by his army recall and subsequent business career.

While we were living in Chicago our 11 year old daughter Charlotte insisted on riding lessons, and we bought her a small horse, Mischief. Moving east in 1964, bringing Mischief with us, we fell in with the Fairfield (CT) Hunt Club. I rode a bit with Charlotte and older daughter Edie at the Hunt Club, but my heart wasn't really in riding around a ring.

*Edie with Buster and Charlie, 1949*

Raising children loomed largest in my life. Riding lessons and small school-ing shows became part of the girls' regular activities, and another addition to their mother's daily schedule. One day Emerson Burr (the professional in charge of riding at the Club) turned to me and said:

*"Mrs. Smart, I think you'd like foxhunting."*

My reply was something along the lines of *"Don't you have to be an excellent rider and have a string of hunt horses?"*

Emerson said:

*"Not at all." .*

So I found myself a member of the Fairfield Hunt field, first on a hunt club "packer" (a leased hunt horse), and then soon enough on Mischief, who had never had to deal with Connecticut rocks before. He got used to the uneven footing quickly, but found it almost impossible to wait quietly for his turn to take a jump. He would rock back on his haunches and catapult himself for-ward in the general direction of the fence. Fortunately he was a very good jumper and could clear the wing of the fence if that was where he was headed. Each day I went out I was sure it would be my last one. It took years before a hunting day was unaccompanied by a case of butterflies in the stomach.

Some time after we arrived in Fairfield I bought a young Thoroughbred geld-ing, Tam, as a yearling, because the breeder assured me he would make a hunt horse. With some help I broke him and started him towards his coming career. Charlotte outgrew Mischief, and moved to a bigger horse.

Now it became Tam's turn. He was only four years old, but he spent the summer being schooled in a ring over small fences. He was agile and quick. Emerson told me he was ready for the hunt field. Perhaps that judgment was a little previous. The hunt field fences occasionally cowed him. I especially remember one fence – a coop going into a wood from a field. Tam thought it scary, and refused it several times. At that point Emerson left me, saying:

*"I think he'll go over it."*

And he did. Emerson had the ultimate talent of a good horseman – he could get inside the horse's head and know what he was thinking. As the years passed Tam proved to be a kind, eager hunt horse, with an incredible jump in him.

One day in late November, while on a hard run, we came to country not usually hunted. Hounds had crossed a narrow dam that created a pond with a skim of ice on it. Tam and I were riding about third behind the Master. We were about half way across the dam when the two horses ahead slipped or fell off the dam into deep and distinctly chilly water. Both riders became separated from their horses, each horse and rider swimming independently for the far bank.. As Tam came to that fateful spot he, too, slipped off the dam and started to swim for the bank, which was steep and slippery. Somehow I stayed on him.

We hunted for about two more hours in our wet clothes before going in. It took weeks for the tack to recover from its total immersion. Needless to say, that swimming meet has been the subject of much reminiscing.

Tam's glory day came one fall at the annual hunter trials of the Fairfield Hunt. Bruce had accepted a luncheon at Pocantico Hills with David Rockefeller and some World Bank officials, which I believe he felt would be more interesting than grooming Tam for me at the trials. So we split forces, and I recruited neighbor Barbara Burian to be my groom.

Tam was entered in the Field Hunter Division, and in every class he jumped the course nicely, with a good, even pace. He just never put a foot wrong. When Bruce got home we had four blue ribbons, two championship ribbons and eight pieces of silver arrayed on the top of the station wagon. Since Bruce is known to be at least casually competitive, I suspect he regretted his decision to go banking that day. Barbara, however, has been eternally grateful for her moment in the sun.

Incidentally, Harry Huberth, a remote acquaintance at the time, was the Judge at those Hunter Trials. Harry, now living at Scuffleburg, near Delaplane, VA., has since become a very good friend and is a fine show rider, winning a championship at Upperville in 2000.

*Edie, Tam (r), and friends*

When we later moved to Washington, nothing was more logical than to bring down my new hunter, Tor (registered name Baratero), so that we could hunt in the fabled area around Middleburg. Our friends George and Danielle Kuper had facilitated our renting an apartment in the building in which they lived. They were members of the Fairfax (Virginia) Hunt, and easily persuaded me to join.

In Virginia, Tor and I competed for two or three years in the

Fairfax Hunt hunter trials. Sadly, that event no longer takes place, outside courses over hunting country generally having given way to the show ring and to urban sprawl. So I am now purely a foxhunter.

Happily Tam had a chance to retire to Virginia, and Tor to end his hunting days with the Fairfax, Middleburg, and Piedmont hunts, delighting in the greatest hunt country in the world.

Many people have tried to describe foxhunting. I find words are poor substitutes for an activity that has so many elements, and they fail miserably to convey the sense of excitement of all the participants in the chase.

First of all, man's partner, the horse, is a most important component. He enables his rider to enjoy not only the glories of the countryside, but gives a sense of exhilaration and well being as the chase progresses. A seasoned hunt horse is a wise and careful companion. He (or she) watches the hounds as they work, seeming to understand that until they stream off after a good scent, giving tongue as they go, the horse should be patient and stand quietly (though mine are not too good at this, perhaps sensing my own eagerness to be off and galloping again).

While running, horses must avoid rocks, holes in the ground, and other horses. They must be willing to check (stop) if the hounds do, and not run over them or kick out at them. We often cross fields laced with groundhog holes. Sometimes these are visible as we approach, but often the rider sees them only as the horse is jumping over them. Most hunt horses have a strong sense of self-preservation, which is fortunate for similarly inclined riders.

*Barbara, Tam and Edie — back from the wars*

PHOTO BY ANITA BAARNS

*Hunting with Piedmont*

They also develop a working knowledge of the game. They seem to know that a gallop, followed by a check while the hounds work a covert, is likely to be followed by another wonderful gallop. One day the field came in while the huntsman was still calling in hounds. As I was untacking Lenah she left me and trotted off to the crest of a small rise where she stopped and just watched. She knew huntsman and hounds should be coming in, and she wanted to be sure they were doing just that; she couldn't check on them adequately from down by the trailer.

For the last several years with Fairfax I have been leading the so-called "hill-topper" field. This "second" field skirts most of the fences, accommodating young or green horses (or riders), horses coming back from an injury, and riders who prefer not to jump fences at high speed.*

---

* [Ed. note]: Edie's "hilltopper" field seems quite pleased to refer to themselves as "Edie's Chickens", and I am careful at home to say nothing about old hens. And they take especial pleasure if they can beat the "first field" to the scene of the action.

———

PHOTO BY ANITA BAARNS

*A flock of Edie's Chickens*

Romeo still can't believe it when I pass up a jump instead of going over it. This is often the longer way around, and so to get to the hounds we have to go faster, but occasionally doing so gives us an early view of "Charlie"* if I guess rightly which way he will turn, and remember where the gaps are. Occasionally we do jump if some in our field want to.

We have had many wonderful "views" where everyone has been able to see the fox crossing the field before us. One fine day huntsman and pack ran down a hill and into a wood, where the pack split. A fox and half the hounds emerged from each end of the wood, giving each field a fine view. Of course, sometimes the huntsman forgets to sound his horn, which leaves the Field Master guessing as to which way he and the hounds will turn.

Hounds hunt with their noses, and when they hit a fresh scent they give tongue – "make music" – that raises the adrenaline in all of us as we take off in pursuit. When hounds start feathering their tails you know there is a sure scent to work with, but not enough for them to give tongue. The fox has been there, but probably left several hours ago.

Each hound knows his name, which is more than most of the field does.

---

* **Charlie** is sometimes used as the name for the fox.

———

177

[Ed note: This is exactly how Edie wrote it. Perhaps she meant to indicate that the field did not know many of the hounds' names, and, again, perhaps she meant exactly what she said.]

As for me, I know that Ruler and Crocus are distinctive and can be counted on. Ruler is an old patriarch who has sired many, and Crocus is a red bitch with a slightly less bushy tail than a fox. Sailor and Saffron are pale, mostly white hounds with fine noses. Alfred seems to have his own agenda, and that for me is about all I can recognize.

The hounds themselves gain stature in the pack as they become more seasoned. The huntsman knows each hound and its capabilities. Some young hounds may give tongue too readily, and if so the other hounds will not honor him or her. A puppy opening up on deer (a no-no) has a higher cry than that used for a fox. Roger is one of those vociferous ones. Our huntsman, Kevin, said, on one windy day when the scenting was atrocious, that…

*"I brought Roger along just so we'd have something to listen to."*

PHOTO BY ANITA BAARNS

Hunts have several breeds of hounds from which to choose – American, English, Penn-Marydel (named for the states in which the breed originated), and Crossbred. Each has its own characteristics of speed, endurance, voice, nose, and appearance, so to some extent the nature of the particular country and its game influences the choice – western hunts chase coyote and a Virginia hunt recently unintentionally treed a bear! Some Huntsmen and Masters go deeply into the breeding of their pack, a specialty that has not yet engulfed me.

*Tally-Ho!!!*

*Some Fairfax hounds – Crocus in the center*

The fox himself has to be a willing participant. If he is not, and goes to ground right away, there is nothing to chase. Some days provide better scenting than others, and therefore longer runs. We know that if the scent is high, if it can be smelled by those of us on horseback, it is likely to lie above the level of the hounds' noses, and they will have trouble following it.

We also have learned that foxes have a pretty set way of running. If one leaves the wooded covert on the hill he most likely will run to the bottom and follow the tree line to the next wooded covert, unless the hounds push him out into a field. Foxes sometimes travel in the water of a stream, rather than crossing directly, giving the hounds a scenting puzzle to unravel.

Deer we see in abundance, and the occasional wild turkey. They favor the same sort of covert as do foxes. Often a red-tailed hawk soars over our heads, probably hunting the quarry favored by the foxes. Then there is the changing seasonal landscape. We start cubbing (hunting with young hounds to train them) in September with the late summer foliage, which turns more glorious as the fall progresses. By November, when the leaves fall it is easier to watch the hounds work.

Finally, there is the community of foxhunters – the field. These are a diverse group of people whose interests converge at the horse, the meet, and the desire to chase after hounds who are running a fox. In the field one finds people from many backgrounds. We have the proverbial doctors, lawyers, merchants (read "business people"), and chiefs – but Fairfax recognizes only one of the latter, MFH Randy Rouse!

*Randy Rouse in the center, arm raised*

We also have emergency vehicle drivers, stock brokers, realtors, nurses, farriers, diplomats, military and government people, housewives and youngsters – in short a wide sampling of those who love the horse, the outdoors, and the sport. These common interests draw them together, and from them a fraternity of life-long friendships is forged.

Foxhunting faces a number of threats to its future, as will be discussed later in the sequel to this volume. For my part, I am well aware that nothing lasts forever, whether ended by personal disability, competing interests, or lack of access to a hunt or hunting country. But I am philosophical. Hunting has added greatly to my enjoyment over many years, and provided yet another dimension to a full life. Whatever the future may bring, the memories of days afield with friends, my horses, the hounds, the foxes, and the beautiful countryside will remain always fresh.

*Piedmont Foxhounds at a check. The Blue Ridge is in the background.*

The fraternity of each hunt has its legends, and Fairfax is no exception. In years past the exploits of an absent minded member, Jeff Davis, eventually gave rise to an annual award for emulation. The Jeff Davis Award was inspired by the day when Jeff, often late, drove up to the meet on time, parked his car and trailer, and set about opening the trailer's rear door. No sooner had he done so than he – and everyone else – noted that something was missing – there was no horse inside! Jeff had forgotten to load him!

Then there was a meet where a hunt member complimented Jeff on his new horse. *"Why that's the same horse I've always had."* said Jeff, patting the animal. *"I thought your horse was a gelding,"* said the friend. *"He is,"* said Jeff. *"But that horse you're on is a mare!"* At the stable Jeff had unwittingly loaded someone else's horse into his trailer and brought her to the meet.

Often one picks up snippets of these legends at hunt parties. Here's a recent sampling:

A horse and rider have just galloped past the Master, a serious breach of etiquette. Master:

> *"Boy, you take that horse to the rear, and if you can't keep him there you take him home."*

The horse was regularly out of control. So, according to the storyteller:

> *"They put a bit on that horse that would stop anything. Rider pulled him up, horse give a "Grrcchht" and threw a lot of dirt – Jeff Davis riding and Jack Sanders and John Heckler following, and the only thing kept them from ramming into the hounds was they was ramming into each other."*

Another conversation overheard:

> *"He and I were friends – drank out of the same flask. [Then…] This horse just grabbed my coat, I could hear him breathin' in my ear – 'have another drink' – that was some horse."*

I never did learn whether it was all about the same legendary animal, and whether the origins of the remarks lay in field experience or at the bottom of a wine bottle. But then, I am not a foxhunter.

Sally Irish tells this story of life in the Orange County Hunt country:

> *"Dick [her husband] was at home alone late one Saturday morning in his usual position, prone on the living room couch, a fire ablaze in the fire-*

---

place, and our Collie-Shepherd bitch secured indoors, being in heat. Then the Hunt, in full regalia, came charging through our property, the hounds circling the house, baying and generally disturbing the peace.

"Panicked, Dick lay flat on the floor behind the couch lest any huntsman (or huntswoman) think someone was at home. Meanwhile the dog flew from French window to French window watching the action, the hounds acting like a pack of bull moose in the rut, refusing to resume chasing the scent of the fox.

"Melvin Poe made a vain attempt to rally both riders and dogs but to no avail. Dick heard many huntswomen swearing like sailors and peeked to see them shaking their riding crops at the heavens.

"In time Melvin managed to call off the hounds and regroup the hunt. A few days later, when we happened to meet, Melvin reported that 'The fox went to ground right under your house!' "

It is unclear whether Sally ever told him what scent the hounds were on at the time.

PHOTO BY DOUGLAS LEES

*Melvin Poe and the Orange County hounds*

# – Memorable Hound Work –

*by Anita Baarns*

It's 3 o'clock in the morning, late in January; I'm laying awake reliving my joy at seeing the greatest hound work I've ever seen, witnessed close-up during yesterday's hunt.

Fairfax met at Farmer's Delight at 1:00 PM. Riding with the hilltoppers I followed Edie. Our elite group of four included Julia Theriot and Jean Stafford. For one and a half hours we followed the hounds, who presently picked up a fox headed for Hibbs Bridge Road. Just before Bolinvar he turned and headed back to Trough Hill in full view of the first field. We galloped around enjoying the country despite the fox's retreat.

Edie led us into the woods behind the Garity's, following Jim's "roller coaster" trail along Beaverdam Creek (my least favorite). After sliding down and galloping up the steep path for a while, regretting my decision not to quit early, suddenly hounds poured over a steep incline and descended to 30 feet in front of us in full cry. Kevin [the Huntsman] watched from above as the hounds stopped briefly at a big fallen tree laying across Beaverdam Creek, which created a bridge across the water.

There the hounds regained the scent, and turned towards us, still in full cry, passing us on the narrow trail. Just past us, hounds lost scent and began to scatter, but the lead hound returned to the fallen tree and spoke. All the other hounds looked up and honored him. We then saw the lead hound crossing the creek by walking on the log, nose down and giving great music. Following hounds jumped into the creek, giving tongue and swam as a pack to the other side, where they left us in full cry. What a sight! Kevin later called it *"toungin' and swimmin' at the same time."*

Edie on "Romio"

SKETCH BY ANITA BAARNS

Kevin turned and headed downstream, seeking the closest crossing. We followed Kevin and were on a run. Following the path brought us to a long plank bridge. We clattered over the planks, ascended a narrow driveway along one side of a small house, and burst forth by squeezing between a parked car and the front of the house, scaring a woman washing windows on the front porch.

Arriving onto Snickersville Turnpike, we turned west and followed the road as fast as we could, soon turning into the surveyed land opposite Egypt Farm. Having lost Kevin and the hounds, we galloped field after field, dodging surveyor's stakes and holes until we finally found Kevin, who was calling back hounds. The fox had disappeared. There we were, the four of us and Kevin, feeling pretty good about ourselves.

Finally, Linda and Jacob [the whips] arrived, and eventually the first field caught up. We greeted them with the biggest grins on our faces, telling them about the most wonderful hound work we had witnessed. Hacking back to the meet took an hour, which we spent reliving our run. When Kevin blew "Going Home" the sunset showed the reflection of hounds and huntsman in a pond. I knew it was the end of a perfect day in God's country!

## – A Matter of Gravity –

The other day Douglas Lees, a noted photographer whose work frequents these pages, showed me a picture of Leff Lefferts falling off a horse, and I took it with me when I went to see my friend Leff, now seriously ill. I found him at home and in bed, resting, surrounded by a life's worth of hunting and steeplechase memorabilia. Among his many pictures was a framed duplicate of Douglas's print, and Leff was happy to talk about it.

Leff Lefferts has pursued foxhunting for many years, in England and Ireland as well as in the United States. As he tells the story today, some years ago he became interested in what is now billed as "The Hunter Championship of America." To compete one enters with a favorite horse. Performance of both rider and horse is judged first by mounted judges in the hunt field. From this a few horse-rider pairs are selected from each hunt to participate in the championship finals run over a set course, including jumps, laid out over hunting country.

Back then, circa 1980, Leff had a fine mare named Simona…

> *"Finest hunt horse I ever had, and I've had some good ones. We won the Hunter Championship that year. Anyone could have done it on her, she was that good."*

———

PHOTO BY DOUGLAS LEES

*Leff Lefferts falling*

The rules called for the prior year's winner to lead the field of finalists around the course in the next competition, so that became Leff's duty in 1981. Simona was not available, so Leff set out on Truffles...

> *"She was a green mare, and when I galloped her into the first fence she suddenly stopped, and I kept going. Nick Arundel told me later 'that picture sold the most papers since Jackie's [Kennedy] fall years ago.' Anyhow, I climbed back on, circled the fence and she went right over it. She must not have liked how it looked."*

We fall to discussing riding accidents, and Leff recites his menu of orthopedic misfortunes. Then,

> *"Falling off is just part of the game, it's to be expected. You just can't worry about it. Early one summer some years ago our son 'L. L.' , then about seven, was learning to ride. He came home a bit mussed up, so I asked 'What happened?'"*

---

185

*"I fell off seven times!"*

*"Seven times? Well, you'll have to get used to it. You'll fall off a hundred times before you're a good rider."*

Late in August, L.L. came in again from riding, and Leff asked him: *"How was your day?"*

*"Eighty-eight, Dad!"* was the triumphant reply.

A few days later I went back to show Leff what I had written, to make sure it was accurate and that he wouldn't mind it being printed. I met his wife Bea in the driveway, heading for the stable. After greeting each other she wondered:

*"Do you think it's too cold to go riding?"*

The mercury said it was about twenty. *"No, it's OK. Edie's off hunting."*

*"Well, just walk right in, he's expecting you."*

And so I do. Leff is in bed, just as I had left him before, tired and pale from the medication and the chemotherapy that he is taking to fight his disease. I hand him the paper, and he reads it, slowly. Then his face breaks into a smile.

*"Every time I think of Simona it makes me happy."*

Then he finishes it, chuckling over the thought of L.L. that summer, and hands the paper back to me.

We talk about many things, mostly about what had meant a lot to Leff: playing baseball in school and college, how he had ridden steeplechasers. How he and a friend had ventured into the management of prize fighters, and dealt unsuccessfully with the Runyonesque characters that inhabit that milieu...

*"You wouldn't believe what those guys can do, working on a fighter in the corner between rounds!"*

Apparently Leff had worked in the corner once during a fight.

We talk about his efforts to find new territory (of which he is very proud) in order to save the Bull Run Hunt. How vivid and happy life's high spots seem as one reflects on them, and how lucky we all are to live in this beautiful place. Then he turns to his illness:

*"I know it would be a miracle if I can beat this thing. But I can try, and get a couple more years to do some things that need doing. We've got to sell this place, its too big for Bea to handle."*

As he talks my mind's eye sees Douglas Lees' picture of Leff suspended in air, and I'm thinking that this time he knows he may not get up so easily from the landing, so he's suspending the gravity that is his illness for as long as he can.

———

While I am musing, Leff remembers a piece of furniture he had made to hold his hunting boots. He climbs out of bed and leads me downstairs to his personal tack room to see it. There we are surrounded by years of accumulated hunting equipment, arrayed in disciplined order. I observe that there are 15 pairs of boots present for duty, several on the special boot rack.

Leff explains how you must allow the inside of boots to dry out after use – the boot rack facilitates that by hanging them upside down – before you put in the boot trees.

*"Otherwise, the leather will rot,"* and he gives me a short course in the general care of leather.

Then he picks up a boot, reflecting on the perfect shine on its toe. And, as he looks into that shine I realize, as Adrienne Hewitt said of herself, that Leff is seeing God again, "in the fox and the rocks and the light."

## – Opening Meet –

The telephone monitor of the Middleburg Hunt advised all callers that Saturday, November 2nd., is scheduled to be the Hunt's Opening Meet, and that it will take place at Groveton at 9:00 AM. The day dawned clear and cold, with the first frost of the fall evident in the distress of the dahlias in the

*Middleburg Masters Penny Denegre (left) and Jeff Blue*

PHOTO BY THE AUTHOR

garden and the skim of ice on the puddles in the driveway. It was a fit day to say farewell to Indian Summer and its casual cubbing, and get properly and traditionally geared up to chase foxes.

Groveton is a pleasant 20 minute drive from home over winding back roads. The residence itself is a small manor house, vintage 1820-40, set back from the road in a grove of large trees. Across the road to the north is an ample stone barn, to the west of which a field is rapidly filling with cars and horse trailers by the time I arrive at 8:30.

PHOTO BY THE AUTHOR
*Field assembling near trailers*

An opening meet is in every sense a welcoming of the new hunting season. Ratcatcher jackets are exchanged for scarlet and black (if you have one), horses' manes are braided, and a large field turns out – to greet each other, to hunt vigorously, and often to enjoy a hunt breakfast of some substance thereafter. Along with the Hunt Ball (and some hunts don't bother with having one of those) and the Hunt's spring Point-to-Point steeplechase meet it is the high point of the season.

PHOTO BY THE AUTHOR
*Sandra Markus and Amadeus*

I park the truck up against the inner side of the wall enclosing the assembly field, and immediately run into MFH Jeff Blue. Through Edie he is aware of my purpose in being there, and his welcome is cordial. Then we part, Jeff to find his horse – which appears to have come separately – and I to acquaint myself with the Middleburg Hunt. Surprisingly, familiar faces are scarce. One of them is Mayo Brown, leaning on an unaccustomed cane. Another, Sandra Markus, smiles down from atop a large chestnut gelding. As I pet him she comments:

*Proceeding up the road to the Groveton lawn*

> *"He's an Irish Thoroughbred, not like those sleek race horses you breed."*

And indeed he isn't. Instead he is large, heavily muscled, plenty of bone – in short, designed for durability, not speed. She tells me:

> *"His real name is Amadeus (as in Wolfgang Amadeus Mozart), so we call him Wolfie."*

And he makes music for Sandra. She bought him because, on a trial run hunting at a gallop on a foggy day, he effortlessly jumped an unexpected five strand wire fence that Sandra didn't see blocking their path. After the hunt she said to the owner:

> *"Here, give me the papers so I can sign right now."*

And so Wolfie is hers for Middleburg's opening meet.

One sees all types of horses in a hunt field. On my brief exposure my horse was a Thoroughbred – Percheron cross named Tiberius. Charley Matheson likes a cross of Thoroughbred and Cleveland Bay. Kids hunt all kinds of ponies, and Garen Stutzman hunts with Fairfax on a mule. Some perfection-ists feel this latter is a bit *déclassé*, and I note that Edie sticks carefully to small, racy Thoroughbreds – but then she also is small, and likes to go fast. The most important thing is to have a horse that is safe, comfortable in a crowd, able to jump, durable, and suited physically and temperamentally to the rider. I have never heard a foxhunter disparage another's horse for looks or breeding, but only for its faults of commission – it kicks, bites, can't jump, runs away, etc. And usually those faults can be traced to poor horsemanship, past or present.

Today the turnout for the meet is large, 70 or 80 horses. When all are at hand, and the hounds have debarked from the hound truck, the huntsman blows his horn and the assemblage leaves the parking area and proceeds up the road – huntsman and hounds ahead, next the whippers-in, followed by the two Masters and then the field. Assembled on the lawn under the trees a stirrup cup is waiting, accompanied by music from stringed instruments on the manor house porch.

After a brief pause for refreshment the Masters thank the owner of Groveton, Jan Evans, the Hunt staff and the members. Then Master Penny Denegre announces, *"Let's go find some foxes,"* and they are off over the field behind the house and into the woods beyond.

Most of the crowd of spectators moves up the steps of the house and enters it. Like a lemming I follow. Inside the doorway the hostess is greeting people. I introduce myself, thank her, and sign the guest book as she points the way to the bar and the Bloody Marys in the rear. On the way one notices the high ceilinged central hall, comfortable rooms on each side, the attractive art and fur-nishings and the molding and other woodwork that say early nineteenth century. Surprisingly, the crowd includes very few familiar faces. But then, we live in Upperville (Piedmont territory), and this is Middleburg country.

PHOTO BY THE AUTHOR

*Masters outlining coming hunt*

The bar tender is busy mixing Bloodies carefully – and slowly, as if his pay will be inversely propor-tional to his output – so I slip around the bar where there is an

*Middleburg huntsman and whippers-in (above) and field (below) moving off from opening meet*

attractive bottle with an old, dusty label indicating its contents to be Port. As I grasp it someone on the other side of the table asks, *"Is the label the same as the stuff inside?"*

I find this question out of order in a nice lady's house, so I pour a glass of the dark amber fluid, test it, and say, *"Yes, can I pour you a glass too?"*

Port is not a family specialty – gout, you know – but this does taste like a fine old version the real thing. Then, glass in hand, I observe a dining room table laden with all the elements of a hold-you-for-the-day breakfast. Someone offers a plate to me.

*"No thanks, I've had breakfast at home,"* and I drift out of the dining room to a front room where friends Wendy Bebie and her husband Bob Gordon are enjoying the hospitality of this gracious home.

Then it's back to the hall. Standing quite near the hostess I hear Nicky Perry say to her – they are connected through a school –

*"Thanks so much for inviting us."*

Oops! It strikes me that I have just crashed my first party since I was in college. Nicky's new husband Andrew Stifler consoles me:

*"It's forgivable if you do it with charm."*

So I apologize to the hostess, who explains that she spends most of her time in Washington, this is her country place, and she has invited a bunch of Washington friends out to see the meet and have breakfast after. To them she has added a select few immediate neighbors and friends such as Jim and Barbara Wilson, and Nicky and Andrew. But she is gracious, and urges me to stay, even if I live 15 miles away in the boonies. (Some days later, someone suggests that the real act of Southern courtesy would have been for her to apologize for her oversight in failing to send me an invitation. But we are perhaps too far North for that.) The personal upshot is: (a) a quick departure, and (b) a desire to know that nice lady better.

Leaving Groveton with minimum embarrassment, I have driven not a half mile when a lone black-coated gentlemen on a sweaty chestnut horse comes into view, going the other way. Stopping, I ask, *"Is he lame, or have you lost a shoe?"*

*"No, I've lost the hunt, I think they are over there."*

and he points with his crop whence I came. Then he adds:

*"But it's OK. We saw two foxes right away."*

Two views have made it a great opening day for him.

———

As has been indicated previously, sidelights that often bracket an actual hunt are the "Stirrup Cup," served at the site of the meet where riders, hounds and spectators assemble to await the action, and the "Hunt Breakfast" which follows the day in the field.

Just as the reader supposes, a stirrup cup consists of a back-bracer to warm the blood on a cold morning, and to summon up nerve for the excitement ahead. For the abstemious there are coffee, hot cider, pickled eggs, doughnuts or sandwiches; for the hardy there is sherry or port; and for the truly fool-

PHOTO BY THE AUTHOR

*Ruth Solbach and Isabel Ferguson serving a stirrup cup*

hardy, or the non-riding observer wearing off the previous evening, there is occasionally a jigger of single malt Scotch whisky.

Usually the servers of a Stirrup Cup are ground-bound non-riders, such as spouses, designated to perform that duty. Occasionally the Stirrup Cup host is the landowner on whose property the day's meet has been "carded" (i.e. scheduled). Passing a tray of potables among a melee of excitable horses, riders, itinerant dogs, pedestrian spectators and stray children can approach foxhunting itself in physical insecurity. But then the tray passer has the remedy for his unsettled nerves immediately at hand. And his role as host, and his wares, confer a modest degree of status, falling of course far below that of the Masters, Huntsman, and mounted members of the field, but fitting in nicely somewhere between the better hounds and the lesser spectators, loose children and farm dogs.

For those not hunting the meet reaches its crescendo as the Huntsman rides up, surrounded by a sea of hounds, and then the meet dissolves all too soon as he blows his horn, and moves off with his pack and the Master to "draw" the

PHOTO BY ANITA BAARNS

*Huntsman and hounds entering a covert*

first covert.

The field follows, and the spectators disperse, occasionally to follow the hunt as best they can by car, more often to a lonely encounter with the Saturday list of chores that awaits at home.

The Hunt Breakfast, though inaccurately named, is a more collegial affair, starting after the hunt is over and the horses returned to their homes or at least to their trailers. In its simplest form it is a luncheon picnic at the site of the meet – beer, wine, sandwiches, cold turkey, whatever – no big deal.

Spouses, children, and loyal hunt followers are welcomed on approximately equal terms with those who have survived the day's action in the field – approximately equal but not quite. I have found it hard to interest fox hunters, as they wind down after four hours spent careening across hunting country, in the intricacies of planting daffodils, splitting firewood, or the subtleties of the latest Washington brou-ha-ha.

Post-hunt, fox hunters' minds and their conversations revolve securely around such key subjects as the superior performance of a new young horse, the awkward riding style of someone conveniently out of earshot, great hound work, a spectacular spill, or the number of times a fox was viewed. In these conversations the non-hunter feels himself an outsider – possibly even an unwashed impostor – suffered only to sip his Bloody Mary in silent awe of the company he is keeping.

———

In this practice of conversational exclusivity fox hunters are precisely as single minded as sailors second-guessing tactics after a race, quail hunters re-living a double on the sundown covey rise, or golfers replaying the decisive hole. It is now suddenly possible for me to sympathize with the non-participating spouses that trail forlornly after those other breeds of sportsmen, for in the case of fox hunting I too have become a trailer.

## - The Hotel California -

One dreary day in the dark of the year, the gray period between Christmas and New Years, when every one is recovering from the excesses of the year end shopping frenzy, family gatherings and whatever else, the snow turned to mud sufficiently for the Fairfax Hunt to hold its joint meet with neighboring Loudoun. Three hours in the field were to be followed by a "breakfast" at an adjacent comfortable but modest farm house lived in by Ann Heacock, a member of the hunt.

*Rusty Cline and John Anderson with guitars*

Arriving at the breakfast, I learned of a sad accident that had befallen a veteran and well-loved horse, casting a pall over the crowd that matched the overcast sky. But, slowly, as is the way with horse people, old friendships, food and – dare I say it? – a glass or two of wine restored a modicum of holiday spirit among those not directly affected by the accident.

Then, the meal over, John Anderson and Rusty Cline pulled out their guitars from somewhere, and tuned up, drawing the small crowd of people still there to the living room. Soon we were engulfed by the music and lyrics of a haunting song, "The Hotel California." The beat was unfamiliar to me – I am of the generation of "Lili Marlene" and "The White Cliffs of Dover" when it comes to haunting songs – but perhaps our children know it. In any event the music and the story, about a hotel and a profession you wouldn't recommend for your daughter, drew the crowd together in a warm and embracing moment, and in those few minutes I felt that I too was of their fraternity.

---

PHOTO BY THE AUTHOR

*Kinross manor house*

## - Kinross Farm -

But the hunt breakfast can be far more elegant than a trailer-gate picnic in Virginia's November outdoors, or a small group listening to guitar music in a farm living room. And no one hosts a better one than Lisa and Zohar Ben-Dov.

Their beautiful Kinross Farm lies a few miles southwest of Middleburg, about on the border between the Piedmont and Orange County Hunt territories. Both Ben-Dovs are active fox hunters who fill in the non-hunting months by campaigning a string of talented steeplechase horses. Zohar began life in Israel, and found eventual success and happiness in America. No one we know is more enthusiastic about the beautiful countryside in which we live, or the America that some natives take so much for granted.

PHOTO BY THE AUTHOR

*Lisa Ben-Dov greeting guests*

This particular year that enthusiasm overflowed at the Ben-Dov's hunt breakfast, an annual event taking place on the Saturday before Thanksgiving.

The invitation said "One PM", but since few would have finished hunting that soon I dawdled on my way there. Edie was to come later, as her hunt duties required her to stay afield until the end, and then there was her horse to trailer home, wash, blanket, and lead up to its paddock.

Dawdling was a mistake. The Kinross Farm manor house – a period Virginia masterpiece – is spacious as houses go, but it proved no match for the Ben-

*Linda and Vas Devan arriving at Kinross Farm. Vas is proud of his role as his native India's emissary to the Virginia foxhunting community*

PHOTO BY THE AUTHOR

Dov's inclusivity in sending out invitations, or their friends' eagerness in accepting them.

When I arrived the house was already comfortably full, and more were arriving by the minute.

Lisa was eagerly greeting everyone, as if only a few guests had yet arrived. Wedging through the crowd towards the double bar in the back sun room I had time to note a splendid collection of hunting pictures, safely up on the walls and away from the crush of bodies blocking my path to suitable refreshment. Familiar faces in the crowd included a cross section of the hunting fraternity, steeplechase people, those from other horse-related pursuits, neighbors, and local notables. Even devotees of other sports were accepted, as indicated by Hank Woolman's necktie, decorated with a fisherman playing a trout (though Hank also has a horse background).

Despite proximity to Washington, no political figures were in evidence. Before she died Jackie Onassis was often at the Ben-Dov's breakfast, and Senator John Warner, a dedicated fox hunter, would not have been out of place. But then, the election is over, and Zohar's enthusiasms may not run to politics.

Looking out the sunroom windows to the east the eye ran over a formal allee of small trees leading to a gazebo, and beyond to a pleasant valley glowing in sunlight and late fall colors. It was a good day to be out of doors, but here we were at a sumptuous hunt breakfast, not a bad alternative.

Inside there were a few eddies of space where one could pause, as I did to talk to Jackie Eldredge about the Keeneland auction, and the phenomenal seven million dollars paid there the prior week for an aging mare.

There were familiar faces from Church – the Slaters, Bob Newton, Patricia O'Brien among them. Joseph Keusch and his wife Jan Neuharth were relaxing over food in the paneled library, two of a small minority to find seats. Joseph asked me if I was going to "our" Breakfast at 2:30. Edie had not told me there was such a Fairfax event, since she planned to play hooky and go to the Ben-Dov's instead. Joseph promised to go and represent the Fairfax Masters, thus playing a double-header on hunt breakfasts.

PHOTO BY THE AUTHOR

Then someone reported that Edie had arrived and was looking for me. By this time the tide of people at the door was shifting from flood to ebb. Edie, wearing her favorite red felt hat, was easy to find. She quickly insisted that I have something to eat, as she had no plans to cook at home. So we circled the dining room table as the caterers restocked it, and had a delicious meal talking to all sorts of people about all sorts of things. Suddenly it was four o'clock and, after proper good-byes among the few still present, we sped home to feed the horses while it was still light. A welcome quiet cup of soup sufficed to close the day. After all, we had just finished breakfast.

## – A Blessing of the Hounds –

This Thanksgiving Day we are gathered – three generations of our family, friends mounted and afoot, horses, and hounds – for the annual "Blessing of the Hounds" of the Fairfax Hunt. Reverend Mark Andrus, Rector of the Emmanuel Church in Middleburg, is there to conduct a brief service of thanksgiving for the sport whose roots run so deep in our community. This will be

*Reverend Mark Andrus doing the honors*

Mark's last service for us, as he is soon to leave to become Bishop of Alabama.

On the back lawn of Black Oak a mass of horses, people, and hounds mill around us. Below us lies the Loudoun Valley, framed in the west by the Blue Ridge, the hills' signature color set off by the lighter blue of a clear morning sky. To the south the twin peaks of The Cobblers rise from the mist of the valley floor. Immediately below us, the sunlight yellows the meadows, and the tan, gray, and brown of autumn woods in the middle distance merge and blend into the ridge beyond.

A stirrup cup is passed among the field as we meet Mark Salser and his family, the new owners of Black Oak. We give silent thanks that this beautiful land has passed to hands that love and respect if, and welcome the hunt to its hillside.

Master Randy Rouse calls the crowd to order, flanked by his two Joint Masters. Mark is introduced, heads are uncovered, and the service begins with the Book of Genesis:

> "...And God made the beast of the earth according to its kind, cattle according to its kind, and everything that creeps upon the earth according to its kind. And God saw that it was good."

It proceeds to:

*"Bless, O Lord, rider and horse and the hounds that run, in their running and shield them from danger to life and limb.*

*"May your children who ride, and your creatures who carry, come to the close of the day unhurt and give thanks to you with grateful hearts,*

*"Bless those over whose lands we hunt, and grant that no deed or omission of ours may cause them hurt or trouble.*

*"Bless the foxes who partake in the chase, that they may run straight and true and may find their destiny."*

PHOTO BY THE AUTHOR

*Tom Hulfish and Tennessee Graham following the words of the service*

And ends with the 121st Psalm:

*"I will lift up mine eyes unto the hills; from whence cometh my help?*
*My help cometh from the Lord, who hath made heaven and earth…"*

After the final "Amen" huntsman Kevin Palmer blows his horn, and hounds and field move off down the hill in the sunlight to draw the first covert. Next to me a little boy whines: *"Mom, can we go home now?"* His even smaller brother declares: *"I don' wanna."* Opinions are divided on foxhunting.

Some may wonder whether this ceremony is a reversion to some pagan rite calling for success in the hunt. If so, it is surely ineffective. No foxes are caught, in fact none at all were killed during the entire previous Fairfax season, or to date this year. For that "failure" no hunter is sorry. God willing, the foxes of Black Oak will for many years, in the way of nature, live, run, procreate and die, just as will their pursuers, and their successors will re-enact in future years their rivalry with the hounds, to the excitement, pleasure, and benefit of those who follow after them.

What really is a Blessing of the Hounds? I believe it is an affirmation of life – of the relation between man and horse and hound, of the natural order of things, of predator and of prey, of God's creation, and of all the glories of the

PHOTO BY ANITA BAARNS

fall countryside through which each participant passes on Thanksgiving, taking another small and joyful step on his or her journey to some final destiny.

But it is also more than that. It is recognition that, by adding risk and effort to pleasure, skill and courage are affirmed, senses sharpened, and understanding of self and of life enhanced.

Finally, it is a celebration of affection, of the bond between human and animal, each essential and of equal merit in the sport they share, and of the bond of community that is created among the human players.

I am not a foxhunter. My connections with nature lie in the moving waters of a river, in the spring garden, in a rising breeze on the ocean, and in the quiet of a broodmare's stall. But there is something special about the beauty of a hunt meet, and the enthusiasm of the sport's devotees – horse, hound, and hunter – and, through foxhunting, the love and respect they have gained for one another and for the fox.

Going home in the car we have a discussion of how some clergy are happy to participate in blessing hounds, horses and the fox, and some are not. For the latter, including the blessing of animals in a religious service may seem to run counter the belief that man alone was created "in God's image", and thus is an inappropriate use of scripture and religion whose purpose is to promote human spirituality.

Our New England daughter Priscilla reacts crisply to this concept:

*"You're only blessing them, you're not worshipping them, for God's sake."*

Her teenaged son Will is equally direct in response:

*"That shows how little you know about foxhunting, Mom!"*

PHOTO BY ANITA BAARNS

*Piedmont leaders crossing a bridge near Unison*

*Erskine Bedford*

## – Erskine –

Last Sunday the community was stunned by a tragic accident. Erskine Bedford, Joint MFH and field master of the Piedmont Hounds was fatally injured when his horse suffered a heart attack and collapsed under him while galloping in pursuit of the sport they both loved. From the wide outpouring of shock, grief, and sympathy it was obvious that Upperville had lost one of its most favorite sons.

Erskine seemed to Edie and me to be a man in whom all the segments of our community came happily together. He was a gentleman of the country, but not a "country gentleman" in the slightly pejorative sense of that term. Trained in agronomy, he loved his farm, Old Welbourne, as passionately as any dirt farmer, and was never happier than when driving his beat up old truck around the place to work on it, unless it was when foxhunting. He was a stockbroker by vocation, modestly successful but never rich from that pursuit. He was well liked by the ladies, but never seemed to take undue advantage of that

---

condition. He was close to people from all walks of life, of whatever origin or age, never either reverent or condescending. He enjoyed a party, but he was not socially self-indulgent. He was a thoroughly nice guy.

Edie first met Erskine when she started hunting with Piedmont shortly after we moved to Trappe Hill. She calls him *"the finest field master I ever rode behind."* We both got to know him better during one casual supper at the Crenshaws' several years ago, and were flattered as newcomers to be invited to his daughter Cricket's wedding. I have shot doves in his cornfield and looked unsuccessfully, while birding, for barn owls in his abandoned silo. The latest of several social occasions we attended at Old Welbourne was a party he and Karen gave for her New Zealand parents. The eclectic group of guests – neighbors, farmers, fox hunters, family, and assorted acquaintances to whom no label could be easily attached – was evidence of his wide and diverse friendships.

Erskine had a lively wit, and a touch of irreverence that he occasionally used as a gentle needle on those – myself included – whose current balloon he thought needed pricking. My guess is he never used this talent with any intent to hurt, or on anyone who could not defend himself with a humorous response. He was too kind for that.

PHOTO BY ANNA BRARNS

Now it is the day of Erskine's funeral, a time to say good-bye to this fine man. From her vantage point as church bookkeeper, Betsy Crenshaw has warned us that a large crowd is expected, and that if we wish seats we should be early. A hasty lunch at noon sees us at Trinity Church by about one p.m. for the two o'clock service. There is already a considerable crowd assembled in the courtyard.

We chat briefly with Sergeant Jeff Brown of the Sheriff's Department. Jeff is an old friend who once held the door open for me as I shot a deer in the twilight from the kitchen steps. Jeff allows that this is indeed a sad day for Upperville, then asks how the farm is going. We reply that all is well, and that the deer hunters seem less numerous. He brightens at this and reports that he has apprehended nine trespassers attempting to shoot illegally off of Route 601 at the top of our mountain.

The Church is now filling – it is one fifteen – and we find seats about half way forward, sitting between Bucky Slater and Dodie Vehr, two of our

*Erskine (in blue) conferring with MFH / Huntsman Randy Waterman*

Upperville friends of longest standing. By one thirty the seats are filled and a line is gathering to stand along each wall. We can only imagine those who come later and must remain outside in the cold.

Looking around, Erskine's appeal to people is evident in all the faces we see. We know perhaps a quarter of the crowd, but almost everyone we expect to see is there. Who are all these other people whose lives he has also touched?

At last the service begins. The casket is preceded by an honor guard of about twenty Huntsmen and Masters of Foxhounds in "Pink", and followed by a like number of honorary pall bearers. We know many in each group, and spot several Masters in civilian clothes attending as well. Bucky recognizes several old -time foxhunters, now retired. Erskine's fraternity is out in force.

———

Edie notes that the casket is actually carried – not wheeled in – by six sweating professionals obviously unaccustomed to the heavy load. Farmer Erskine would appreciate the work ethic in evidence. The eulogies are succinct and moving, touching on his life as a father, a farmer, and a foxhunter. For us the high point is the superb singing of "Swing Low, Sweet Chariot" by a ten voice group from the Willisville and St. Louis Village Singers. These are African-American communities who have come to honor him – Erskine's friendships knew no racial bounds.

A New Englander is struck by the emotion evident in the congregation, subdued but obvious. Perhaps it is the ceremonial aura of the scarlet coats, the many pall bearers, and the spiritual singers – or possibly it is the expression of a Southern approach to life and death and the hereafter that differs from what a stiff-lipped New England upbringing has instilled in us. And then, might it be only a very human reaction to the sudden snatching away of a dearly loved person? Whatever, it is not a dry-eyed experience.

Leaving the Church we exchange somber greetings with various friends, ending up on the Church office doorstep with Betsy and Kitty Slater. Kitty is Bucky's mother-in-law and a noted expert on Upperville history. The two ladies estimate the attendance at six hundred. Betsy reports:

> *"We printed five hundred programs and ran out"*.

Kitty believes that this is the largest crowd ever to attend an Upperville funeral. Heading for our cars, another old-timer, Jamie McCormick, agrees:

> *"Erskine didn't have a single enemy, only friends"*.

Interment is to take place in the private cemetery at Old Welbourne. Getting there, a distance of perhaps four miles, is a slow process, giving us a chance to let our emotions down, until we pass the jump and field where he fell, and see the flowers left there by mourners.

Following a slow line of cars we eventually reach our destination. We park and walk across a large field to join a crowd congregating just above the wall of the small wooded cemetery plot. When all are assembled the familiar burial service begins….

> *"We commit his body, – earth to earth, ashes to ashes, dust to dust"*.

In the background one hears the low bellow of a bull, and the musical calling of unseen Canada Geese. As we join in prayer for him, Erskine is duly buried in his favorite spot on the land he loved so well, while the natural life he adored goes on about him.

Then we hear the mournful notes of a huntsman's horn blowing "Gone Away".

----

Four mounted scarlet-coated figures, a Master and three hunt servants, appear from behind the trees below the graveyard, their horses surrounded by a pack of murmuring hounds. They move slowly at first, then at a canter, across the gently rising field beside us towards the sunset. After several hundred yards they crest the rise and disappear silently behind it. Gone Away.

The crowd slowly disperses, walking across the large field towards the Old Welbourne manor house and the food and drink awaiting. As we proceed three large V's of Canada Geese pass overhead, calling in their plaintive fashion, as if to make a last fly-over celebrating Erskine's life. The party is pleasant enough, but the magic of the day has passed on with the horsemen, the hounds, and the geese.

*The northern Virginia hunt country*

# Steeplechasing

PHOTO BY ANITA BAARNS

*The water jump at Great Meadow*

*"I love the visuals of steeplechasing: the immaculately groomed horses, the silks of the jockeys, the flags marking the fences, the white rails that line the homestretch, the colorful party tents, and, above all, the beauty of the landscape at the country race meets…"*

—Peter Winants, author of *Steeplechasing: A Complete History of the Sport in North America*, and former amateur race rider

*"The best feeling I have ever had is riding in a race. They [horses] give you everything they have. It's amazing that something so big will do that for you. You feel so privileged – and honored."*

—Jonathan Thomas, 20-year-old steeplechase jockey

Steeplechasing's origins are uncertain, but the best guess is that the first race, from one church steeple to another, took place in County Cork, Ireland in about 1752, to settle a dispute over the merits of two horses, take your pick as to the route to follow. Racing over jumps in open country soon caught on in the British Isles – a logical extension of foxhunting.

In 1834 the sport crossed the Atlantic, with the first race in Rock Creek Park in Washington. For those interested in its subsequent history Peter Winants' book cited on the previous page is a must. Today steeplechasing is well ensconced from Saratoga to Atlanta, with outpost meets elsewhere.

As the quotes on the prior page suggest, the ingredients of steeplechasing – beauty, emotion, the connection between horse and rider, risk and courage – make the sport addictive for its participants and followers. If a quiet trail ride on horseback is the equivalent of a Sunday drive through the countryside, then steeplechasing is the equine parallel to a NASCAR race, happily free from the noise, fumes, hype and commercialism of that activity.

PHOTO BY PAT MACVEAGH

*Jumping a timber fence together*

Virginia is by far the nation's leader in number of steeplechase race meets, holding more than twice as many each year as the next state. Not surprisingly, the Virginia hunt country is the scene of almost all of the action, and its hunt people the biggest participants, sponsors and enthusiasts.

Most flat races for Thoroughbreds are now at distances from five furlongs to a mile and a half, run most often in America on an oval track with a dirt surface. Steeplechase races are two to four miles, run on grass. Thus the best flat racers may not have the staying power or prefer the racing surface called for in 'chasing. Selecting steeplechase prospects, and teaching them to jump, are skills that define the best steeplechase trainers. Often these horses are flat track graduates, though not always the fastest, maturity, staying power, and athletic ability being more critical than blinding speed.

About 25 race meets are held in Virginia each year, each meet consisting of six to eight individual races. Meets are divided into two categories:

- **Point-to-Points** are essentially amateur events, usually put on by a local hunt. Prizes are small engraved mementos of nominal monetary value, though larger "permanent" bowls or cups are often the keep-it-for-a-year award for winning a featured race, some trophies going back to the beginnings of the race meet.

*Horses jumping a National Fence*

PHOTO BY PAT MCVEAGH

Programs include a selection of races – over jumps and on the flat – some including a Foxhunter's Timber Series race limited to horses that have seen substantial service as field hunters in the past season.

Often a "hunter pace" is held in connection with a Point-to-Point. Here teams of two foxhunters each compete over perhaps three miles of hunt country, going as fast as they can (fast time) or to match a typical hunting pace (optimum time) established but undisclosed prior to the event.

- **Sanctioned Races** are run under the rules of the National Steeplechase Association, and involve purses of from $5,000 to, in a few instances, six figures. Since there is, with one or two exceptions, no pari-mutuel betting on steeplechase races in Virginia, the purses come from commercial sponsors as a means of promoting their products.

Within a meet the "card" (program) consists of hurdle races over brush or artificial brush* jumps, typically two to two and a half miles, and "timber" races over higher, more solid obstacles, going three to four miles. Within the category each race specifies the conditions entrants must meet to qualify, such as: maidens (horses that have never won a race of this type), non-winners of two, claiming price (if any) for which the entered horse may be bought, etc.

Additional conditions may vary the weight each horse is to carry – for example a novice jockey may be given an allowance of a few pounds off the standard to take account of inexperience, or a horse that is a multiple winner may have weight added. The purpose is to establish a field of horses for each race that have a relatively equal chance of winning it.

---

\* ***Artificial brush hurdles***, consisting of a padded steel frame topped by simulated brush made of plastic, are called ***National Fences***, and can be moved from one meet to the next and positioned as needed, saving much investment in permanent fences and labor cutting cedar trees, as well as adding flexibility to course design.

National Fences were developed in Ireland by Earl Harrington. Randy Rouse tells how they came to America: *"I was hunting in Ireland and saw these fences. I said to Bill Harrington 'That solves our problem,' so I had two of them flown over here and tried them at the Fairfax meet. The Jockeys didn't want to jump them, but we made a deal. If they didn't work we'd draw lots for the purse money. They agreed and we ran the races over them with no problem."* Randy, a long time race rider over fences, does not mention whether he won that day or not. National Fences are now the standard hurdles at all but a few U.S. steeplechase meets.

More recently the National Steeplechase Association has been testing plastic come-apart wings for jumps to lessen the hazard (compared to permanent wooden wings) if a horse decides to or is pushed into running through the wing of a jump.

---

*Lady Rider Timber Race at Oatlands, 2003 — Forever Silver (Beth Newman) leading Bavario (Tiffany Mueller), and Double Redouble (Julie Bonnie)*

In Virginia there are about 17 different race sites. Almost all are in beautiful, rolling country, with a backdrop of pastoral or mountain views. Careful location of jumps and finish line assures spectators of an easy view of most of the action. Races are held, rain or shine, from the last weekend in February through the middle of May, and again, in the fall from mid-September into November, capitalizing on the best weather for both spectators and horses.

Because of this variety of season and site each race meet assumes a character of its own. For us Casanova, coming in late February, is the beginning of spring, weather or not. Blue Ridge, two weeks later, may have traces of winter still showing, but we treasure past wins there. Perhaps our favorite, though, is the Old Dominion Hunt's Point-to-Point at Ben Venue near Amissville. Set in a bowl of fields, surrounded by woods with a spectacular backdrop of mountains, it is the perfect setting in which to enjoy Virginia's early April sunshine.

Attendance at races varies from a thousand or two at Point-to-Points to up to 50,000 at the Virginia Gold Cup in May. Steeplechase meets in Virginia and surrounding states are social highlights of almost every spring and fall weekend, drawing spectators and horses from all over the Mid-Atlantic states.

---

*Tailgate on the rail…* *and headed for the start at Glenwood Park, Middleburg*

*The Greyling leading Hendler at Glenwood Park*

*Fall Gold Cup views at…* *Great Meadow, The Plains*

PHOTOS BY THE AUTHOR

*Start of a steeplechase race — when the flag drops, "they're off"*

## – Getting Initiated –

Edie and I met steeplechasing through George and Daniel Kuper. One fall evening in 1985, shortly after we moved to Washington, they invited us to the Fairfax races the coming Saturday at Belmont Plantation near Leesburg.

I remember the festivities well: the glorious day, a great tailgate, exciting racing, and meeting up with my old college friend "Pete" Beauregard (christened Pierre Gustave Toutant Beauregard IV after his famous Confederate General ancestor). It all seemed so "Virginia," and so far removed from the realities of Washington. And it was fun. Maybe some day…

"Some day" came five years later. We had bought Trappe Hill Farm in 1987 from Ellen and Randy Waterman, and in 1988 my government service ended. We rented part of our new stable to Juliet Graham, one thing led to another, and we ended up owning a veteran steeplechase horse called Mocito Bien, who Juliet rode for us in our new yellow and blue silks at Casanova that spring.

The years came and went. Mocito graduated to be a hunter, succeeded by our first Point-to-Point winner, Shore Casting – nicknamed "Radar" because he had only one functioning eye. Eventually we obtained our first really good Point-to-Point horse, Dawn's a Pleasure, who ran well but eventually succumbed to an incurable infection. So we were again without a 'chaser, attending races but missing the adrenaline surge that goes with REALLY CARING who wins.

PHOTO BY DOUGLAS LEES

*Zohar Ben-Dov congratulating Neil Morris and Frost a Lot for winning the Rockeby Bowl*

PHOTO BY THE AUTHOR

*Dawn's a Pleasure*

- *Chartering a Horse* -

Early in 1997, just before Casanova, Donny Yovanovich left a phone message. He has a hurdle horse that is for lease. Are we interested? Of course we are. We go to Donny's farm to "interview" Murray's Ruler.

Donny's lease terms are reasonable with an option to buy. That evening we enjoy a nice dinner at the Ashby Inn with Zohar and Lisa Ben-Dov. Zohar remembers Murray's Ruler as a *"nice steady horse but not brilliant."* He will ask his trainer Neil Morris more about him.

Thursday morning, Edie, Wayne and I watch Murray work out at the training track. He moves well and hates to run behind any other horse. We like his attitude. Zohar calls to say Neil endorses our leasing Murray. Over an early supper Edie and I agree with each other to do so.

Friday morning, lease agreement in hand, I drive to the track. Donny reviews the proposed lease, then signs it. I will get him our silks prior to race time Saturday. We are back in the steeplechase business, just in time for the new season.

Saturday – Casanova Day – dawns clear and unseasonably warm. A sharp shower announces the passage of a small front, followed by clearing skies and a brisk wind. The clouds are spectacular. The temperature remains warm. The sun comes out, shining on the puddles and the wet grass. By 10:50 we are on our way to the Casanova course near Warrenton, arriving in time to catch the first race. Murray is to go in the fourth, a one-mile flat race tune-up for horses that have previously run over jumps. Donny is optimistic, but a lot of well-bred horses are entered. Anywhere in the first five is OK – 11 are in the field. Peter Walsh will ride.

It is hard to pay attention to the early racing. Finally, our race impends. At the paddock, Henry Wood reports that he has galloped Ray Moffett's Double Found, a graded stakes winner. He thinks that horse is too tough for the rest of the field, including Murray, whom he considers...

> *"...a nice, consistent horse."*

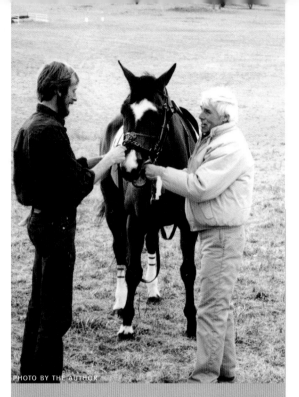

PHOTO BY THE AUTHOR

*Murray's Ruler with groom Marshall "Peanut" Campbell and trainer Don Yovanovich*

We learn later that Murray was brought to steeplechasing by Ray Moffett. The horse made maybe 25 starts over four years, mostly in Point-to-Points. Ray wanted a horse to win in sanctioned company, which Murray had never done. And Murray treated hunting as a race to be won. He was a professional racehorse stuck at a level that did not meet Ray's aspirations.

Off the start we are next to last, improving to the middle of the pack at the halfway point. Double Found has meanwhile pulled away to a big lead. Three furlongs from home Peter energizes Murray, and they move into contention for second. As they come down the stretch Murray is on the rail. Peter taps the horse twice. Murray responds. In a mad finish, with five or more horses vying for second, it seems to us we have prevailed. Double Found has of course won by several lengths.

Peter thinks that with a better start he could have won. We like the attitude, but doubt it. There is a long, long delay in announcing the sequence of finish after the first horse. When it is announced, Murray is not mentioned. As those who know my Puritan attitude towards injustice – and losing – will suspect, I am upset. So is Donny. So is Edie. The jockey and the groom know we got second. Wayne is quite sure of it. Those near the finish console us: *"Your horse was indeed second".*

Donny exchanges polite words with Jimmy Young, a perennial steward at these affairs. Finally Donny asks,

*"Will you concede that I did actually have a horse in the race?"*

The stewards send us to the video people, Fred and Paula Myer, whose tape has been used to judge the close finish. It is obvious, from their vantage point across from the judges' stand, that the saddle cloth numbers on the horses nearest the rail have been obscured by outside overlapping horses. They will review the tape. Back at the van Murray has cooled down quickly and seems happy. He knows how he did, and has no knowledge of placing judges. He is to be envied.

PHOTO BY THE AUTHOR

*Cameraman, Fred Myer*

We revisit the paddock for a later race. Jimmy Young approaches and apologizes for the mix-up. The placing judges are embarrassed. They did not note down the numbers of the horses nearest them, and apparently forgot them when their numbers did not show on the tape. I say *"forget it"*. Double Found has clearly won. Second doesn't count in Point-to-Points.

The wind is rising as the last races go off; late February can still be aggressive, even if spring is finally touching Virginia. We come home via the Marshall IGA, opting for filet mignon to be cooked in the fireplace to celebrate our return to steeplechasing, and the advent of a new spring. We are happily speculating on Murray's coming campaign when the phone rings. It is Fred Myer. They have looked at the tapes, including one made from the judges' side of the finish line. Fred reports:

*"Your horse was second. The stewards are thinking about correcting the results."*

It has been a typical Smart day* in the competitive arena, but I am mellowing right now, a condition my children will suspect is unlikely to last the season.

In the next weeks Murray gives us many thrills. At Rappahannock he races to a big lead, so big that Peter pulls him back to save him. We have not yet learned that Murray must build and keep a good lead during the race, as he does not have the foot to hold off the charge of fast closing horses. Murray comes into the last fence only slightly ahead, bobbles it, and is passed by two horses. The stretch at Rappahannock is uphill, and Murray's finishing kick catches one of his two rivals, but not the other, Gorfen Letch, the oddly named

---

* For those less familiar with our family's sporting past, a **typical Smart Day** is one of moderate success marinated in minor controversy.

Moffett horse that will ultimately win the 1997 Virginia Point-to-Point Hurdle Championship.

At Blue Ridge Murray puts it all together, and wins the Open Hurdle convincingly by eight or ten lengths, wire to wire. Donny, Peter, and of course the Smarts, are overjoyed – a first and two seconds in three outings. The season has started well. Two weeks later at Piedmont it is another story.

PAT MACVEAGH PHOTO

*Murray's Ruler winning at Blue Ridge, Peter Walsh up*

Again Murray races to a good lead around the tight hurdle course, but by the next to last fence the lead has diminished to three lengths, and we fear he will be outrun. Instead, as he lands over the jump he slips and falls on the wet ground. Murray gets up quickly and heads down the track, galloping after the other horses. Peter sits up in the mud, helplessly watching him go.

To our horror Murray then veers off to the right, jumps the high orange plastic fence that separates the course from the crowd, and gallops down an alley between rows of parked cars, tailgate parties, and spectators until he reaches Donny's trailer a quarter of a mile away. Blissfully, no one is hurt.

Next it is time to see what he can do in sanctioned company. The races at Foxfield, three miles west of Charlottesville, provide an opportunity, a Maiden Hurdle Race with a purse of $7,500. If you have never been there, the Foxfield Races offer a new and different experience. Coming in late April, a crowd of perhaps 20,000 attends, many of them students from the University of Virginia, for whom this is a major spring bacchanal. It takes an extra hour to go the last three miles over a winding two-lane road clogged by cars overloaded (in more than one respect) with revelers.

The occasional policeman attempting to maintain a minimum of decorum is overwhelmed by celebrants seeking relief in the neighboring bushes, then running to catch up with their car – or any car – as the traffic slowly moves westward. Edie is spared the roadside scene, having been deterred by some unavoidable duty at home. Eventually the race course looms ahead as the first race goes off. Luckily we are running in the sixth.

On the infield side of the finish line, just back of the judges stand, is a tent for owners and trainers, providing a bit of insulation from the raucous crowd. In this oasis I find Ray Moffett, just as it is time for the third, a hurdle race for non-winners of two, in which he has entered Double Found, our nemesis at Casanova. Ray leads me as his guest to the elevated stand provided for owners so that they can see the action on the more distant sections of the course. The regular spectators must watch from ground level, a difficult feat given Foxfield's rather flat terrain and large crowd. Few celebrants seem to care.

The third race is a triumph for Double Found. Back in the owners' tent Ray explains that he got the horse for a song, after he was injured at the end of his great flat race career. Following a year or two layoff, Ray has been running him occasionally over hurdles, doing very well in that program. Today is just another example. (Two years later, at 13, Double Found won six Point-to-Point races and the Point-to-Point hurdles championship.)

The Foxfield program profiles the season's six leading trainers and six leading jockeys. Four of each are listed as entrants in the sixth race, The Michelob Hurdle, which will have a full field of twelve horses. Murray will be up against a new level of competition. Ray and I return to the observation stand. Murray runs his normal race, jumping cleanly, and eventually taking about a three length lead. This is not enough. By the final fence he has been caught and jumps in company with another horse, with three more close behind. Quietly I resign myself to third. But a strange thing happens. Peter touches him with the whip, a final surge of energy is released, and Murray drives ahead to a one length lead and victory.

Ray and I are ecstatic as we descend, he to the owners' tent to celebrate, and I to the winner's circle to collect a pretty crystal trophy. Edie will be pleased, but disappointed she missed it. Then Ray and I spend the next half hour in the tent, warmed by the day, the horses, our duplicate crystal bowls, the

*Ray Moffett*

complimentary libations – including Michelob – and an acquaintance that is blossoming into a fast friendship. I decide not to mention that Murray's time was more than two seconds faster than Double Found's over the same course.

So we have many things to thank Murray for. However, now that he has broken his maiden under rules he seems unlikely, at nine, to be competitive in open company, and we must decide whether we want an aging Point-to-Point horse, or whether we should return him to Donny to find employment with others. Two more starts prove the horse needs a rest, and we reluctantly decide his future lies elsewhere.

Based on Murray's later success as an owner-rider horse it is a wise decision. George Kingsley and Murray's Ruler win the 1998 season series for Owner-Riders. Ray Moffett and Lynn become two of our favorite friends, and in 2002 Ray joins Edie as a Joint Master of the Fairfax Hunt.

## – Anatomy of a Point-to-Point –

The Saturday morning after St. Patrick's Day is bright but cold. A stiff frost has browned the magnolia blossoms, and knocked the blooming daffodils flat on the ground. Until today we marveled at the year's very early spring. Now, as Wayne notes,

> *"Spring has taken a U-turn back south."*

Nevertheless, today is also the Warrenton Hunt Point-to-Point, and Sally Tufts, Warrenton MFH, has persuaded us to subscribe to a Patron's parking place. We have thus financed a better view of the races, the company of adjacent friends, and an excuse to invite others to join us in a tailgate party. We plan to go early and dress warmly.

Six years ago Dawn's a Pleasure, won the Open Hurdle Race at Warrenton, our first win over fences, and we have had a hankering ever since to repossess the big Riverland Bowl that is the "perpetual" trophy for that race. Our current horse, Devil's Reach, is entered in today's Open Hurdles, so we have a shot at

*Dawn's a Pleasure winning at Warrenton, Matt McCarron up*

a second leg on the Bowl. But it is bad luck to mentally polish silver that you have not yet won, so we keep our hopes in check.

Meanwhile, Edie has cooked up a big pot of chili (to complement the weather?). I am assigned the potables department, which includes mixing up a bunch of Virgin Marys, to which vodka can be added later if necessary. A foam container that once held iced salmon suffices for wine, beer, soft drinks, ice, cups, the bottle opener, and the Mary mix. We load the chili pot – now encased in newspaper and a corrugated box – plus dishes, utensils, munchies, a pitcher of reviving daffodils, and the informal salmon cooler in the back of the Explorer, and leave for the 40 minute drive to Airlie Farm and the races. We decide not to bring our stuffed fox, and we have no ribbons to fly from the car's aerial. We will lose the "prettiest tailgate" contest to those who have taken some pains to win it.

Arriving at the course, we detour by the horse van area to inspect Jimmy Day's new trailer. Devil's Reach is there, looking out the window, along with Jimmy's own veteran horse Joli's Summer (by Lejoli out of Sensational Summer), and Beluga – named for the caviar from the sturgeon of that name. He's by the stallion Black Tie Affair. (The thoughtful reader may now reflect on the subtleties of naming horses.) The horses are keyed up, sensing the excitement of their season's first race. Jimmy is not around.

We proceed to our assigned parking place, # 306, up on the side of a grassy ridge overlooking most of the course. It's a 75 yard uphill sprint from there, through some pine trees at the crest, to where one can see the other side of the course. As a result, spectators will get in some running to match their horses' effort, but there is probably no correlation between the speed of the fans and that of their animals. At our age we find that consoling.

*Will O'Keefe and Michael Hughes*

Up against the pine trees is the tower for the race officials, manned on its top level by the long-term Point-to-Point announcing crew of Will O'Keefe, race caller, and Mike Hughes, facts and color. Will trains for this important assignment by managing the various equine activities at Morven Park during the week, and Michael teaches music at Notre Dame Academy, having before that been a bloodstock agent. We have listened to a lot of race announcing teams, but they are our all-stars. No one beats them for knowledge, voice, and drama. And we envy them their view from the tower.

*Andy Martin and Peggy Castrelli*

As we set up our tailgate we see that friends Andy Martin and her sister Peggy Castrelli are in the next space but one. We exchange greetings, and note that their table sports a mounted red fox not unlike the one we left at home. Opening our cooler we learn that by some mischance the vodka has failed to make the trip to Warrenton. Not to worry – Andy has two bottles, and we take temporary possession of one. (Later, Bloody Marys sell poorly, and after the races we return it almost untouched.)

Jimmy will ride Joli's Summer in the Owner-Rider Hurdle race, next on the program. Jimmy gave up race riding ten years ago, trading in his silks for the

PHOTO BY THE AUTHOR

*Warrenton Point-to-Point tailgating and racing*

PHOTO BY PAT MACVEAGH

responsibilities of fatherhood. Nevertheless his comeback is at hand, and his wife Emily and his parents, over from Ireland for a few weeks, are there to see it. The parents' pride is obvious. Emily's emotions are concealed. As a veteran horsewoman and past race rider, she knows that part of the excitement is the risk.

Jimmy's return to the races isn't quite as hazardous as it may seem. He has spent the last ten years training horses, which in his case involves galloping some of his charges each day, and teaching the green ones to jump. So he is pretty fit, but as he says, it takes a race to really tighten a horse up. That no doubt goes for the rider as well. I conclude that by owning Jo-Jo (the stable nick name for Joli's Summer) Jimmy has found his excuse to get back in the competitive saddle, at least this one time.

*Jimmy Day at Blue Ridge, ten years before*

Now it is time to leave for the paddock, and then to saddle up and canter to the start. Jimmy's troupe of minions follow, while I stay in sight of the trailer to make

*Florry Day, Emily Day, Edie Smart, Winkie Mackay-Smith, Jim Day, Sr.*

sure no one bothers Devil's, who is now calmly awaiting his turn four races hence, munching hay. He is unaware that he is a stable favorite, and that his handlers refer to him affectionately as "Devil Dog."

Jimmy's race is a good one. Joli's is among the leaders, and occasionally in the lead, most of the way. He jumps the last fence even with Tom Kirlin's Deal Again (out of a mare called Second Hand), but doesn't quite have the endurance to outlast him, and finishes second by half a length or so. Since Tom is already leading this spring's Owner-Rider series, Jimmy has nothing to be ashamed of. Back at the trailer we greet an elated old pro. He had a…

PHOTO BY THE AUTHOR

*Watching the race intently*

*"…great time, lots of fun, Joli's was wonderful. The race was what he needed. No one will beat him again this year. Those horses aren't good enough."*

I refrain from asking Jimmy, *"Who will ride Joli's next time?"* Jimmy's "come-back" may be a sensitive matter, and its continuance best left to the Day family to work out. We go up the hill to the tailgate. Jerry Toray has now joined us, adding more food to our pile. The Garitys, Brenda Milne, and a number of others from the Fairfax Hunt have stopped by, and our party and Andy's have begun to merge. Jimmy appears and grabs a beer and some food. He is obviously happy, as are his folks, who have also joined our tailgate. We are getting plenty of mileage out of the chili and Sally's patron's spot. The day is bright and cold, the wind is blowing, and our faces are getting burned, just as they would be if we were spring skiing.

Now it is back down hill to the trailer. Devil's is out and being walked to loosen up. Danielle Hodsdon will ride him. Because Devil's won last year under rules he was scheduled to carry ten more pounds than the rest. By having Danielle, a novice, ride we get an offsetting ten pound allowance. But, because Danielle is light, many lead weights must be added to bring rider and tack up to the required 160 pound burden. Dead weight is a little harder on the horse than if his burden is all live weight in the person of the jockey.

Danielle is excited. Though she was the runner-up novice rider on the flat last year, she has only raced once before over jumps. Today she will be up against several professionals with many big wins to their credit. Jimmy calms her:

> *"Take it easy, but keep close, second or third. The most important thing is that Devil's has a good time."*

Jimmy uses Point-to-Points as workouts to prepare for serious stuff to come. He has no use for silver plated hardware, and does not know of my interest in the big bowl. There is no purse money to be earned at Point-to-Points.

Jack Gold, the bookie who is a fixture at these races, has Devil's as third choice, in part, I suspect, because of the novice lady rider. The favorite, Ponsonby, broke his maiden here two years ago for our now-deceased friend Colonel Bob O'Brien, who bred and raised him. Bob named his horses for military figures. Ponsonby, a gray horse, is named for the commander of the Scots Greys at the Battle of Waterloo. His trainer, Donny Yovanovich, now owns Ponsonby, and has nursed him back to health from an injury last season. Before being injured, Ponsonby beat Devil's by a length at Orange County, and we would like revenge. On the other hand, if we can't win, Ponsonby and Donny are our sentimental choice. They are no doubt the crowd's.

Again the race is a good one, with Devil's duplicating Joli's earlier experience. Midway through the race a horse loses its rider and the loose horse, running along with the rest, gives Danielle a bit of a hard time. She finishes a close second to Ponsonby. A spectator remarks, *"It's too bad the Colonel wasn't here to see it,"* to which Edie replies, *"Oh but he was, looking down from his little pink cloud."* Back at the trailer Devil's, who is hardly sweated up, is relaxed and happy. Jimmy is all enthusiasm:

> *"He ran a great race, just what he needed to tighten him up. She gave him a wonderful ride. None of those horses will beat him again."*

I conclude that Danielle has made the Varsity. Gay Estin has brought a bottle of champagne to the tailgate, adding as she hands it to me:

> *"I hoped it would be for a win, but he ran a good race so we can drink it anyway."*

And we do.

There is one race left for the Daybreak Stable team, the ninth, a Novice Rider Flat Race for Danielle and Beluga. The competition is stiff, as owners are using it as a tune up for experienced jumping horses. Included in the field are Zohar's Gold Quoit and Company Eight. Last year Gold Quoit beat the great Saluter over timber at Middleburg, and finished second to him in the fall Gold Cup. The sun has now left us, and the day has turned raw. In the paddock

Danielle is shivering, and I lend her my parka. Jimmy's advice is the same:

*"This is his first race after a year's lay up. He needs the work. Keep him close, but let him have fun."*

Then it's "Riders Up" and they leave for the start. The race is a reprise of Jimmy's prior two. Beluga does well, finishing a close second to Company Eight. Again Danielle rides well. Jimmy is enthusiastic:

*"The horse did great. Just what he needed. No one's going to beat him again this year."*

Then he turns to me,

*"We'll talk Monday about what's next for Devil's. Gilded will go in the Maiden Hurdles at Orange County in two weeks."*

I get the impression Danielle will ride him. I surely hope so. But it is time that the owners, as well as the horses, have some fun. A couple of wins, even in Point-to-Points, would make a difference. We will speak to our star rookie rider about it.

*Devil's Reach and Danielle Hodsdon winning at Orange County*

PHOTO BY BETSY PARKER

EPILOGUE:

Two weeks later, on a beautiful spring day at Orange County, Devil's Reach wins the open hurdles. His rider? Danielle Hodsdon, who chalks up her first win over jumps, and then spends the afternoon dodging buckets of Gatorade.

Some time, long ago, some one must have said, *"Bet mine is faster than yours,"* and horse racing was born. Those who could not afford to own a race horse shared in the excitement by calculating the chances of the contestants, and backing their handicapping skills with a wager. Everyone could play. As the years passed, Stephen Foster's Camptown Race Track matured into Churchill Downs, Saratoga and Belmont, and the man-to-man betting of the past evolved, through the book maker – where bettors bet against "the book" – into the pari-mutuel tote board. There everybody bets against everybody else electronically, the odds set by the amount bet on each horse. Then the track, the state, and the purse account take their cuts before returning most of the "handle" to the successful bettors.

At steeplechase meets there is not sufficient betting volume to justify the electronic machinery of the pari-mutuel system. So the book maker prevails, giving bettors a chance for action at a level modestly above the "one dollar, pick a number" lottery of the typical tailgate betting pool.

The book makers at Virginia steeplechase races are the father and son team of Jack and Lenny Gold, occasionally supplemented by Jack's other son Norm.

Today we are at the Piedmont Foxhounds Point-to-Point, a small crowd, small fields, and threatening weather. Jack and Lenny have set up shop – actually a blackboard on which to display odds – near the spot of maximum pedestrian traffic, the crossing from one side if the course to the other, close to the finish line. Business is at the moment slow, and they have time to visit with an interloper.

Jack is a retired type setter from a big printing company, displaced after 27 years of service, at 49 years old, by the computer. Since then he has "got by," aided by his many years of handicapping horses. Lenny owns and runs a restaurant, which he keeps tabs on by phone while at the races.

I speculate with the Golds on the day's handle, guessing, *"Maybe between one*

*Lenny and Jack Gold explaining the system - picture taken at Middleburg*

*and two thousand dollars."* They allow that I am a bit high:

*"At Middleburg it would be more. We'd be real busy."*

At the moment they are not. Lenny tries to correct that situation, calling in a loud, sing-song voice,

*"Bets! Place your bets here! Place your Bets!"*

Right now they are struggling with a problem. In the upcoming fourth race, a four horse field of owner-riders over three miles of timber fences, they have had the favorite, Monster Monster, at even money. Last week he won impressively, and someone has just placed a huge bet of $100 on him to win (the only bets they take are win bets). Quickly they cut the odds to 1 to 4 – bet $4 and you get $5 back if he wins. They want to discourage more betting on this hot horse. If he wins they already stand to get killed, because the total bet on all the other horses won't reach the extra $100 they would need to pay off the big early bettor.

A man comes by who seems to be new to the game. Jack explains it as I watch.

———

He points to the blackboard on which he has chalked the horses' numbers and the odds on each for the upcoming race.

*"This horse is 3 to 2. You bet two dollars, you get five dollars back if he wins. This next one is 3 to 1, bet two you get eight."*

The man leaves without betting. Perhaps he has engaged his mind and figured his chances. He is running uphill against the Golds. The total payout won't match the total pay in. Jack and Lenny are not doing this as a public service, even though they seem to enjoy it.

I see Henry Wood about to cross the track and I wave to him. Jack says to me:

*"Real gentleman, that Mr. Wood."*

I agree, wondering nervously how Jack rates others in the crowd. Jack adds:

*"We always rated him the favorite, at least when he had Topeador."*

PHOTO BY DOUGLAS LEES

*At Piedmont: Be Nimble with Henry Wood up – actually WAY up – and Monster Monster with Rob Banner up. Henry was indeed nimble, he didn't fall off!*

Topeador was Henry's great horse with which he won the owner-rider timber series seven times.

Another man comes by, looks at the odds, and places a bet on Mr. Rokeby, the coming race's long shot at 2 to 1. Someone remarks on the symbolism of the bet. The late Paul Mellon's Rokeby Farm is nearby, and the feature race later in the day is for the Rokeby Bowl, four miles over timber. Lenny is busy on his mobile phone, talking to the restaurant, Apparently the refrigeration unit has broken down. He tells the man which repair service to call. Because of this off-site crisis it is now hard for me to get in a word edgewise.

Eventually I have a chance to ask Jack how he does his handicapping. He describes his many years watching and analyzing the race results. As he does I recall last spring at Potomac. They had our Devil's Reach as the favorite at even money. Anonymously, I had asked why. Answer:

*"Devil's Reach. Class of the field. No one here going to beat him."*

And they didn't, at least at Potomac last year. Last week at Warrenton they had Devil's rated third behind Ponsonby and George Ohrstrom's horse. The Ohrstrom horse lost his rider, Ponsonby won, and Devil's finished a close second. Clearly they are good at their business. Jack allows that the internet makes things easier. Every Monday all the weekend steeplechase results are there…

*"Just log in to morvenpark.centralentryoffice.com."*

Lenny Gold disappears. A few minutes later he is back with some printouts of prior races, samples of what you can get on the Internet. There we are in a printout, big as life, Gilded winning on the flat at Blue Ridge – grist for the Gold mill when Gilded Life runs next week at Orange County.

Now it is time for the fourth race, and I leave to watch it. As I do a man is trying to bet on the race after this, the fifth. Lenny tells him he'll have to wait until they know what horses are scratched. Patiently he explains that until that is known you can't make the betting fair. I'm not sure the customer understands. He wants to bet now and get back to his tailgate party.

The race goes off. About five minutes later Monster Monster finishes nowhere as Mr. Rokeby wins. Back by the chalk board people are crowding around Jack, holding out their winning tickets, asking to be paid. Jack says:

*"Wait 'til it's official."*

Then the loudspeaker comes alive:

*"The results of the fourth race are now official. First, Mr. Rokeby, owned,*

*trained and ridden by Eben Sutton…"*

Jack pays off the winners, and begins scrubbing off the board in preparation for taking bets on the fifth. Lenny has gone across the race course to the place where horses are checked in, so that he can determine the scratches. I try to get in a word to Jack, like, *"You guys dodged a bullet with that $100 bet on Monster Monster – guess it pays to be wrong sometimes."* But he doesn't hear me.

Lenny is still waiting for the final word on the scratches, and Jack is yelling at him to get it quickly, while telling fifth race bettors to be patient until he does. The fourth race and Monster Monster are history. It's the next one that counts. The Golds are now all business, no more idle conversation with bystanders.

Book making looks like fun, and less risky than horse ownership. I think of trying it, briefly, then remember it took Jack thirty years of study and a lost job to get good at it. I don't have – or want to develop – those credentials. But now the Golds are race day friends, not just a part of the anonymous background scenery.

*"Place your bets! Place your bets here!"*

PHOTO BY PAT MACVEAGH

*Saluter in the paddock ready to go for his sixth Gold Cup, May 1999*

*Steeplechase silhouette*

PHOTO BY ANITA BAARNS

## – First Saturday in May – 2000 –

PHOTO BY ANITA BAARNS

*Saluter, riders up, May 2000*

In the American race horse world the height of the spring season comes on the first Saturday in May, with the playing of "My Old Kentucky Home" at Churchill Downs in Louisville, immediately preceding the Kentucky Derby. Here in Virginia there is a competing tradition earlier on the same day, at Great Meadow, near The Plains. It is the Virginia Gold Cup, the featured timber race on a varied card of eight jumping races, preceded by pony races and Jack Russell Terrier competitions.

Last year the great Saluter won the Gold Cup for the sixth straight time and a huge crowd is expected to see him try again. This year, the great day dawned clear, hot, and humid, projected to hit above 90° by mid afternoon.

We leave home early. The crowd will be immense,

with nearly 50,000 visitors expected. Gilded Life is running in a maiden hurdle race – the fourth – and so we dress with the formality expected of owners – jacket and tie in my case, cool dress and straw hat in Edie's. We are careful to add our National Steeplechase Association pins, tickets to the areas reserved for insiders, and protected by fences and gate keepers from invasion by the masses.

Because we are early we find a shady parking spot under a tree in the horse-man's area. At 11:00 the heat is building rapidly. By post time at one it will be unbearable. Protocol gives way to comfort. Tie and jacket abandoned, we proceed to Members' Hill, passing through various check points to reach this premier location set aside for owners, trainers, riders, race officials, and those willing to pay in more direct ways for the privilege. Enroute, we hear an exchange between a guardian and a casually dressed young man:

*"Where's your Members Hill ticket or steeplechase button?"*

*"Don't have one. What do I do to get in?"*

*"See that lady over there."*

The young man moves to the side towards the lady, letting several credentialed people pass through. He asks her:

*"How much for a ticket?"*

*"Fifty dollars."*

There is a moment of stunned hesitation, then he decides he can see the races almost as well from whence he came – and besides, his friends have a cooler full of beer back at their car. He does a U-turn and leaves.

From Members' Hill one gets a beautiful view of the race course, with an unspoiled vista of the countryside behind, at first falling away to the little valley in which the course is laid out, and then rising and falling gently over fields and woods to the Bull Run Mountains five miles to the northeast. One can see only an old red barn and a silo in a field behind the course, and, much further away, two farm houses peeking out from the old trees that shade them. But for the commotion of the day's event, it is as pastoral and as shimmering hot as it must have been when Confederate and Union troops fought nearby at First Manassas, almost 139 years ago.

I pause briefly to think how the gentle landscape might have been changed, had the Walt Disney Company prevailed in their plan for a giant theme park and surrounding city, its downtown to be centered about six miles northeast of where we stand.

The Virginia Gold Cup was first run near Warrenton in 1922. The Great Meadow site is much newer, the land bought in 1982 by Arthur (Nick) Arundel, a local newspaper publisher who once was an amateur steeplechase rider. Competition came from a developer who envisioned many houses on the tranquil ground lying ahead of us. Instead, Nick and his friends have created a horse Mecca, with the race course, a polo facility, and areas for horse shows, eventing and other equine contests, all forever protected as open space. In 1985 the Gold Cup moved here. Now it is run for a purse of $50,000, with smaller purses for the races on its under card.

The race course itself is special. In addition to the hurdles there is a water jump, a challenging timber layout, and a special "steeplethon" course with a 60 yard "splash" gallop through a ten inch deep pool of water, and obstacles

*Horses splashing through Swan Lake*

– wall, bank, ditch, chicken coop – more typical of fox hunting that today's formalized jump racing.

The pond contiguous to the "splash" is called Swan Lake, no doubt in recognition of Dr. Bill Sladen, Nick Arundel's brother-in-law, who is an ornithologist attempting to reintroduce trumpeter swans to America's eastern flyway.

There are well over 100 white tents arrayed around perhaps two thirds of the periphery of the race course, accompanied by railside parking spaces, open air boxes, and other amenities. At the summit of Members Hill, next to the permanent building reserved on race days for the special supporters of Great

PHOTO BY THE AUTHOR

*Tents along the far rail, as seen from Members Hill*

Meadow, are three dozen or so larger "corporate" tents for use by race sponsors and others interested in entertaining their customers or special friends.

Overhead a small aircraft flies back and forth, trailing a blue and white banner advertising "Sideware.com", a name until now unknown to the writer and not (yet?) listed on the NASDAQ. The marketeers have classified the Gold Cup crowd as belonging to the "new economy."

The terrier races conclude, and the pony races take their place. Most spectators pay little heed, leaving the caring to the child riders and their parents. Usually one pony has proved clearly superior in earlier meets, and form almost always tells. That doesn't discourage the small riders from addressing their tasks with utmost seriousness. Win or lose, they are part of the big day, learning about appearing in public and taking winning or losing in stride.

Then it's on to serious business. The announcer calls attention to the color guard parading by the three story tower that serves as the stewards' stand. A lady with a high and occasionally tremulous voice sings the Star Spangled Banner. The crowd is respectfully silent.

I recall a more participative past — football games where thousands sang the anthem, lustily accompanied by a college band, rendering to Caesar his due

PHOTO BY DOUGLAS LEES

*Remy Winants finishing a pony race*

before shifting to "On, Wisconsin," "Anchors Aweigh," or "Bulldog, Bulldog, Bow Wow Wow." Substituting a performer, usually one who feels the song and the shining moment are his or hers alone, still seems to this old soldier to be a sacrilege, despite its current universal acceptance. In any event I miss singing our country's song, my off key efforts drowned by thousands of better voices.

The second race is the first division of the maiden hurdle (Gilded Life is running in the fourth race, the second division of maidens). The field includes two Virginia horses that have beaten us in the past, Echomont and Ponsonby, and we breathe easier knowing they are not to run against Gilded. Ponsonby finishes third, with the top two spots going to unheralded newcomers with Pennsylvania trainers. This sets the tone for the day, as Virginia-trained horses will gain only one win, two seconds and a third in the seven regular races on the card. As a friend observes later:

*"There's plenty of money in Virginia, but they don't spend it on race horses."*

Our fourth race proves the exception. In the 12 horse field at least half are Virginia-trained. We join Jimmy Day in the paddock as Gilded Life is saddled and mounted by jockey Jonathan Thomas, a young friend from our church. We then follow Jimmy to the viewing stand next to the stewards' tower and the finish line. The race proves typical of Gilded's spring. After a decent start he settles comfortably in the middle of the pack, jumping easily and well. With three-eighths of a mile to go he has eased up to third as a couple of horses have fallen or pulled up. At the last fence he is even with the leader, the Ben-Dov's Fields of Omagh. Our excitement builds, but Gilded is no match for his rival's closing kick, and we settle for second. Jimmy is pleased:

*"He ran well. He'll break his maiden soon enough. Don't worry."*

Why should we? Gilded has a win on the flat, and two seconds and a third

*Gilded Life at Great Meadow, Jonathan Thomas up, Danielle Hodsdon leading.*

over fences so far this spring, a fine start to his steeplechase career. Between races we seek shelter in the Equine Medical Center tent which offers both shade and a breeze, and the supply of ice and soft drinks is inexhaustible. Hot and listless, we watch the crowd go by outside the tent. It is mostly young, casually dressed and happy. Their many naive questions suggest it is not a sophisticated horse crowd, but it is admiring. *"Oh, they're so beautiful"* refers equally to the horses and to the girls in the crowd.

Soon enough we must bestir ourselves to watch the preparations for the Gold Cup itself, and we go to the paddock near the steward's tower. With such an assemblage the pull on politicians is irresistible. The presence of our local member of the House of Delegates, the Lieutenant Governor of Virginia, and our two United States Senators is noted by the announcer. Happily he does not surrender his microphone to any of them. Instead we watch the participants in this race – not next November's – parade in the paddock.

The race itself is introduced by the strains of "Carry Me Back to Old Virginny." Gold Cup management is not averse to copying what builds tradition elsewhere. The star of the show is Saluter, an 11 year-old bay gelding trying for his seventh Gold Cup in a row. His extraordinary record has never been approached, the closest competitor being Leeds Don, who won it three times in 1965-6-7. Saluter has also won the fall International Gold Cup twice.

Saluter is not yet a graybeard, but one has to empathize with Mrs. Stern, the owner, and Jack Fisher – trainer and rider – as they deliberated during the spring on whether to take a shot at extending the string to seven, or whether Saluter should quit at the top after last year's win in the fastest time in Gold Cup history on the Great Meadow Course. Now, despite the awful heat, it is too late to change their minds – Saluter is the crowd's favorite, and scratching him would be a public relations disaster for all concerned. Of course the potential critics of any such move are not middle-aged specimens facing an all out effort over four miles on a 95° humid afternoon. With Saluter in the paddock, and Jack Fisher in Mrs. Stern's pink and green silks the die is cast. Saluter is going.

Of the nine horses entered only Ironfist is scratched. He won two races earlier in the year, and almost $50,000. At seven years old he looked to have a good shot here, but now he won't run. So the most likely challengers are local horses: Gold Quoit, second to Saluter a year ago, who has beaten him in shorter races, and Bavario, Nick Arundel's seven year-old by Theatrical, a sire of stayers who run well on turf. Of course steeplechase form does not always follow flat race breeding, as the more modest pedigrees of Saluter and Gold Quoit make clear. As in any sport, it is what you do today that counts, not what your press clippings said you did last week, or who your father was.

The other contestants are less well known to this crowd. Father Sky and Hopewell, both local, have not won since 1998. The English visitor Pennybridge shows no recent race record in the program, but is eligible for a $100,000 bonus based on wins at home if he wins here. J J Hansel and Priceless Room (by Bates Motel out of Priceless Asset) have both won this year, but in lesser races. A careful student would have noted – as we did not – that 10 year-old Priceless Room, a mediocre flat race veteran, won his maiden race over timber only a week ago at Foxfield, but by 20 lengths. If the careful student was a Gold Cup handicapper, he would mark the horse down for having inadequate rest between starts, compounded by age and inexperience. Then he would note the margin of victory and wonder.

Soon enough it is "riders up", and the horses are on the course, then "under starter's orders," lining up for the start, and quickly "they're off!" and headed for the first fence. Saluter's proven pattern is to coast along in the rear for almost all of the four mile, 23 fence course, then accelerate over the last three fences, passing tiring horses on his way to another win.

The pattern reasserts itself. At three miles Pennybridge leads Gold Quoit by a length, with Priceless Room third and Saluter last. By the 21st fence, as Pennybridge surrenders the lead to Gold Quoit, Saluter begins his trademark charge. The crowd, well aware of what is happening, comes noisily alive. Over the last fence and down the stretch five horses battle to the wire. Priceless Room ultimately prevails over Gold Quoit by half a length, with Saluter in third by a length more. After four miles, only three and one half lengths separate the first five horses. In that crowded finish an era has ended. An unknown horse, owned by the one horse syndicate Big Wood Stable, has dethroned the great Saluter.

So the champion goes down, but in gallant fashion. We suspect he will be back at Great Meadow in the fall. As Jack Fisher says in his post race interview:

*"Losing is not going to hurt his legacy."*

A maiden claiming race wraps up the program, and we retire to the hospitality tent reserved for owners, trainers, riders, and any one else who can talk their way in. The tent is hot, the beer good (if you can crowd through to get some), the wine marginal. At each end of the tent is a TV screen, its attention and that of the crowd tuned now to Louisville. Talking heads explain the Derby, the horses, and the sport, with the twin towers of Churchill Downs visible in the background. The four million dollar yearling Fusaichi Pegasus, now three, is a consensus choice to win. His story and his Japanese owner are

*Saluter after losing in 2000*

both colorful. The sport needs new heroes, and it yearns for a Triple Crown winner. It's been 22 years since Affirmed won that title in 1978.

The band plays – or is it a singer who sings – "My Old Kentucky Home." As nineteen horses enter the starting gate, the mood is that of a coronation. Then "they're off," and three year-old Fusaichi Pegasus does not disappoint, threading his way brilliantly through his competition and the blur of the Great Meadow television screens to win with relative ease.

Saluter's reign in Virginia may be over, but within a couple of hours, in Kentucky, a presumed new champion has taken his first step towards greatness. The Great Meadow crowd disperses, and we work our way through traffic and towards home, happy to have been a minor part of a great day of racing.

Saluter sat atop the timber side of U.S. Steeplechasing for six years, rivaled only by the great hurdle horse Lonesome Glory (now retired), until meeting his fate at the hands of the lightly regarded Priceless Room.

Fusaichi Pegasus' reign has been notably shorter. After only two weeks of acclaim, an inexperienced but talented colt named Red Bullet cut him down in the Preakness, extinguishing any hope of a Triple Crown this year. Fusaichi Pegasus then skipped the Belmont and has now been pointed at a final racing effort in the fall Breeders Cup, to be followed by a lucrative career at stud, his sale for that purpose already consummated. For Saluter no such blissful Elysian Fields await – he is a gelding – but he will

PHOTO BY ANITA BAARNS

*Lonesome Glory, Blythe Miller up, making a curtain call at Great Meadow*

own his special little piece of Great Meadow forever. We look forward to his return. As for Fusaichi, we know only that we cannot afford to breed to him.

## – *Planning Ahead* –

It is a crisp spring day at the end of May, and I have a date with Jimmy Day to go over the coming schedule for Devil's Reach.

Devil's ran well last Monday – Memorial Day – at Fair Hill, finishing second in the Miles Valentine Stakes, just where the odds makers had him. Losing a close one to Quel Senor, a Group III winner in Europe and a rising star over jumps, is no disgrace, and some very good horses finished further back. Devil's latest fine effort puts distance between us and the distressing memory of the recent Temple Gwathmey Stakes, which Devil's won, only to be set down for presumed interference, a call that made no sense to many. Finishing first three times and second once in four starts is a spring to savor.

This morning I find Jimmy in an equally good mood. He has had a wonderful spring, despite a shortage of hands to help with the sixteen horses he has in training – active 'chasers, jumping prospects, and youngsters being readied to run on the flat. His biggest client is his landlady, Martha Cook, owner of the stable and track that Jimmy leases just north of Millwood in the Shenandoah

Valley. Jimmy and Emily Day own several broodmares and foals, and Emily trains and sells hunters from her family's farm some miles to the south. Daybreak Stables is a family horse conglomerate, of modest size by Kentucky standards, but large for Virginia.

I have been thinking that Devil's is a bit thin, and might be helped by a little break to freshen up. If so, now is the time to give him a vacation. There is only one race available for Devil's – the Zeke Ferguson Stakes at Colonial Downs – before the Saratoga races in August. We inspect the horse. Jimmy is of the opinion that Devil's is fine and should stay in training, aiming at the Ferguson. He doesn't feel he is too thin:

*"He's a race horse – that's how he should look."*

Then he runs his hands over the horse's legs…

*"His wheels are cold. No problem. And he's eating well. He goes out in the paddock for three hours in the morning, if I left him longer he'd blow up on grass and not eat his grain.*

*"Devil's gives you everything he has. If we'd been on the inside at Fair Hill, instead of on the outside, he'd have won. That other horse is a bloody good horse. I'm thrilled with how Devil's did. He might surprise you in the Ferguson."*

Looking to the Fall, there are three starter handicaps scheduled for horses that have run for a claiming price, so these races have to be on our list, beginning with one in August in Saratoga. Then there is the Maryland Million steeplechase in October, limited to Maryland-bred horses. Here's another good spot for Devil's – there aren't a lot of Maryland-bred 'chasers in his league. That evening Jimmy calls:

*"Thinking it over, maybe three weeks off would be a good idea. I'd still have time to get him ready for Saratoga."*

*"OK. We'll pick him up tomorrow,"* I say. So much for the Ferguson; it reminds me of an old racing axiom:

*"Keep yourself in the best company, and your horse in the worst. …You have to run 'em where they can win."*

Next day, as we load Devil's, Jimmy has the final word:

*"He's up to date on everything except he's due to be wormed. And have him back in three weeks – no more – I have to get him ready for Saratoga!"*

Devil's is now in a stall at Trappe Hill, and Wayne has already wormed him. We are leaving keeping in the best company to Grade 1 winner, Flasher, and Canta Ke Brave, and will aim Devil's to win where he can.

Bay Cockburn with Donna and Joe Rogers at Glenwood Park fall races

PHOTO BY DOUGLAS LEES

## - The Fall Season Opens -

It is now September, more than four months after Saluter's Gold Cup defeat. Steeplechasing resumed last week at Glenwood Park, and today I am sitting on a hill at Morven Park, examining the program for the Fairfax races now in progress in front of me. Thumbing the pages, I note to my surprise that Saluter is entered in the Bowman Bowl, the feature timber race, against a small and less noted field for a modest purse of $10,000.

As I am studying the program a tall, lean man lowers himself to the grass beside me, settles down comfortably, and says:

"Hello. I'm John Fisher. "

I give him my name, and add, "You're Jack's father?"

"Yes."

Dr. John Fisher is one of the legends of the sport, and I start to pump his brains on all manner of subjects, from horse breeding theories, to where to find steeplechase prospects, to how to arrest sprawl in the beautiful country around Unionville, PA (his home), and Upperville, VA (ours). Eventually we get around to Saluter, and whether he will run in the International Gold Cup this fall. Dr. Fisher comments about as follows:

———

*"Jack and Henry didn't want to let him be one of those athletes that hangs on past his time. On the other hand, he just loves to train. Saluter will tell them when he's had enough."*

Then he goes on:

*"The story of how the Sterns got Saluter is interesting. Some years ago my mother wanted me to find a horse for her that Jack could train. I had been going to yearling sales, and there was about then a dispersal of horses of all ages. This young gelding took my eye, and I bought him and sent him over to Jack. I heard nothing for two months, which was unusual, so I finally called Jack up. What I heard on the other end of the line was…*

*" 'Dammit, Dad, you sent me a pony. What do you expect me to do with him?' "*

Apparently Dr. Fisher's eye was still focusing on yearlings, and the older horse he bought was judged against that size standard. My new friend continues:

*"Well, I took him home and every couple of months I put a stick on him and he inched up from 15.2 to 15.2½ to 15.3 hands. When he finally hit 16.0 I sent him back to Jack and told him, 'Now teach him to jump.'*

*"Sometime in there my mother died, and we thought the horse was coming along pretty well so I sold 50 percent of him to Henry Stern. After several starts I became disenchanted with his temperament and potential and I sold my 50 percent to Henry. Henry took him to the Faifax races, over at the old Belmont course. Well, he got to the starting line and he wouldn't start, just stood there as the others took off. I was so mad at the horse that I told Jack, 'If that was my horse I'd shoot him and be done with it.'*

*"But of course he didn't. He continued to train him for Henry rather successfully. Eventually Henry sold him to Jill Waterman. That horse was called KY Mint Julep, and she had a lot of success with him later at Point-to-Points.*

*"Jack was so upset by KY Mint Julep's performance at Fairfax that he offered Henry a 50 percent interest in a young timber horse that had just broken his maiden at Geneseo. That horse was Saluter, and as you know he turned out OK. Jack and Henry have had a wonderful relationship."*

Now the Bowman Bowl horses are headed for the paddock, and Dr. Fisher rises and takes his leave. Down the hill I check the chalk board, where Jack Gold, has Saluter at 1-to-2. As I watch people coming up to bet, Jack tells his son Norm to erase the 1-to-2 and make it 1-to-3. Five minutes later it is 1-to-4. Jack says:

---

*"They just keep betting Saluter. I have to change the odds, but they don't know what they're doing. How do you know whether the horse is here to win, or just here for a good work?"*

Back at the paddock Saluter and Jack Fisher are all business. In the warm up Jack canters the horse down the stretch, giving the fans a good view of the immortal – perhaps their last chance. During the three mile race Saluter stays close to the leaders, not back as usual, but jumping well. Perhaps the pace is slow. As they turn for home it is a three horse race, including Saluter.

But this is not his day. In a three horse photo finish Saluter comes in third. He does not know of the silver lining – his loss has made Jack Gold's afternoon. Jack will keep all that money people bet on Saluter. The winner is a six year-old gelding named Dr. Ramsey, trained by – who else? – Jack Fisher, and ridden by a rising young star, Jonathan Thomas. We hope they will be around a long time. Familiar names add greatly to the sport's appeal.

As for 11 year old Saluter and the International Gold Cup some weeks hence:

*"Maybe yes, maybe no."*

EPILOGUE.

Saluter does go in the International Gold Cup, finishing second. After what would for most horses be a brilliant year – three seconds and two thirds, at the highest level – he has been retired. Jack Fisher explains:

*"He lost a step this year. We don't want to disgrace him."*

Saluter will be missed by all, but long remembered. Dr. Ramsey was stakes placed at Genesee Valley, but did not enter the International Gold Cup and did poorly in Camden. The week after his win in the Fairfax meet Jonathan Thomas suffered a frightful fall at Colonial Downs. At first he was paralyzed from the shoulders down, but over the time since then his recovery has been remarkable. He is now able to walk – initially predicted as an impossibility – and will eventually return to a normal life. Whether that will include the abnormal activity of race riding is yet to be determined.

Erstwhile "wonder horse" Fusaichi Pegasus finished sixth in the Breeder's Cup Classic at Churchill Downs, and is now being promoted by his owners as the coming king of sires. He will stand next spring for a fee of $150,000. Breeders can save a lot of money ignoring the hype.

This business, like life, has a way of cutting down its early bloomers. But for Mays to come the music of Stephen Foster will fill owners' ears as they dream of their promising young horses.

---

PHOTO BY DOUGLAS LEES

**JULIE GOMENA BEATING THE BIG BOYS**

*(LEFT TO RIGHT):* **Tom Foley**, *Champion Apprentice Jockey, 2001, on Fast Steppin Man;* **Robert Massey**, *Champion Jockey, 2002, (Earnings) on Sovereign Storm;* **Julie Gomena**, *Winner of this race, her first sanctioned win, on Double Redouble;* **Mark Griffiths**, *Veteran of many sanctioned races on Fifth Creek;* **David Bentley**, *Champion Jockey, 2002 (Number of Wins), on Young Dubliner*

Along with the horses, steeplechasing depends on the riders, young and not-so-young people who balance risk against thrill as participants in one of the world's most beautiful and exciting sports. Every other aspect of riding jumpers is unattractive – the pay is low, the rides uncertain, the travel onerous. If you win, the horse is a great horse, well prepared for the race – just ask his owner and trainer. If he loses, he was set up to win but you gave him a bad ride. As owners we confess to having entertained those unkind thoughts once or twice, but mostly we think back to the many fine riders who have delivered to us our vicarious thrills. Without them, and their counterparts, there would be no steeplechasing. The story of the sport is their story.

———

247

I ask Matt McCarron, *"Why do you do it?"* His answer is prompt:

> *"A horse like Devil's is a joy to ride. He was genuine. He had a great personality and he always gave his best. Riding him was a high."*

Three riders we know are profiled in the following pages, a varied sample of the many more who for lack of space are not. From among the latter here are five who have given us special moments to remember:

PHOTO BY THE AUTHOR

*Matt McCarron and son Trevor*

- Danielle Hodsdon, who had her first win over jumps on Devil's Reach.

- Rob Massey, who quietly shared two heartbreaks with us.

- Matt McCarron, who won with Dawn's a Pleasure at Warrenton and rode a perfect race on Devil's to win the Region's Bank Imperial Cup at Aiken.

- Peter Walsh, inseparably successful with Murray's Ruler, except when falling.

- Henry Wood, who taught so many what the term "gentleman rider" really means.

No doubt every owner and trainer has his or her special list as well.

## – *Jonathan Thomas* –

When I called Jonathan, two months after his accident, to ask to visit him, I was stunned to hear:

*"No, I'll meet you. I can drive fine."*

And so he came to see us one Tuesday in December. That morning the Piedmont Foxhounds were scheduled to meet at Trappe Hill. Our little band of hosts – Edie, Betsy Crenshaw, Jonathan, and I – offer the small field a stirrup cup to ward off the nor'west wind coming in on the heels of a front which luckily has dropped its snow further west. Then, hospitality duties over, we return to the house to catch up on how Jonathan is mending.

As we go up the driveway we see Gilded Life in the paddock. Jonathan, who rode him last spring at the Gold Cup meet, stops now to mourn over the bowed tendon that has diverted the horse's career from racing to a quieter future as a hunter. Later it strikes me that Jonathan's life may have taken a similar turn.

Jonathan's story really starts before he was born. His mother and father were amateur Point-to-Point riders then, and trained flat horses and steeple-

Jonathan Thomas

chasers for a living. His mother galloped horses until she was six or seven months pregnant with Jonathan, finally taking time off for the baby to make his appearance. For ten years Jonathan lived at Paul Mellon's Rokeby Farm with his mother, his parents having been divorced when he was two. His father, John Dale Thomas, migrated to Delaware Park, where he eventually became track superintendent.

Growing up, Jonathan was always around horses. He remembers that by six he was hot walking and grazing them at the Middleburg Training Center. Later he spent summers in Delaware with his father, and learned from the ground up how to care for a race horse, how to groom him, put on bandages

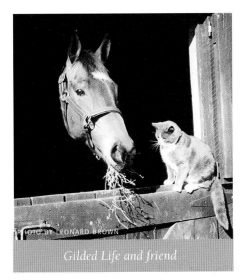

Gilded Life and friend

and poultices, and how to muck stalls. During this time his riding, though, was limited to ponies.

By twelve, however, he had decided that horses were not "cool", and he had little to do with them for the next four years. Then he came to one of a modern teenager's life crises:

*"I wanted a car, and that meant I needed a job in order to afford it."*

He found work handling steeplechase horses at Point-to-Points for trainer Mairead Carr. Then his aunt, Chrissy

Jacobs, who worked for Col. Bob Newton, got him riding again, but he had no thought of race riding. Galloping horses was just a job – a means to an end – the way he could get that car.

Jonathan also worked for Rosemary Bogley, where he met Tony Bencivenga, an old time jockey who had taken care of and galloped Citation at the great Calumet Farm in Kentucky. While Chrissy taught Jonathan equitation, Tony was a font of knowledge on how to ride in races. And so Jonathan started to think about becoming a race rider. His first mount was No Wonder, trained by Susan and Pat Cooney. The race was on the flat at Southern Pines, and Jonathan and No Wonder won it.

> *"When we won that race I started crying, the feeling of connection with the horse was so amazing. Then I won my second start over hurdles – on Have Plan Will Travel – and my first start over timber. It was a picture perfect beginning to a career."*

I asked him what he liked best about it.

> *"What I like most is the whole life style. Every day you wake up excited about going to work and riding. The better you get, the more you want to do it. My life was all caught up in the game. Get up at six, work 'til twelve, ride some more horses, go to the gym to work out…"*

His voice trails off a bit. Then…

> *"I started riding over fences at 19. I wanted to stay in Virginia, but I only got about six rides that first year.*
>
> *"Then Tom Foley invited me to go to Ireland with him, and I skipped my high school graduation to do it. [not to worry, parents – Jonathan has his diploma]. I planned to be there a week but I stayed several months, riding for Charlie Swan. Charlie was one of Ireland's greatest jockeys, and he had just started training.*
>
> *"Charlie taught me a lot about racing, and how to conduct yourself with trainers and owners. He talked about the business side, and how to promote the game, tell people how wonderful it is, not just say you're a jockey. He was a great mentor."*

When Jonathan returned home he worked for a while for Janet Elliot, for whom he galloped horses and rode a few flat races. Then jockey Andy Wilson helped him get a job with Jack Fisher, and in due course he was riding Fisher-trained

*Tom Foley, at age 17, was a brash young Irish lad breaking into American racing. He since has matured into a competitive professional rider. Pictured here, he is bringing in Pal's Pride after the horse's first win. Tom subsequently rode Pal's Pride to the 2002 Three Year Old Championship*

horses over fences. He sums up his brief career to date:

> "80 rides, 11 wins over jumps in sanctioned races, plus one on the flat, plus one Point-to-Point – I haven't ridden in many Point-to-Points."

Now we come to another turning point in his young life, the disastrous fall at Colonial Downs two months ago.

> "I was riding Darn Tip Alarm. I'd won a 50 thousand dollar race with him before, so I knew him. Towards the end of the race at Colonial the horse was tired, but things had been going so well for me the past two weeks that I thought maybe we could still pick up a small check, even though the horse hadn't run in six months. Going into the last fence I could feel the fall coming, but I went for it anyway, when I should have pulled up. In nine out of ten cases it would have worked, but this time it didn't. It was 100 percent my fault.

> "The horse hit the fence, and his head and shoulders just disappeared in front of me. I don't know what happened to him. I've had four falls, and in

251

*the first three I hit the ground and rolled. This time I hit the ground and
just stuck to it. I couldn't move from the waist down. I wasn't scared or
anything. Then in a minute or so I went into shock.*

*"In the hospital it was pretty scary when I found out I couldn't move. Then,
each day as I started to heal, I learned something – good or bad – about
my injury. But what it meant for my future didn't really hit me until, after
a week, they put me in a wheel chair, and I couldn't walk."*

Jonathan's recovery has been remarkable, perhaps miraculous. I asked him to
what he attributed his healing.

*"I was lucky. Lucky to be very fit physically. And having a great medical
team in Richmond near where it happened was lucky. The support from
family and friends was very helpful."*

I comment on one way-point in his recovery, *"We all cheered when we learned
that your bodily functions were under your own control again."*

Jonathan turns from gastroenterology to describing the metal structure placed
in his back, which keeps load off the injured vertebrae while they heal. It is to
be removed next spring, and the prognosis is for normal mobility thereafter.
Meanwhile, he has physical therapy several times a week. I ask him what the
injury means for his career. His answer has been well thought out:

*"I never questioned that my future is with the horse. I always planned to
ride as long as I could do it well, and then become a trainer of flat race
horses – there isn't much money in jump racing. So whether I ride again or
not – and I hope I do – the plan is the same.*

*"I've applied to business schools – University of Louisville, University of
Arizona – where they have courses in equine business. I know a lot about
the horse, but I wasn't very good in math. I need that side of it.*

*"Then I'd like to be assistant to a really good trainer – like Bill Mott or
[Neil] Drysdale – and eventually be on my own, someday at that level."*

One matures quickly when contemplating the rest of one's life in a wheel chair.

Now it is time to drive Jonathan back to his car where we met at Trinity
Church. This time we go down the back driveway, past the weanlings. As we
stop they amble over to be petted, and I note the eye of a future trainer
appraising them all. He is especially delighted that we have a colt by
Gentlemen – a race horse he admires. Perhaps one day trainer Jonathan
Thomas will buy one of Trappe Hill's youngsters for a client, and we will all
come together, dreaming, on the first Saturday in May.

---

*Kassie Chatfield-Taylor – in dark shirt – on the way to beating the boys.*

## – Lady pioneer –

*"The horse has been my whole life, my friends, the way I raised my children, the thing that has sustained me."*

—Kassie Chatfield-Taylor Kingsley, pioneer lady steeplechase rider.

When Kassie Chatfield-Taylor was six her family moved to Waterford, Virginia. As a girl she had access to a pony, shared with several siblings, and spent summers at the Foxcroft School, riding Miss Charlotte's ponies in "riding class."

Her competitive spirit showed up early. Kassie was a member of the first Loudoun Pony Club team, one that went to the National Rally in Nashville, competing against teams from all over the country. It still galls her that they finished second, four and a half points out of first, because their barn manager left a pitchfork on the floor, and the team was docked five points for careless horse management. During that time she began hunting with Middleburg and Loudoun, thanks to friendly members, and…

> *"…local farmers and people that worked in Washington, with Joe Rogers, Hunton Atwell, and Miss Anna Hedrick as Masters. From 12 years on, I rode with and for Joanie Moore DuPont. She – and later we – would go to the Front Royal Livestock Market and buy green or unbroken horses and ponies that we showed and hunted and turned into wonderful children's mounts."*

After graduating at seventeen from the Convent of the Sacred Heart in Noroton, CT, she had a job breaking polo ponies for Hap Puelicher. A fall dissuaded her from this, and she ended up as riding instructor at the

---

253

Garrison Forest School near Baltimore. After five years at Garrison she returned to Loudoun County, riding horses for various owners and trainers, including Hall of Fame trainer Mikey Smithwick and Dr. Joe Rogers.

In her first race, she rode a hunter called King Chick, who belonged to a local carpenter and farmer, Clayton Kephart. At fence after fence, as King Chick jumped clean and in the lead, she could hear the rattling of rails behind her. Glancing back, she could just see the nose of a competing horse. Curious as to why he could hit so many fences and still keep up, she looked again, and saw that he had lost his rider, and was just following King Chick around. They had a large lead. Surprised, she eased her horse, wondering what to do. She was caught, unable to get King Chick's momentum back, and so finished second. To her vast relief, Mr. Kephart commended her on a good ride, never bawling her out for throwing away a win, a valuable lesson in how to coach rookies.

During one season, she had a spate of races in which she went off course and was disqualified, because while in the lead she was not sure of the proper course. Since her siblings had poor eyesight, Dr. Joe Rogers insisted that she have her vision checked before riding his Bally Guy. She went to the eye doctor, expecting to have glasses prescribed. Instead he said:

> *"Your eyes are perfectly fine, just open them and look."*

Before the next race for Joe Rogers he gave her a little lecture about staying on course, the theme of which was:

> *"Now, I've never gone off course, or been bitten by a dog, or got a speeding ticket,"* [implying that he was always careful].

Kassie opened her eyes and won the race for Joe, but seems secretly pleased to report that Joe "broke his maiden" in all three of those unpleasant experiences within the next year. I ask her, *"Which was the best horse you ever rode?"* The prompt answer:

> *"Lenoso, an Argentine-bred horse. Riding him was like riding a wonderful locomotive."*

She came to Lenoso by way of a Christmas party at the George McGhee's. There she ran into Arch Kingsley, who owned Lenoso. One thing led to another, and she married Arch, himself a fine steeplechase rider, in 1969, and also rode Lenoso for him for several years. Kassie was the "Martini and Rossi" leading lady rider in 1968 and 1969, *"because of Lenoso and several other good horses."*

Shortly before her marriage she became one of the first three women licensed

*Kassie on Lenoso*

by the National Steeplechase Association to ride in sanctioned races, which she did in 1969. This door was opened by the court battle fought in 1968 by Olympic rider Kathy Kusner in order to get a jockey's license from Maryland. Kassie's son Arch later asked Lonesome Glory's jockey Blythe Miller:

> *"Have you ever thanked my Mom for making your riding against me possible?"*

Six years later (1975) Kassie was schooling a horse at Warrenton. Something startled him, and he ran through the wing of the jump and broke a fence post. The resulting fall fractured the back of Kassie's head and smashed her cheek bone. For hours she was unable to move at all, but slowly recovered. For over a year her memory was fuzzy, and even now, when she gets tired, she says she *"reverses things terribly."* Race riding became a thing of the past, but when she sees a line of hedgerows or fences now she still feels herself…

> *"…go dum, te-dum, te-dum, te-dum, as I mentally gallop up to and over them."*

She was, however, able to keep up foxhunting for many years after her accident, blending it in with the upbringing and riding development of her two sons, George and Arch, Jr. Though she has been divorced for many years, without her marriage she would not have had her two boys. Both of them are now race riders and she is intensely proud of them. One of her special moments was hunting with both boys on her birthday, when they were six and seven. Another was when son Arch, at Christmas, baked 24 loaves of bread and took them around as presents to all the people that had helped him over the years.

George Kingsley has steeplechased successfully as an amateur. He is now…

> "…working hard. He has a barn full of sport horses, and is riding for Mairead Carr."

Arch Kingsley, Jr. has become one of the nation's best professional steeplechase jockeys, ending up first or second in numbers of wins over the last three or four years. I ask their mother, thinking of her own accident, *"Do you worry about their riding?"* The reply is crisp:

> *"No. I like the fact that the boys are riding; I only worry that they might not get to do all they could."*

Kassie remains very active in the steeplechase world, officiating at race meets and point-to-points. Her greatest thrill, though, is that her boys still think she knows enough to want her to critique their races.

## - Sean Clancy -

Sean rode Devil's Reach to a second at Saratoga in 1999. Sean loves that track and all that goes with it, and has written a book about it, *Saratoga Days*. So it seemed logical to look to him for a veteran's insights into race riding (we will report on his literary career in a subsequent volume).

Sean grew up around the race track. His father trained horses - flat racers and jumpers - for Mr. Donald P. Ross, Jr. at Delaware Park. As a kid Sean hung around a bit on the backstretch, but usually he bummed a ride over to the grandstand to watch races. He

PHOTO BY STEEPLECHASE TIMES

*Sean Clancy*

didn't ride much as a child, but his heroes were jockeys, especially Joe Aitcheson, who rented a room one summer in the Clancy's house. Sean tells how he started race-riding ponies at 13:

> "There was this pony Red Raven, fastest race pony ever, a Thoroughbred twin by Gun Shot. Ricky Hendriks, Sanna Neilson, Blythe Miller, Bernie Houghton had all won on him. Dad was by then working for Mr. Strawbridge – Augustin Stables – and he had found the pony – he was in bad shape – and fixed him up. Sanna had grown out of him, and one day Dad said 'I think you could ride Red Raven.'

> "It was like saying 'you can fly to the moon.' Dad was able to instill confidence even when he didn't feel it himself. So he put me on Red Raven in a port-a-paddock [a small round portable enclosure]– that's how much confidence he had – and I rode him in there to start. Dad was careful never to over-face me. Someday, if I have kids, I hope I can do that as well as Dad.

> "Then, on October 29, 1983, I rode Red Raven in a race, and won, beating my best friend, Chip Miller, whom I'd never beaten at anything. It was the first success I ever had, and I'll never forget it. Of course, it wasn't perfect. I stood up at the wire, like I'd seen winners do, but the stirrup leather came off the bar, and the stirrup fell off the saddle, and five strides later I'm on the ground and the pony runs over me. They had to put seven stitches in my wrist."

Sean shows me the scar, then continues:

> "So then I started riding flat races at hunt meets, and eventually they let me ride a ten year old horse, Student Dancer, over fences. I rode him in Point-to-Points at Warrenton and Fairfax. In 1988 he won at Foxfield, my first win in a sanctioned race. It was the greatest day of my life."

A check of the records shows Student Dancer to have been a durable race horse of modest talents. His only notable achievement was the race at Foxfield, where he and Sean set a new course record. Last week Sean won the Maryland Million Steeplechase, on a day at Laurel Park when the purses total $1,000,000 (the jumper's share is quite modest). It was his 150th win, tying him for 10th overall, lifetime, with Dougie Small, a childhood hero.

I ask Sean about Jonathan Kiser. Jonathan, the year's leading rider at the time, was killed earlier this year when he fell off a rope swing at his family's home. Sean wrote a beautiful obituary in Steeplechase Times (Sean and his brother Joe founded the paper), in which he noted that Jonathan had quit school at 16 to ride, and that steeplechasing was his whole passion. Sean thinks a minute before answering:

*"Jonathan was the best, and everyone liked him. You've noticed that we all are wearing black helmet covers with J.S.K on them. But he thought of nothing but riding. I always worried what would happen to him when that was over. But I'd rather have that worry than what did happen."*

I have a final question in mind, but I fear the interview has taken too much of his time, and say so. The reply is quick:

*"Don't worry. I can talk forever."*

So I proceed, *"What is it about horses that draws you to them?"* Sean's answer is succinct:

*"It's the generosity of the horse. The pureness of them. They are peaceful, and people gravitate to them. They're honest. Any bad habits are usually man-made. [Then, almost wistfully] …It's so sad – so many human relationships are based on what someone wants. It's our underlying nature. Not so with the horse."*

### EPILOGUE

The Saturday after our meeting Sean was scheduled to ride Campanile, one of the favorites in the fourth race, the $250,000 Breeders Cup Steeplechase. In the third however, Sean's mount Indispensable fell and Sean was injured. In the fourth Campanile finished last without him. Three weeks later Sean came back at Camden, with two wins – one of them on Indispensable – and a second in three tries. He retired at the end of the year with 152 career wins, tenth on the all-time list.

## - Coming Back -

A few weeks ago, at the Warrenton Point-to-Point, Gus Brown rode White-wood Farm's Loughbed Rambler to a not-surprising win in the open timber race. Gus was, after all, twice the NSA's leading rider, and now has over 100 career wins to his credit. There aren't many Pennsylvania-based professionals riding at Virginia Point-to-Points, and Whitewood horses have until recently been suffering from a long absence from the winner's circle. So I was curious about the horse-rider hookup. As Gus tells it:

*"I grew up at Kinlock Farm near The Plains, where my Dad handled hunters, show horses, race horses, a bit of everything. George Ohrstrom's Whitewood Farm was a couple of miles away, and when I was 12 Dad and John Coles arranged for me to work there in the summer and on weekends.*

*"For my last three years of high school I studied at home so I could work*

*seven days a week at Whitewood. Two days after my 16th birthday I started riding novice races on the flat for Mr. Ohrstrom, but I never won, and in due course I moved to Pennsylvania. After Richard Valentine started training at Whitewood Mr. Ohrstrom said to Richard 'Put Gus on the horse,' and eventually I won for them on Wesley Chapel.*

*"This year, at Aiken , I won my 100th race on Whitewood's Michele Marieschi. If I had to picture my 100th win it would have been for Mr. Ohrstrom and Richard Valentine. Growing up on the farm I saw how much George Ohrstrom did for the kids that came and went. I'm truly blessed to have the experience of knowing him."*

Gus Brown and Loughbed Rambler at Warrenton

Before the Warrenton win Gus had spent several weeks in England, catching rides where he could, and has this to say about that experience:

*"England was phenomenal, such a different life style. The level of professionalism is high and they put the horse first. The most ignorant English fan knows more than our well-informed ones do. In the pub at night the English talk about horses with the same depth of understanding that Americans would about the NFL playoffs.*

*"While there, I think I rode well, but not on very good horses."*

The reason? There is a surplus of riders in England, the purses are small, and the trainers make sure their regular riders get the best shots. Gus continues:

*"The English are a very generous, accommodating people, and I got a lot of help. I had eight rides total, two of them great although I didn't win. But I felt like a winner with what I gained from it… The sport in England is about the horse and the everyday guy."*

Gus's return from England has coincided with a comeback for Whitewood.

The Ohrstrom family – the senior generation includes George and his sister Maggie Bryant – has raced horses over jumps forever, it seems, scanning the previous winners listed in race programs. But for quite a spell Whitewood wins were scarce. Now, by late April they have already had five sanctioned wins, six more at Point-to-Points, and one training race win on the flat. Some people have told me the Whitewood renaissance started when Richard took over in 1996, so I asked him about it.

*"Last year [2002] we missed the chance to train in the south, and we won only two races. This year we went down to Camden. That made a difference."*

*George Ohrstrom*

Then, indicating his two exercise riders – Jill Waterman, an experienced race rider, and Alice Clapham, who *"comes from an eventing dynasty – these girls have been a great help."*

George Ohrstrom has for some time been plagued with a debilitating illness that has left him wheel chair-bound and with great difficulty speaking, though his mind remains first class. The other day I congratulated him on the recent Whitewood wins – one at our expense – and his whole face lit up with pleasure. Richard comments:

*"Horses are the thing that picks his head up."*

Changing the subject, I ask, *"But you don't have a regular 'house' jockey?"*

*"No. But we get good riders. People love riding for Mr. Ohrstrom. Gus and Chip Miller are good friends, that helps. And Mr. Ohrstrom got a great kick out of Woods Winants riding Bowman's Crossing in the Maryland Hunt Cup, and Gus winning his 100th on Michele Marieschi."*

Then Edie and I pile into Richard's "off road" SUV, along with three dogs, and drive up through a series of high meadows to where the girls will gallop a pair of horses. The sun is out, the air is fresh, the view is superb and the horses love running through the fields and over the fences laid out for their training. Richard adds:

*"We have an aerator and a roller, so the ground is good."*

Richard is tall, young, intelligent and articulate. He clearly knows his

———

business, but there must be more than a good trainer and beautiful fields behind the burst of Whitewood's success.

Research gives some hints. Six horses have run this year under the Whitewood silks. All but Bowman's Crossing are between six and eight, prime ages for jumpers. Perhaps the best, Michele Marieschi, is just coming into his own at six. Whether home-bred or purchased, every horse is either from Europe, or out of a French or English mare and by a sire with success on the grass. George knows how the right breeding will improve his odds.

Now, when his spirit needs it most, the effort is paying off. Our only regret is that we have to run against Whitewood. Does anyone know where we can find a nice young French jumper – cheap?

*Alice Clapham and Jill Waterman galloping horses*
*in the high fields of Whitewood Farm*

PHOTO BY THE AUTHOR

*Practice makes perfect*
*Schooling for a show under the eyes of groom and trainer*

"Why do I like horses?

"It's the beauty of the animals, and the love and affinity I have for them. I show them for those two minutes when you are one with the horse in an effortless ride. I love their personalities. I've had the arrogant horse, the punk, the sweet one – they're all different."

—Pam Dudley, amateur show hunter owner and rider, commenting on her sport

———

Showing horses is perhaps the horse sport enjoyed by the greatest number of participants in Virginia. In what the telephone company calls "The Piedmont Regional Calling Area" – roughly from Leesburg and Winchester south to Orange – there are at least a dozen hunter-jumper events each month that are listed in the magazine *Horse Talk*. There are many more not listed, held by Pony Clubs, riding stables and other less formal groups.

It is impossible to cover this vast expanse of activity comprehensively in a single chapter, so we have selected a spectrum of four events to represent the genre and convey its flavor and its mood: St. Peter's, an informal junior event; Warrenton, a rated but locally oriented show; A-rated Upperville, including its Grand Prix jumping; and the new Grand Prix at Great Meadow.

## – St. Peter's Horse Show –

On the last weekend in May Nancy Dillon's Chimney Hill Farm becomes a Child's Garden of Horses (apologies to Robert Louis Stevenson) when the St. Peter's Schooling Show takes place for the benefit of St. Peter's Church. The show is part of an organized group – the Short Circuit Horse Show Association, membership $10 per year, no admissions committee interview required.

CHILCOTE FAMILY PHOTO

*Pinning the class*

Chimney Hill is not easy to find, at least if the breakfast table directions are, loosely summarized, "somewhere northeast of the corner of Route 611 and the Snickersville Pike." After bumbling around in this region, between corn fields, cut hay and overbuilt subdivision houses, I set out by dead reckoning to the hamlet of Philomont. There, in the general store cum post office, a kindly man behind the counter

*Sam Chilcote*

interrupts the sale of coffee to a policeman to help me.

> *"Go thata way,* [he points to his left, whence I had come] *...second left, sign says 'Horse Show,' you can't miss it. Must be a million and a half cars."*

His directions prove precise, his car count excessive by about 1,499,930. But we are there. By chance the rail fence I belly up to is at the entrance of the upper ring, where there will be three classes each for the categories of:

- Lead-line • Pre-Short Stirrup • WARM UP – 18" • Beginner • Young Entry Equitation • Baby Green Pony.

The Pre-Short Stirrup Division is just ending. A small bespectacled boy on a tiny pony emerges from the ring through the gate next to me. His pony is wearing a huge Championship rosette, its long blue, red, and yellow ribbons almost trailing on the ground. In addition to a large hunt cap and appropriate shirt, jacket and jodhpurs the rider is clad in a huge smile. A shrill young voice emanates from among the crowd of ponies, riders, parents and coaches awaiting the next class:

> *"Good job, Sam. You earned that one!"*

I am soon to learn that *"good job"* is the most used phrase of the day, applicable as much to those who tried but finished last as it is to victors such as Sam.

---

Judging by the crowd of young girls waiting for their turn at WARM UP – 18" ( the number apparently designates the height of the WARM UP jumps) the win by a boy is statistically unlikely, and so to be treasured.

Next to me, over the fence, is a sleepy bay pony named Wanoon, and his rider Katy. Katy is properly dressed in a dark jacket, her outfit topped by what seems like a huge hunt cap. I am reminded of days years ago coaching a group of large, visored baseball caps, under each of which it was possible for a discerning eye to discover a small boy with a baseball mitt.

Katy and her friends all seem to have their hair braided into two pigtails, each tied with a bow of bright ribbon. I ask Katy about her show experience.

CHILCOTE FAMILY PHOTO

*Lauren Hair*

*"This is my second show."*

*"Ever get a ribbon?"* I ask.

*"No."*

*"Maybe today."* She smiles.

Katy explains that Wanoon is one of Nancy's ponies (all the kids call her Nancy), and that most of the others are too. Katy turns to her friend Hannah mounted next to her to explain some detail of the WARM UP course, and Nancy notices me and comes over.

The maestro of Chimney Hill is a lean, weathered woman of uncertain age, quiet spoken and seemingly unflappable. She is clearly the role model, probably the heroine, for the young that chatter with each other and with her as they await their turns in the ring. Nancy exudes calm, confidence, enthusiasm and encouragement, qualities instantly transmitted to those around her. She seems to know exactly why I am there as she welcomes me, so I ask, thinking of Wanoon *"How many horses do you have on the farm?"*

*"I don't know. I was a math major in college but I don't know how many*

horses I have." [She seems pretty precise, though, on the number of her grandchildren – six.]

*"You see that little girl in the blue jacket over there? That's one of mine. She's four, she's going in the walk, trot, and canter this afternoon."*

Across the ring there is a pick-up truck parked along the rail. In its bed the judge is sitting in a folding chair, scoring what is going on. Nancy turns to her charges...

*"Hannah, have you got the course?"*

*"Yeah."*

To another:

*"Be sure to keep your reins up. Don't look at us at all... Keep her on the base, then she won't outjump you."*

I notice two girls not in riding clothes, but mingling in the mix of ponies and riders – *"Those girls aren't riders?"*

*"They're Greer and Louise Chapman. They're here to support their friends. They ride, but they're not ready just yet to show."*

A lady nearby overhears us, and introduces herself:

*"I'm Martha Chapman, their mother. Our daughter Bess is an acolyte at Trinity Church. And we have a Halloween trail ride for kids each fall."*

I should have recognized a fellow parishioner, but then we go to the eight o'clock service, and most young families go at eleven. Nancy has 40-50 kids coming to her at any one time, perhaps 20 of which are regulars who often help out with the novices. She adds:

*"I've probably taught a thousand. And every pony here we broke and trained. We don't go to a lot of shows, we mostly do hunting."*

Then Katy enters the ring, and Nancy says:

*"This kid just learned to jump two weeks ago."*

Katy finishes, her round marred by the fact she trotted between jumps. As she exits Nancy explains:

*"You trotted because you made the turn too sharp. You have to come to the fence. I'm telling you this so you'll learn."*

Her voice is kind. Then she turns to the child about to go in...

*"You have to ride this pony in. She's a little bit herd-bound to the other ponies."*

———

A red-haired freckle-faced lady comes up – Kim Hurst, Katy's mother. As we are talking they award the ribbons, and we hear:

*"Second, # 609, Wanoon, ridden by Katy Hurst."*

Hannah gets fifth, and there are *"good jobs"* all around.

Katy dismounts so her sister Jessa, #610, can get on Wanoon. Nancy adjusts the stirrups while Katy tightens the girth. At the gate for the next class – I think it is "Pre-Short Stirrup" walk, trot – Nancy is talking to #485, her four year old granddaughter, Haley Alcock. Her parting comment:

*Katy and her red ribbon*

*"Get your heels down."*

Then we watch Haley go, posting properly when she trots, but looking all around at the crowd. Quickly the results are in. Haley gets a pink ribbon. Nancy:

*"At least she beat one."*

Silently I wonder if she expected more of a Dillon – even if the class was for up through nine year-olds.

Looking back one can see Katy and Hannah inspecting the posted course diagrams, which Katy is explaining. Are we looking also at a budding teacher – or executive? Then the class is over, the one in which Katy's sister rode Wanoon. The six participants emerge, carrying their ribbons. Jessa's is green, sixth, and she is having tear trouble. Katy consoles her:

*"Good job."*

Soon both girls are smiling. Katy explains to me later:

*"Last time she got a third and I didn't get anything. I know how she feels."*

As I am taking in the scene there is a commotion in the lower ring, where the more advanced riders are competing. A bridle-less horse is galloping madly around, while his ex-rider is dusting herself off by a jump. As you by now would expect, Katy has the story:

*"It was Nan and Mono. Nan is my friend, Mono is a horse. She kicked him right after going over the jump. He stepped on the reins and pulled off the bridle. Mono is normally very, very good."*

He is also soon caught, and no one is hurt. In another class, a girl enters the ring, loses concentration, goes off course, and is dismissed. Graham Alcock, Haley's father, sighs…

*"It's all a learning experience."*

The mood of the parents is healthily relaxed. As the girl leaves the ring someone says:

*"There you go. Head up, shoulders back."*

I half expect to hear Katy say *"good job."*

Nancy has told me to get the program and the tag that outlines the Dillon philosophy, and so it's time to go to the secretary's table located behind the judges' pickup truck. On the way I pass an older girl carrying a coat hanger holding six ribbons in order – blue, red, yellow, white, pink, green. Nancy explained that the ribbons awarded are "recycled" from the collections of others, I suspect mostly her own. The ribbon carrier's hat says "Barn Kid."

We pass a man shooting pictures, with a little boy tagging along. The boy turns out to be Sam, now out of uniform. I admire the man's camera and long lens. He is not a professional but he shoots a lot at horse shows. Sam, who has his own camera, is candid:

*"My dad burns up a lot of film. …I took pictures of Mackenzie – she's my friend. Willie is the horse."*

Willie and Mackenzie have won a red. Probably it was Mackenzie that said *"good job"* when Sam was awarded his big ribbon.

At the secretary's stand I collect the written material. Entries will exceed 350 today; they are still coming in. Nearby is a kitchen, manned by two gray-haired ladies, set up in the farm house garage. I ask, *"How many people do you serve?"*

[First lady]: *"We should have kept count."*

———

CHILCOTE FAMILY PHOTO

*Mackenzie Canard on Willie*

[Second lady]: *"We can't even count well enough to make change."*

But she does, precisely. As I sit on a tack box under a tree to eat my barbecue sandwich, two tiny girls, one in jodhpurs, play around their mother, whose appearance suggests they will soon have a new sibling. Nearby their father, a farmer by his clothes, talks with friends. (I learn later that the farmer is Neal Dillon, and that the expectant lady is Neal's wife Becca. The jodhpured child is Nancy's granddaughter Gracie.)

As I am eating, an anachronism, a boy in a gray and red baseball uniform, strolls by. On its front his uniform is emblazoned "PHILLIES." On its back, in smaller letters, one reads "MOUNTAINEER PIPE CORP." Possibly he has given up riding, tired of losing to girls in horse shows.

Behind the one and a half story stone farm house is a fenced-in swimming pool, and further back, an old wooden barn surrounded by paddocks, one of which slopes away to a pond. Woods on all sides hold at bay the unrelenting development that is replacing annual crops of tall corn with a crop of much taller and more permanent houses.

The barn area is a center of activity. There are a number of saddle racks

269

and nine tie-up stations for grooming and tacking up horses. Several girls and a lone boy are at work with their animals. A friendly, freckled girl of fourteen – Kristin Dillon – gives me a tour. As we visit the horses I ask her about her riding.

> *"I rode a four year old paint today – no ribbon. But I also ride in pony races. Won at Old Dominion. Third at the Gold Cup. And we've won the family class several times at Upperville."*

The fact is that six or so Dillons have proven almost unbeatable for years in that particular venue. Kristin continues

> *"I don't care that much for the competition. I just do it for the fun."*

In the barn we meet Mistique Bear Tracks, a paint horse with little marks all over him that gave rise to his name. Outside is a pretty bay animal – *"Master Key. He just made a horse."* – by which she means that he has grown beyond the 14.2 hand limit that determines whether an equine is classified as a pony

*Katy and Jessa Hurst working on Wanoon's tack*

or a horse. This promotion is not a financial triumph, as the market for large and pretty ponies is strong, but prices are far less for under-sized horses. My guess is that Nancy Dillon doesn't care. After all, by Kristin's count…

*"We have 66 horses and ponies."*

As I drive away from Chimney Hill Farm there is an enameled sign on a tree by the road at the edge of the woods. It says, in large letters:

STEWARDSHIP FOREST

Further down the road, beyond the farm's boundaries, there are new houses under construction. Any forest that preceded them is gone.

And here is the tag that Nancy was anxious that I have:

**St. Peter's Horse Show**

S taring at the jump
T o get a perfect stride,
P reparing to give reign with
E quitation while I ride.
T o win is not important,
E ven though it makes it fun.
R eserve or maybe Champion
'S ymbolizes a job well-done!

H appily we welcome you to
O ur annual event.
R ibbons awarded were won before
S urrounded by memories to be
E njoyed again.

S urely horses are God's own treasure
H aving been given to us from above.
O nly made by the Father's hands
W ere these creatures He sent us to love.

- The Dillon Family
2002

– *Warrenton* –

The Warrenton Horse show takes place on Labor Day weekend and this year marks its 103rd anniversary. Next to Upperville, it is the most significant event of its kind in Northern Virginia. Yet it differs greatly, starting with its length – four days versus seven. And Warrenton's entire Saturday program is devoted to breeding stock, draft animals, and a special division for Cleveland Bay hunters – essentially the purpose for which Richard Dulany founded Upperville in 1853. There are 17 Futurity classes (not counting the special Virginia Thoroughbred Association exhibition of future race horses), divided by sex, age, and Thoroughbred from non-Thoroughbred, followed by two for "Full Draft" animals, and four for Cleveland Bays.

Entries in the breeding classes are, according to the program, *"To be judged on conformation, quality, substance and suitability to become or produce hunters. Broodmares and foals to walk; yearlings, two year-olds and three year-olds to jog."*

Most will be led in and exhibited by professional handlers, some of whom may have more trouble with the "jog" bit than their charges.

On other days Warrenton has the traditional classes – from leadline to side saddle to hunters and jumpers, to Master's Class and Hunt Teams, but today the emphasis is on breeding fine animals for the future of the sport.

After each paying the five dollar admission fee and parking we are in the immediate presence of horse trailers and horses. The mood of

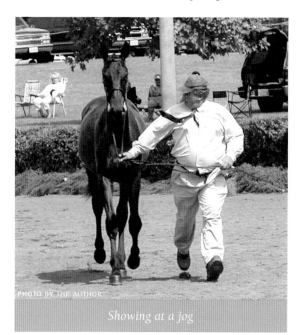
*Showing at a jog*

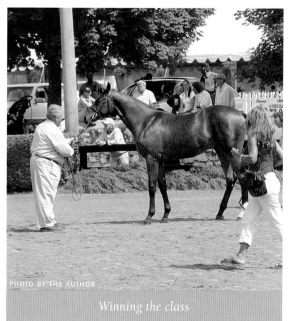
*Winning the class*

Warrenton is relaxed, a country event engaged in by area residents – with occasional visitors. The crowd, the pressure, the tension of a major horse show are blissfully muted.

Mary Ann Gibbons is here with her yearling filly, Love and Glory, ready to be shown. Mary Ann is a close friend, and as a horse person's "spouse of" I ask about her husband, *"Is Jack here?"*

*"Of course not."*

Mary Ann is quick to reply. Horses are Mary Ann's thing, not Jack's. I ask, *"Well, how about if I interview you?"*

*"Oh no, you're not going to. I don't know a thing."*

*"But why do you like horses?"*

*"I've always loved horses, always had one. I like them for their elegance, grace, their personalities – how they interact with each other. I love to watch them. And I love ponies and children. I bought my first horse with*

*my first $200, and the family didn't know it. My mother rode a bit, but my grandfather was a big horseman. He had steeplechase horses and was on the equivalent of the US Polo Team. His name was Walter Scott Hobart, from San Mateo, California. I still race under his colors."*

So much for the "non-interview." Of course we already know a lot about Mary Ann: how she has two or three Thoroughbred mares that she breeds to regional stallions, how she fusses with them and their babies in her paddocks and small stable near The Plains, and that she has a nice young filly running at Charles Town.

Here at Warrenton, a bit later, Love and Glory leaves the ring, accompanied by a fourth place white ribbon and Charlie Brown, who showed her. Charlie comments:

*"She's a right nice filly, should have been* [placed] *a little higher."*

I ask: *"Is Mary Ann going to run her?"*

*"That's what she says. But not until she's three, though."*

Charlie and I then reminisce on the Hard Scuffle Stakes at Churchill Downs in 1999, when we were on the same plane going to Louisville. There his traveling companion, horse owner Charlie Strittmatter, saw his underdog Popular Gigolo win that big race, the first leg of the steeplechase triple crown. (Our own underdog, Devil's Reach, finished tenth.)

Later Mary Ann concurs with Charlie:

*"That horse pinned ahead of her wasn't properly groomed or anything."*

Relax, Mary Ann, that's what races are for – not for who's best groomed but for who comes in first. I'm sure Mary Ann appreciates that, but like most of us she hates to lose, whatever the game.

PHOTO BY THE AUTHOR

*Mary Ann Gibbons with her filly, Love and Glory*

Next we run into Charley Matheson. He extends his left hand in greeting – his right arm and shoulder not yet fully recovered from a horse-related barn accident last spring. Charley is a driving enthusiast whose interest in that ancient pastime has led him into breeding Cleveland Bays and crossing Cleveland Bays with Thoroughbreds to create fine field hunters. With Charley are his associate in the breeding operation, Marty Venburg, and a large yearling, a Thoroughbred – Cleveland Bay cross, that Marty will show for the gelding's new owner. My immediate reaction is *"That's a very big yearling!"* Charley concurs:

> *"Yes, I suspect he'll be 17 hands. He'll be a hunter. Personally I don't want driving horses bigger than 16.2. Everyone wants a five year-old made hunter – you can get a lot for them. The trouble is, someone has to spend the time to make them, so they're scarce."*

The large yearling is shown, and does not place high. Charley is philosophical:

> *"The judges lean towards the Thoroughbred look, even in the non-Thoroughbred classes."*

But Charley's time will come. He has three horses here for the Cleveland Bay Division later in the day – *"probably after dark,"* observes Charley. And there is a special Cleveland Bay event down at his operation at Montpelier next weekend – horse auction, show, and benefit dinner. I ask, *"Are you the largest Cleveland Bay operation in America?"*

> *"I guess so. We bred 18 mares this past season."*

Meanwhile Edie is touching base with old friends – Mark Deane and Tommy Lee Jones, the show manager – among them. As we leave we pass by a pretty gray three year-old in a cooler, standing sleepily in the warm-up ring. His handler explains:

> *"There's six more classes to go before his, but the stalls here are small, and he's big, and he gets cast\* in them, so we decided it was better to wait out here."*

I ask, *"He seems relaxed. Has he done a lot of showing?"*

> *"Yes. He won as a weanling, as a yearling, and as a two year old. We're trying to make it four straight."*

About that time two weanlings also in the warm-up ring start cutting up, prancing, bucking, and generally giving their handlers a hard time. The "old"

---

\* A horse is said to be **cast** when he lies down and then is unable to get his legs under him to get up because of the interference of an adjacent object such as a wall or fence. In the panic that occasionally follows some animals injure themselves.

boy snoozes on, oblivious
to the youthful foolishness
taking place behind him.
After all, he is now a graybeard – actually he has
been for most of his life –
and it's six classes to his
moment of truth.

Along the rail

Overnight it rains, but it is
only drizzling by noon, so
we go back to the show.
The program today includes hunter classes and the Ladies Side Saddle Division.

The ring is muddy, with occasional puddles. Most horses handle it well, but
as we watch one objects to a fence, stopping so abruptly that he projects his
pink-coated rider over the jump while remaining on the take-off side himself,
watching the flight of his passenger, and the effect of gravity and mud on the
pink coat. Proceedings are interrupted for a few minutes while the rider
checks himself for damages – none – and the fence is put back together –

A last minute check of the instructions

*Joseph Keusch jumping*

easily. The jumps for these hunter classes are not imposing, though in the jumper classes held Friday evening they were substantial. For all its atmosphere of informality the show attracts a competent crowd of horses and riders, and is rated at the "C" level by both the Virginia and the Maryland Horse Show Associations.

After touring the on-deck area – a mélange of horses, riders and mud – we mingle in with a festive crowd whose casual approach to showing creates a relaxed atmosphere not found at the very large professionally oriented events. At Warrenton, many if not most horses are trailered in for the day, usually attended to by their riders or rider's relatives. Few paid grooms are in evidence.

Again, we find many acquaintances among the crowd. Edie's Fairfax Hunt is out in force to cheer on members Joseph Keusch and Heidi Stirrup who are riding.

As if the Fairfax group needed an excuse for a party there is a birthday cake for Chuck Borchetta, a new member, and singing to go with it. As one would expect, a knot of children gathers around the cake and helps cut it.

Joseph, his round finished, joins the crowd, remarking:

*"Did you see that crow perched on the top rail of that jump?"*

He points at the nearest fence.

*"Yes, but he flew off when you came up to it."*

*"I know; it startled me, but it didn't bother the horse at all."*

Horses that live outdoors in Virginia see hundreds of crows on fences every day.

Other groups are collected along the rail, and clusters of spectators are seated or standing on a small hillside overlooking the ring, a crowd not unlike that at a Point-to-Point. Halfway around the ring, past the small grandstand, I visit with John Zugschwert and John and Penny Denegre, MFH of the Middleburg Hunt. Nearby is a box in which friends Pam and John Wooley are part of an otherwise unfamiliar group.

*Pam and John Wooley*

The largest entertainment tent is sponsored this year by the Old Dominion Hunt, and the loudspeaker invites all at the show to enjoy the food and potables.

Later, taking up the invitation and talking to Old Dominion members we learn that the hunts in the area take turns serving as hosts at the Warrenton Horse Show.

The Warrenton message seems to be *"Come and have fun watching us have fun too."* Warrenton is the kind of crowd that if you didn't know them all you'd like to.

# – The Upperville Colt and Horse Show –

The Upperville Colt and Horse Show started in 1853 with two classes, one for colts and one for fillies, competing for silver trophies crafted by Tiffany.

Now it lasts seven days, with about 1100 horses entered in 205 individual classes. Classes are grouped into Divisions of up to five classes each, organized by category, age, size, and experience of the horse and in some cases the age and professional or amateur standing of the rider. They range from a leadline class for children three and under to Grand Prix jumping by Olympic veterans and hopefuls.

PHOTO BY KELLY MEISTER. COURTESY OF HARRY HUBERTH

*Harry Huberth winning the Invitational Hack (Veterans) Class*

Hunter Divisions are the most numerous category, each Division consisting of a variety of tests over fences and on the flat. They account for half the classes at Upperville. Most of the action takes place across the road from the Piedmont Point-to-Point racecourse, with two show rings and two schooling areas spread under the grove of ancient oak trees. An old covered wooden grandstand flanks the main ring on one side, while on the others a number of ringside parking places are designated for subscribers.

Outside this central area are eight large stable tents, each with numerous stalls, some of which serve as tack rooms or grooming areas for the contestants. To the north, across Route 50, are two rings for jumping competitions, two schooling areas and four more huge stable tents, three of them colored in a blue and white striped pattern.

Intermingled with the competition areas and the tents are perhaps 50 commercial activities – booths selling everything from hot dogs and sodas to tack, horse trailers, old horse books, stuffed horse toys, riding clothes, and art *objets*

*Jumping in front of the old grandstand*

to suit many tastes and pocketbooks. There is a blacksmith's stand, a tack repair trailer, and an agency for the golf carts used for quick transportation around the premises. One vendor will videotape of your round so you can have proof it was better than the score the judge awarded it. You can also show it to your friends at cocktails, along with the ribbon you won.

The horse trailers are particularly noteworthy, whether for sale or already owned and in use. The larger ones not only transport horses, but some provide dressing rooms and even living quarters for the support people necessary to campaign a string of horses. Few people lavish more care on the decor and maintenance of their homes than do the trailer owners on their vehicles and accompanying tack boxes – large trunks often emblazoned with farm name and colors.

Upperville Show competitors range from very small children on ponies to professionals with international reputations. In seven days there is something for everyone. Many exhibitors spent most of the prior week showing at Devon, Pennsylvania. A week hence they will be in Atlanta, or at Ox Ridge in Darien, Connecticut. Points earned by performance in these A-rated shows can qualify one for the fall indoor circuit, culminating in the National Horse Show in New York.

Leadline at Upperville

PHOTO BY ANITA BAARNS

## – Upperville 1999 –

Some months ago Edie learned that the late Theo Randolph had created an award for a young horse person who gave promise of future success in the field. Foxhunting involvement would be weighted heavily. So Edie nominated Jacob Puleo, who was whipping in for Fairfax. Last week we heard from Tommy Lee Jones that Jacob had won, and was to receive his award at noon on Saturday at the Horse Show.

Because of the large number of entries and the Saturday crowd, the show program has fallen behind schedule, so we watch a couple of lead-line classes before Jacob is at bat. The first is for two and three year olds. There must be fifteen tiny contestants, almost all properly attired and each sitting on a fat pony. The ponies are led at a walk around the ring while the judges attempt to find some criteria to separate the competitors into winners and losers.

(Actually there will be no losers, because after the first five ribbons every one else will get a green sixth place ribbon.)

In some cases the person leading the pony, presumably a seriously competitive parent, is aided by another walking along side to secure the small novice to the saddle. One contestant had two such out-walkers, one on each side. Another was equipped with what Mary Clark called a "stopper" in his mouth – to me it looked like a baby's blue pacifier. A third wore a wild west suit with a cap gun. Presumably these accouterments helped the judges narrow the field to those able to handle it with a single adult and conventional riding garb. But then, every rider can say in later years that he/she has been showing since two years old, and one of them will remember clearly that...

*"I won at Upperville when I was three."*

The four to six year-old class, even larger, is enlivened by one boy severing connections with his mount. In this class the second place finisher was last year's winner. Lead-line competition is getting tougher every year.

Finally it is Jacob's turn. He is called to the center of the ring, while his fans watch from the rail. Edie's letter of nomination is read over the loud speaker. Jacob is handed a silver trophy and an envelope.

PHOTO BY ANITA BAARNS

*Jacob Puleo, Whipper-in, Fairfax Hunt*

Pictures are taken. The trophy is taken back by the Indian-giving presenter, but Jacob keeps the envelope and presumably the check therein. His dozen fans applaud vigorously as he returns, smiling, to them.

Everyone else is otherwise engaged. Jacob may well be the most accomplished and rounded young horseman on the grounds, but there are probably a hundred others, each of whom believes that he or she is. For confirmation, just ask their parents.

*- Taking a Break -*

On Friday night we attend the Firestone's garden party, a frequent adjunct to the Upperville Show, in which the Firestones, both Diana and daughter Alison, are regular participants. The Firestones live at the very top of the local horse world. Not only is Alison a fine rider and a strong contender for a place on the US Equestrian Team, but Bert and Diana, as noted earlier, were the breeders and owners of Genuine Risk, one of only three fillies to win the Kentucky Derby.

Their Newstead Farm is located, as the crow flies, just one farm removed from our Trappe Hill. We arrive rather early, as does our friend and vet, Dr. Gary Spurlock. Gary remarks that he thinks this year's crop of Trappe Hill yearlings is special. We allow as how...

> *"We hope the auction buyers agree with you."*

From the valet parking dismount area one goes through a gate into a tiered and walled garden sloping down to a landscaped pond. Two large tents house dining tables and adjacent bars. We do not remember tents in former years, and with the dry June day they prove unneeded.

On the way to the first drink we run into Connie Rucker and Jerry Hall. Jerry, as manager of Foxlease farm, is an across-the-road neighbor of Newstead, but we have known him and Connie as cattle people, not horse lovers. We are glad to see them, and even more delighted to learn that they are engaged to be married.

The next contact is also a surprise – Charley Waddell, our former state senator. Charley is introducing his son-in-law, Mark Herring, who is running for county supervisor . His platform is "slow growth", so we are supportive. "Slow growth" is now in fashion politically; we pray the fashion lasts through election day.

As the crowd builds to well over one hundred we note a lot of young – mostly show people from away – mixed in with familiar faces such as the Wilsons, Ben-Dovs, Gay Estin and George Beavers. We are especially glad to see Bill and Susie Katz. Bill has been recovering from a serious auto accident – he wasn't driving – and is just starting to get out and about.

As usual we are a bit late joining the buffet line, and eventually find two vacant seats at a table otherwise occupied by a trainer from North Carolina, four of his girl clients, his wife and young daughter, and a stray boyfriend of one of the riders. The group has done pretty well at the show, their combat is now over, and we have a relaxed, fun time with them. At one point I ask the trainer's daughter, Sarah, how old she is, guessing out loud, *"Nine, or Ten?"* The prompt, definitive reply:

*"Ten!"*

*"How old do you think I am?"* It is a risky question. Sarah pauses, looking me over carefully in the dusk. Then,

*"Fifty-three."*

*"You're wrong by twenty-three years."* There is another pause. Then Sarah asks:

*"Up or down?"*

As the table breaks into hysterics, I glow. That little girl will go far, but by the time she does I really will be a bit long in the tooth.

## – *Upperville 2000* –

This year we decide to see the show during its mid-week sessions. Pulling into the gate marked "General Admission $5" we are greeted by a nice sandy haired lady who takes our money and points out a parking spot. Curious, I ask her, *"Why do you do this? Are you a volunteer?"*

*"Sort of. We get things like free lunch, and my son is manager of the show."*

*"Tommy Lee Jones?"*

*"Yes, he's my son."*

*"You look younger than he does!"* She assures us we can get back in this afternoon without paying again.

Mrs. Jones has been doing this for ten years, ever since she retired. The show benefits the Upperville Community Outreach and Upperville Volunteer Fire Department, which as its contribution runs a food stand near the main ring. Vilda Royer has for some years helped with the food service. She has told us about some of the other volunteers, one a lady of ninety who is still active helping her community.

Behind this group of front line helpers is a management structure of some depth. Pam Dudley, Vice President of the show, has this to say about the work that goes into putting it on:

*"Cathy Newman, a professional trainer and rider, is the unpaid President of the show's Board. Tommy Lee Jones reports to the Board of Directors, made up of local citizens with roots in the horse world. The Board meets monthly,*

*Lady jumping side saddle at Upperville*

*addressing such matters as capital improvements, selection of judges, insurance, trophies, and fee schedules, in some cases appointing committees to handle specific aspects.*

*"The land used by the show is made available by its owners without charge, with the show maintaining the grandstand and other improvements in accordance with Tommy Lee's wish list."*

Today the weather gods have smiled on the Upperville Colt and Horse Show. Blue skies dotted with cumulus clouds stretch from the Blue Ridge on the west nearby to the eastern horizon. The temperature drifts up from 65° in the morning to a high of around 80° later on.

As we enter we pass by the trailer and tent section of Mr. and Mrs. John Barker of Middleburg. The entry to their aisle of stalls is arranged as an open air tack room, surrounded by flower boxes on which Staci Young is putting the finishing touches. Later on there will be a contest for "best tack room", rivaling the tailgate contests at Point-to-Points.

Tommy Lee drives by in a tractor hitched to a watering cart, spraying the roadway to suppress the dust. Traffic runs heavily to electric golf carts, a

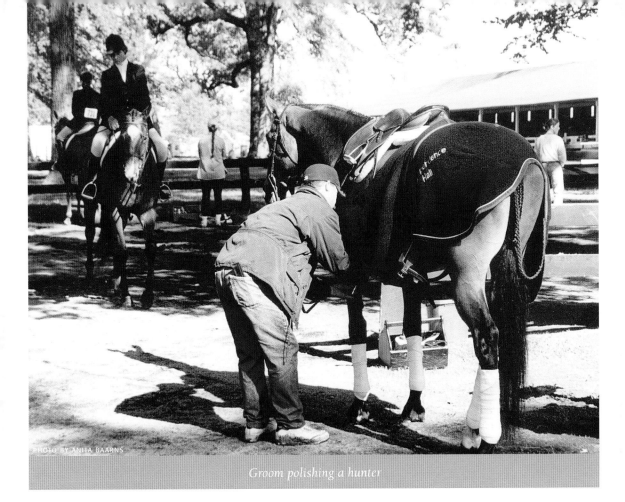

*Groom polishing a hunter*

painless, silent way to move quickly from stall to ring, but dangerous when a careless pedestrian crosses the path of an unobservant driver. In another nod to modernity, every second support person walking by – groom, trainer, exercise rider – seems to be talking into a mobile phone.

People less engaged in readying a horse for combat are often being led around on leashes by their dogs. Welsh Corgies and Yellow Labrador Retrievers are especially "in" this year; the once ubiquitous Jack Russell Terriers have been left at home, their temperament more suited to guarding the stable and killing rats than to calming horses. Just beyond the entry to the ring, on the way to the grandstand, we note a big sign that says "ABSOLUTELY NO HORSES BEYOND THIS POINT." Right beyond the sign are two show hunters, leisurely grazing, their reins held loosely by their guardians. No one seems concerned at this display of slack discipline – or illiteracy – take your pick.

Show hunters differ from the field variety used in foxhunting, though some may also participate from time to time in that rougher sport. Most tend to be more placid, less excitable, and of more perfect conformation than their country cousins. They lack the lean and hungry look of a much used field hunter. It goes without saying that the good ones are more expensive, and that they lead more sheltered lives. They are incredibly beautiful.

Overall, the feeling in the "on deck" area next to the entry gate is of gentle motion but without hurry, and of quiet, almost languid, purpose. The sun drifts down through the oak canopy, dappling the ground and the creatures under it. Voices are soft, subdued in the bright stillness of the day. Next to the ring, sleek hunters, trim riders, and attentive grooms wait patiently to be called to perform over the course laid out under the great oaks. Close by, a Mexican family blends into the scene, the father following instructions from his horse-owning employer, while his small children perch on the board fence, chattering softly in Spanish with their mother.

Despite this quiet ambiance one senses suppressed competitive tensions. Trainers review the course and tactics with their charges. Attendants polish every bit of the horse, tack and rider they can reach. Then it's into the ring to test the ability, training and teamwork of horse and rider, built up over hundreds of hours spent working to reach this moment. It is a picture worthy of Sir Alfred Munnings at his best, and the cover of the Show Program, by local artist Anita Baarns, shows the children and ponies of last year, surrounded by their handlers, in just such a setting.

PHOTO BY ANITA BAARNS

*Children waiting*

Winning at horse shows depends on approaching perfection in control and movement, a choreographed dance routine, rather than a mad scramble over fences in a race to beat exhaustion to a distant finish line. It is a contest of attention to detail, of patience and gentle grace, a test of emotional as well as physical control, rather than a test of speed, courage, and stamina.

Edie has now drifted off elsewhere to chat with friends. At the on-deck area I meet several show veterans. Kenny Krome is a trainer and rider from Maryland, but is spending this week nearby with the Ben-Dovs. Kenny reports he...

> "...has been doing this since I was eight. I guess I've ridden in every
> division of the show, including the Grand Prix jumping."

He does not mention "Lead Line" or "Ladies Side Saddle", however. This time

PHOTO BY ANITA BAARNS

*Clearing the green and white bars*

Kenny was placed second in the Handy Hunter class just finished, giving him sufficient points to win the Championship of his Division.

Nearby, Gary Baker, a friend of ours from steeplechasing, is advising local rider and trainer Tony Workman – or vice versa. Tony lives nearby in Hillsboro, Virginia, where he maintains a string of about 30 horses. He has a staff of four or five girls (or young women if you prefer), two of whom are at the gate, watching. Both have cell phones. I ask them about their jobs. They seem to like their work, but the words that stick in my mind are:

*"…and we don't have to muck out or anything!"*

My eye is taken by #532, a lovely horse called Mesmerize. We learn that he belongs to Mary Braga, and is being ridden by Patty Heuckeroth, a horse professional from Southern Pines, NC. Patty is busy grooming the horse, aided by a girl in riding breeches with a white tee shirt over her riding shirt.

As she finishes primping the horse it is time for Patty's round, and she turns in a good one. Then, after the last rider has finished, the best performers are called back into the ring for inspection by the judges and the awarding of ribbons. Soundness and conformation count, as well as performance, and so the horses must be examined close up. Mesmerize is called back first, and maintains that position to win the class, on his way to winning his Division Championship with a record of two firsts and two thirds in its four classes.

Mesmerize – not his registered name – came into the fold very soon after the day Patty and Mrs. Braga first saw him. That evening neither could forget him. According to Patty, Mrs. Braga called and said:

*"I can't get that horse out of my mind."*

*"Neither can I,"* replied Patty. So Mrs. Braga concluded:

*"I really don't need another one, but lets get him."*

And they did. And so he is called Mesmerize, for the spell he casts. As we part, Patty sums up her situation as a professional trainer and rider:

*"I've done it all my life. It's a living, and it's fun."*

Who could ask for more? Billy Abel-Smith, husband of our friend and equine advisor Mimi, appears and spies Pam Dudley arriving for the next class on a pretty horse. Turning back to me he observes:

*"That girl is one of the best. You know her?"*

Billy seems pleased that we do. We watch her two rounds. The first includes a refusal, the second is pretty good, but there will be no ribbon this time. Smiling optimistically, Pam observes:

*"He'll be OK. I was going too fast down the little hill in the ring, and got him too much on his forehand. It was probably my fault. He'll get better. He's a very nice horse."*

There's a lot of good sportsmanship on display at Upperville, though somewhere, hidden from the crowd, there may be tears as well. Show people are also human beings.

Now it is time for us to move on. Near the gate there is an officials' station where ponies are being measured for height to see whether they qualify for the Small, Medium, or Large Pony Division. Standing in line are a girl and her mother, the daughter Erin tall and slim, her physique currently clinging to both sides of the divide between child and young woman. We introduce ourselves to what we quickly find is a charming twosome, preparing to compete for the first time in a big show. The family lives near Haymarket, and the pony, Merrylegs, is boarded in a stable nearby.

Merrylegs was bought cheaply at the livestock auction in Marshall, for sale because the prior owners had trouble catching her in the field. Now she comes whenever Erin calls. Merrylegs is measured in at 13 hands, 3/4 inch, which qualifies her as a Medium Pony. Erin receives a paper to that effect. I ask Erin what she hopes for in the show.

*"To have fun."*

*"No, I mean do you have a particular ribbon in mind?"*

*"Not really; if I got one it would be wonderful."*

Erin is a true amateur, and a realist. The competition will be tough and experienced. She will ride in the afternoon, and I resolve to return to see her. Meanwhile it is time to rejoin Edie and go home for lunch.

Back an hour later, Mrs. Jones has a place for my car; Edie has opted for farm work. My wanderings take me by a trailer with the sign "Charlie's Tack Repair" from Hempstead, Maryland. Charlie is away on his golf cart making a house call, but his assistant, Beth Richards, is on duty. Above Beth, posted on the trailer wall, is a sign:

**IF YOU'RE GROUCHY, IRRITABLE, OR JUST PLAIN MEAN,**
**THERE WILL BE A $10 CHARGE FOR PUTTING UP WITH YOU**

A girl comes by with a broken boot zipper, which Beth decides the trailer lacks the equipment to fix. The girl leaves, and Beth is happy to visit for a bit. She has a Bachelor's degree in Math and Computer Science from Illinois, and a Master's from George Washington University in Telecommunications Engineering. Meanwhile, she is *"helping out Charlie, he's trying to retire."* I find out Beth spent five years in Germany, where she *"learned not to coddle horses."* Now she has a jumper, which her trainer has been showing. She explains:

*"The horse is strong and fit, and I'm not, because of time off to get the Masters. I need to get back in shape before I can show him."*

Then Beth comments on the other booths around the show:

*"They do a lot of business. Some people come to horse shows just to shop. I once took a horse show friend to see the Baltimore Orioles. Between innings we left our seats to get hot dogs and beer. A dog and a beer in hand, under the stands, my friend asked 'Where are the shops?' She was stunned, and disappointed, by my answer – 'There aren't any. This isn't a horse show.' "*

Near Charlie's tack trailer there is a tent booth named "The County Seat", which features fancy English saddles and related gear, and is "manned" by a nice blond English girl. She shows off a new type of curvy girth, designed to position the saddle a bit aft of normal, in the optimal spot for comfort of both horse and rider. The workmanship is superb, and the price reflects it. Defending the fancy price, she replies:

———

*"It's a new invention, hot off the press. We have the patent. You can't get one anywhere else."*

As she speaks, one is reminded both of the reason for Bill Gates' success, and that in Britain "patent" rhymes with "latent". Caught up in the shopping mood, I decide to get one of the new girths for Edie, just as soon as I can learn the proper size for her hunters. Then the subject changes to employment of immigrants: I ask, *"Do you have a Green Card?"*

*"No, but I have a work permit. I don't know about getting a Green Card. It's the next step, but it's lots of money and lawyers."*

Welcome to twenty-first century America.

At the auxiliary show ring the Local Medium Pony Hunter Class is just starting. Erin's fan club, ten strong, is resting in the shade, awaiting her effort. Members range from Grandma to mother, aunts, small cousins and neighbors. I decide to watch separately. Her first round is a bit rough. She gets in too close to the second and fourth fences, and stops the pony too soon at the end. But the second round is much improved. Her coach claps, and Erin smiles. No ribbon is likely, but the trend is upward. I tell Erin *"much better"*, and leave.

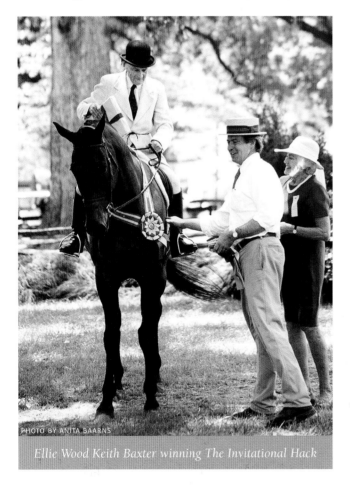

PHOTO BY ANITA BAARNS

*Ellie Wood Keith Baxter winning The Invitational Hack*

On the way out two ladies share their private horse show thoughts with me.

Anita White asks where Edie is. I tell her. She responds:

*"I'd rather be home spraying thistles, too."*

Jackie Eldridge, who is not riding, shares my view of competition exactly. She says:

*"Winning anything is fun."*

On this beautiful day many people who didn't get ribbons won anyhow.

Grand Prix jumping represents the pinnacle of the sport of show jumping. Some Grand Prix events are associated with horse shows, others held independently. At the top level less than a third of the horses are ridden by their owners, the sport being so difficult and the training and showing on the Grand Prix circuit so time-consuming that most riders are professionals. In this sense the horse-owner-trainer-rider relationship differs little from international level eventing, sanctioned steeplechase races or flat racing. And Grand Prix is widespread: there are 38 Grand Prix events scheduled in the US for July, 2002, 10 of them in the Mid-Atlantic states (including Virginia) and New England.

PHOTO BY PAT MACVEAGH

*Kim Frey on Bergerac*

Scoring is based on faults, the fewer the better. Pulling a bar costs four, refusals cost three for the first, six for the second, three refusals and you're eliminated. A maximum time is established for each course, above which each additional second costs one quarter fault in the initial round, one fault in a jump-off. Ties are broken in favor of the faster performance.

At a Grand Prix event the crowd is attentive, quiet and polite, clapping at the end of the effort of each contestant, even those that "voluntarily withdraw." A neophyte observer is struck by the intense concentration of the riders, the occasional apprehension in the eye of the horse, the huge and bizarrely colored jumps, the tight turns, the short – and slow – run-up to the jump, and the immense thrust of the horse's hind quarters as he (there are only a few mares in this game) takes off. A neighbor tells me:

> *"That's why so many are European warm bloods. They need that great big engine in the rear."*

---

291

## – Upperville Grand Prix –

The final Sunday of the Upperville Horse Show week is set aside for this purpose, with a $50,000 purse supplied by the day's sponsor, Budweiser. This year there are over 30 horses entered. A fine day draws a crowd of several thousand people. Just outside the ring's perimeter is a circle of boxes assigned to those who wish – and can afford – chairs and a front row view, plus a red ribbon denoting box holder status. Behind the western side of the ring and its boxes the land rises to form a spacious amphitheater where the general admission spectators can sit on the grassy slope, or on folding chairs they have brought, their children running loose, their dogs hopefully leashed, and their coolers and picnics spread out around them.

We enter at the southeast corner, immediately finding friend Jeanie Perin in her box, concealed under a straw hat and behind dark glasses, relaxing after the League of Conservation Voters benefit she put on last night for 300 people. Our casual attire is not amiss – Jeanie has selected blue cotton slacks and – at the moment – bare feet. Only the riders will be formally attired – black or scarlet jacket* (scarlet for past or present members of national equestrian teams), white breeches, hunt cap, white shirt and stock.

If one looks across the ring from the east side one sees the Blue Ridge rising above and far beyond the crowd on the grassy slope. Towards the north end of the slope is a large white tent, its three conical peaks gleaming in the June sun. Were this the field of Agincourt, the tent might be the headquarters of the French commanders, the Dauphin and the Constable of France, for it is too large to suit the battle-hardened and – according to Shakespeare – more democratically inclined King Henry the Fifth of England. But resident within the big tent there is indeed a King – Budweiser, The King of Beers – entertaining his many royally endorsed friends above this peaceful field.

To the south of the royal tent are the general admissions hordes, enjoying the almost-too-warm day. Among them a scraggly youth sets the nadir of the dress code, lying on his back, blue jeans perilously low, shirt off, gold earrings glittering, a series of black Chinese characters stenciled or tattooed on his sweaty, hairless chest. We are perhaps fortunate not to understand what they say.

From this vantage point one sees to the east a line of trees immediately behind the far boxes, screening a warm-up ring and the stable tents beyond. To the south are more boxes, behind them a huge television truck, and numerous vendor tents backed up to Route 50, no doubt relocated overnight from the main show grounds across the road.

But one's gaze is drawn quickly to the center of the action, the "lists" – oops, the "ring" – which holds 17 jumps of all shapes and sizes except easy. Horses and riders enter this arena by passing under a red and white banner emblazoned "Budweiser."

---

* In very hot weather it is sometimes permissible to eliminate the jacket.

PHOTO BY THE AUTHOR

Once inside, they find that the course designer's imagination has run wild, hoping to challenge each horse with something it has never seen before. One jump is a fake brick wall, behind which is one flanked by two large replicas of Orcas (killer whales), marine mammals infrequent in horse farm ponds. Two nearby red and yellow rail jumps have Monarch butterflies, with three foot wingspans, perched on the posts in a take-off position. A wingless green and white jump is only six feet wide, offering the lazy horse an invitation to skip it by passing to one side. The final fence is a solid red wood wall, topped by a red and white rail, and flanked by two 12-foot brown bottles decorated with the Budweiser label. They promise a reward for horse and rider as they complete their effort, and suggest an immediate option for thirsty spectators. Few if any fences are less than five feet high.

The prescribed course weaves through a complicated series of eight tight turns, three of them at 180 degrees or more, encompassing all 17 of the fences, some of which are placed so close together that there is only room for one stride between them. Maximum time allowed is about 85 seconds. The undulating ground at Upperville – most Grad Prix events are on the flat – and the highly "technical" nature of the layout make it a difficult test.

As horses and riders are introduced by the loudspeaker it is obvious from their credentials that this is a game at which most have excelled. We note only one rider entering his first Grand Prix, and his inexperience shows; he does not complete his round. Another contestant falls as the result of a refusal. Nothing except pride is hurt, but a bystander comments:

> *"That's show jumping. First you're soaring over a big fence, then you're lying flat on your face, inspecting real estate!"*

Another horse splashes through, instead of leaping over, the pool of water that is obstacle #8. A steward at the side of the pool waves a red flag while the splashed water is still sparkling in the air. Four faults. The horse must jump when you ask him to, whether he thinks it is necessary or not. Thinking is the rider's job. Jumping is his.

By this time I have settled into the box of Edie's cousin, Peter MacVeagh, and his wife Pat. Pat is a former show jumper, once competing at a modest level, but now an inveterate photographer of horse events, currently totally absorbed in her hobby. We chat briefly about enlisting her help in illustrating this book, then she returns to her camera. Peter, meanwhile, is keeping score. About half the horses have gone, and there are several tied at four faults, but there has been no clear round yet. If there is, those tied behind the zero-fault leader(s) will be placed in accordance with how quickly they completed the course.

---

With the exception of Alison Firestone, the riders' names are unfamiliar. No doubt many are from "away" and Grand Prix jumping is perhaps a sport apart, without the cross-connections one often sees among hunter-jumper exhibitors, steeplechasing, endurance riding, eventing, and foxhunting.

A horse named Gardenio enters the ring. Peter knows him from past exposure:

*"That's my horse!"*

Peter's excitement builds as Gardenio goes clean over fence after fence. Then comes the moment the four-fault club has feared. Gardenio completes a clean round. So later do Bergerac and Quintin. The fastest of the four-faulters must now settle for fourth; one rail pulled by jumping an inch too low in the first round will separate a possible first from perhaps eighth. A jump-off will decide the first three places.

The jump-off course has eight obstacles, again finishing with the three closely spaced one stride jumps and the beer bottles. The contestants are the three with perfect scores: Gardenio and Todd Minikus, Bergerac and Kimberly Frey, and Quintin and Candice King. King has been riding Quintin for only six months; the other two have had much more experience with their horses.

Gardenio goes first, and pulls a rail at the butterfly jump. The other two now can shoot at his four faults. Candice King is next, going cautiously, knowing that a clean though slow round will assure her of second, and that is what happens, as Kim Frey, from nearby Hume, also goes clean on the 13 year-old Bergerac, but in four seconds less than King, thereby winning.

Were he here today, Colonel Dulany would be surprised at and proud of his handiwork. The first Upperville show in 1853 had two classes. In 2002 there were over 50 division champions – typically four classes per Division, and 15 riders won leading rider awards in their category. Since Dulany's time the horse has made the transition from economic and military necessity to agent of pleasure without missing a beat in Virginia. He remains an object of affection and beauty, and a superior teacher of patience, responsibility, teamwork, and caring for others.

The surrounding countryside still retains the beauty of Dulany's day, despite modern pressures for change. The children of today will remember their time under the great oaks, and because of those memories will become the future guardians of the Colonel's vision. His Upperville Show still brings his community and the wider horse world together in a common endeavor providing sport, friendship, and fun for themselves, and support for a worthy cause.

May it always be thus.

A new local September fixture is described on its program cover as:

2ND ANNUAL GREAT MEADOW GRAND PRIX AND BLUE RIDGE WINE WAY WINE FESTIVAL,
FEATURING THE $100,000 MOORE CADILLAC HUMMER CLASSIC, AND
BENEFITING THE MEADOW OUTDOORS FOUNDATION FOR OPEN SPACE PRESERVATION

PHOTO BY THE AUTHOR

*Great Meadow row of merchants' tents. Large tent in rear is for wine tasting*

As a stand-alone event the organizers have made it a happening, with both a morning $10,000 Junior / Amateur jumping event, a wine tasting, tents housing booths of merchandise, opportunities for the public to walk the course with its designer, and to meet and get autographs from the winning riders. The "opening ceremonies," will take place just before the main event, featuring a rider galloping around the ring carrying Great Meadow's flag that flew over the Pentagon on 9-11.

We decide to explore Grand Prix from the inside, to meet and talk to the people behind the scenes, so our first stop is the stable tent.

Passing down an aisle we meet Jessica Saalfield tacking up Lavarro for the Junior / Amateur event. She owns her horse, as do most of the riders in this Division. We find her pleasant and polite but also tense and busy; with her approaching round her adrenaline is rising. We know how stomach butterflies feel, and we leave her to investigate a less pressured situation.

Near the stall of Rio (owner McLain Ward) is a baby parked in a stroller, who is being gushed over by a nice lady not his mother. We enjoy the baby momentarily and then move on, finding him unable to explain his connection to Grand Prix jumping. Further along is Kelly Strock of Somerset, Virginia, who works with La Rocca and his rider, Paul Matthews. Kelly is busy cleaning tack, but happy to talk:

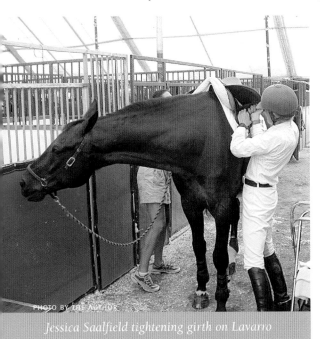
Jessica Saalfield tightening girth on Lavarro

*"I've been riding since I was nine. I went to Averett College and got a degree in Equestrian Studies and Business. Freshman year there were 35 girls and 2 guys in the class; when we graduated there were three girls and one guy. It got too hard, and they changed their minds when they saw how early they had to get up."*

Kelly figures she has been getting a lot of basic management experience, but isn't yet fixed on any particular career path:

*"I could run a business, or go in some other direction."*

Meanwhile she is focusing on getting La Rocca ready for the afternoon's Classic (where he will later finish among the also-rans). After the competition she is philosophical; there will be another day and her pay check does not depend on La Rocca's purses. Even in Grand Prix jumping almost no one can cover expenses with winnings.

In the next aisle two young girls, Bianca and Rachel, are talking together near a non-descript dog guarding a tack box by lying on it.

Kelly Strock

*Bianca, Rachel and Erica Valdivia*

*Collie Valdivia and Modra*

Rachel is the daughter of Linda Gordon, who is now riding in the Junior / Amateur; Bianca's mother and father are nearby. The mother, Erica Valdivia, tells me:

> *"My husband Collie and I take care of the horse, his name is Modra."*

She spells it for me. *"Where do you come from?"* I ask.

> *"From Mexico – Guadalajara."*

She has been working for 7-8 years in the US, for how long with her current employer, rider Barbara Bancroft, I do not learn.

Finally there is Cari Furze, a lady from Calgary who has just finished her round on Geneva, and is taking the tack off her mare. *"How did it go?"*

> *"Well, we had two rails down. But that's OK. We've never done a course that big before, but because of my rapport with her I thought we could do it."*

I ask her about the horse and her future plans. She answers as she takes the studs out of Geneva's shoes:

> *"She's a Dutch Warmblood – got her in Germany. We only have four horses now, so we take care of them ourselves. We're in the US for two months – two horses. I'm training with Joe Fargis – he got a gold medal in the 1984 Olympics. We're staying in Middleburg now, then we go to Florida."*

It is almost lunch time, but first the wine tasting. For this you need a blue ticket, which gets you into a line at the entrance to a big white tent at the far end of a line of vendors' tent booths. The man asks for identification – we are being carded for the first time in five decades. Fortunately we pass, and

PHOTO BY THE AUTHOR

*Susan Strittmatter*

each of us is given a small wine glass. Inside the tent there are eight vineyards represented, all from Virginia. Samples vary in quality, but are uniformly minuscule in size, no doubt a conspiracy with the twin objectives of saving money and avoiding civil disturbance.

We enjoy a happy encounter with our steeplechasing friend Susan Strittmatter, and then leave stone sober for our picnic lunch.

Unfortunately the ring and spectator areas are so positioned that photographing the jumping will be hard. The problem is solved when Leslie gives me a green "press" ribbon – we are after all writing a book – and suitable areas become available. The rest of the story is best told in pictures…

*The feature event opens with a parade of the flag*

*Contestants school before entering on the course*

*Jumping in front of Great Meadows signature tower*

*Riders and fans await their turn*

*Hurry, time counts*

*Nonix le Parc and Aaron Vale – a clean round*

*Flying over an oxer*

*The Swedish oxer*

*A photographer's view toward the spectators*

*Leading riders signing autographs*

During the jumping, four contestants have clean rounds, assuring a jump-off. The Great Meadow announcer does a fine job of color commentary. And as the jump-off approaches he interviews those whose first rounds have been clean. Two are riding Thoroughbreds, two have Warmbloods. The latter are apprehensive – a tie will be decided by the fastest time – and their comments

Nonix le Parc and Aaron Vale in the jump-off

PHOTOS BY THE AUTHOR

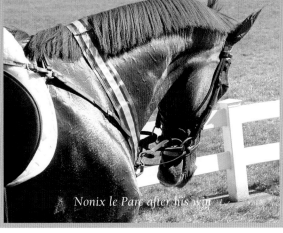

Nonix le Parc after his win

go about as follows:

> "My horse is jumping well, but I'll have to push him hard to keep up with the Thoroughbreds' greater speed."

And they are right. The first horse to go in the jump-off is Nonix le Parc, a Thoroughbred ridden by Aaron Vale. His round is clean and blazing fast. The second fastest horse, McLain Ward's Rio, is 0.23 seconds slower, and he pulls a rail trying. The others are far slower. Edie, a Thoroughbred fan to her bones, is delighted. Nonix le Parc looks as if he is too.

As a final benefit for the fans, the top riders in the event autograph programs and posters.

Less than a mile down the road from our Trappe Hill is Windsor Farm, for some years now the home of Francis and Margaret O'Neill, and, judging by the paddocks, an increasing number of horses. One evening, before dinner, I discussed show jumping with Margaret's daughter, Alexa Lowe, who is back home after a year in Holland and Germany.

Later on, one October morning, we arranged to watch Alexa school, to get a better understanding of the many months one must put in to make a top

PHOTO BY THE AUTHOR

*Preparing for the schooling session*

level jumper before enjoying a few minutes of success in the show ring. We are to meet her at the ring near her mother's house.

As is often the case at this season the morning is misty, the brightness of yesterday now held back by a high overcast, behind which pale sunlight is struggling to reach the ground. Overhead, nine Canada Geese pass us on their way to link up with skeins of their kind assembling for the morning journey to the cornfield of their leader's choice. As they pass Alexa appears, horse and rider dressed against the morning chill.

As Alexa dismounts to remove the mare's blanket and make adjustments to her tack, we ask how her program is coming. The answer is cheerful:

*"Champagne and I won the Amateur Grand Prix at Harrisburg last week and got reserve for the division. In a few days we'll take four horses to the Washington [DC] International Show.*

*"Today we'll work with Quintilla. She's in rehab from an injury and she's having trouble relaxing. She was my best horse in Europe, but she's been out of it, and doing small fences is the way to get her back.*

*"We'll be doing small fences like this all fall. She's a competitive, experienced mare – 14 years old – and she can do big fences. You don't need to jump big – it's all about rideability between jumps. Riding with the reins in one hand relaxes them. That's how cowboys do it, they need the other hand for the lariat. My trainer learned a lot about it from reiners."*

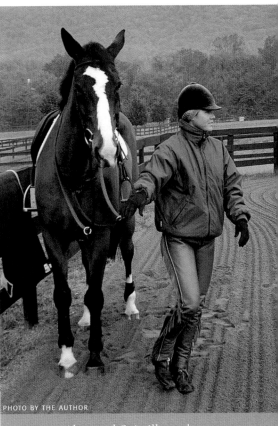

PHOTO BY THE AUTHOR

*Alexa and Quintilla ready to go*

As she readies her horse and then schools her, I reflect on what she told me some weeks ago about her career:

*"I'm on the cusp now. I've definitely been a professional, if you judge 'professionalism' by time devoted to the sport. I've been doing it full time for the last five years, but technically I have not yet declared myself 'professional' to the AHSA\*. Now I have to see whether I can make a career of it... As a little kid I was put on a pony, and by four I was screaming for riding lessons."*

Her goal was to go to the Olympics. At times she thought that was unreasonable, but she always wanted to ride at the top level.

---

\* American Horse Show Association

*"I believed it all depends on how hard you work and how much you want it."*

But there were also doubts along the way. There may be more to it than hard work and desire.

*"It's important to have a goal. The hardest problem is having such a high goal. There are ups and downs, and the downs put me further away from the goal. I had an older Grand Prix horse, and I had to retire him and go back down to the amateur division riding young horses. There were also bad decisions and bad luck with horses. It was hard. Making a show jumper, let alone one of Grand Prix caliber, takes weeks of schooling and attention to detail for every minute in the show ring."*

I ask her about her earlier life.

*"I went to high school at Maret, in Washington, then two years of college at Mount Holyoke. Then I dropped out and got an internship on Capitol Hill with the Republican Senatorial Committee. I did that full time, riding two horses in the evenings. I just wanted to prove to myself that I could do something else successfully before I gave the horses 100 percent of my focus and put the rest of my life on hold. The internship went very well, I could do that.*

*"But I got a late start in show jumping, switched to it when I was twenty, so I missed all the experience and exposure at the junior level. I had a bad fall in Florida in 2001, and couldn't ride for three months. As soon as I healed I headed for Germany."*

Alexa's stay in Europe has clearly been a formative, maturing experience.

*"I went to Europe to become a pro. I learned to judge myself on how I'm riding, not just by the results. My trainer, Albert Voorn, is a genius and a mentor, who won a silver medal in the Olympics at Sydney when he was 44. In the US the trainer goes with you to the shows, and points out the pitfalls in advance. It's a cultural thing. In Europe you do your training at home, go to shows alone. It registers faster when you make the mistakes on your own. Get the video, and let the trainer help you after the show. Then Albert told me 'Go home, and when Caletta [now seven] is ten come back and we'll work on her.' "*

Alexa also has had other good teachers.

*"In the States I have worked with Katie Monahan Prudent, Kim Frey and Jimmy Wofford. I learned a lot about fitness from Jimmy. There's a lot of psychology in sports. Kim gave me a book\* on that. And this show jumping*

---

\* *Golf is not a Game of Perfect*, by Dr. Bob Rotella

*Alexa schooling over jumps*

*is a game of inches and milliseconds. Sometimes you hit a rail hard and it stays up, other times the slightest nudge brings it off."*

As I am writing this I am reminded of a quote in *Practical Horseman* by trainer Jack Le Goff: *"Practice doesn't make perfect, perfect practice makes perfect."*

Alexa has come home confident that she can do it herself, but there are problems to be solved. She wants to become a better rider, and to find a way to finance her ambitions.

> *"I want to take reining lessons. I think it would help with show jumping – the principle of highly disciplined, relaxed horses that act with the slightest amount of pressure. And I want to know how – and why – the reiners do it with tough bits and sharp spurs.*
>
> *"Then there is the matter of finances. You need a reputation with which to get a sponsor, or pupils, or have enough money to do it yourself. If you prove yourself as a successful junior you can get jobs and sponsors early. But I'm too late for that."*

I can't help but ask, *"What if you can't make it?"*

> *"At the moment I'm not thinking about that. But they've told me I could go back to the Hill. I'd only want a job I was passionate about. Before going to*

---

*Europe I volunteered at the PEC\*, editing their newsletter, and I hope to do that again. But I want to stay in horses and make enough to carry myself. I want to keep my seven year old Caletta long enough to see how she does – she has Olympic potential."*

*"So what do you do to make ends meet?"*

*"I've been home a month, and I get some help from the family. My goal is to bring horses here from Holland and sell them. In the '80s many jumpers were Thoroughbreds. Now it's European sport horses. The Germans and Dutch have been studying bloodlines and breeding them. So everyone is going over there to buy Grand Prix horses, it's quicker."*

*"But what about all those mares and foals in your paddocks?"*

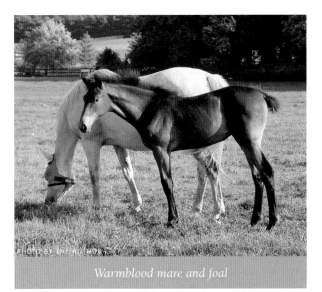
*Warmblood mare and foal*

*"They're all my mother's – Dutch, German, French. She has about ten mares, and she gets the semen from Europe. All the stallions gallop down the driveway in a FedEx truck. I've told her I don't want the babies, I'd rather buy four and five year-olds, but that's her hobby and she loves it."*

Silently I ask myself: *"Is Margaret dreaming that she will breed one good enough for Alexa to want?"* Alexa returns to her own horses – two four year-olds and five show horses, including a six year-old to sell and help pay the bills. There must be two more somewhere, because she reports, when asked about her schedule:

*"I'm riding nine horses a day now, that's 45 minutes times nine horses, plus time in the barn."*

I ask her about help.

*"Well, a good farrier is the hardest thing to find, next is a vet. I use Greg Ramsey for shoeing. So does Kim Frey, and she's pleased with him. But on the road you need a farrier to travel with you."*

I'm curious, maybe too pushy: *"How about social life?"*

---

\* **Piedmont Environmental Council**, the area's leading environmental organization

*"Social life is different. On the road you're a band of Gypsies. Most of your close friends are ones you see along the way, nine months of the year. Your social life becomes the horse show. I've lived here in Upperville – 'based here' might say it better – for five years and this is the first time I'm starting to meet people. I don't yet have a feeling of community. But young horses will let me stay around and do that. We won't have to spend all that money chasing the big tour."*

At Upperville this year (2002) Alexa showed in the low amateur (4'3" jumps) and the high amateur (4'6" jumps). Grand Prix jumps are at least is 5'0" and in the past she has competed in it. But she is pleased with this year's results.

*"We don't have a Grand Prix horse right now, but at Upperville we won one of the high amateur classes, and got fourth in both of the low amateur classes. So I got a check for $85 after they deducted my entry fees from the $700 gross purse money! And next week, at Leesburg, there's $10,000 purse money, and the competition may be easier."*

There are softer ways of making a living than the horse show business, but for some horse people that may not matter very much.

*Looking to the future*

# XII
## DRESSAGE

*Mozart, ridden by Phoebe DeVoe*

*DRESSAGE*
*"The art or method of training a horse in obedience and in precision of movement."*
*(See "Haute Ecole")*

*HAUTE ECOLE*
*"A series of intricate steps, gait, etc., taught to an exhibition horse."*

—Random House International Dictionary

*"Dressage challenges our intellect while it satisfies our compassion for the horse… results are obtained*
*through cooperation and guidance, rather than force or coercion… for junior riders it is an important*
*tool in stimulating attention to detail and planning… dressage can be a way to approach life."*

—Barbara Burkhardt, in *Dressage from A to X*

---

In ages past the most extreme use of ridden horses was in war, so it is not surprising that superior methods of training them and their riders emerged from the work of Cavalry officers. The roots of modern dressage lie in these methods, originally conceived by the Greek general and historian Xenephon about 400 B.C., and further developed over many years to school military horses in maneuvering at close quarters. Later, dressage became recognized as useful in teaching horse and rider the fundamentals of horsemanship – working as a team. Eventually it became a sport, as well as an element of three-day eventing.

My father was both a student and a perfectionist, and he approached his sports in that fashion. At two years old he had contracted polio, an affliction which left him with a wizened leg and a permanent limp, further stimulating him to seek the best possible information on proper form, in order to maximize his ability to compete athletically. Growing up as a minister's son in Vermont he had little exposure to riding horses, and so he did not connect with horse sports until after college, and when he did he started with books.

In his library I found a little book entitled *Exterieur et Haute Ecole*, by Captain Beudant of the French Army, translated into English as *Horse Training: Outdoor and High School*.

Horsemanship starts with an understanding of the physical and psychological makeup of the horse, accompanied by empathy. Beudant begins by demolishing those theories of horsemanship that he sees as over-control, blaming the horse for the error of the rider. He sees the…

> "…*main requisites of training to be to observe the horse at liberty, to reflect, and to strive to perfect one's self.*
>
> "*The rider must reduce his actions to the very minimum and leave the horse the greatest possible freedom in his.*"

In other words, let the horse be a horse, but train him to do so in the manner the rider wishes.

In most of his treatise Beudant and the authorities he quotes call for balance, lightness, patience, calmness, and impulsion from the rider.

> "*A teacher must first get the confidence of his pupil, then evince kindness,*

*gentleness, and a will that though calm is inflexible."*

He then quotes from *Equitation Actuelle* by Gustave LeBon:

*"The legs [of the rider] create impulsion, the hands prescribe the manner in which it is to be expended. The reasoned training of a horse is a mental gymnastic, a character builder for the rider."*

In short, the beginnings of dressage are also the fundamentals of good horse-manship, in whatever activity it may be later employed. And so we come to the modern sport, the ultimate blending of horse and rider into an inseparable minuet of motion and control.

Just as not everyone relishes galloping over open country and fences in the risky pastimes of foxhunting and steeplechasing, not everyone finds happiness in the detailed and patient training and execution necessary to advance through the levels in dressage.

*"Chacun a son gout."* Each to his own taste.

But the sport of dressage is growing. Last year 3,400 new horses were registered with the USDF, up substantially from the previous year. There are now over 40,000 dressage horses registered in the US.

The formal dressage competitions are separated into levels of competence. While riders are scored, and winners established, many participants compete mostly against themselves, trying to better their score as a means of demonstrating the improvement training has accomplished.

Competitions are held in a defined rectangular "ring," either indoors or outdoors, the "standard" ring being 20 x 60 meters, compared to the "small" ring at 20 x 40 meters. The ring is bounded by a low white boundary fence, a foot or so high, along the outside of which are placed markers with letters on them. Each competition is based on performance in a specific "test," calling for a series of sequential movements that the horse and rider team is to carry out, and the lettered points between which they should do so (see diagram, which in this case also shows the course to be followed while performing movement 20 of this test). Other letters on the diagram identify unmarked points on the centerline of the long axis of the ring, which are also used as reference points.

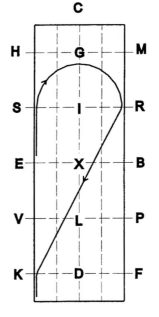

Each test is composed of 25-30 components, each specified as to route, gait, speed, lead (if at a canter), and accompanied on the score sheet by "directive ideas" defining what the test is intended to demonstrate.

Having come this far in our book learning it is time to visit the real thing, in this case a VADA – NOVA Championship Schooling Show scheduled for a November Saturday at Morven Park near Leesburg.

I arrive about 9 a.m., and find that the show is a two ring affair, compared to larger shows that may have five or six rings in simultaneous use. Classes are divided by level and by type of test to be taken. Competition began at 8:00 a.m., and contestants are scheduled by name at six-minute intervals throughout the day – much as tee times are assigned at crowded golf courses – with an hour break for lunch.

Piko and Kimberlee Couch

PHOTO BY THE AUTHOR

The show is in progress in a large sheet metal structure, the "Swiss-American Arena." This building, or rather complex of buildings, is laid out in the shape of a "T" – the lower three quarters of the stem of the "T" being the main arena in which there is a dressage ring, opening on an assembly and administrative area at the top of the stem, this area in turn connected to a smaller schooling arena that forms the cross piece of the "T."

Well turned out horses are being groomed near their trailers, or ridden in the schooling arena by riders uniformly attired in black jackets, brass buttons, white shirts and stocks, white breeches, and black boots with spurs. The breed of their horses varies as does horse size, but few if any seem to be Thoroughbreds, a calmer disposition being preferred.

On the wall of the assembly area are sheets giving class designations, names of horses and riders entered, scheduled time for performance by each, and for completed classes the individual scores and placings. I note that in Class 1, Introductory Level 1, there were originally 10 entries, three of which were scratched. The winner was Opalescence, ridden by Sara Eberly, with a score of 66.818. The lowest score in that class was 48.636.

There is also a small sign announcing "$50 Fine For All Loose Dogs." Unlike hunt meets, horse shows and steeplechase races there are no dogs here at all, loose or otherwise. Dressage is a restrained, quiet, serious business.

Tucked in at one side of this area is a table with ribbons laid out for later presentation, each ribbon accompanied by a carrot for the horse. Perhaps dressage people really do care more about improvement than winning, but the magnum size of the championship rosettes on the table suggests person-to-person competition is also alive and well. And, unlike the "winner take all" policy of Point-to-Points, there is a ribbon for everyone down to the eighth place finisher in each class.

Along one side of the ring near point "B" there are some bleachers. Here I join an older man and his wife as the only spectators. In front of me is an announcer with an impressive array of electronic equipment. I note that three women are seated on a little stand at the far end of the ring, behind point "C." One is clearly the judge, and I learn later that another is her scribe, and the third is a "runner."

Now a contestant, Michelle Capello on "Casa Blanca," enters the ring at point "A", the end opposite the judge. Horse and rider move down the centerline of the ring at a "collected" trot, halt in the middle (point "X"), and salute the judge. This entry is the first test item scored, shown on the score sheet as:

| | | TEST | DIRECTIVE IDEAS | POINTS |
|---|---|---|---|---|
| 1. | A<br>X | Enter collected trot<br>Halt, Salute<br>Proceed collected trot | Straightness on centerline,<br>quality of trot, halt and<br>transitions | |

The judge rises and returns the salute, following which the test proceeds to element 2, normally silently. In this case, however an assistant to the competitor stands at "E" and reads aloud the directions for each of the 28 elements of the test just prior to its initiation. Prompting is allowed in lower level shows, though most riders do not use it.

In this case the "reader" tells me later:

*"Cassie hasn't been ridden in a closed arena before, and Michelle was afraid the horse would freak out, and Michelle would lose concentration. So she*

*asked me to help."*

I ask, *"How did you happen to get picked to read?"*

*"She keeps her horse in my barn, and I'm showing later today so I agreed to help her."*

Further queries disclose that "my barn" signifies where you board, not ownership of a stable.

Back in the bleachers the announcer, a photographer and I wait to watch a class being "pinned." In front of us two volunteer show officials debate whether to pin the horses winner on down, or eighth place on up. In any event they call all nine contestants to the ring. Eight get ribbons. The ninth is the only rider not wearing a jacket. Did she just assume that she would not have to join the ceremony, and was caught unawares by the call to the ring? In any event, she cheerfully joins the others cantering in a "victory lap" around the ring and out the exit, one rider carrying her ribbon clipped to her boot top, the seven other prizes fluttering from horses' bridles. Tolerance for ribbons flapping in the horse's face is apparently not a dressage requirement.

It is becoming obvious that I need help in understanding dressage, even if actual riding is beyond me. I approach a nice young lady wearing the coat of arms of Oxford University on a gray (or in this case perhaps "grey") sweatshirt, and explain my mission and lack of dressage qualifications to her. The lady, Tracy Brown, turns out to be the "runner" for the judge. She suggests that if I'm nice maybe the judge will let me sit near her and hear what goes on. We head around the outside of the building toward point "C." Then Tracy seems to have second thoughts:

*"Maybe I'm overstepping my bounds to take you there."*

But we keep walking. The judge is clearly a person of eminence in the dressage world, perhaps equivalent to a Colonel, and a volunteer runner is still just a runner. First salutes, now rank, recall the military beginnings of the sport. After five and one half years of that in the US Army I feel right at home. I assure Tracy I'll behave. We arrive at "C" just as the next horse and rider enter the ring. There is no time for explanations or pleasantries, but I am invited to take a chair – there isn't time for the judge to make any other choice, like telling me to get lost.

Immediately the judge starts stating grades in a low voice, "6", "7", "6", "5", as each segment is completed, plus comments such as:

*"Needs more bend… slight late behind… needs more ground cover… oversteps… late, not enough transition."*

These ratings come at perhaps 10-12 second intervals, and the scribe seated next to the judge enters them on the score sheet along side the printed description of the test element just completed.

Then, test over, the contestant returns to the center of the ring, salutes again. The judge rises and returns the salute. A small covey of supporters clap. Most riders then paste smiles on their previously expressionless faces, ride up to the judge, and thank her, then leave the ring whence they came. Meanwhile, the judge completes that part of the score sheet that calls for rating the general aspects of the round – gaits, impulsion, submission, rider's position and seat. That done, she rings a bell and the next horse and rider enter the ring, moving to the center at a collected trot, stop, salute...

For several rounds I remain silent, fascinated by the concentration of the performers, and particularly the intensity with which the judge and scribe attend to their duties. Slowly I begin to differentiate between the horses and riders that are just trying to comply with the test requirements and those that can do so with confidence and also show a little panache in their performance. It will be interesting to compare this schooling show with one for horses at a higher level of development. And so we reach the lunch break.

The judge rises, turns to me and introduces herself.

*"I'm Susan Carr."*

I respond, stating my mission and telling her a bit about this book. Then I add, *"The judge has the hardest job here – no time to relax all morning."* The scribe also has a tough job – she mustn't lose her place and put the score and comment in the wrong box on her sheet. Susan's reply:

*"Well, the riders pay a lot of attention to the score sheet and the comments on it. We need to be accurate. Some of them even have their round taped and later watch the tape with the score sheet in hand..."*

*"Like checking up on you by instant replay?"*

*"Yes, I guess so."*

I learn that Susan is a dressage trainer, lives in Maryland, and judges shows almost every weekend from March to November. She offers to help if I need it, and gives me her telephone number. But now it is time for lunch. She has to be back promptly for the afternoon session.

I thank Tracy for her help, and leave, marveling.

A day later, in our office, I tell Betsy of my encounter with dressage. Betsy recollects:

*Dressage warmup at Foxcroft — Suzanne Sherwood on Absolute Mazeppa*

> *"I remember the girls — Libby Crenshaw and Annie Bishop — when they were about 12 — putting letters all around the living room rug, and walking the course so they could remember their dressage routines. Then they did the same thing on the lawn and at a swimming pool."*

As Barbara Burkhardt said:

> *"...for junior riders it is an important tool in stimulating attention to detail and planning... dressage can be a way to approach life."*

Libby and Annie are now in college, perhaps helped to succeed there by dressage training many years before.

Some months later there is a two-day dressage event at the Foxcroft School. There are a total of 48 classes, divided into a dozen or so levels and divisions, and further divided into different tests. Most horses and riders are in more than one class — and four rings will be used for the total of 330 entries. The thermometer is flirting with 90, and so jackets are forgiven — the uniform being white shirts and breeches, black hat and boots.

———

As soon as I have parked the car my eye is drawn to a handsome chestnut – #134 – performing in ring three. As in last winter's event only the judge, scribe and runner are watching, plus one or two connections of the horse. As the test concludes, and the salutes are exchanged, the horse leaves the ring and I introduce myself to his owner-rider, Phoebe DeVoe, the owner, and to Mozart, her Dutch Warmblood. The ride has been good, and I compliment her on it. She responds:

> *"He went well, better than last time. It was slippery out there* [the grass is dry and the ground hard] *but he has borium cleats on his shoes. He hasn't been to many shows, and he gets nervous."*

Mozart is stabled in the barn down the hill, but first I need a program. Somebody nearby is helpful: *"See that door on the left, the one with the front of a white truck sticking out? You go in there."* And I do.

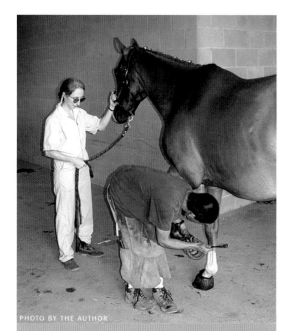

*Amy Nostradt holding Parceval while Ramon Rodelas works on a shoe.*

At the back of the truck a horse is being re-shod by the farrier, Ramon Rodelas of Leesburg. Holding the horse – his halter identifies him as Parceval – is Amy Nostrandt, a slim young woman who identifies herself as, *"Owner, rider, and general horse person."* Most dressage riders take care of their own horses, at least at shows.

Beyond the shoeing area, but short of the table with the printed material on it, several young ladies are chatting, while other contestants examine the wall-mounted sheets on which results are posted. I ask the three conversationalists – Alison Head, Sara Spofford, and Margot McAllister, all Virginia residents: *"Why do you like dressage better than eventing or foxhunting?"*

Here's what I hear, reported at their request without specific attribution:

> *"We're neurotic perfectionists."*

> *"Also a little bit chicken."*

> [One adds] *"A little???"*

> *"We get to bond with our horses better than in other sports."*

This I doubt, so I ask, *"Better than eventing and foxhunting?"* and I hear:

*"Better than eventing. If they make the jump OK they're happy. We would worry if it wasn't perfect."*

*"Foxhunting? They have to be bonded – if they're not they're going to get their necks broken."*

Margot and I discover that we both live in Upperville, though she is a newcomer – here only a year…

*"I grew up in Colorado – Boulder – but it's too developed, so I came here for the horses. I knew the Virginia horse country from taking a semester at Sweet Briar, and from showing in the area, and I used to foxhunt."*

She invites me to go see her horse, Kandinsky. *"How's he done?"* I ask. It's the right question…

*"He won class 20 this morning, he got a 70."*

Going into his stall I meet a large, friendly dark brown – almost black – animal. Margot elaborates:

*"He's Russian. His papers are all in Russian. I couldn't read them so I call*

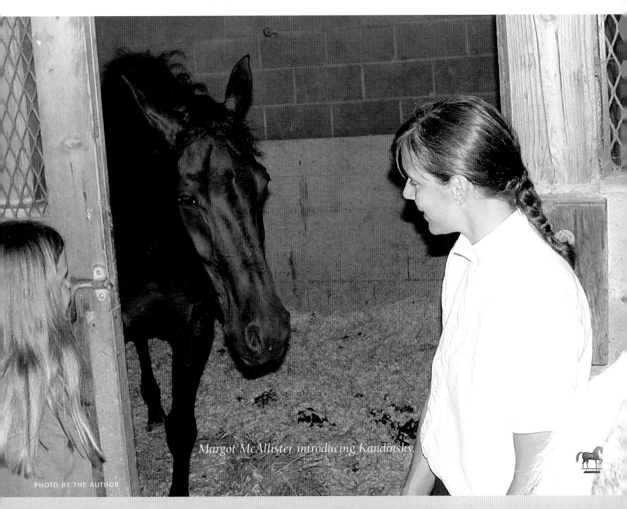

*Margot McAllister introducing Kandinsky.*

*him Kandinsky. I think he's a Trekhener."*

She explains the origin of the horse's name, but the notes I took are insufficient, so the next day I look up Kandinsky. Here is what *Benet's Reader's Encyclopedia* has to say:

> *"Kandinsky, Wassily (1866-1944). Russian painter, …in 1910… he evolved a style of turbulent, vividly colored abstractions. After 1920 his style gradually became orderly and strict…"*

Margot looks 25 years old, but her real age is well beyond that, and I ponder whether the name choice is subtly autobiographical – exuberant youth metamorphosing into the careful control and patience her sport requires. Dressage people really do get closely bonded to their horses.

In the next stall – more accurately in the aisle beside it – is a pretty gray mare, Katrina, being braided by her rider-owner Shannon Pedlar. Shannon and Margot are playing out a fantasy – a fantasy because Kandinsky is a gelding. Shannon:

*Shannon Pedlar braiding Katrina*

PHOTO BY THE AUTHOR

> *"She's in love. She likes big bays. She'll bypass a chestnut any time for a big bay."*

Kandinsky sticks his head out of the stall to inspect Katrina, who seems well fleshed compared to our Thoroughbreds. Kandinsky appears to approve. Shannon explains:

> *"These dressage horses carry more weight than Thoroughbreds in training. In dressage they develop slow-twitch muscles, not fast-twitch like racehorses. And the added weight conceals some flaws."*

I learn that Katrina is 11 and an Andalusian / Thoroughbred cross. And, *"Her great grand daddy was Count Fleet."*

I ask, *"How did you get involved with horses?"*

> *"I started riding at a cavalry post, Fort Knox. Yes, right on top of all that*

*gold. My father was a career Army officer."*

"In the Cavalry?"

*"No, he's a priest [we presume Episcopal, since he has a daughter]. He was Post Chaplain. When he retired he bought a farm in southern Virginia."*

"Did you ever do Pony Club?"

*"No, 4-H. it was more affordable than Pony Club. In Pony Club you had to have a horse trailer and all that equipment."*

Around the corner there is a wash stall. In it is another gray horse, Hideaway's Flicker, being washed by owner Kathy Mathers. Suddenly, fully soaped up, he takes it into his head to trot back to his stall. As she goes after him Kathy exclaims:

*"At least you know where you live!"*

PHOTO BY THE AUTHOR

*Kathy Mathers washing Hideaway's Flicker*

Back in the wash stall the horse is bombproof to the flash of my camera.

Leaving the building I again pass by Ramon, working on a front foot, and giving advice to a young lady on foot care for horses; no doubt he hopes to add her to his list of regular customers.

Edie spent Saturday clearing trails in the Fairfax hunt country and so she has so far missed the dressage. We decide to take a reprise and go back to Foxcroft on Sunday after lunch. As we park at Foxcroft there are a lot of horses in the dusty warm-up ring, and we watch them for a moment, then go to ring three where #20, a handsome, husky bay horse is performing. He does well but must strain to achieve the quick elegance that a smaller, lighter horse would find natural.

PHOTO BY THE AUTHOR

*Hunt country trail clearing crew*

As he leaves the ring we compliment his rider, and ask whether his size is a disadvantage.

*"He's a big boy, 17.2, and sometimes in tight circles… but no, not really, at this level."*

The horse is friendly – and hot – as we pat him. We learn his name is Piko, that he is listed as a Rhinelander, a Westphalian / Hanoverian cross, and his owner is Kimberlee Couch. She adds:

*"He's doing well, but he doesn't like big shows – too much pressure and too much crowding in the warm-up ring."*

Piko is the last contender for the day in ring three, so we adjourn to the indoor ring. As we pass by the white truck Ramon is at work on a dun colored animal, and I remark, *"He's almost another gray."* Ramon is literal:

*"Nah, he's yellow."*

The indoor ring has a very high ceiling, along the centerline of which is a wide strip of translucent roofing, providing a band of pale sunlight along the center of the sand surface of the ring. Instantly I realize that this feature may be camera-friendly.

By great coincidence the contestant in the ring is #64, our friend Katrina

*Shannon Pedlar on Katrina*

from Saturday. Shannon, riding her, has on her black jacket, and the rider, the gray horse, and the band of sunlight provide a sense of drama we have not seen elsewhere. The movement is fluid, projecting the elegance that gives the sport its special appeal. Katrina is followed in the ring by a nice bay animal, but its movements are not as flowing and the drama of the

contrasts and the band of sunlight are gone.

Back at her stall we find Katrina munching on candy treats being fed to her by Shannon. The mare is sweaty. Shannon now has on a cooler shirt, and is wearing a long skirt over her riding breeches. The black boots are gone. Shannon says:

*"I like to let her cool down a bit before washing her off in cold water."*

We note a blue ribbon hung on the wire mesh of the stall.

*"That was from this morning. We scored a 67."*

She sounds pleased. Yesterday was good, too. I ask, *"How about this round just now? We thought it was good, and we took some pictures."*

*"There were some little mistakes — maybe not quite as good as the morning."*

*"Why did you wear the jacket when no one else is doing so?"*

*"Well, its more formal, and shows more respect for the judge and the sport. And it's only on for a few minutes."*

I am reminded of yesterday's remark about *"neurotic perfectionists."*

Two girls come by with a large red cooler full of free Popsicles, and we each take one. Three quarters eaten, the rest of mine falls on the floor. Shannon scoops it up as I think *"neurotic compulsive cleaner."* But quickly she feeds the sweet mess to Katrina, who licks her lips in happiness. Change *"compulsive cleaner"* to *"bonder."*

Shannon is interested in her round, so we go see the sheets. Her score is now posted, 67 point something, the best so far in the class and only the bay that followed her still to go. It seems certain Katrina has another blue. As we watch the poster puts up the last score, 60, and there are congratulations all around. We promise to send Shannon a picture, and wonder how soon Katrina will be moving up to the next level.

On the way out we again pass Ramon, holding a horse's foot up and explaining its defects and indicated treatment to the horse owner. As we pause, the Popsicle girls come by again, and we each take one. Bonding to Popsicles is easy on a hot day.

Then, leaving, we note a young boy taking his first lesson in horse bonding…

———

*Starting at the bottom*

# XIII THREE-DAY EVENTING

*Olympic victory lap – David O'Connor and Custom Made*

---

*"The courage, initiative, and seemingly limitless energy of a fit three-day event horse are difficult to reconcile with the obedience, calmness, and stability required for the dressage test. ...The three-day event is not for every horse. It requires courage, tenacity, perseverance, and both moral and physical strength from horse and rider."*

—James C. Wofford, *Training the Three-Day Event Horse and Rider*

Three-Day Eventing, also called Combined Training, is the most comprehensive test of horse and horseman, demands the most versatility and is surely one of the fastest growing among horse sports. There are now 19,000 registered event riders in the US, the vast majority amateurs in every sense of the word, topped by a very few at the pinnacle, the International and Olympic competitors for whom training a string of horses takes several hours daily. With world famous coaches and several Olympic medalists living within the area, the Virginia Piedmont can claim to be at the nation's center of the sport.

Eventing grew out of cavalry training of horse and rider, and first became an Olympic sport in 1912. Interestingly, this shift from military purpose to sport preceded the start of World War I by only two years, the war in which the machine gun rattled *finis* to the role of horses in close combat.

Three-day events test the ability of each horse and rider team to perform at a high level of competence in three different disciplines: a day of dressage, followed by a day of cross-country riding, up to 20 kilometers at varying speeds, including a difficult and dangerous series of as many as 45 jumps, and then a day of show jumping over imposing fences. A shorter version, called a horse trial, takes one, two, or three days, but in horse trials the cross-country element is reduced in scope and the difficulty of the jumps may be less. Consequently, the ability of a horse to complete a physically very demanding cross-country phase, and have enough energy left to do well over jumps in a show ring is not tested as severely as in a full three-day program, and so is less influential in the final outcome.

Entries are separated into a number of divisions, established to place horse / rider teams of relatively equal experience and skill against each other. Since each horse-rider pair is a team it is possible for a rider to be paired with two or more horses, and thus be a part of several teams, often assigned to different divisions based on the ability and experience of the particular horse.

Dressage (see prior chapter) scoring (from 1 to 10) is done for each of the 20 or more movements in the test. For compilation with the other elements of a combined event, the dressage score is deducted from the maximum score possible, in order to convert it to the equivalent of a fault-based number.

Cross-country calls for jumping skill, endurance and speed. In a full three-day event this day has four phases (standards shown are maxima for the highest level of international competition):

> Phases A and C – (roads and tracks) – 16,000-20,000 meters combined total distance over country at a speed of 240 meters / minute
>
> Phase B – (steeplechase) – around 3,500 meters at 690 meters per minute with perhaps ten jumping efforts
>
> Phase D – (cross-country) – around 7500 meters at 570 meters per minute with 30-35 jumping efforts

Total distance for the day is thus around 27-31,000 meters (17-19 miles) and total time around one and one-half hours of sustained physical effort.

Cross-country jumps at the top competitive level are up to four feet high, but some are also as much as five feet wide. Some are uphill, others drop down to perhaps six feet below take off. Occasionally the landing or take off is in water, or the next jump is placed close to the last, occasionally requiring a 90 degree turn in between. At the Sydney Olympics one obstacle to be jumped was a farm wagon. At Lexington in 1978 horses jumped into and out of a roofed pavilion. Courses and jumps increase in difficulty as the level of the competition advances. Faults are assessed for jumping failures and excessive time taken to complete the courses. And the final cross-country phase is run after the horses have endured many miles of slightly less strenuous exercise.

In addition to great endurance, jumping ability and speed a horse must have complete confidence in the rider in order to do what must seem to him to be totally unfamiliar and challenging things. Comparing an international three-day event cross-country ride experience with a Virginia trail ride is about like comparing the National Football League with tossing a football with your ten year-old kid.

As the competition progresses, each competitor knows exactly where he or she stands versus rivals, and how little margin there is, if any, for error. So the tension builds with each day, reaching its height in the show jumping. Fences are high, varying in appearance and painted in gaudy colors. Crowd noise can be unsettling to nervous and perhaps tired horses, and disorienting to riders. Jumping consistency and the agility to make quick changes of direction as the course twists are essential, just as in the Grand Prix jumping

*Navigating a water jump*

classes common at major horse shows. The score of each round is based on jumping faults and penalties for failure to finish within the specified time.

The final three-day event score is the total of fault points assessed over the three days, low score of course winning.

## – The Trainer –

Jim Wofford, son of an Olympic rider, was for twenty years a member of the US Equestrian Team. He participated at the highest level of eventing, earning several Olympic medals and a World's Championship. He has also served as President of the American Horse Show Association. Perhaps his greatest contributions to his sport, however, are the riders he has trained over the thirty years he has been engaged in that activity, operating from his farm "Fox Covert" in Upperville, Virginia. I asked him how he became involved. His reply:

> *"I had no choice. I was born and raised in it. Every morning I wake up wondering why I am so lucky as to be doing this."*

In 1995 he distilled his approach to eventing into a classic book, *Training the Three-Day Event Rider*, that takes both novice and expert through the steps that lead from taking up the sport to performing at its highest levels, pointing out the pitfalls along the way and explaining solutions to them.

Chapters include: "Selecting a Horse," "Equipment," "Dressage," "Cross-Country," "Show Jumping," "Conditioning," and finally "Putting It All Together."

Jim is candid in explaining that the sport is *"complicated,"* and then dissects its complexity with an easy to read text larded with photographs and perceptive observations, such as, on selecting a horse:

- *"Don't buy him if you don't like him the minute you see him."*

- *"Look him in the eye… the look of eagles is alive and well in the horse world."*

- *"The eye should reveal an unquestioning acceptance of human presence."*

There follows a comprehensive discussion of conformation, temperament and breeding desirable in an event horse. Then on to Equipment:

- *"The connection between the rider's hand and the horse's mouth is the most important part of riding, and we had better start there."* [Discussing in this case the selection of bits.]

- *"The answer in the long run is always more training, not more bit."*

Next come skills needed and aids used in riding the various phases of eventing:

- *"The purpose of good position is to influence your horse, …supple and elastic, not posed and rigid."*

- *"Once you become, in effect, the perfect passenger, you must learn to combine the perfect position with an ability to follow the horse's motion by balance alone."*

- *"Ride your horse with your seat and legs, not your reins."*

- *"The end result of classical riding is that the horse is always perfectly balanced between the rider's hands and legs at all times."*

- *"Horses tend to go the way we ride them."*

Under training and participating in competition, he offers:

- *"It's much easier to survive a mistake caused by aggression than to get out of a situation caused by timidity."*

- *"Part of the fun of training three-day event horses is feeling them change and improve."*

And finally, a Wofford after-thought:

---

- *"You get mixed emotions when your students start to show you up."*

In short, Jim's book shows that eventing is about pervasive horsemanship in all its aspects, and thus the most demanding, and to its practitioners the most satisfying, of all horse sports. Having read the book I looked forward to a chance to watch trainer, rider and horse work together.

It is a warm June morning. Jim's classes start at eight at Fox Covert, and I am standing just outside the ring as the three students assemble and Jim introduces them to each other and to me. Aside from the fact that they all have gray horses, and are all older than Jim's typical student, there is considerable diversity among them.

Jim Wofford setting rails
PHOTO BY SUSAN MCHUGH

Will Coleman is a sizable man, a show jumper living near Orange, VA., give or take 50 years in age, riding a huge (17.2 hand) Holsteiner gelding, seven years old, named Krackie.

Barbara Lawrence is a seasoned eventer and a riding instructor from Haymarket, with a well schooled nine year-old gelding, Que Verdad, which she bought at two.

Gillian Clissold is an event rider from Nokesville, VA., here to cool down a rather hot, small mare, Sports Car, who, according to her owner *"needs this at the beginning of each season."*

While the horses are trotted around the ring, warming up, Jimmy and his helper, Hans Gehrling, position and adjust the cavelletti* rails and the jumps for the drills that will follow. Looking at the bars lying on the ground and the small jumps I am surprised, for Jim's book is profusely illustrated with event horses soaring over difficult cross country obstacles, and no such jumps are in view.

But then, Jim's book also does say:

> *"The end result of classical riding is that the horse is perfectly balanced between the rider's hands and legs at all times... it's the horse's balance*

---

\* The use of rails lying on the ground to train horses is an Italian innovation, the name **cavalletti** coming from the Italian word "cavelletto" which means "small pole." In English usage the word "cavalletti" is both singular and plural.

---

329

*Jim Wofford and Will Coleman*

*that controls his speed, and not the pressure of your reins on his mouth. …once you become, in effect, the perfect passenger, you must learn to combine the perfect position with an ability to follow the horse's motion by use of balance alone."*

He calls his small squad to the center of the ring. Standing before them in shorts and a polo shirt, red hair peeking out from under his cap, he is both informal and in complete command:

*"We'll do gymnastic jumping, my favorite. I'll have you as close to a rat in a maze as I can. We'll do four exercises. Some fences will be all height and no spread, others all spread and no height. The object is to get the horse to adjust. We'll help them if they don't understand."*

Soon the horses are trotting over five cavelletti, the rails placed apart at distances measured to produce a regular trot step. Gillian's horse heats up and she turns her sharply. Jim complains:

*"Oh, don't turn her like that, she's not a dirt bike. Watch the rail, Gillian."*

---

Now the drill switches to four cavaletti followed by a small jump. Jim adjusts the spacing by pacing and by using his feet as measures. He shows what he wants by demonstrating. His body rises from the knees up, as if following the rise of a jumping horse, as he says:

*"I didn't jump, I allowed the horse to push me into position."*

On the first try Will's big horse has trouble. Jim notes:

*"He's jumping off four steps, not five. It's difficult for him, but we have to teach him to jump with both front feet, not just one."*

On the next try it is better. Will reports:

*"I slowed him down a bit, and it helped."*

He sounds pleased. Jim collects the riders' crops and issues each a thin dowel rod. The object is to hold the stick in both hands, along with the reins, and keep it level, thus assuring that the rider controls his hands. A second jump has been added to the sequence. Jim explains:

*"Will, now that he's taking the fifth step there's a split second more before he pushes you up as he jumps,"*

The drill is now four caavaletti at a trot, then a jump, one stride at a canter, and a second jump, then a caveletti, as in the diagram below.

```
>>>>>>   o   o   o   o   i            i   o  >>>>>>
CIRCLE  AND  TROT    TROT    JUMP  1 STRIDE  JUMP      CANTER
```

Will does it well. Jim: *"Oh yes, oh yes."*

Eventually the exercise expands to four cavelletti and four jumps, two of them oxers*. Jim sets another rail diagonally across the oxers' two top rails to show the horse that he is to jump both rails, and not put in a stride between. Jim explains:

*"If you miss at the start the whole sequence will be wrong."*

One rider appears to over-control her horse. Jim:

*"Let her deal with it, let her deal with it. I want to teach the horse to jump, to build in a margin of error."*

---

* An **oxer** is a widened jump having both a front and a back top rail, in this case with the rails set about three feet apart.

---

At 9:20 it's getting warm, and Jim announces that *"we've about run out of gas,"* and the lesson is over. My brief post-game interviews elicit the following:

[Will]: *"Jimmy's a great guy. He teaches in a way that gives you confidence in your horse, and your horse confidence in you."*

[Barbara]: *"Why do I like eventing? Because it makes you the best all-around horseman. I like to see a horse develop its full range of physical and mental capabilities. As they say of people, 'a mind is a poor thing to waste.'"*

[Gillian]: *"It's a good outlet for my aggression. When we got married we reduced the number of horses to save money and so I could spend more time with my husband. It didn't work. He said 'get more horses, you're pleasanter to live with when you have them.'"*

[Jim]: *"The hardest part of teaching is lifting those rails around and adjusting them."*

The Wofford philosophy is to teach the horse so there is more margin for rider error. On his stable wall is a list of favorite quotations, including:

*"A short cut is the longest distance between two points."*

When it comes to riding, Jim Wofford is a classicist.

PHOTO BY SUSAN MCHUGH

*Juliet Graham on Buckley Boy*

The next student is due at 10:00. Jim describes her as more typical of the people he teaches than were the experienced and older amateurs of the last session.

Ayla Turnquist is from Minneapolis, young, blond, and a rising sophomore at Johns Hopkins in Baltimore. She hopes to qualify for the "Young Rider" series in Area IV, which includes Minnesota. Friends have steered her to Jimmy, and this will be her second lesson with him. She's driven the two hours from her Maryland stable in a truck pulling a big trailer, with a traveling companion, a sizable young man named Bill, who also goes to Hopkins.

Ayla's lesson is similar to the one before, but it seems to me that her horse (he's 3/4 Thoroughbred, 1/4 Morgan) is a more typical event horse, and that she, while athletic, is a bit less experienced than the ladies in the other group. Jimmy's comments during the lesson include, among many:

*"When you're posting, let the horse's motion bring you out of the saddle."*

*"I want the horse looking at it [the cavelletti] and thinking 'what shall I do with my feet?'"*

*"You don't want to rob him of his initiative."*

Bill and I are standing together, watching. Bill allows:

*"I can't imagine taking five hours out of the day to do this – two hours of travel each way – for a one hour lesson."*

As Heidi Stirrup said many pages earlier, Bill obviously *"just doesn't get it,"* at least not yet. At 11:00 it's pretty hot, and Jimmy concludes the lesson with:

*"Very good. He can have an easy day tomorrow."*

After she's dismounted, I ask Ayla why she does it.

*"Because there's nothing I'd rather do. I enjoy being with this big lug… [she pats the sweaty horse, not the nearby Bill] and making him better, and me too. I enjoy the competition, too, but that isn't all that often."*

Next day, Jim Wofford calls on another matter. As we finish that business, I thank him for yesterday's insights, adding, *"Eventing seems to me to be the ultimate test of horsemanship."* His answer is crisp:

*"Its proponents would agree with you."*

## – Cross Country –

This weekend there is a CDCTA horse trial taking place at Great Meadow, and Leslie VanSant, newly appointed as the executive director of that facility, suggests I attend. CDCTA stands for Commonwealth Dressage Combined Training Association, a mouthful that its principals hope someday to replace with an easier handle. CDCTA manages an ambitious annual schedule of 44 events in Virginia, from pony club and schooling shows on up, though stopping short of the American pinnacle of eventing, Rolex CCI ****, more simply known as Rolex Kentucky, held each spring.*

Sunday is the day for the cross-country phase of the competition, dressage and jumping having taken place the day before. It is also the day of the Foxhound Show at Morven Park, a must on Edie's foxhunter's calendar, so we split forces. Cross-country will be a new experience for me.

Great Meadow seems little changed since the Gold Cup three weeks before,

---

* Three-day events are graded for difficulty – from one to four stars. Four stars (****) signifies the highest level, and Rolex CCI **** is the most prestigious three-day event in North America.

*Jumping at Great Meadow – Nina Fout on Wild Frontier*

except that the crowds and the tents are gone, and there is easy parking in the space designated "Horsemen." Nearby is a bulletin board listing the times at which each horse and rider team will go, and under that, piles of dressage score sheets for perusal by contestants. Despite the unstarred rank of the event the names of the players cover a wide spectrum, from recent Olympians David and Karen O'Connor, and Nina Fout, through international veterans Juliet Graham and Torrance Watkins, to those on eventing's lower rungs, where Katie Gordon and Teddy Mulligan are recognizable local names. Clearly the course is challenging enough to be useful both for bringing along less experienced horses and tuning up accomplished performers.

Nor is it entirely "Commonwealth." In addition to Virginia license plates there are trailers and vans from WV, NY, MI, MD, PA, KY, AL, and VT. Some car licenses indicate the owner's passion – "EVENTR" and "WOH NELY" for example. And trailers come and go as contestants time their arrivals around the posted schedules.

———

The stewards' tower at the finish line of the steeplechase course provides a fine view of the cross-country jumps, laid out in and around the steeplechase fences, and using some of the same facilities such as Swan Lake. On the top level of the tower is an announcer, keeping the tiny crowd – mostly off-duty contestants and connections – abreast of what is happening on the course.

Because of the time each participant will use to complete a round (about six minutes) it is necessary to have more than one horse on the course at any one time. Horses start at two minute intervals, and so are always well separated, for each horse and rider team is competing against the course, not head to head with an adjacent rival.

For this event there are separate courses (though using some of the same jumps) for Novice, Training, and Preliminary Divisions (at a higher level event there would also be Intermediate and Advanced Divisions), each further

PHOTO BY THE AUTHOR

*Jumping into Swan Lake*

broken down into categories "A" and "B" (in divisions best handled in two sections), "YR" (young rider) and "JR" (junior). For each course there is an "optimum time", a slightly slower "speed fault time" and a much slower "maximum time." Deviations outside of the prescribed range will result in time penalties, as will "stops" (refusals) and other jumping failures.

Optimum speeds vary from 350-400 meters per minute (mpm) for Novice to 520 mpm for Preliminary, the length of the courses varying from 2000 meters for Novice to 3120 meters for Preliminary. This calls for galloping at no more than moderate speed. For comparison, a steeplechaser racing over hurdles for the same distance (3120 meters = 1.94 miles) might run at 800 mpm, about the same speed as a "two minute lick" in a flat race training work.

In a three-day event at the highest level, the cross-country phase would be far more extensive and severe, and thus the most critical of the three elements. Event trainer Jim Wofford says:

> *"It is also the hardest to learn, because the effect of the terrain and the speed make jumping so complex."*

In horse trials some or all of cross-country phases A, B, and C may be eliminated, as they are at this event. The challenge lies in getting the horse to jump unusual obstacles sited in peculiar locations, a test of the confidence horse and rider have in each other. At Great Meadow there are about 40 separate obstacles to choose from in setting up a course, several involving water. Many are peculiar, such as the white picnic table located near the steward's tower. Obviously the highest level, in this case Preliminary, calls for the greatest distance and the fastest speed, and includes the most challenging obstacles along a route incorporating the most complex turns.

Fence names are descriptive: Wave Ramp, Mushroom Oxer, Quarry, Lobster Pot, Spillway Ramps, Chevron (a V-shaped jump, not a gas station), and at the finish, either Gate House or Last Log.

A girl in a yellow shirt helps me:

> *"A refusal here costs 20 penalty points, that pretty well kills you."*

I note she is wearing a light cast on her arm – *"You're not riding?"*

> *"No, I broke my arm."*

*"Doing this?"*

> *"No, galloping a race horse, actually."*

Boundaries between equine pursuits are permeable.

---

PHOTO BY JANET HITCHEN

*Complex jumping problems*

PHOTO BY JANET HITCHEN

The U.S. Eventing Association (USEA) has this to say about safety:

*"...all horse activities contain a certain amount of risk to horses, riders, and even bystanders. Eventing asks much, but properly conditioned, trained and ridden, life and limb problems become the exception. ...the USEA is constantly educating event organizers to use only the appropriate design for Cross Country and Show Jumping for each level."*

The progress of riders on the course comes to us intermittently over the loud speaker:

*"There's a stop at The Quarry for Diamond Monkey and Sara Kozumplik... [then] ...One stop at the Log Slide for Chelsea Reinhardt, but now clear there... [And, then] ...Unfortunately that's a third refusal at the water for Wendy Masemer and Mr. Jingles. They're eliminated."*

Occasionally the announcer leaves his favorite subject – describing the misfortunes of others – to make a public service announcement such as:

*"Young Rider Division – Christain Trainor, First Place. Your ribbon is at the Secretary's office... [or] ...If you're missing a Jack Russell we have one at the Start House."*

Jack Russells are apparently the favorite dog of eventers, followed by Labs, and the program for this event is emphatic regarding them. At the bottom of page one, it says:

*"All dogs must be on a leash!"*

*Spectators and dogs*

However, no penalty points are specified for infractions. In the background the announcer reverts to type:

> *"One stop at the Spillway for Little Cheap Shot and Sandy McCormack… [then]… Looks like another stop at The Quarry, no, unfortunately a third stop at The Quarry – they'll be retiring."*

His tone of voice suggests he is inured to the trials of eventing.

Our small group on the tower includes a man busy with a camcorder – a father? a coach? – and Olympic gold medalist David O'Connor. A girl comes up to ask David about improving the surface of the area in which she trains –

PHOTO BY THE AUTHOR

*Bob Hilton – grounds manager at Great Meadow*

it has too much clay. He has some ideas, and asks about what they are willing to invest. Her reply:

*"I don't think expense is much of a factor."*

She is probably thinking of a patron, not a parent. David:

*"Then tear it up and start all over."*

So much for clay. Another girl asks about course maintenance:

*"When is the best time to aerate?"*

*"Do it in the spring, maybe six weeks before you want to use it. [Then the salesman in David emerges] …We bought special equipment to do this, we charge $250 each time we do it for someone, to help pay for the equipment."*

The girls leave without placing an order, and I ask him, *"What do you think of the surface at Great Meadow?"*

> *"It's the best in the country; these guys are turf specialists."*

David wears his champion's mantle modestly. Would that all sports notables were as helpful, polite, and self-effacing, but then, humility is a natural result of long association with horses. Cheers from the crowds that worship touchdowns, slam dunks, or home runs have a less healthy impact on the authors of those feats. Score one for the horse. And I can't wait to tell Leslie and Bob Hilton about David's turf endorsement. But it's time for lunch.

# – Show Jumping –

(Originally and still sometimes called Stadium Jumping)

This year the Morven Park Horse Trials falls on Easter weekend, and Darby Smith has urged me to go and learn more about her sport. Friday and Saturday produced conflicts – a house guest and a Point-to-Point – but Sunday's schedule is clear. Unfortunately the day is not. As I drive to Leesburg a cloudy sky gives way to a drizzle, which later becomes a cold rain.

At the Equestrian Center the jumping phase of the trial is in progress. A Division of Intermediates is competing in an open air enclosure studded with brightly painted jumps, each topped with one or more rails. Some are solid below the top rail, others have only three or four light rails and present an airy, open and insubstantial look to the approaching horse. A prescribed course weaves a circuitous route around and over the jumps, which are arranged to present two or even three obstacles in quick succession. Clearly the contest calls for consistent pace, nimbleness in changing direction, ability to control strides to reach the desired take-off point for each jump, and consistently smooth and sure jumping ability. The jumps, however, are about four feet high, challenging enough though significantly smaller than the obstacles in a Grand Prix event.

PHOTO BY PAT MACVEAGH

*Phyllis Dawson on Enniskerry Imp at Morven Park*

Contestants enter the ring in reverse order of their standing in the trials to date – that is, their score after the dressage and cross-country phases that took place on Friday and Saturday. Because this is a horse trial, even though held over three days, the cross-country segment has less elements than would have been used in a regular three-day event. Thus, faults accumulated in cross-country are in some cases few or even none. Friday's dressage has "set the table," and a lead there is easier to defend over the next two days than would be the case with a more demanding cross-country phase.

---

As each contestant enters the ring his or her score to date is reported. Then, at the conclusion of the jumping round, the number of jumping faults*, if any, are announced, and the final score totaled. Several horses complete faultless rounds, though there is one particular jump at which a few others pull a rail. Whether this is because the rail's green color makes it hard to see, and the horse aims to jump only the solid white panel underneath, or because of some striding difficulty in the approach to the fence, is unclear. In any case it is a troubling spot.

PHOTO BY PAT MACVEAGH

*Karen O'Connor and Joker's Wild negotiating the troublesome jump*

In this Intermediate group the ten leading contestants going in to the jumping phase remain the top ten at the end, though there are two or three shifts in placing. When all complete their rounds the ten best are called to receive ribbons (equine trivia: light blue is for tenth place). In this case, both the first and second place horses are ridden by Phillip Dutton, who has been a member of two Australian Olympic gold medal teams (though he is now based near Unionville, PA). This win is his third of the day. When all are pinned, Dutton leads them in a victory lap while the loudspeaker produces a lively rendition

---

* **Jumping Fault** penalties: Four faults for "pulling" (knocking off) a rail, three for a refusal, six for a second refusal. One fault for each second elapsed over the standard time limit. Disqualification for exceeding the maximum time limit, usually reached if the rider falls off.

*Phillip Dutton on Janraffole, winning the CIC\*\* Division 1 class at Morven Park*

of John Philip Sousa's "Seventy Six Trombones." Then the announcer calls for an intermission while the ring is rearranged for the more difficult course for the Advanced Divisions, which will begin jumping at noon.

After a break, under cover and out of the rain, it is back down to the jumping. Juliet Graham is there, standing on the hillside above the ring. She wonders what I am doing here. I tell her, then ask about her new horse.

*"He's doing well but he's a couple of years away. I'm on the Canadian Olympic Selection Committee, so I'm here checking out some Canadians."*

There are seven Canadian horses and five riders in the Advanced Division coming up. Under the maple leaf hat she is wearing Juliet is shivering. It has turned a lot colder since early morning. Near Juliet a Ford Explorer is parked with its open back towards the ring. Edie's cousin Peter MacVeagh and his wife Pat are hunched inside, camera and telephoto lens aimed at the action. They invite me into their shelter, observing:

*"Camera lenses don't like rain much."*

A few cars away *Loudoun Times-Mirror* reporter Betsy Parker is covering the event in much the same way, pointing her camera out the left front window. As we chat, the Advanced Division One jumpers start, and Betsy's camera clicks as each soars over the nearest fence. That way she's sure to have a picture of the winner. This Division has the best collection of riders, and Betsy points out how much smoother they and their horses are than those that went earlier. They should be, given the star quality of the group. Phillip Dutton wins again, his fourth of the day; that will probably be the feature of Betsy's story. His clear round in jumping has moved him up from third to first. The legendary Bruce Davidson is second, David O'Connor third (up from fifth), his teammate-wife Karen O'Connor sixth and Nina Fout tenth.

Down in the officials' tent Pam and John Wooley are preparing to give out the ribbons. Pam coaches John on what to do if the horse doesn't want it on his bridle. Obviously, since Pam is a Morven Park official, today it's John's turn to be "spouse of." Then, the ribbons awarded, Dutton leads the victory lap, the loudspeaker again filled with Sousa. Perhaps the record player forgot to bring a record of Waltzing Matilda with him.

Is three-day event jumping a spectator sport? On this rainy Easter Sunday a sampling of the best event riders in the world has drawn about 40 cars and perhaps twice that many people. Perhaps it's the weather, but that didn't seem to deter any competitor. And the fences aren't as big as they will be at the Grand Prix at the Upperville Horse Show in June. Or perhaps this particular event is mostly for practice; the Rolex four star is coming up in Kentucky in about three weeks, and it will attract tens of thousands. In support of the "practice" theory one notes that in today's four Advanced Divisions, averaging 16 entries each, the O'Connors have ten horses, and Bruce Davidson and his son Buck have six.

Up at the headquarters on the top of the hill I find Will O'Keefe, yesterday's race caller at the Orange County Point-to-Point, overseeing this latest of the many events that take place at his Morven Park fiefdom. He gives me permission to drive out through the forbidden back gate. It will save four miles going home and I am cold, damp and late for Easter lunch.

*Getting ready to ride – note the right hand in a cast*

Clearly eventing is growing in its appeal to horse lovers. Who are these people? Where do they come from? And why do they love their sport?

## – Teddy –

We met Teddy through a horse. Actually, it wasn't a regular horse – it was a rocking horse, primitive folk art, an antique child's toy. This horse had seen hard service – it was old, paint partly missing, no reins, a docked stump of a tail, head worn smooth by the caresses of generations of small owners. And it wasn't Teddy that we met first through this horse – it was his mother, Dee Mulligan, proprietress of the Delaplane Antiques Center.

Her evident passion for her rocking horse, her love for it and for other equines, was evident in her hesitation about entering the rocking horse for a claiming price of $1,250 in her booth at the Oatlands Antiques Show. But there he was, stabled under a table in the booth, standing for a tag, because she was anticipating future college bills. Edie admired the rocking horse, too. But our stable of folk art is full, we have no small grandchildren, and we had just bought a broodmare. So we did not enter a claim.

The source of the incipient college bills soon showed up, Dee's son Teddy, accompanied, as is the wont of 17 year old boys, by an attractive young lady he had brought to meet his mother. After introductions the conversation turned to horses – real ones. Teddy is hooked, has been since he was very small. He now whips in for the Blue Ridge Hunt, and wants to study equine management in college. We agreed to meet later.

*"Later"* turned out to take some time, as it often does. We were at the Great Meadow horse trials one May. By chance I noted the program entry, #128, Felton Lea's Sionach and Teddy Mulligan, and resolved to look him up. The chance came when the loud speaker at the course announced him. All proceeded well until the announcer reported one stop, then a second, and finally a third at the jump called The Quarry. Teddy was excused. I found him riding dejectedly towards his horse trailer. Reintroducing myself, I said something imaginative like… *"Tough luck."* Teddy was philosophical:

> *"He's a good jumper, but he doesn't like ditches. [Then, wistfully] …We were fifth going into the cross country."*

By this time Teddy has dismounted, removed his tack, and is hosing the horse, while Dee is scraping the water off. She looks up at me…

> *"I'm the mom."*

*"Yes, I know. Did you sell the rocking horse?"* She did. She adds:

> *"It was a really nice piece."*

———

THREE-DAY EVENTING                          *344*

I ask Teddy if he's still whipping in for Blue Ridge.

*"I did last season but I'm going to have to stop. I'm going to Roanoke College in the fall."*

*"What about horses?"*

*"I'm looking at a career with them. First I'm looking for a young horse I can ride and bring along down there. This guy's getting older. He's 15.2, all Connemara."*

*"Not enough size and speed?"*

*"Well, you need Thoroughbred blood. Seven eighths Thoroughbred, one eighth Irish would be perfect. My dad's Irish."*

With a name like Mulligan, who would have guessed? Teddy continues:

*"I want to study biology, maybe go to vet school later. But I'd like to continue eventing, if I'm good enough. "*

*"You should meet Dr. Matthew Mackay-Smith. He knows a lot about endurance riding, too."*

*"And a lot about foxhunting. I've talked to him."*

So much for volunteering to introduce members of Blue Ridge to each other. It must be the heat. Dee takes pity on me and gives me a bottle of ice water. Then she finishes scraping off the horse, and Teddy takes him away to graze and dry off. Teddy will bring the horse and the truck and trailer home later. Dee is headed there now, and says good-bye, adding:

*"Drop by the store sometime."*

Perhaps her farewell comment is a marketing gambit. She will need to sell a lot of antiques to support Teddy's studies and his hoped-for new horse.

## – Reaching for the Stars –

After the ribbons were pinned for the Intermediate Division I went up to the building at Morven Park where I had watched dressage some months before. Inside was a young girl, perhaps 12, sitting on a hay bale and holding lead shanks attached to a gray and a bay horse, each covered by a handsomely embroidered blanket that said "Bates." As I started to talk to the girl a large man appeared behind her, eyeing me with what I took to be suspicion. In defense I introduced myself and stated my purpose for being there. He responded:

*"I'm Peter Kozumplik, those horses are my daughter's, Sara, same surname."*

*"But it says 'Bates' on the blankets?"*

> *"Bates is an Australian saddle maker, one of Sara's sponsors. They gave her five saddles, and $4,000 a year worth of equipment. Sara was Young Rider of the Year in 2000. She's too old for that now, she'll be 23 in two days. Bates products are sold in the US by WeatherBeeta."*

As I am taking notes he spells it out – *"W-E-A-T-H-E-R-B-E-E-T-A."* Then Sara rides up on yet another horse, I am introduced, and Peter and she have a typical father-daughter exchange relating to the Advanced Division Three in which she will soon be jumping. Sara rides off, and Peter begins to tell me a lot about his family and eventing.

Peter himself has retired after an Army career. Sara started riding at three, benefiting from the fact that her mother is a dressage coach – according to Peter *"a bloody good one."* Mother has been able to continue teaching as the family has moved about, following Peter's military postings. Now they have settled nearby, and run a stable in Clifton, VA. As Peter tells it:

> *"Sara grew up in the Pony Club orbit – made A Level at 17. Here in Virginia, as Sara rose the whole barn switched from dressage to eventing. We have a string of eight event horses now, some owned jointly with sponsors, and some school horses for the students. The girl that was holding the two horses [they have now left] is one of Sara's pupils. We've never been able to afford a 'made' horse, so we buy prospects and Sara brings them along. That makes her a better rider, and closer to the horse. When you buy a made horse, and then he goes lame or dies you are left high and dry because you haven't learned enough."*

I'm curious about this eventing life style: *"Where did she go to school?"*

> *"She hasn't gone to college. She got this horse, As You Like It, and Jim Wofford – he's her coach – said 'you'll never have another horse like him,' so she couldn't let up, and she just kept going."*

I ask: *"As You Like It, as (like?) in Shakespeare?"*

> *"Yes, Sara's really into Shakespeare. We also have Richard III, Henry the Fifth and his half brother Agincourt, and Measure for Measure. She wanted to name one Hamlet, but I put my foot down – can you imagine an event horse considering whether 'to go, or not to go, that is the question.' One day last year the announcer introduced her as 'Sara Kozumplik, riding for Team Shakespeare.' All but one of our event horses are Thoroughbreds, some off the track. As You Like It is Prudent Pass on his Jockey Club papers."*

Later research discloses that Prudent Pass made 31 starts, winning twice. His new career suits him much better. *"Tell me about him."*

> *"He's a fast learner, got to Rolex Three Star in two years. But he's a bit weak in dressage. In a two star CIC in Georgia he was 23rd out of 35 at the end of the dressage, then 12th after the cross country, and finished 11th."*

[Ed. note: According to Nina Fout a fit Thoroughbred race horse is likely to get impatient doing the slow intricacies of the dressage tests.]

I ask, *"Can he win today?"* Peter is a realist:

> *"Not likely. He's fifth, and with Karen O'Connor and Regal Scot leading, they won't make many mistakes. But we're happy with how he's done."*

> *"Sportsmanship still exists in eventing. Riders will help each other with advice on the course, like 'watch fence #6 because it doesn't ride like it walks,' or 'be sure you get your extra stride in here.' …That attitude is great for young people."*

Then there is the small world department. The Kozumpliks are neighbors of Chuck and Inez Youree of the Fairfax Hunt, and Adrienne Hewitt's sister is one of Sara's sponsors.

## – The Confidence Builder –

Betsy Crenshaw describes Juliet Graham as:

> *"…the finest, most knowledgeable horse person that I know. Her attitude is that with the right prompts, training, and care any horse can make good at some job. In 17 years I've only seen her give up on one horse."*

The first steeplechase horse we owned was Mocito Bien. No foxhunter could get him over a chicken coop; when it came time to sell him there were no takers. So we sold him for a dollar to Juliet, for whom he became a fine field hunter, coops and all. Betsy has this theory:

PHOTO KINDNESS OF JULIET GRAHAM

*Juliet and Mocito*

> *"She was the only person that could get inside Mocito's head. He was a frightened horse, and she gave him confidence."*

Betsy continues:

*"I met Juliet through our pre-school daughters, Annie and Libby, who were in the Piedmont Child Care Center at the same time. One day many years ago several of us – Juliet, Heather Hooper, Libby, Annie, me – were riding around back of Ayrshire, playing horse show, laughing, dogs under foot, a regular circus.*

*"Then Juliet said to Heather 'Let me try that horse.' Heather's horse Count, an Arab, just seemed to us like another barnyard horse, but Juliet got on him and proceeded to put him through some complex dressage moves. That horse knew more than he was letting on, and Juliet had spotted it.*

*"All horses respond to the same aids, and Juliet knows what buttons to push. It's her body that does it, and her confidence. The horse senses it, becomes confident himself. I believe she could ride without any reins."*

We too have known Juliet Graham almost since the day we arrived in Upperville 15 years ago. Yet one recent fall afternoon, sitting in our living room, was the first time we had actually pieced her career together. Here is how it went. I ask, *"You were a Canadian?"*

*"Still am, but actually I was born in England. My parents moved to Canada when I was three – bought a ranch outside of Calgary. …I was bitten by the horse bug early, started riding at three, showing at six. My family was breeding horses and into three-day eventing in the 1960s, early for western Canada."*

*"How did you come to this area?"*

*"Well, my family had a friend who was the riding instructor at Foxcroft."*

*"So it was a way to combine riding with a fine education?"*

*"I guess so. I had a great time at Foxcroft. After graduation in 1972 I went to England for a couple of years. Took my own mare, Sumatra, bred by my parents, to compete at Burghley. Sumatra had spent two years with me at Foxcroft, and was eight years old."*

*"Wouldn't that be considered precocious – for both of you?"* Juliet is characteristically candid:

*"Fairly. Sumatra had done the Pan-Am Games in 1971."*

Juliet tells me something about Three Day Eventing, and I learn that during her stay in England she competed in the four star events at Badminton, and Burghley again, and in the World Championships, where she finished eighth. The big riders that year were Bruce Davidson, Mike Plumb, and Jim Wofford, all-time household names in the eventing world.

I ask her about further competition.

> *"Sumatra went on at that level for seven years — pretty amazing. I did the*
> *Montreal Olympics in 1976 as part of the Canadian team, and was with*
> *them in the 1978 World's Championship when the team won the gold*
> *medal. I missed the 1980 Olympics — I was pregnant. Then I rode in the*
> *1982 World Championships."*

PHOTO BY TERRY BRANHAM, COURTESY OF JULIET GRAHAM

*Juliet Graham on Sumatra — Montreal Olympics 1976*

*"Did you win it?"*

> *"Nah, --- I fell off!"* [She laughs.]

Juliet evented for a few more years, then took up steeplechase racing. I ask why.

> *"It seemed like a good idea at the time. I worked and rode, mostly for*
> *Randy Waterman — he was phasing out as a race rider about then."*

In 1988 she won the lady rider championship in the Virginia Point-to-Point
circuit on Mocito Bien, but by then her marriage had come apart, and she

had to get some income from what she was doing. Sometime in there she tried her hand at selling tack and horse supplies, but gave it up because she'd rather spend her time with the horses. Juliet also was a source of horses for fellow foxhunters. One day Edie needed a new one, her old Tor having been retired, and Juliet had the answer. Edie tried and liked the horse.

*"What's his name?"* said Edie. Answered Juliet:

*"Romeo!"*

True story, and Romi is now Edie's favorite hunter. I ask, *"Were you ever tempted to go back to Canada?"*

*"No. It's too spread out up there, so you don't get the concentration of horse sports. This is the place for hunting, racing, eventing. I went back to eventing in 1994, but didn't have a good horse until a couple of years ago."*

I ask Juliet about how she made a living boarding horses and giving lessons, which she's done for a dozen years until recently.

*"That's the 24/7 of the horse business. Generally I boarded foxhunters, tacked them up and took them to the meets so all the owners had to do was show up, get on, and ride. Plus some teaching, and exercising horses between hunts. When I was at Catesby I had 42 horses, a wonderful Mexican to do stalls, and two exercise riders. Fortunately some of the boarder horses were not in work."*

I do not ask how the Mexican made out with 42 stalls, horses in work or not, but instead, *"Can you make any money that way?"*

*"Only if you don't have too many of your own horses. I had to have three hunters so I could go out with my clients, and there were two event horses. My vocation is also my avocation.*

*"It was total insanity. So when Milton Sender, one of my clients, decided to keep his horses at home, he offered me a job, and eventually I couldn't refuse. Of course there were six horses then, and now we have seventeen! Milton's business takes him all over the world, but hunting is his passion. He's really supportive – does a lot for the Piedmont Foshounds, and my job allows me to do more hunting and be a Field Master or Whip. And I have this new event horse that Milton owns."*

Juliet is obviously excited. The new horse, Buckley Bay – Bucky for short – is five years old, and now at the Preliminary level. I ask how far he can go.

*"With luck, he has the class and ability to go all the way. I had a lesson the other day with Jimmy Wofford, and he said 'with this one you better dust*

PHOTO BY SUSAN MCHUGH

*Juliet training Bucky at Jim Wofford's*

*off your pink coat.' "*

*"But at your age, can you do it?"*

> *"Why not? I've been there before. I think I've never been riding better, I know more. There are people my age at the top level. It all depends on what you're sitting on."*

Jimmy Wofford (now coach of the Canadian eventing team) concurs:

> *"She's got the knowledge and experience. She's very fit. And she's got a good horse. She's a couple of years away. Maybe in 2004…"*

The conversation turns reflective. I ask Juliet, *"If you hadn't gone to England after Foxcroft, what would you have done?"* The answer is prompt and direct:

> *"Gone to Vet School."*

I ask her about the common belief that one of the challenges of eventing is to get the horse competent in what seem like the contradictory skills of dressage and cross-country. Juliet sees it from another angle:

> *"The technicality of dressage improves their jumping ability. The more they learn in dressage the better they can jump. It's all about getting 'broke'. So technicality is not much of an issue anymore. As for cross-country, rather than being the antithesis of dressage, dressage is what makes it. The more broke they are, the faster they go. Jimmy's definition of broke is 'You pull on the reins and they stop. You kick them and they go.' But you must teach them to do all of that correctly."*

*"But how about another Olympics?*

> *"I want to take Bucky as far as he can go."*

Those who subscribe to the magazine *Practical Horseman* were treated in November, 2000 to a dramatic cover photo of David O'Connor taking his victory lap after winning the individual Three-Day Eventing Gold Medal at the Sydney Olympics. In the picture O'Connor, wearing his scarlet coat with blue and white collar, holds his reins in his left hand while using his right arm to hold aloft his riding cap and his crop, to which is tied an American flag that streams out behind him. At first glance one sees a handsome and triumphant athlete at the pinnacle of his career.

The cover – based on the photo at the start of this chapter – suggests a more intriguing story. Splashed across O'Connor's chest, between his collar and the gold medal dangling from a blue ribbon around his neck is the magazine's headline – "Custom Made Gold!" Below the headline and the rider's body is the head of the pretty bay gelding that O'Connor rode – make that "teamed with" – to the Olympic win. As the headline suggests, the other athlete that shares the gold medal with David O'Connor is named Custom Made. It's the first Olympic gold for an American horse and rider since 1984, and David's face says it all – national pride, disbelief, and a sense of humility.

This great moment was shared retrospectively with a group of perhaps 70 horse people gathered at the National Sporting Library in Middleburg one November evening. The event was billed as "A Conversation with Olympians" and starred O'Connor and two of his three Virginia team-mates, his wife Karen (riding Prince Panache) and Nina Fout (3 Magic Beans), who together with our neighbor Linden Wiesman (on Anderoo), had won the team Three-Day Event Bronze Medal as well.

As the program unfolded, highlighted by movies of the action, the intensity, difficulty and risks of high level three-day eventing became clear to those more accustomed to other aspects of horse sports.

Because of the huge variety of skills, training and experience necessary to bring a talented horse to the top level, event horses are much older than typical race horses, in the case of the US team ranging between 10 and 16 years. By the time a horse is 17 or 18 he tends to have lost enough to be unsuitable for international competition. Serious event riders need to have younger horses coming along behind their current stars, just as major league baseball teams have farm systems.

But there is far more to winning an Olympic equestrian medal than a horse and rider team bonding through intense training and competition, and then navigating their way through a grueling three-day test of precision, courage, and endurance. As the O'Connors repeatedly emphasized, a winning Olympic team is made up of many elements. Karen puts it this way:

*"Competing in the Olympic Games is a privilege unparalleled by any other experience I have ever had. Every athlete that participates shares a sense of patriotism for one's country. David and I have both been fortunate enough to win medals. When you stand on the podium to receive your medal, you are overwhelmed by the sensation of all the people standing there with you. You are the lucky one that receives the medal. You occupy the hallowed ground the Olympic podium provides you, for your moment in time.*

*"But, there are literally the tens of people directly involved, the thousands of people indirectly involved, not only the O'Connor Event Team, but also the US Equestrian Team, and of course there are the millions of people that are there through their association with the US Olympic Committee and the USA itself.*

PHOTO BY PAT MCVEAGH

*Karen O'Connor on Travis – show jumping locally*

*"All are sharing in that awe-inspiring sensation of success in the Olympic movement. The Olympic Games encompass a worldwide appreciation of the level of excellence the champions have achieved, which is recognizable by hundreds of millions of people, regardless of your sport or country. No one stands there alone.*

*"The key to success in our sport is teamwork. Teamwork is the ability to make every person feel that his or her effort is vital to the success of the mission. For David and me, our mission is sustained competitive excellence throughout not only an Olympic quadrennial, but over multiple Olympic cycles. Everyone's job is crucial to success.*

*"To that end, teamwork is never more profoundly demonstrated than in the partnership between horse and rider. The horse, for which we owe so much, has always been there for man as a team player. The horse has had such an amazing impact on civilization itself. In today's modern world he is enjoyed by millions as a wonderful friend and sporting companion. And so our plight continues: to understand the language of the horse."*

This brings us to those often unseen but essential members of the extended team – the horse owners. It is unusual when a skilled rider also has the pocketbook to own several expensive event horses. So, perhaps half or more of Olympic-caliber horses are owned by someone other than the rider. At Sydney only Nina Fout and Linden Wiesman rode and trained their own horses. The team was lucky to have Jacquie Mars as owner and sponsor of two Olympic horses – Prince Panache and Giltedge, David's horse in the team contest.

Horse owners were clearly critical to the success of the Olympians, and the

PHOTO BY THE AUTHOR

*Nina Fout competing locally*

applause given Jacquie at the Library showed that everyone there knew it. And all the other owners, whether of Olympic horses or those against whom they compete to get to the top, are also contributors to Olympic success. Competition is what brings out the best in the best. The Olympians were quick to note also the help that Jim Wofford had been to them during their careers, even though he was not part of the group in Australia.

The Olympic team depended on Chef d'Equipe Mark Phillips in the role of non-riding coach and Jim Wolfe to handle administration and logistics. Since the riders were all highly experienced, Mark's job was to keep them focused on the work at hand, and to see to it that each entered the course or ring at a peak of confidence and determination to have the best possible round.

Juliet Graham sees the ideal management structure slightly differently: *"The Chef d'Equipe need not necessarily be the Coach. In some cases the Chef d'Equipe handles the paperwork – hotels, cars, transportation;"* all the logistical details of a large group of people living and working far from home. She continues:

> *"The Coach does the horses and riders, fitness programs and focus for both. And there may be a sports psychologist involved. The game is so fine-tuned that the riders must have their minds in the right place. You get to the Olympics by years of concentrating on an objective. Then the 'elite athlete syndrome' comes into play. You suddenly realize 'Holy S---, THIS IS THE OLYMPICS,' and all sorts of distractions rise up in your face. You need someone to help you resist them and stay focused."*

As Juliet implies, media pressure can be intense. At Sydney a tutorial was held for the US riders to help them in handling media contacts.

What the coach does for the riders, the grooms do for the horses. There may be four horses that will compete, and another four as spares. At one groom to a horse – the normal ratio – that's eight grooms. Backing them up will be vets (three at Sydney for the whole USET), a farrier, perhaps a horse masseuse. Feed and equipment companies will have specialists along, to help with nutrition and tack and for the publicity they receive. And then there are the officials of the Olympics and of the relevant national horse associations. So the extended team will have several times as many support people as there are riders competing.

Putting such an organization in place, and maintaining it in a foreign country for some weeks calls for funding well beyond what Olympic horse owners can give. So sponsors and individual donors are essential. Nina Fout estimates the cost of sending a horse and rider to Sydney at $40-50K or more. Without those many, many supporters the results at Sydney would not have been possible. But with them it was a great team effort, and a huge stimulus for Three-Day Eventing in America.

Two years later, Nina sums it up:

> *"What was the greatest thrill? Just being there, one of only four compared to all the thousands of eventers who didn't have a chance to go. Sydney was one of the best sites ever, incredibly well organized, great national pride, real sportsmen. It was a wonderful way to start the new century. In a neutral political climate we all felt safe – it was just perfect."*

*"Would you like to do it again?"*

> *"I'd love to. But you have to be realistic. If it comes, it comes. You have to have the right horse to do it."*

## – Next Stop, Jerez –

In geologic time there is only an instant between the American success of 2000 at Sydney, and the next international team challenge, the World Equestrian games at Jerez, Spain, in 2002. Two centuries ago Napoleon's army traveled to Spain, among other places, on its stomach. Today's American eventing teams also travel on "bread" – in this case the financial contributions of private supporters, rather than their home government as may be the case in other lands.

This August evening our neighbors had a chance to see their local eventing heroes in action in one of the tests that will determine the makeup of our team in Spain. About a dozen "short list" American riders, some with more than one horse, and a few international visitors, held a show jumping element of this trial in a ring conveniently located behind Virginia Gunnell's house, Banbury Cross, just east of Middleburg. The invitation to attend, and share the Gunnell hospitality as well as watch the jumping, made clear that this was a fund-raiser through which locals should show their support for the people who in 2000 had placed our horse country in the first rank of world equine-dom. Several hundred were there, check books in hand, to do so.

The course was designed and then described to the crowd by Sally Ike. Brian O' Connor (David's brother) announced the horses and riders, as he does regularly at such events.

The horses and riders performed with professional smoothness over Sally's tight circuit of challenging jumps. The crowd was knowledgeable and appreciative. After the event Middleburg Mayor Tim Dimos made cogent observations about the contributions of these riders and horses to our community, and the need for supporting them. Then the riders were given awards, after which they mixed effortlessly with the crowd, which included in many cases their parents, coaches, friends, or acquaintances from eventing, showing, fox-hunting, steeplechasing or even yesterday's Pony Club.

It's a long way to the 2004 Olympics, but Middleburg, The Plains, Upperville and adjacent parts of our Community of the Horse plan to get us there in fighting trim.

The only complaint, a muted one, came from the photographers – professionals like Janet Hitchen and Betsy Parker, and amateurs such as the author – that the overcast evening light was a little weak for shooting at 1/800 of a second.

PHOTO BY THE AUTHOR

*A fundraiser for the USET Eventers at Banbury Cross*

To my knowledge none of the broader audience cared a whit for that optical inconvenience. They were too busy enjoying each other and their special connection to international equestrian stardom.

EPILOGUE

A few weeks later the US Eventing team of David O'Connor, Amy Tryon, Kim Vinoski and John Williams won the Gold Medal at Jerez. And as Karen O'Connor pointed out, everyone that had been at Banbury Cross was at Jerez in spirit.

*Event riders at Banbury Cross*

But it is evident that reaching the competitive zenith in this sport – and perhaps in any other – calls for extraordinary long-term dedication of time and self on the part of the players. Many participants will enjoy – and their lives benefit from – the sport of eventing. Only a very few riders will have the talent and be willing to pay the price that success at the top level demands.

## – Second Thoughts –

Darby Smith came to eventing the old-fashioned way – everyone around her was doing it.

She grew up in Stafford, Vermont, a rural horse community, where her grandfather had been the Congregationalist minister. Since the 1960s the area around Stafford and Woodstock had been a center of eventing. As a young girl she…

> *"…had a lot of horse books that I read obsessively, even before I had a horse. When I got one, I rode bareback, tried to vault onto him from the ground, raced with my friends, explored trails to see where they went. It was all informal, but those are all the elements of eventing. My mother didn't ride competitively, but she liked having horses around. There were many small*

*farms with horses, an economical way to have them, not like today, board-ing at a stable. …I knew I wanted to jump, and to go fast. I even thought of being a jockey, but I got too tall and outgrew it."*

Then she started watching the people at Huntington, a big training center nearby. At 13 she brought her horse there, and started eventing. Her first horse, a Thoroughbred/Quarter Horse cross, eventually was deemed too small by her trainer and was replaced. The style then was for larger horses. Soon she was 16, and ready to go "Preliminary" with the new horse. I ask her about eventing: *"Isn't it the most diverse of horse sports, and the most demanding?"*

*"Not really. The three disciplines are inter-related. The aids in dressage are the same as those used in cross country, which is the heart of the sport. Cross-country, that's the real challenge – speed, danger, fun. The horse has to be good in this. For him it's a puzzle to be solved. They enjoy it. And stadium jumping is just dressage over fences."*

Soon fate, in the form of an auto accident and a broken leg, intervened and eventing took a back seat. Next came college – Bryn Mawr, and a degree in film studies. After college she…

*"…rode a bit here and there. I spent four or five months in England – the Isle of Man – galloping race horses."*

Next there was a job with a publishing company, and a film job, mostly to pay for her eventing.

*"Then I came here with my horse – Middleburg is the center of the eventing world – and worked at* The Chronicle; *now I'm taking care of Charley Matheson's horses. At first the job and the horse seemed to reinforce each other, but later they started to pull me in opposite directions. It's hard to do both well, hard to keep one from interfering with the other. …One problem here is the lack of cross-country courses on which to school. It's a matter of land availability and insurance. I go back to Vermont in the summer and ride cross-country where I know the places.*

*"I've reached Preliminary level in horse trials, but never my original goal, taking part in a regular Three-Day Event."*

*"Why not?"*

*"It is harder to get there than I thought. The great thing then was, anyone could do it. Now it's much more expensive, and the rules make you compete more and do better at the horse trials in order to qualify for the three-day events, where the entry fee may be $500. It's getting more professional – the rules acknowledge this, and are encouraging a split between levels.*

*"To get to the top you need a lot of money, or a patron, or to be a professional and earn a living from selling horses or training."*

Darby is a realist, and she wants a career in which she has a chance to excel:

*"I think I'm done with eventing. Of course, I've said that before, and I have a lot of friends in it. But my present horse Shoeless Joe is 15, and has done all he can do. I plan to sell him. Shoeless Joe helped me see that the horse business can be a 'Field of Dreams.' When I was a kid I thought 'How can I arrange my life so I can ride? What school also has a barn?' My schedule was dictated by making time for riding, and when I had to feed the horses. Now I'm planning to go back to school, get a Masters in Education or Writing so I can teach."*

*"Did you ever know anyone else who gave it up?"* Darby thinks for a while, then:

*"Yes, an older friend, Patty VanCise. She was a trainer in our barn, came to Vermont after a year of college. She competed, got to the preliminary level. Her first horse was a mare, which she bred. Sadly, she lost both the mare and the baby in foaling. Then Luc, her second horse, had a chip in his ankle. Patty went back to Colorado, got a Masters, and started a career in social work. Later, she went back to riding, and then died of Lou Gehrig's disease. Some of us think she went back to riding when she learned she wasn't going to live much longer."*

It seems time to get on a happier tack, so I ask, *"At what level do you want to teach?"*

*"College. I like ideas and stories, methodology, theory. It takes my mind beyond the physical relationship with a horse. I'm looking at Columbia and Dartmouth, maybe others. I've been out of the academic loop for a while."*

*"Would you quit riding?"*

*"I imagine myself always riding, but it's hard for me to ride and not be goal oriented. I might just pleasure ride, that's not high maintenance, might do that. There's something about riding – people out there striving, some people on a spiritual path. Doing horses incorporates these things. You communicate without words with a beast."*

*"Clearly you have an emotional attachment to horses. Why?"*

*"They seem to be all heart. They're doing their best for you, willing to communicate, to have fun. They're gentle, affectionate, kind and noble creatures. There'll always be something there for me, watching a horse in a field, swishing his tail, taking a roll… the only song that can make me cry is 'Run for the Roses'. "*

---

Some day, at some college, somewhere, a lot of people who are now little kids are in for a great educational experience. And on her day off their professor will no doubt unwind on the back of a horse, meditating on paths not taken.

## – Advice to the Young Eventer –

I asked Nina Fout what she would offer as advice to the young hopefuls whom we have met earlier, given the long odds against getting on an Olympic team. Here is what she had to say:

PHOTO BY THE AUTHOR
*Nina Fout*

*"Having a passion, a dream, a focus is good. Children who grow up without one have a void in their lives, so it is good to follow your dream. Whether you get there is not as important. It's your enthusiasm and fortitude that count.*

*"Having to take care of a horse is a responsibility, and you must learn to handle the misfortunes that can come with owning a horse."*

Nina is currently training four event horses, of which she owns two. Though they take up half her day she tries to have a balanced life, and interact with a broad spectrum of people.

*"A balance in life helps when horse things go really wrong. Then you should remember that eventing is, after all, a sport."*

## – On Being an Owner –

Jacquie Mars has been a horse person all her life. As she tells it:

*"When growing up my pony was my best friend. Then came everyone else."*

She followed that with a love of foxhunting, won the junior division of a 100 mile ride, and has owned flat race horses and steeplechasers, though horse shows have never had much appeal for her. Now eventing is Jacquie's passion, despite her own event riding career having stopped well short of where her horses now are.

> *"I had two children and a non-riding husband. I could do horse trials, but there wasn't time for the Three-Day Events. But it was fun anyhow."*

I ask her how she became interested in the sport.

> *"I went to Rome in 1958. I'd never seen horses perform like that. It was remarkable they could get horses to do what they were doing, because of the relationship between the horse and the rider. Event horses aren't sold very much, rider and horse tend to stay together as a permanent team. There's no other horse sport like that. I love the idea.*

> *"There isn't much money to be made in eventing. But it combines it all – grace, discipline, bravery… I'm too much of a foxhunter to like dressage a lot, it's too confining, but the rest of eventing is as close as you can get to wild man foxhunting."*

I ask how she met the O'Connors, who now operate out of her farm.

> *"A girl that worked for me had an event horse she was bringing along, and I met Karen through that – it must have been about 24 years ago, before she was married to David. Karen can tell you more about it."*

*USET Eventing hopeful show jumping at Banbury Cross benefit*

PHOTO BY THE AUTHOR

*Water obstacle at Great Meadow*

The conversation returns to her horses, and Jacquie wraps it all up:

> *"My event horses live down in the barn. I go see them every day, bring them something, and they nicker at me. They know me as the 'treat lady.' I even ride them occasionally. It's a relationship that you cannot have with a race horse in training. Eventing is the only competitive equine sport where as an owner you can have that close personal connection with your horse."*

And she could have added – though she did not – that as the owner of Olympic horses she was a vital part of the team's success.

## – The Case for Eventing –

Together with the previous pages, Jacquie Mar's experience summarizes the case for eventing.

- It captures the imagination of young Pony Clubbers and gives them the incentive to become proficient and serious horse people.

- It requires the most complete understanding of the horse and the

*Juliet Graham – riding the dressage phase of the 1978 Eventing World's Championship*

fullest development of the horse-human relationship, both physically and emotionally, of any equine sport, at least in the eyes of its proponents.

- Success is not easily or quickly achieved. It requires planning, dedication, and hard, detailed effort over a span of years.

- Eventing calls for tough-minded athleticism, and develops both physical and moral courage.

- No eventer can become proficient single-handed. Eventing fosters cooperation not only with the horse, but also with competitors, trainers, and service providers of all sorts, even parents.

- Eventing builds an intimate and enduring relationship between an individual horse and its rider.

- When an eventer moves to other fields, the instilled habits of dedication, discipline and cooperation remain lifelong assets.

- Because there is so little money to be earned from it, eventing escapes the adverse pressures that can plague "big money" sports like flat racing.

- Even in success, the ups and downs of eventing and of horses maintain a suitable degree of humility in its devotees.

---

- Its rewards are based as much on perceiving self-improvement as on competitive success; both can be immensely gratifying.

- After one's active days are past there is still an opportunity to stay intimately connected, helping others as an event horse owner, sponsor, event volunteer or enthusiastic friend for those active in the sport.

Perhaps most important, no "player" encountered by the writer in the preceding random walk through eventing circles wished to be any place other than where he or she was at the moment. Eventing surely builds character, but for its disciples it is first and foremost ... a great deal of FUN!

*Jumping into Great Meadow's Swan Lake*

# XIV
# STEER ROPING

PHOTO BY THE AUTHOR

*Ropers in the big sand arena at Big Sky Ranch*

**B**rian Smith has invited us to join him at The Big Sky Ranch this evening to watch them practice roping, and to learn more about this transplanted western sport as it is practiced in Virginia.

Raleigh Kraft, owner of Big Sky, is a native of Montana. He has scraped off the top of a shale hill in the Shenandoah Valley and made a 150 x 300 foot arena with a deep sand cover in which to practice his hobby, team roping. As we drive up the hill, Brian, mounted on a 15 hand, stocky Quarter Horse, opens the gate, normally closed to contain the small herd of small Mexican cattle that provide practice for the ropers. We drive through and park next to Brian's trailer. Indicating his mount, horse-shoer Brian comments:

> *"It's a lot more fun on top of these things, but I can make more money underneath."*

We pat the horse, noting the great difference in temperament and physical structure between this animal, bred for patience, agility, toughness, and quick speed and the larger, more graceful, delicate and sensitive Thoroughbreds with which we are most familiar. The horse has a brand on his shoulder: "D / M".

*"What's his name?"* I ask.

> *"We call him Mo. That's because I got him from Dave Mazurko, who is known as Mo."*

So the D / M brand is explained without asking. Raleigh appears, and we say hello (or was it *"howdy"*?). After I introduce Edie, Brian and Raleigh chat briefly about a recent roping event. Apparently there were a lot of "Buckle Bunnies" there.

*"What's a Buckle Bunny?"*

> *"They're young girls that hang out around ropers – like 'groupies' with ball players."*

*"Oh."* Brian and Raleigh are both unattached, and young enough to be noticed – so the subject is not pursued, though we conclude roping is a sociable sport. Raleigh confirms this by pointing to a beverage cooler…

> *"There's beer and soft drinks over there. Help yourself."*

It's getting cool, and for the moment we demur.

Suddenly Raleigh lets out a long, deep, melodious sound – *"Hoo-oo-aw, Hoo-oo-aw"* – like a Montana bull elk, and in a minute about fifteen small cattle with wide horns emerge from a dense pine grove and crowd to the top of the hill. There the animals are directed to a small pen at the far end of the arena by Brian and a medium-sized, low slung, black dog. We ask Raleigh about the cattle.

> *"They're about 17 months old now, and good for a year or two. Then they get too heavy, or too smart to rope. Then you can eat them, or breed the females to produce a new crop. We have a Mexican 'Coriente' bull – 'Coriente' means mongrel – that gets the animals we want."*

Now another trailer pulls up, its side labeled "REG. QUARTER HORSE." The driver dismounts and is introduced as J.R. Shockly. As JR unloads his horse I note the saddle, made of carefully tooled leather, with the inscription: "G P I R A – All

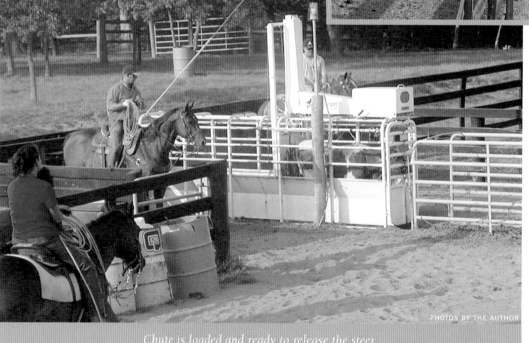

*Chute is loaded and ready to release the steer*

PHOTOS BY THE AUTHOR

Around Champion." JR is modest:

*"The saddle was a friend's."*

We later learn that "G P I R" stands for "Great Plains Indian Reservation."

Tonight's practice is to help JR school his horse for an event coming up in Morgantown, West Virginia. Everyone here is a team roper, the team consisting of two riders – a "header" to catch the animal by the head, after which the "heeler" completes the capture by getting his rope around the hind legs, usually by throwing a loop under the belly of the steer, and tightening up on the rope as the running animal steps into the loop on the ground. We learn that…

*"…best time wins. If the heeler only gets one leg it's a five second penalty. The header can rope the neck, or both horns, but not just one horn. If he*

PHOTO BY THE AUTHOR

*Header and heeler pulling alongside a running steer*

*does get just one horn he has to maneuver his rope until it is over both before he can turn the steer for the heeler. That's called 'fishing without a license' "*

The capture is complete when both ropes are taut, and the riders are facing each other with the steer in between them.

JR is a heeler, while Brian and Raleigh are headers.

Raleigh has been uncertain whether to join the practice or not, but when Edie says she would ride he asks:

*"Western or flat saddle?"*

*"Well, I've ridden more, recently, in a flat saddle."*

Brian is helpful:

*"Western, and bring Comet Man for her."*

Raleigh leaves to get two horses. We ask about the ropes, obviously carefully made of some synthetic material.

*"They're a blend of nylon and poly. Poly adds stiffness and doesn't stretch. The header's rope is 30 feet long, the heeler's 35."*

As we chat, Brian turns philosopher:

*"You can come up here and rope and forget about everything. Not that shoeing horses is a high pressure job, but it can get on your nerves. [Then he adds]... Jimmy Ellis is sure enjoying fishing in your pond. He likes to take the kids there Sunday mornings."*

Jim is the new farrier for our yearlings, recommended to us by Brian.

Now to business. Brian and JR mount and start warming up their horses. Both are small, solid Quarter Horses with short necks. They are bred this way to allow the roper to get down to the level of the animal he is roping. Then the horse must be strong enough to take the strain as the rope tightens up and stops the roped steer. Sometimes, for speed and endurance, a Quarter Horse will be crossed with a Thoroughbred. The result is called an "appendix." I ask Brian, *"Why that name?"*

*"At one time a horse was 'appendix' until it qualified as 'permanent'."*

Raleigh arrives with two more horses, and boosts Edie aboard Comet Man, and adjusts her stirrups. Her uncertainty is apparent, though Comet Man, stocky and quite fat, is hardly moving. She is holding the reins in both hands, as if he is a hunter. Brian notices:

*"One hand, Edie, one hand. And it's OK to hold onto the horn."*

———

Now the cattle are moved to a pen at the near end of the arena. That enclosure in turn feeds cattle single file into a chute, at the end of which is a gate much like the one we use to work Angus, only smaller. Unlike our Angus arrangement, the exit gate is remote controlled electronically by a horseman, so the roper can release his quarry much as a skeet shooter can say "Pull!" to have his companion press a button that launches a clay pigeon from a machine several yards away from either of them.

After a bit of warm up rope twirling Brian and JR line up alongside the chute, the header (Brian) on the left, the heeler (JR) on the right. They wait

*The header's rope is about to connect*

for Raleigh and Edie to get out of the way, then the gate is tripped and a steer rushes out, headed for the other end of the arena and safety. The two horses sprint along on either side of him, Brian's rope drops over his horns, tightens, and the steer is pulled into a ninety-degree left hand turn, a required maneuver. JR then takes a shot at the hind legs, but misses. Brian slackens his rope, and follows the steer to the pen at the far end of the arena, where he releases him.

Another steer is loaded and "fired", this time with

Raleigh as header. Again the horns are roped, again the heeler appears to miss. JR explains:

> "I only got one leg. I don't like to dally on one leg – you can hurt the steer. This time I'll get two, and dally."

Now the third animal is set free. Brian heads him quickly, turns him, and, good to his word, JR gets both legs. His rope tightens around them and both riders stop, their horses facing the steer immobilized between them at the end of two taut ropes. Game over. Bravo!! – or is it Ole!!

We conclude that the heeler has the harder job.

*Just out of the chute…*                    *…the header (Doug, in white) ropes first, then JR catches the heels.*

JR is anxious to school his horse to follow his commands, not anticipate them, so on some occasions he delays his turn, or makes some other unexpected move, to force the horse to listen to him. I ask JR about his horse…

> *"He's seven, I've had him 14 months. I call him 'Sorrelly' 'cause of his color – sorrel. He's bred super. It takes at least a year from breaking until they are ready to go anywhere. Longer if you have less time to work on them."*

I gather from all of this that some ropers do it full time, no regular job to get in the way. Obviously it's hard for the regular working stiffs to compete – just as it was when us weekend sailors went up against the sail loft's full time pros. I ask our new friends about it. The answer:

> *"Oh, but it's so sweet when we do beat them!"*

Reaching back to a moment on Long Island Sound, many, many years ago, racing a boat with a crew of Edie and two half grown children, I think *"Yes indeed, I can still taste how sweet it is."*

Now all the cattle have had a trip down to the other end, and Brian and I go down to bring them back for another round. As we start down Brian cautions:

> *"Watch out you don't get some atmosphere on your feet!"*

Perhaps he has forgotten that we, too, live on a farm. As the evening progresses we learn more about our ropers. JR is a native Virginian, from Winchester, and a construction worker. Raleigh is trying to persuade him to start his own house building business, but that hasn't quite happened yet.

Raleigh headed east as a young man to go to West Point, but ended up graduating from Georgetown. After some exposure as a staffer to Justice Brennan, he gave up the idea of earning a joint JD/MBA graduate degree and went on to a successful career as a financial manager, which led to owning Big Sky Ranch.

I ask how many ropers there are around these parts. The answer:

———

*"Maybe 40 or more guys live within an hour of here. Within five hours there are two roping events every weekend, Saturday and Sunday. Everyone brings their family. All the prizes are money, or fancy belt buckles, or horse equipment like saddles. The biggest event we ever had, the prizes totaled 21,000 dollars. Mostly they're a lot smaller."*

## – Malcolm Baldridge –

All this reminds me of Malcolm Baldrige, a fellow roper that Raleigh knew, who was a member of the Cowboy Hall of Fame.

One Monday morning, long ago, in Secretary Baldrige's walnut-paneled office in the United States Department of Commerce, I asked my then boss, *"How was the weekend, Mac?"*

Baldrige, a native Nebraskan, hoarded words as well as any movie cowboy. In this case he used none at all to answer me – he just reached in his pocket and pulled out a huge roll of bills, which he proceeded to thumb through slowly as I watched. Mac had just spent a great weekend, team roping.

He was a heeler.

*Malcolm Baldridge practicing roping in Aldie, VA – the header's rope has just tightened*
PHOTO BY PARKER

Months later Raleigh calls:

> "We're having a big do – auction, food, drinks and some trick roping – at the Big Sky Ranch on the 20th. Can you join us?"

So I do, early enough to watch some more steer roping before the festivities get serious. The first person I meet is Doug Pitts, an insurance adjuster for State Farm. He's also candid about his job:

> "It's something I do so I can support this."

Doug Pitts

Two of his favorite ladies are with him. One is a palomino mare…

> "Her name is Lily's Oro – Lily here is my daughter, Oro is Spanish for gold. But her stable name is 'The Hussy.' She's pure athlete, and intuitive about the rider."

"The Hussy"

At the moment she is tied to the fence and seems asleep. Doug reassures me:

> "Soon as I get on her she'll wake up. [then about Lily]… "The kid's been riding since she could walk. It's something we can do together."

But now it is time for some roping, and I go to the tower where Randy Goldhizen is announcing the goings on for the benefit of perhaps 10 spectators. The first team of Doug and JR is quick to get their steer. Randy observes:

> "5.65 …it's going to be hard to beat."

> [Someone adds] "Way to go, JR, he's my man."

Next steer, the heeler misses. Randy:

> "Looks like Brooks had the right things

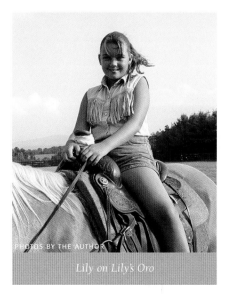

PHOTOS BY THE AUTHOR

Lily on Lily's Oro

*going, and Lydia did not…* [then] *Doug Pitts on the heading side, JR on the heeling side…* [a pause, then]… *No catch."*

Then, as the next steer is released from the chute…

*"We've got the head wired, it's JR heading. The lady in red is my wife, fortunately,"*

But she misses the heel. Randy explains:

*"She spends her time taking care of me."*

Soon all the steers have accumulated at the far end of the arena and it's time to bring them back and reload the chute. Three riders are dispatched for retrieval

duty. As they herd the cattle Randy is on the horn:

*"They're goin' on a trail ride, folks. If you'd a-done that we could've rode some horses, had a couple of beers."*

I learn that the head wraps on the cattle are to prevent the rope burning them, and that when the heeler gets only one leg they loosen up and they let him go…

*"Don't want to stretch him. Steers are expensive."*

Next a steer is caught quickly by Brooks Staples and JR, and someone asks the time.

—
375

PHOTOS BY THE AUTHOR

*Brian Smith in Raleigh Kraft's Big Sky Ranch tackroom*

*Kevin Staples, trick roper*

*"Randy's got the watch and went down stairs."*

Randy hears and calls up:

*"7.2... [then he adds] Didn't look like that, did it?"*

Randy comes back up, and he tells me a bit about himself, his career on the Front Royal police force, how he's now retired and recovering from diabetes. As soon as he was well enough they lifted him on a horse, but he's not ready yet to start roping. I take his picture, face peering out from under his black hat, and since the camera is digital I show him how he looks, adding *"That's some leer."* Randy shoots back:

*"There was a time when that leer meant something. Not any more."*

A lady in the tower is listening, and is quick to add:

*"He had his day, though."*

Now it is time to go down to the party starting outside the tack room. Here a crowd of 50 or more is gathering, mostly ropers and their families, soaking up Raleigh's hospitality and just visiting as they look over the silent auction material spread out on tables.

Brian Smith, through whom we have become acquainted with Randy, is there and introduces me to the trick roper, who will perform later. Since I have to go soon to join Edie elsewhere he shows me a few of his specialties, including rolling the loop over the back of his neck. Fortunately he does not head himself.

Up in the ring the ropers are still at it.

——

STEER ROPING

376

Old folks like me

Party scene and auction tent

The next generation

# XV

## POLO

*"I play polo because I love the horse, and because I love team sport competition. It's a way to enjoy both at the same time... the action, the element of danger, to be in sync with your horse at high speed, to out-think, out-maneuver, out-ride the other team..."*
—Garrick Steele, amateur polo player and entrepreneur

378

One late summer day in 2001 a platoon of giant yellow earth moving machines – bulldozers and scrapers – appeared in an open field diagonally across Route 50 from the Upperville Horse Show grounds. On another day, as I drove by, they were stripping the topsoil from a large section of the field.

A man was on the field watching. Assuming he was the supervisor, I turned in through an open gate, my curiosity aroused. Sensing my interest, his comment was direct:

*"They're building a shopping mall."*

Using the pronoun *"they"* instantly demot-ed him from supervisor to casual passer-by, and so without much credibility. *"Come on, that makes no sense out here. What do you really know about it?"*

Grass polo

*"Well, it's a polo field, so they can attract the Olympics. They wanted to have all the horse events at Great Meadow, but Eve Fout wouldn't have it, so they're doing it here. And they'll have to widen Route 50 to handle all the traffic."*

PHOTO BY THE AUTHOR

Important conservationist though she is, Eve Fout has little to say about Great Meadow, and if she wanted the Olympics at all she'd probably rather have them there than create another tourist event site in this as yet unspoiled countryside. So it was obvious my sidewalk superintendent friend was toying with me, playing the cat to my mouse. But the scrapings did look like an embryonic polo field.

Time passed, summer turned into fall, and fall into winter. The original machines were joined by graders and backhoes. Cutting and filling, collective-ly they have created a level surface, gently crested to provide drainage. When the earthwork is complete the yellow behemoths will no doubt re-spread the topsoil presently stored in long berms at the sides of the now-leveled ground, then seed the surface in the spring. Their now-obvious objective is a first class polo field.

Years ago we were introduced to polo in Milwaukee by Bob Uihlein, who doubled as the captain of the Milwaukee polo team, and as the key operating executive in the Joseph Schlitz Brewing Company, the largest account of Continental Can Company, and my direct responsibility as Continental's local sales manager.

Edie and I promptly developed a liking for polo. Attending the games led to being invited to the Uihleins' for after-game cookouts, which in turn led to steak and beer acquaintances with many players, including Bill Ylvisaker, for

COURTESY OF THE NATIONAL SPORTING LIBRARY

*Polo in olden times as Illustrated in* Harper's Magazine

a time owner of Salamander Farm (see Page 74). Not coincidentally, the cookouts also led to an occasional tip on nefarious moves by our competitors, most helpful in preserving Continental's large market share in beer cans. Learn of a competitive threat Sunday evening, react with a successful counter move Monday morning. So we played the game as professionals, without ever touching a mallet, owning a pony, or being rated as players.

Sadly, both Continental and Schlitz have been absorbed by other companies, but the practice of extracting business information at social events goes on unabated. Privatize the CIA?

Like dressage and three-day eventing polo has a military heritage. It was born in central Asia around 600 BC, and imported to England via India, reaching America in the nineteenth century. For years it prospered as a sport for training Cavalry, and many of the best players hatched in the 1920s and '30s were army officers.

In concept, polo is a simple game, the object being to hit a ball through a pair of goal posts, using a long, flexible mallet, while galloping at top speed on a horse. In practice it is exceedingly difficult. To achieve your objective the rules call for three similarly equipped teammates to assist you, and four opponents to thwart your efforts. The ball may be struck from either the near or off side of the "pony" (actually the "pony" is a nimble small horse), either backwards or forwards. Strokes may also be made under the pony's neck or across his tail.

PHOTO BY SEBASTIAN LEZICA

*Arena polo. Eye on the ball.*

To prevent outright mayhem there are a limited number of rules, a principal one being to restrain a player from crossing the line of the ball – think of a horse crossing the line of the fox – to avoid collisions, and other rules to discourage extreme or dangerous forms of interference. As in its distant cousin ice hockey, the limits of aggression in polo are established by a mounted referee, whose job is to put the ball in play, rule on fouls, out of bounds shots, and goals, and generally to preserve a modicum of safety and control of the game.

Polo may be played on a large, flat grass field (about 160 by 300 yards), usually bounded by low boards on the sides ("outdoor" or "grass" polo), in a smaller sand floored enclosure (100 x 50 yards), with high board sides ("arena" polo), or indoors in an armory or like facility ("indoor" polo). In the latter two versions the teams are reduced to three players each, the ball is larger and softer – think softball vs. croquet ball – and the speed of the game somewhat constrained by the size of the playing area.

---

## – Polo in Virginia Today –

Compared to foxhunting, showing, eventing or steeplechasing, polo seemed a boutique sport in these parts, but construction of the new field is a sign that something is stirring. Investigation was called for, and so I found myself headed for Great Meadow one May morning.

At Great Meadow Leslie VanSant, newly appointed as the facility's executive director, introduces me to Juan Salinas-Bentley. I learn that Virginia is a center of American "amateur"* polo – the big boys in Florida (and Milwaukee?) play at the "professional" level. Juan, a professional, is the operations manager of "Polo Great Meadow (hereinafter PGM) 2002." Our arrival diverts him from a scrimmage between eight inexperienced players, four to a side, practicing for the coming season. He looks at his watch, blows a horn, and ends the chukker (a polo game is divided into six periods called chukkers, each lasting seven and a half minutes.) I ask him about himself.

*"I'm a polo professional, a 'Tex-Mex,' born in San Antonio. I found out*

---

* It seems that "**amateurs**" are those who play for fun on evenings and weekends, while "professionals" treat polo as their principal activity, whether for pay or not. Many "amateur" teams recruit professionals to their ranks.

---

*recently that my grandfather played for the Mexican Generals, against George Patton and other Americans. I work full time for Phil Staples – here in the summer, in Florida in the winter.*

*"We practice and play 2-goal on this field, arena polo over there* [he points to a fenced but uncovered enclosure a hundred yards away] *and 8-goal at the old Phipps Field* [now called the Goose Creek Polo Club Field] *south of Route 50. We rent that."*

Polo players are rated according to skill on a range of minus 2- to plus 10-"goals" to establish handicaps to keep the team competition even. The sum of the ratings of the players on a team is the team's rating. "2-goal" means that the team will have, perhaps, two players that are rated 0, and two more that are at 1-goal each. An 8-goal team might have a 4, a 2, and two 1's, or any other combination that totals no more than eight. If the team an 8-goal group is playing is rated at only 6-goals, the lower rated team starts the game with a two goal credit on the scoreboard. In some cases, as at PGM, the minus to zero ratings are called C, B, and A, no doubt to bolster the self-confidence of the less skilled. Horse sports are humbling enough without using negative evaluations.

I note one change from years ago. *"Those players are all wearing face masks. That's new."* Juan is in favor of face masks:

> *"There were too many eye injuries, but there is a downside with masks. If you fall they can catch in the ground and twist your neck."*

In polo, as in all other horse sports, falling is both undesirable and inevitable. Juan offers to let me borrow his book of old clippings to catch up on polo history in the area. Then he leaves to set up the next practice session.

PHOTO BY DOUGLAS LEES

*Betsy Manierre at Great Meadow – note face mask*

We are standing next to an array of large trailers, most with horses tied to rings along the trailers' sides. Moving around and between horses, washing them, cooling them out, tacking them up, are the players and grooms. The horses seem calm and relaxed, the day warm. I fall in with one of the players, an older (for polo) man in his fifties. Tom Leonard is in the heating oil business, in Woodbridge.

*"I have time in the summer, winter is our busy season so I can't foxhunt."*

*"How long can a guy play polo?"* I ask.

*"I'm 55, I'm in the twilight. Some play into their 60's. But you lose the quickness, the hand-eye coordination. By their 40's the pros are in a pretty steep decline."*

*"And the horses ....?"*

*"A horse can play until he's 19 or 20. Ideally you need six, one for each chukker. Maybe with a young one he can double up. It used to be three was enough, but the game is faster now, and the horses better. When I started you could buy three horses out of the stockyards for $200 each. Now an old one costs $8,000. For what I want you have to go three times that. And some are successful race horses, and go for much more."*

He pauses, then concludes:

*"You need Thoroughbred types that can really roll it."*

PHOTO BY THE AUTHOR

*Ponies in waiting*

PHOTO BY THE AUTHOR

*Juan Salinas, Nelson Gunnell and Phil Staples*

Tom used to run the games held in Washington on the Lincoln Mall, and fills me in on some of the players and polo fields out here. A few names among them are familiar.

> *"There's Phil Staples, Dick Reimenschneider, the Reinharts, Garrick Steele, who's building that new field near you. Then there's the Doughertys, Kevin and son Matt, daughter Erin is an All-American at UVA. Maureen Brennan just bought Kent Farms, there's a field there. The Steiners at Foxlease have two fields. Nelson Gunnell has a field behind his grandmother's house. The Muldoons started in show jumping, but switched over. Jack Sanders used to play polo…"*

Juan returns to continue my lesson. As he does so a player trots by, calling to his groom in Spanish, so I ask Juan, *"Are there a lot of Hispanic players?"*

> *"It's very international, Chileans, Argentines, Mexicans, Aussies, Kiwis, Brits… we play five or six days a week. Our 'Ride for Charity' program is a 501-c3 corporation. We get a great Friday night crowd for arena polo, 300-500 people under the stars, very family oriented. The 'Chief of Protocol' cup was put up years ago by Joe Smoak, then it was discontinued. We're going to revive it at Great Meadow this September."*

Juan pauses for breath, then concludes:

> *"There are so many things that could be going wrong in the world, but my biggest dilemma is 'Who's going to be playing polo on Sunday?' "*

---

HOWARD ALLEN PHOTO

*Hap Puelicher, Wayne Brown and Dick Reimenschneider*

## - *Recent History* -

Leslie has delivered Juan's books – the polo scrapbooks of William West, from his days as a cadet player and captain at West Point (Class of 1939), to his role as Colonel West in international "cultural exchange" polo in Pakistan in 1962 and, locally, on through1968. Included are West's stints playing for a series of teams in northern Virginia and Maryland from 1950 on. From these papers one learns that *"in 1955 Warrenton poloists were once again seen"* after a hiatus beginning in 1951.

The 1955 resurrected team included Bill, John, and Mary Gulick (Bill's wife, and *"one of the country's most prominent women players"*) and John Hopewell. Nick Arundel, Buzz Rogers and illustrator Wesley Dennis are listed as *"alternates."* By 1961 a nine team Maryland-Virginia polo league had been formed.

A *Loudoun Times-Mirror* story describes the new Goose Creek Polo Club, whose president, Hap Puelicher, says *"With all the interest in horses and in sports, I certainly think – well, I hope – that this sport will be a very popular one here in the County."* Mr. Puelicher adds that he *"would be playing on the team, as would Colonel William West."*

The article goes on to say *"the club also hopes to get Will Farish, present captain of the University of Virginia team* [later a well-known Kentucky horse breeder, and now US Ambassador to the Court of St. James] *and Richard Reimenschneider, who was captain of the University's team in 1959."* Puelicher adds, *"...there wouldn't be much interest in anything second rate. So we will try to get the best there is,"* which appears, perhaps stated unintentionally, to include Mr. Puelicher himself.

Random reports of the 1950s and '60s show West playing for several local organizations – seemingly as a recruited gun – occasionally teaming with individuals such as Col. Bob O'Brien, Dr. Jack Sanders, and (then) Major Joe Smoak.

### – Arena Polo –

We now fast-forward to the near past. In 1992 the Meadow Outdoors Foundation approved the formation of a polo club and facility. To make polo more afford-able an arena was built, arena polo being less demanding, and thus requiring only two ponies for a four chukker game. A Friday series of twilight games was born, lasting from June through early fall. This has proved immensely popular, attracting several hundred spectators who bring their picnic suppers.

PHOTO BY THE AUTHOR
*Picnicking family*

The 2002 PGM roster totals over 70 area players, of whom about a third are women. The group is clearly amateur, two thirds rating zero goals or less (A, B, or C), and only two as high as four goals.

One cool June evening we decided to see what arena polo was like, and headed promptly for Great Meadow. We need not have rushed. Only two small groups precede us. We commandeer a bench abreast of what might be

PHOTO BY THE AUTHOR
*Ready for arena polo*

called the thirty yard line, and set up our picnic in front of it, failing to note that the back of each bench has a sign with neatly lettered names of its season subscribers. "Our" bench is at the crest of a gentle slope, giving us a fine view of the playing surface fifty feet away.

By 7:00, the presumed starting time, perhaps 100 people have arrived. At 7:06 a large silver horse trailer pulls into the parking lot across the way. Sipping a glass of wine we watch the crowd; it is young, many groups having children and a few with dogs. The mood is relaxed, casual happiness. In front of us is a table and table cloth set up just in back of the permanent box seats. Behind the table are two ladies who look like Friday evening veterans. I introduce myself, asking, *"Are you here because you have arranged for the space, or can anyone move down here?"* The lady in charge is polite, and up on local protocol. She answers gently:

> *"This is our space."*

The name on the box just in front of her says "Dr. & Mrs. Stephen Seager." Dr. Seager is president of PGM (his rating is A). Adair Seager, their son, is however a 4. Daughter Fiona is also an A, and she will be playing later in the evening. I learn from Mrs. Seager that where we have landed is OK, but probably at the forward limit for general admission patrons – us.

At 7:13 the first rider enters the arena, and warms up, cantering and stick-and-balling. The scoreboard now has the names of the two team leaders, D. Barnes (in blue) and J.D.Olinger (in white). Each will play position #3, the most critical. The announcer explains that this contest is a cultural inter-change – two slots on each team will be filled by lady riders who are currently competing at the Upperville Colt and Horse Show.

At 7:22 the game starts. The ladies seem tentative, and the two men limit themselves to keeping the ball moving. There is a lot of swinging and missing, and over-riding the ball, but eventually there is a score. A horn blows, red lights over the goal flash. It looks to us as if the pony deliberately kicked the ball into the goal, perhaps in frustration. (An expert later assures me it was an accident, as ponies don't kick balls deliberately, a point on which there are two views, neither substantiated by a pony.) But there is a lot more to polo than just being a good rider. Some of it is having good ponies.

Leslie comes by, and we learn that,

> *"Everything is sold out. This is very popular."*

One girl, Alexa, seems better than the others. Leslie adds:

> *"That Alexa has played polo before."*

---

We realize later that Alexa Lowe is the daughter of our Trappe Road neighbor Margaret O'Neill. By now the Whites – or is it their ponies? – are ahead by two, but Alexa scores to narrow the margin at the end of the chukker. In the second chukker a Blue "garbage goal" (or so it would be called in hockey) – Alexa again? – evens the score. This is REALLY LOW GOAL polo. Leslie's associate Marie joins us, commenting:

*"They finally got the score keeper to tell the truth and we're tied."*

Leslie announces:

*"We have to check out the porta-johns, we had a crisis today."*

She and Marie leave. They are still on duty. The game ends in a tie and every player gets a prize. A lady with a fat Corgi goes by us, the dog's belly almost scraping the ground. Someone says – was it the announcer? –:

*"Come to Great Meadow where your pet is a VIP"*

A man passes, pushing a baby in a stroller, with a toddler in tow. He explains gratuitously that the older child is not his. We refrain from inquiring more deeply into its provenance. Now it is payback time for the expert lady show jumpers turned polo tyros. The intermission will exhibit three polo players riding their ponies over eight jumps. Only one does a presentable job (over 18" fences) and one is really bad.

But it's time to get serious – opening day for PGM. There is the National Anthem, followed by a rider galloping back and forth carrying the flag that was at the Pentagon on 9/11, accompanied by appropriate remarks. We estimate the crowd at 250-300 people and well over 20 dogs. Alexa comes by, commenting:

*"Those polo ponies are unbelievably broke. They're really obedient, know their job. And yes, I played polo before – once, last year. I learned that if the ball is up against the end wall you can place your horse next to the wall, blocking out the opposition, and just nurse the ball along the wall 'til you get it to and into the goal."*

A tractor comes out, dragging sand bags to smooth the arena surface. The announcer pipes up:

*"We'll start the feature game, soon as we get this arena drug."*

By now the arena lights are on. A car with four people has pulled up behind us, including Yolanda Brittle, whose name is on "our" bench. She does not object to our staying. The referee "throws" (actually, he rolls it) the ball in to start the game. The play is fast and reasonably skillful. The announcer jumps on top of the action, excited and involved.

*"In the goal! What a shot that was! [a pause, then] ...I'll fix the scoreboard in a minute. This is electronic – I can't handle it. Score's 1-1."*

He returns to his play-by-play:

*"Tap in set up by J.D. Olinger..."*

Then *"Oh my goodness!"* as the finishing tap-in is flubbed by Olinger's teammate.

We find Juliet Graham and Annie Bishop, among the few familiar faces in the crowd, and visit with them. Then the conversation turns to polo. As usual Juliet's thoughts are on the horse:

PHOTO BY SEBASTIAN LEZICA

*There is a lot of scoring in arena polo... later*

*"A polo pony tries to kick the ball in the goal; he knows that when the buzzer goes off a goal is scored. And they know how to put the rider on the ball."*

We go back to our bench for dinner as the half ends, and the tractor drags (or drugs?) the surface again. It's maybe 60 degrees, no one has left, they're all having too good a time, but those in shorts are getting a mite cold. Children solve the problem by racing around and through the crowd, some dancing on the benches to the loudspeaker music. Some of their parents find a beer. Then, there is a public service report from the announcer:

*"Ladies toilets are down beyond the lights there, we changed the location, but it's not in the bushes."*

The game resumes. The 8-4 score is suddenly 8-6. The announcer:

*"See how quickly scores can change in arena polo."*

We are told that Phil Karber is playing with two replaced hips. In 2001 he received the PGM President's Award for service to the club. Soon enough it is 9:24, with the last chukker coming up. Then Kevin Dougherty scores to make it 9-6 for Hidden Creek. Edie notes that their lady teammate – it is Fiona Seager– *"is not bad."* Quickly it's 12-7, and a free shot is coming up as a result of a penalty.

*All eyes on the ball*

"Whap!" the shot is straight on goal, but high, high enough to clear the 12 foot wall above the goal, and out into deep center field – or more precisely, the parking lot. The loud-speaker says:

*"No goal.* [adding] *...someone will get a dollar for returning the ball."*

Edie is packing up our things as the game ends, 13-8. There's no rush for the exits, and we are among the first to leave.

There is a lot of scoring in an arena game –

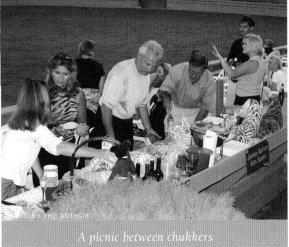

*A picnic between chukkers*

seven goals in the last chukker – and a lot of fun to be had at Great Meadow every summer Friday evening. We are quite likely to come back. We may even bring our Chesapeake Bay Retriever, Smiley, who has practiced for it for years as a VIP at Trappe Hill.

Garrick Steele went to prep school at Culver Military Academy. He describes his run-up to polo:

> *"I'd ridden all my life, showing, jumping, so at Culver I was in the riding program, though football was my first love. But I was pretty small for that in college."*

Garrick is now, in his late forties, slim, trim, about 5'11" and 160 pounds dripping wet. He continues:

> *"I'd been at college (Harvard) about two weeks, with no thought of riding there, when a couple of guys from the polo team knocked on the door. They'd learned of my riding background and wanted me to try polo, so I did. Polo was a varsity sport, but there wasn't much University funding. Your friend Bob Uihlein was a great help with that, so that's how I met him.*
>
> *"I played four years, and was captain the last three. We played Yale,*

*Garrick Steele and the tools of his trade*

*Cornell, University of Connecticut, UVA, some California and southern schools."*

This sounds like a major logistical problem, so I ask, *"How did you get your ponies around to all those places?"* Answer:

*"In intercollegiate polo you share the home team's ponies. We only played indoors, so the game is four chukkers. Each pony plays two, one ridden by a home team player, the other by a visitor. That way there's no pony advantage to either side. For a road game all you have to bring are your boots and mallets."*

*"What's your rating?"*

*"Now I'm a one, and strictly an amateur. I used to be a three, but after college I went to work in real estate and the restaurant business, and only played on weekends, so the rating went down — age and not playing enough."*

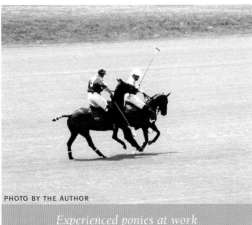

PHOTO BY THE AUTHOR

*Experienced ponies at work*

Garrick describes the local polo here as *"very low key."* Grass games are Friday and Sunday in summer, and he goes to Florida in the winter, but only for weekends. Here they play on different fields around the area. He feels the game here is growing, but that the cyclicality of interest is likely to persist.

*"Sunday afternoon is traditional. Anyone is welcome to come watch, but it's not promoted. Call me up if you want to go, and I'll tell you where the game will be."*

*"How about the horses?"*

*"It takes two years to 'make' a pony. Most of us don't have the time. With the free time I have, I'd rather play than school a pony. And some players wouldn't have a clue on how to do it. Most ponies come from places like Texas or South America, places with big ranches or estancias, where help is cheap and people love making horses."*

*"How about your new field?"*

*"The weeds have been sprayed, the irrigation system is in, and we'll 'sprig' it with Bermuda grass next week. Bermuda is tougher than Blue Grass, but this is pretty far north for its range, so it will be high maintenance. Give me a call and we'll go over and look at it."*

---

Garrick may not have time to make ponies, but he isn't adverse to making fields for them, and proud of the result. Then, finally, I wonder, *"What does it take to be a good player?"*

> *"It's pretty demanding physically, all the pushing and bumping. It's a team game. The biggest hitters aren't necessarily the best players. You must time your swing in cadence with the motion of the horse. The ball is moving, probably bouncing, not necessarily in sync with you and the horse. And it takes a lot of thinking."*

*"What do you concentrate on most?"* Garrick takes a moment to answer:

> *"The ball. Your relationship with the horse has to be second nature, like skating is in hockey. The ball first, then the location of the opposing players, and finally the position of your teammates."*

Then he has a thought:

> *"Give me a call, come over some weekend, I'll lend you a horse, we'll go out to my practice field in the back and you can see for yourself how hard it is."*

*"Thanks, I'd like to do that."* and we say good-bye. Maybe I'll get a C-minus rating. When I get home I tell Edie about Garrick's invitation. Her reaction? Incredulity, quickly engulfed in laughter verging on hysteria. Perhaps she envisioned me in this photo...

## – *Phipps Field* –

I call Garrick a couple of weeks later and learn that tomorrow evening, July 3rd, there will be a game on the field near Goose Creek, the old Phipps field, game time 6:30. (The upcoming horse events listed in the local paper do not mention polo.)

July 3rd is hot – over 90° – and humid, a time for iced tea and indolence rather than exercise. After setting up the sprinkler hose in the garden Edie and I head for the polo field. The air conditioning in

PHOTO BY DOUGLAS LEES

the car is a relief. We speculate that the game will be called, but at least we can get a look at the field. We turn south off Rte 50 onto 624, a one lane gravel track that follows Goose Creek up river from the old stone bridge made famous by the battle in June of 1863. Along Rte 624 we cross a narrow bridge, and Edie remarks:

> *"I don't see how they get those polo trailers over this bridge... Maybe they bring them in from the other side."*

*Garrick Steele*
PHOTO BY THE AUTHOR

After about a mile there is an expansive, level grass polo field on the right in the river's flood plain, blue goal posts at each end. Around the field's northern perimeter are several large horse trailers, each with horses outside on which grooms are working, tacking them up. There do not seem to be any spectators, but the game is on despite the heat. We park as inconspicuously as possible.

As we walk by the trailers no one pays us much heed. One player – identified as such by his white breeches – talks in Spanish to a groom, and then flips into English to visit with a team mate. Is bilingualism a prerequisite for polo?

*Eight horses and players chasing the ball – Phipps field, some years ago*

At the fourth or fifth trailer a player in a blue shirt is relaxing in a folding chair in the shade of a large tree. I introduce myself. He is Kevin Dougherty. I learn that this game is the final one for his team, Woodlawn, in the 8-goal league. Their opponent this evening is Middleburg. The Lineups:

| MIDDLEBURG (7 goals) | WOODLAWN (6 goals) |
| --- | --- |
| Garrick Steele | Phil Staples |
| Joe Muldoon, Jr. | Juan Salinas |
| Nelson Gunnell | Kevin Dougherty |
| Jim McGowan | Matt Dougherty |

I ask Kevin how Woodlawn has done.

*"Not very well. This is our last game for the June season, and we haven't won any."*

He goes on to add:

*"There are eight teams in the league: Virginia Beach, Charlottesville, Rappahannock, and five around here."*

*"Virginia Beach? That's a long way to trailer your horses."*

*"Well, mostly they come up here."* He continues *"We seldom get a crowd, don't promote it. Playing is great for me, I can do it with my kids, I might not be playing but for them."*

*"How about the heat?"* which must still be 88°-90°.

*"It's borderline. We normally start at 5:30, but we delayed an hour today because of it."*

Some players are now out on the field, warming up by hitting balls and following them, though "warming up" seems like an inappropriate phrase today. Kevin is reluctant to go out until he has to. I am now sitting on his beverage cooler, next to him. In front are a dozen or so polo mallets, with more hanging on the door of the nearby trailer. *"How do you choose which mallet to use?"*

*"They come in various lengths and weights. I specify a head weighing 210 grams – that's medium / light. Big hitters might use 230. You need several lengths so you can pick a size that fits the height of each horse."*

He and his groom Pedro look them over, and he chooses one, hefting it as a baseball player might test his bat.

Down the way Edie has found her foxhunting friend, Phil Staples, who is talking with Nelson Gunnell and Juan. Woodlawn will wear blue shirts tonight, and Middleburg red. Nelson is in blue and will have to change. Soon it is game time, and the referee, Martin (pronounced "marteen") throws the ball into the lineup of eight players. My mission now is to get pictures of the game with my unfamiliar new digital camera. This is not easy. At any shutter speed less than 1/500 of a second the image of fast-moving horses is blurred. And the distance from lens to galloping horses changes rapidly, so automatic focus has trouble adjusting.

The contrast with the arena game is startling. First, the smaller ball – now made of a reinforced plastic rather than the old style made of wood, travels faster and further. There is much more room for 100 yard pony races, each player trying to reach the ball first. Several horses moving in close quarters at a full gallop is exhilarating for horses, riders, and fans alike (by now there may be 10 of the latter on hand ).

And there is noise. Galloping hooves, of course, but also the creak of boots on saddles and the shouts of the players. Frequently you hear, *"Leave it! Leave it!"* as a trailing player, invisible to his teammate ahead, tells the latter to ignore the ball he is about to hit and gallop towards the goal so that the trailer can drive the ball up to the leader for a shot. The wider expanse of playing surface

*Twilight action on the field*

permits more spectacular teamwork and calls for more strength and skill from both horse and rider. The comparison with arena polo might be analogous to comparing slow-pitch softball to well played baseball.

Then you add the color and beauty of a wide green field, the fast moving horses, the bright-colored uniforms of the players, the evening sunlight, and the background of the river bottom's tall trees and you have a picture far different from the tailgate party around a wooden enclosure. Watching polo on grass, one can imagine how the wild tribesmen of central Asia that invented the game came to love it so.

After the third chukker there is a break, and we go over to talk to Phil. A girl groom passes, leading a very sweaty horse. We ask Phil about horses,

> *"You should come on a cool day, it'd be faster. The guys don't want to run their horses into the ground."*

We talk about Bill Ylvisaker. Phil reports:

> *"Several guys have had hips replaced, including Bill. He must be 76, 77 now, but he healed much faster than the 50-somethings. He was in such great shape. He even says he's going to play polo again."*

Phil's groom is holding a gray pony nearby. Edie asks about his breeding.

> *"I don't know, He's the best I ever had, but he's just a jug-headed Argentine out of the back country. He's 17, not quite as fast as he was, but he still has all the lateral moves."*

Phil offers us a beer, and I accept. It tastes wonderful. Phil comments:

> *"After a game I drink a bottle of water, then a cold beer really hits the spot. But now that you've had one you can't play any more!"*

Thus dismissed, we say good-bye to Phil as he gets ready for the fourth chukker. As we are leaving we pass Garrick, who is…

> *"Sorry you had to come on the hottest day of the year."*

I ask, *"Why does it say 'Point to Point' on your shirt?"*

> *"Nelson Gunnell's company* [Point to Point Fencing] *sponsors the team."*

*"He pays all the bills???"*

> *"No, he buys the shirts. That's about it."*

It is still very hot as we leave. We never do learn who won. We suspect the players didn't worry much about it either. They were having too much fun, aging athletes galloping around like kids.

---

By late afternoon, despite gloomy predictions, nothing has been heard from Al Qaeda on this anniversary of the strikes at New York and Washington. Meanwhile, Edie wants to take some injured tack to Ridgely White, a nearby horse trainer who has established a cottage industry repairing broken horse paraphernalia. As we drive by Garrick's new polo field we are surprised to see uniformed players riding about on it. I debark with my camera to catch the action, while Edie proceeds to Ridgely's.

On the field the Blues are lining up against the Whites, and a striped shirt umpire throws in the first ball to initiate the playing career of the new field. My camera clicks and I pray the historic shot is good. True to the local game's

PHOTO BY THE AUTHOR

*First throw in at the new field*

quest for anonymity the "crowd" numbers five, all located up on a berm of ground, at about mid-field. The throng consists of Dick Reimenschneider, a lady photographer on whose truck we're leaning, and another man and woman I don't know. Local color is provided by a solidly built girl in blue riding a gray pony equipped with a red saddlecloth and leg bandages; perhaps she is the mascot for both teams?

At the north end of the field, behind a line of trees, are several big horse trailers, many ponies tethered to each, and a gaggle of quietly un-busy grooms – all paying no attention to the historic moment on the field.

*Ponies and trailers*

My fellow photographer is Robin Greenhalgh, a polo player as well as a photographer of the game. *"Are you a professional?"* I ask, noting the huge 400 millimeter lens attached to her camera.

> *"Not really, but I went down to Aiken to play, and also shot some pictures and sold them. Someone said it was to help me pay my bar bills!"*

She then points out that to take polo pictures one should have the light behind (obvious) and be on the mallet side of the attacking team (not so apparent). She concludes:

> *"That's where the action is."*

There is a lot of it on the field, and Garrick's new grass takes quite a beating. At "half time" – the end of the third chukker – Edie appears with her repaired tack, and we drive home.

EPILOGUE

Later, using my picture, Juan Salinas-Bentley identifies the teams and players. Both Mount Airy (named for Garrick's farm) and Banbury Cross (where Nelson Gunnell has a field) are rated at 10 goals. The nine horsemen on the field come from five different countries and four continents. The first game on Steele Field is both international and pretty high goal. Its score – Mount Airy 9, Banbury Cross 5 – goes unreported.

We are back at arena polo at Great Meadow, again early. There we meet Sebastian Lezica who is hanging pictures in a tent behind the announcer's stand. Along with Julie Reardon, Sebastian photographs the action. This evening there is to be a doubleheader, the first game the finals of a handicap tournament, followed by the finals for the Chief of Protocol Cup.

This is Arena Polo at its best – a crowd that will grow to almost 1000, box

PHOTO BY THE AUTHOR

*Sebastian Lezica, Peggy Arundel, Edie Smart*

seats full, spreads of food and drink elegant, the crowd young, ponies and riders highly skilled. The play is rougher than in prior matches we have seen, and only a few players are local. Phil Karber will play in the first game, but now is warming up by walking dismounted on the grass carrying a short mallet. Asked his age, he answers:

*"56 on a good night."*

Peggy Arundel, our hostess, arrives, and we help her set up a buffet table next to their parking spot. Nick will be along later. Meanwhile, some polo trivia:

- The first game is the highest goal arena polo ever played at Great Meadow

- 70% of the ponies are mares

- Many are Argentine Thoroughbreds

- They average about 15 hands

- Their tails are braided to facilitate back shots and to prevent mallets becoming entangled in horses' tails.

PHOTO BY THE AUTHOR

*Phil Karber receiving runner-up congrats*

The first game starts. On horseback Phil Karber's seat seems looser than the others, as his new hips, though well braced, are a bit less effective than the originals. At one point he comes off his pony, and is momentarily stunned, but remounts and continues to play. In the end his team loses.

There are more fouls called, and thus more penalty shots, than in less intense games, so there are more dollars to be made by kids as balls leave the arena with some regularity. There is also more scoring, each game totaling about 30 goals over its four chukkers. The announcer has not lost his touch. Sample quotes:

[A back shot goes over the wall]
*"You'll need a horse to get that one!"*

PHOTO BY THE AUTHOR
*Referees conferring*

*"After the game go meet the players. I've met all of 'em, and most are pretty good fellows."* [He stops short of identifying those who are not.]

The second game is faster – and closer – than the first. At one point tempers flare, two players slash at each other with their mallets and – as in hockey – they are sent to the equivalent of a penalty box to cool off. They shake hands as they leave, and the game goes on, two

PHOTO BY THE AUTHOR
*Alan Nash with his trophy*

players to a side for a time. There is no noticeable effect on the score.

Our tailgate host Nick Arundel – a former player – pays close attention, often transfixed by the skill of the horses and riders that Great Meadow has attracted. This is polo at its best.

Arena polo is clearly back in the community's affections. We arrive home near midnight, wondering if polo on the grass will see a similar upturn in popularity. If it does we would get to bed a lot earlier.

PHOTO BY THE AUTHOR
*Nick Arundel and Leslie VanSant*

*Action on the grass at Upperville*

## – A Year Later –

After the wettest spring on record, by July Garrick's new field near Upperville is dry enough for use, with Middleburg (in white) scheduled to play Rappa-

hannock (in blue). As we arrive a mower is completing a final trim, and workers are setting up the goal posts and corner markers. Officials arrive and grooms begin tacking up the horses.

*Dana and Justine Fortuno*

Last year the inaugural game here drew five spectators. Today, despite the 90 degree heat, a throng of a dozen cars and perhaps 20 spectators has converged on the grassy berm overlooking the action. Several are young ladies, and attached to the players, including Berkeley Gunnell and her baby son Thomas.

Older attendees are perhaps wishing they were playing... or similarly attached.

Nelson Gunnell

Rick Heald

In addition to #4 Dana Fortuno the home team consists of #1 Nelson Gunnell, #3 Rick Heald and #2, Garrick Steele

The new field has matured splendidly since last fall. Garrick is quick to point out, however, the amount of work that goes into developing and maintaining a facility like this. Ambassador Dick Viets, a career Foreign Service Officer, is among the 20 spectators, and I ask him if he ever played polo.

*"Yes, in India, but never in the US."*

Then he volunteers

*"I've seen polo fields in India, Pakistan, England, France and the US. This is the best I've ever seen. Usually after the third chukker they ask to spectators to go out and replace the divots. Here there are hardly any divots. The turf is just superb, it must be special* [as is the elevated viewing from the berm]. *It would get high marks from any player anywhere."*

Perhaps that is why Garrick is smiling. Now, if he could only turn down the heat and humidity… But only the spectators seem to mind. The players and ponies are having too much fun.

By the way, they think the final score was Rappahannock 7. Middleburg 6.

PHOTO BY THE AUTHOR

*Stylish polo ladies*

# DRIVING AND DRAFT HORSES

PHOTO BY THE AUTHOR

*Marged Harris and pair of Hackneys*

*"Driving horses really have to trust you — much more than ridden horses. That's the biggest thing I get out of it — the relationship. They don't have time to question you, they just go. It's so subtle, more like playing with a marionette than a hand puppet."*

—Muffy Seaton, National Champion in Combined Driving with Ponies.

Driving and draft horses today are gentle and colorful vestiges of the time when the horse was a central factor in life everywhere. To develop some historical background I turned to the National Sporting Library. Their "Coaching" collection consists of about 170 volumes, of which many were printed in England.

This British tilt is logical. The great days of horse-drawn vehicles – leaving ancient chariots aside – could begin only with the availability of well drained hard surfaced roads, and had to end with the ascendancy of the railroad and the motor car. Those chronological bookends define a period from 1750 to the beginning of the Great War, 1914. Within that time frame, the period from 1780 to 1850 was "The Golden Age of Coaching."

England was a well developed and tightly knit country, with a structured society in which well-to-do people could indulge in owning classy carriages

*Antique English "Park Drag" coach, lovingly restored*

drawn by stylish horses and staffed by liveried servants. The engineering genius of the Scotsman John MacAdam (1756-1836) developed hard-surfaced roads of crushed stone (later bound with asphalt), a network that tied English society together.

During the same period, back from the seacoast, America was a sprawling collection of small rural settlements linked by forest paths and muddy roads, difficult even for ox-drawn wagons. Outside of its few cities and a scattering of hard surfaced turnpikes, fast travel in America was either by ship or on horse-back. American society consisted mostly of farmers, artisans, and merchants, people with independence of spirit but not yet much accu-mulated wealth.

The nation was well into the nineteenth century before driving evolved beyond utility to a means of displaying one's taste in horses, vehicles and skill in handling them. And, in a country of farmers, there was much interest in the multi-purpose animal – one that could be ridden, driven, or even hitched to a plow.

PHOTO BY THE AUTHOR

*A pair of Belgians haying in Maine*

Uniquely American breeds such as the Morgan and the Conestoga were developed in response. By the end of the nineteenth century equine-drawn vehicles had been designed for almost every conceivable purpose, and specialized breeds of animals developed to fit them.

In England there was a hiatus. In 1914 many coachmen had joined the colors. Those that came back in 1918 often found themselves chauffeurs instead of horsemen. The Depression and another war followed. It was not until the coronation of Queen Elizabeth II in 1952, an event calling for a parade of carriages, that English interest in driving was rekindled.

Today in America the use of working draft horses is limited to groups resist-ant to modernity, such as the Amish, and to situations where a horse can perform as well as a tractor. But he has not been forgotten.

---

*One of the Shires fom Ayrshire Farm*

Driving – as a sport – is making a strong comeback in Virginia; some dedicated horse people are recreating the world of their forebears, and falling delightedly back into it through breeds of horses and antique vehicles or reproductions thereof. If the lure of foxhunting and its more extreme extension, steeplechasing, includes exhilaration and risk, the comparable words for driving are "tradition" and "elegance."

In the United States interest is widespread. The first 345 US names listed as members of The Carriage Association of America show at least one in each of 45 states, with over 10 percent living in Pennsylvania. An area of similarly concentrated interest, per capita, is New England. For those statistically inclined the Virginia contingent in this crude sample is 9 (2.6 percent), about proportional to the Commonwealth's share of the nation's population.

Driving requires one to assemble vehicle, horse and driver skills into a "system" that can deliver what the owner wishes, be it pleasure driving, competitive combined driving, carriage shows, or a show case for his horses.

There is, I think, a parallel between serious driving and antique collecting. In both, one starts with an artifact from a bygone era (and, in the case of driving,

---

a breed of animal as well as a vehicle), often of great beauty, with historical significance, and threatened with irrelevance by the innovations of the present. The connoisseur becomes immersed in the history and customs of the period represented by his collectible. The driving enthusiast is interested in the origins of the breed he favors and the design and provenance of his vehicles. He treasures these expressions of the past, and allows them to carry him back in time to the

PHOTO BY THE AUTHOR

*Bill Allen and his Hackney*

pleasures of an earlier age. Caring for them becomes as meaningful to him as using them, or so it seems to this collector of Americana.

## – A Sunday Outing –

One August Sunday I passed a pair of ponies pulling what I later learn is a scaled down Brewster Coleman Phaeton, carrying a lady and her husband (she holds the whip) along Rte 719 near Newstead Farm. Behind them is a boy on a bicycle, serving as groom and outrider to caution approaching traffic. They thank me as I slow, and I turn my car around and follow them to take their picture. They suggest this would be easier if I wait 'til they turn into Newstead Farm. In Newstead's back driveway the lady calls out:

*"You know this is private property?"*

*"Yes, it's OK. The Firestones are friends – I've just been there taking pictures of Genuine Risk."* She points ahead…

*"You can take the photo as we come towards that bend in the road."*

I pass her, park and try to comply, running to keep enough in front of the trotting ponies. I'm panting – *"Can you stop 'til I get set?"*

*"Well, no. One pony really doesn't want to stop, it gets nervous and fidgets."*

So I race ahead, set myself, and shoot – two misses and an acceptable hit as they pass. I call out my name. The over-the-shoulder response is…

*"Are you Edie Smart's husband?"*

*"Yes,"* I say. As they disappear I hear:

*"I'm Flora Hillman, live across from Sally and Verne Hosta."*

Then, referring to the man in the back of the vehicle:

*"This is Owen Snyder* [her husband] *with me."*

Flora Hillman and her Welsh ponies

PHOTO BY THE AUTHOR

That evening I call up my new friend to explain why I wanted the picture. She seems glad to fill me in:

*"That boy on the bike is our son, Tim. He's 14, and he's my groom. I pay him. Today we went about seven or eight miles, two and a half hours. We take it easy, just a quiet jog/trot."*

*"How did you get into driving?"*

*"I'm an endurance rider, have done some foxhunting. Twenty-five years ago I had an event horse…"*

*"You were eventing then?"*

*"Yes, it was cheaper, you could do it for 25 bucks. My horse got navicular, and I retired her from foxhunting, and decided to teach her to drive. We got a book about driving, and it said to start by hitching her to a tire so she could drag it around. Well, we did that for a couple of rounds and she was fine, so we harnessed her to a vehicle and drove off on the road, just like that. The gods were forgiving, she'd never been driven before. The next time we were more careful. We tried it on a foxhunter – gave him three days with the tire, and he was wonderful. His picture ended up on the front of* The Maryland Horse."

About this time I conclude that Flora establishes psychic confidence in her horses, which would explain this smooth transition to a strange discipline. (Later Edie tells me about her mother's similar attempt with Lady Go Lightly, an ex-steeplechaser: *"She hitched her to a breaking cart and she took off. It was a breaking cart all right, she broke it!"*) Flora continues:

*"I fell into driving because you can take a non-rider with you. My husband*

---

411

*has a stressful job, and it relaxes him. But he thought it was too much for one pony to pull us both, so we got a second pony. Now we needed a vehicle for a pair of medium Welsh ponies. We called Dinwiddie Lampton who had a carriage collection, and we took off the measurements of a Phaeton, scaled them down to three quarter size to fit our ponies, and Owen built our vehicle – the under carriage is antique, the rest is reproduction."*

She tells me that her farm is named Auriga, and gives me its web site address in case I need more pictures. I ask, "Why Auriga?"

*"My first mare was named Capella, a star in the constellation Auriga, which is called the Charioteer."*

It helps a horse person to have the right stars on your side.

## – A Drive in the Country –

At a dinner party in his carriage barn Carey Beer offered to show me something about driving, and we made a date for a Monday morning in March. About 7:30 of the appointed day the phone rang. It was Carey:

*"Brrrrr. It's cold. Driving is supposed to be fun. How about two, it'll be warmer?"*

I agreed, and met him at the carriage barn that afternoon. The temperature had skyrocketed from 28 to about 42. Two horses were already outside, partially in harness as Liz Nicholson, Carey's horse care person, prepared for the event. We start with a short introduction to Carey's and his wife Adrienne Hewitt's collection of 16 horse-drawn vehicles, a few modern ones, but most of them antique with interesting provenance:

*"This one is a Roof Seat Brake, made in Philadelphia around 1900. It belonged to Stacy Lloyd, one of the founders of* The Chronicle of the Horse, *and later was a part of Liz Tippett's estate. Each has a particular use, and requires an appropriate size horse."*

*"This was the property of Adrienne's mother, descended in the family. It's a Bret, made in Philadelphia around 1880."*

We then go outside to meet Olive and Cocoa, two 16.1 hand black mares that Carey has had for about four years. They are a Morgan-Percheron cross (versatility and moderate size bred to massive strength). As Carey and Liz finish "putting to" (connecting them to) the carriage-du-jour I'm told that our vehicle is a relatively new Derby Brake made in Bremen, Germany. The harness is Dutch, by Van der Wiel. Carey:

*Beer / Hewitt collection. Tandem carriage from estate of Liz Tippett*

*"Putting to is the tricky part. Do the reins first so you have some control. If you don't, and something scares them and they decide to bolt with the carriage attached, you can have a bit of an adrenaline sandwich."*

*Carey Beer attaching pole to Bret carriage*

He continues in a more reassuring vein.

*"Some of the finest harness is made in Europe. Competitive combined driving – the driving equivalent of three-day eventing – is big over there, and they need the very best."*

He shows me a strap, made with two plies of black leather with a layer of nylon web sandwiched in between. Then he carefully checks all connections to the vehicle,

413

just as a skipper would check out his boat's rigging before leaving the dock.

Then we mount, clamber on, embark – I do not yet have the proper term at hand. Carey and I are sitting in the front seat, nicely positioned above and to the rear of the engine ends of the mares. Liz is in a seat behind us, able to shift from side to side if stability considerations call for it. In case of extreme instability – Carey has never overturned a carriage, but it does happen – he suggests:

> *"You evacuate by going out over the uphill side if possible."*

With this consoling thought we move out, swaying a bit as a boat would in a light chop. Carey accelerates and slows his team almost entirely by voice, turns them by pressure applied by the reins, and encourages the lazier one – Olive – to do her share of pulling by a touch of the whip from time to time. Occasionally Cocoa gives Olive a nip or two for the same purpose. One is struck with how only a little gentle direction is needed to control this pair.

We pass through a series of lovely open fields, following a seldom used farm road, mostly at a trot, but with a canter up hill to show me that infrequently used gait. Once one gets used to the swaying there is lots of time to enjoy the

*A passenger's view of
the road ahead at Heathfield*

countryside, with the Blue Ridge in the distance. We come to a small, sunny pond, from which about twenty geese depart, honking. The horses pay no attention. As I admire the scenery Carey observes:

*"You need a lot of open country to enjoy driving."*

He is fortunate to have a bunch of it close at hand. Later, prior to fording a stream with a rocky bottom, Carey halts the horses, lets them look it over, and then urges them ahead. The uneven bottom rocks the carriage; I am too concentrated on which side is "uphill" at any given moment to note whether Liz is shifting ballast in the rear, but soon enough we are through and up the far bank. Carey says:

*"Once they have confidence in you, these horses would walk off a cliff if you steered them at it."*

We trot across a small piece of field towards a chicken coop, and Carey is careful to turn the pair well before we reach it.

*"Adrienne and Liz hunt these horses, and if they got the idea they should jump that coop they just might do it. We introduced them to hunting as a learning block, so they would be at ease if we met hounds while driving. They enjoy hunting, and after it they seem keener in their work in harness."*

Pretty soon we come to our only real obstacle, a small black heifer just over the fence along which we are driving. Cocoa lets us know she does not approve, slowing down as she looks over at the heifer by craning her neck to see around Olive. Then she tries to move to the left and away from the frightening, though immobile, bovine. Carey halts the team and talks to Cocoa for about a minute. You can see her relax, and we proceed. Carey explains,

*"When we got these horses they were very green three year-olds, and we rode them by about everything that might frighten them when driving. The road grader was the scariest – it's big, noisy and it blows a lot of air. Pleasant experiences are like today's candy to a horse, enjoyed but soon forgotten, but a bad one stays on their hard drive forever."*

From there we go to an old Civil War era cemetery in a grove of trees, a favorite place of Carey's.

*"We come here in the summer sometimes for a picnic. Even if it's 90° elsewhere it's cool here. I think it was a Quaker cemetery, but I've found no meeting house foundations."*

Back on the road we turn towards home. As we approach a sharp curve a big white truck rounds it from the other side. We stop, as does the truck. Then we pass slowly by, the driver waving and smiling at us. Carey observes:

---

*"Most people, trades people especially, are very nice about carriages. But you have to be careful…"*

His voice trails off. We emerge onto Welbourne Road. Then he turns into the driveway of Welbourne, handing me the reins.

*"Here. It's nice and straight. You drive."*

And I do, down the driveway, around the circle in front of the house, and back to the entrance, trotting, imagining myself as Colonel Dulany, the former master of Welbourne. Then, as we approach the "main" road: *"Whoa, Cocoa, Olive."* I pull back gently on the reins. Surprisingly, they "whoa."

Carey resumes command – I should say "takes back the whip" (even though he never gave it up). Going out the driveway he stops and listens carefully…

*"We almost had a bad experience here once – these little Japanese cars are fast – and quiet. You can't be too careful."*

Today there is no sound, or Japanese car, and we proceed home safely. Turning into his barn I calculate that of the six miles we have covered only about a mile was on a public road. Now comes the reverse of putting to –

*Liz Nicholson cleaning tack*

let's call it "unharnessing" – and cleaning tack. Carey seems happy to leave that privilege to Liz.

Later, back at his house, we move to Carey's library. Carey is an enthusiastic foxhunter, and a caring father, as various photographs on the shelves attest. As I inspect a picture of four polo players, including Carey and Charles, Prince of Wales, I am reminded that Carey's new sport has replaced this former and less quiet pastime. Carey notes:

*"Charles is a very steady and conservative polo player. He is gifted over others in polo because he is such a fine rider to begin with."*

I wonder if the same word "conservative" could have been said of the polo of a younger Carey Beer. Carey tells me, as if in answer to my thought:

*"I don't go much for competitive driving. When I compete in anything I do it hard, and with three kids under 16 there isn't enough time. So our driving is just for fun."*

Then my host continues my education, pulling out his driving library, an eclectic collection of books on carriages, how-to-drive manuals, periodicals, driving club membership lists, and rules of competition. His enthusiasm is contagious, and I take home 25 items for further "homework" on his sport.

## – The Gentle Giants –

*Shire foals*

PHOTO BY THE AUTHOR.

Sandy Lerner is a slim, determined and entrepreneurial woman, captivated by a love affair with the largest, gentlest of horse breeds, the Shire. About 40 of these kind creatures call her Ayrshire Farm their home, and on a visit there we started out by exploring the breed's struggle to persist in the modern world. Sandy began our education:

*"Do you know how many Shire filly foals are registered each year in the US?"*

Of course I didn't, so the straight man in me answered, *"No. How many?"*

*"Only 24..."*

I concluded the demographic comparison *"...versus about 18,000 Thoroughbred fillies each year."*

Sandy sees herself as the guardian of the classic segment of this ancient gene pool. Shires go back a thousand years or more, bred initially to be war-horses capable of carrying armored knights into battle. Thus size, strength, intelligence and disposition were critical. They needed to be oblivious to the confusion and dangers of combat, working fluidly with a rider encumbered by armor and a helmet providing only the slimmest view of the scene around him. Sandy puts it this way:

*"The fright / flight response has been bred out of them over 1,000 years. Battlefield training produced a mind-meld between horse and rider, and an ability to disregard peripheral distractions. Today you could run out among a bunch of them wearing a clown suit, screaming and throwing ice cream cones. They would look at you, think a bit, but not run, no flight reaction whatsoever. Then they'd start happily eating the ice cream cones. They've developed a socialization ethic.*

PHOTO BY ANITA BAARNS
*Sandy and her favorite, "Izzy"*

*"One day when riding my girth slipped, and I found myself on the ground, lying between my Shire's front feet. He didn't move. He knew where his feet were, and where I was. He just stood still while I pulled on his feathers — the long hairs that cover his ankles — and then his mane to drag myself out from under and onto my feet. Any other horse would probably have panicked and might have killed me."*

The invention of gunpowder spelled the end of the war-horse and his armored knight, and so service as a powerful draft animal became the Shire's role, pulling heavy vehicles. In the early 19th century the British system of "Macadamized" roads led to lighter vehicles, which could be pulled by smaller horses bred for speed. Sandy adds:

*"By 1827 the new roads had speed limits — nine miles per hour — and the British mails traveled 16,000 vehicle miles each night."*

And so the Shire once again was moved down on the equine status scale. Sandy:

---

*"If you really want to get me going, you only have to call them 'cart horse' or 'plow horse.' "*

However, she notes that until 1875 Shire owners in England were members of the British Cart Horse Society. According to my hostess, one more indignity awaited the breed:

*"New-style Shires emerged. Where once they were bred for size, intelligence, and disposition, now they are bred principally for size, with longer bodies, four white feathers, and cow-hocked legs so their feet would wing up and out."*

*"So they'll look flashier?"*

*"Yes, and less sound. Hackneys on steroids."*

Sandy is quick to say she is by nature…

*"Anti-prejudice, and for the underdog. These horses haven't had a fair shake. They are beautiful, giving, useful and kind. They want to please you. Once they were war-horses, at the top of the equine heap. …I want to give them visibility, show people how splendid and magnificent they are."*

———

419

Sandy is no stranger to the lot of the underdog. She and her husband Len Bosack started the firm now known as Cisco Systems with technology they had invented at Stanford University, rebelling against the University's unwillingness to encourage commercialization of technical advances made there.

*"For three and one half years we financed the company with credit cards, and finally agreed with Stanford over the rights to the technology. By then we were selling $500K of product per month over the Internet, with seven employees, no sales force. But we had to have capital to grow, so we sold 70% of the company for $2.5 million. Three years later we had to leave."*

*"The personalities of business founders and new owners often don't work well together. You were a burr under the saddle?"*

*"I suppose so. And I was a woman. Most men don't take to female disagreement. Len didn't have to leave, but he went too – out of loyalty. With both of us leaving they let us have our stock that wasn't yet half vested. ...For seven years my life had been put on hold, working 20 hours a day. It wasn't intentional, we didn't plan it that way, but you rise to whatever you have to do. When it's 'do or die' people 'do' – just like animals. After Cisco I got back into life."*

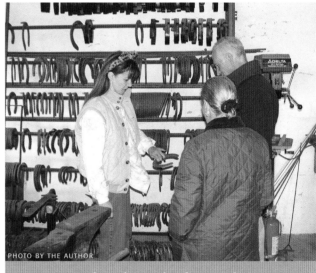

PHOTO BY THE AUTHOR

*Sandy explaining her farrier's shop*

One way she "got back into life" was buying Ayrshire Farm, a beautiful 800-plus acre tract of rolling ground just north of Upperville that once belonged to a man named Ayre. Around 1910 the land, site of much of the action in the 1863 Battle of Upperville, was bought by a Baltimorean, General James A. Buchanan, a noted owner of racehorses and a supporter of local equine activities. In time the property descended to his heirs, one of whom, his great grandson Tom Stokes, farmed it for many years.

Eventually, tax and financial complications made a sale advisable, as the place had only marginal utility as a cattle farm, and its numerous buildings were in growing need of maintenance. A Japanese Golf Club was one rumored buyer, and the threat of break-up for development was continuously in the air. For those interested in saving open space, Sandy's appearance and her restoration of the property have been a godsend, a benefit tempered in the minds of fox-hunters by her opposition to their sport. Realistically, though, neither a golf course nor development would have allowed foxhunting to continue either.

The 40 Shires at Ayrshire include youngsters, pregnant mares, stallions and horses in work for riding, farming and driving. In addition to a main barn with farm office, tack and harness rooms, and a carriage hall, there are several satellite structures, including a second barn, a farrier's shop, run-in sheds and an outdoor schooling arena.

As we toured the paddocks that windy February day Sandy would call to each horse by name, and a large, powerful animal and slightly built, almost willowy woman would come together, subtly exchanging feelings of affection and mutual rein-forcement. Then she would pick up a foot, showing the huge size-10 shoes, and ask me to run my hand over the stout cannon bone that supported the "wheels" of this "gentle giant."

PHOTO BY PAT MACVEAGH

*Ayrshire's Shires at work*

Moving my hands up over the warm body, I too found comfort in his quiet presence.

During our tour I thought back to a Halloween costume party in the Ayrshire stable one evening some years ago. The building was dark, except for black light picking up the white shirts of the bartenders, with piercing white rays slicing through the shadows to give the illusion of spider webs. A bar was conveniently accessible through dim light, the crowd large and the music noisy. In one stall a coffin opened occasionally to reveal an animated "corpse" that groaned and offered hors d'oeuvres. Evidences of witchcraft abounded.

Sandy, dressed in a gray, gossamer-winged fairy dress, flitted through this mélange of darkness, stabs of light, and humanity, assigning jobs to everyone. Edie was to be a costume judge (the winner was a man dressed in leaves as the Jolly Green Giant), and I was to release several Shires at midnight so, as the Horses of the Apocalypse, they could run through darkness, rays of light, and the crowd in the aisles. This seemed madness – huge, moving animals colliding with unstable (dimly lit?) guests in the dark – but it was her party, and I did as I was told; a few minutes later horses and guests were sharing a good time, and no one was hurt. Having now hugged several Shires myself, I can see why Sandy said there was no reason to worry.

During our tour I learned about the typical career of a Shire at Ayrshire.

> *"Shires come in three colors – gray, bay and black. We have, typically, three foals a year. As yearlings they are just big, friendly babies – they know nothing. At two we introduce them to bridle, harness, saddle. We tax them a bit mentally, but not physically, just socialize them. We start them in work at four, though they keep growing until six or seven, often reaching more than 18 hands and over 2000 pounds. Some we sell, others become a part of our driving group or broodmare band. Shires live to about 30. Occasionally we buy a mare that will move our breeding closer to the Shires of 100 years ago. Some we buy to save from slaughter.*

> *"We train them all in dressage. My favorite horse "Izzy" – officially 'Gronant Aristocrat' – was never under saddle until he was 10. At 11 he scored 70 in first-level dressage.*

> *"When we show them we try to win with the natural look, give people an alternative to artificial stylization such as docking tails and altering their horses' feet or gait."*

A casual display of ribbons in the tack room suggests that at least some judges approve of that approach. I ask how she got into Shires.

> *"I wanted to joust, and I'm a small person, so I wanted a big horse. I fell in love with their hairy feet. There are a number of different jousting exercises. For tilting at a gallop, spearing rings the size of lifesavers, you need a smaller horse, perhaps an Arab. In the ceremonial games they use the big horses, and I have a set of 19th Century armor."*

She shows me a photo of herself in jousting garb, then continues

> *"Did you know that jousting is the Maryland state sport?"*

Sandy hasn't given up commercial jousting, either. At last count she had four diverse ventures going – a recording studio, a venture capital firm, a restaurant (where she occasionally tends bar) and an animal critical care center – in addition to the farm.

Ayrshire Farm also raises Highland beef cattle, a rare breed of pigs, dairy cows, turkeys and chickens, all in a natural, organic way. The old buildings have been lovingly restored. Oak timbers cut off the property are incorporated into the new farm structures. Landscaping has been upgraded, fruit trees planted. The manor house is rehabilitated and used for community functions. A professional group controls artifact recovery around the Civil War battle sites, where re-enactments often take place. But it is the Shires that provide their owner the emotional gyroscope, that each of us needs to maintain personal stability in a turbulent world.

PHOTO BY THE AUTHOR

*Highland cattle of Ayrshire*

Betsy Crenshaw, who worked for Tom Stokes and lived at Ayrshire for several years, has this to say about recent developments:

*"I love that land. It warms my heart to see what she's done with it."*

## – The Conservator –

Charley Matheson is an architect, and his professional "eye" has led him to a creatively designed home, "Heathfield," which he is currently in the process of remodeling.

Charley has been a foxhunter for perhaps 50 years, and he remains dedicated to the sport. But in 1970 he found himself in Newport, riding on a coach as a passenger, and he was bitten by driving. On a trip to England a visit to the Royal Mews disclosed the Cleveland Bay as his kind of horse, though he later has come to fancying the Cleveland Bay – Thoroughbred cross. He tells me:

*"Drivers' personalities are reflected in their choice of horses."*

Charley is low key on formality, so it is not surprising that he adds:

*"Some people like grays, and they are beautiful, but they're hard to keep clean-looking so I avoid them. …Hunting is my first love. But I knew the Cleveland Bay / Thoroughbred cross was good for hunting, driving, dressage, eventing. So it fit all needs."*

Before we visit the horses, we tour his stable area. In the carriage barn are six vehicles, the queen of them being a fully restored black and cream-colored Road Coach. Charley confides that when he took up driving it was:

*Charley Matheson and "Andy"*

*"…to learn to drive a four-in-hand."*

Charley likes challenges.

Inspection of the coach displays its engineering features – brakes, stability, and suspension, as well as its immaculate condition and finish. Charley continues:

> *"Coaching exhibitions and contests today are heavily about presentation: horses, vehicle, harness, dress and how they are appropriate to the function and formality of the vehicle. In coaching, every day is opening day. Sometimes I think the pretty ladies' hats decide the winner."*

His comment does not specify whether it is the prettiness of the ladies or that of their hats that is the critical success factor. No doubt he prefers to have both. Charley continues:

> *"To compete with a combination driving team you need four horses and a spare. Then there are the different harnesses. You'll need a practice vehicle, a presentation vehicle, and a cross country vehicle. Then you need a horse van set up to also house the harness, and a van for the vehicle. You'll need two*

*grooms. You'll be judged on all kinds of appointments and turn out rules, as well as the performance of the team."*

Charley tells of an event whose organizers begged him to bring his coach and

*Exhibitor at the Piedmont Driving Club competition at Foxcroft School*

*Heathfield tack room*

team of four because they lacked entries for that class, and wanted to show an example of four-in-hand driving. As he completed half of the first lap of the course the judge blew his whistle. Charley was disqualified – he had only one groom aboard his coach instead of the requisite two. He begged to be allowed to continue the round to show the crowd the rig, and how it was driven – that was why he had come – but the judge – a friend of his – was unbending: *"Disqualified."*

We proceed through the tack room, noting the various styles of harness. On the walls are pictures of Charley and Bonnie Matheson driving coaches and fours with notable buildings as background – Mount Vernon, The White House, Windsor Castle. A particularly dramatic picture is of a team of four galloping across a stream, water flying in all directions. I note with some satisfaction that those able and brave horses are NOT matched as to color.

The Cleveland Bay breed originated in medieval times in the Vale of

Cleveland, in Yorkshire, England. Its origins lie in the "Chapman Horse" of Yorkshire, a horse bred to carry both a load and a rider, a "chapman" being an itinerant peddler. Within its ancestry are strains of both the Andalusian and the progenitor sires of the Thoroughbred. In any event, the Cleveland Bay has now settled into a predictable breed suitable for both draft and riding, it's stud book having been closed since 1884. Charley's paper "Encounters with the Cleveland Bay" describes the horse:

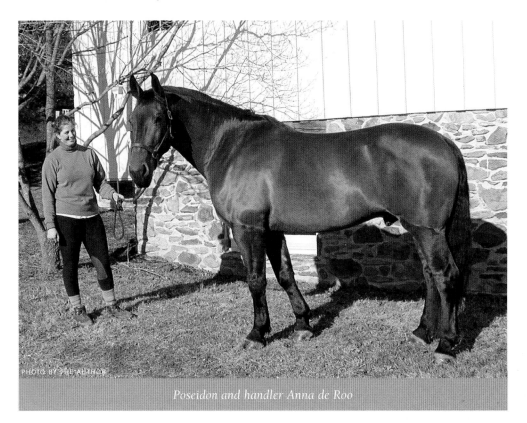

*Poseidon and handler Anna de Roo*

"*Characteristics in the breed: typically a slightly snub convex nose, moderately high knee action, a well collected and balanced frame and a kind eye reflecting a similar disposition. The dense bone, stamina, sloping croup, durability and incredible substance are… from the native Yorkshire stock. The horse is always bay, with no white on it.*

"*In 1823* The Farmers Magazine *called the breed 'best for light work …an original breed …a distinct race from any blood horse and equally distinct from the black (or cart horse) …wonderful uniformity of size and color (blood bay, no white) …great endurance …free action.*"

When Richard Dulany imported Scrivington the Cleveland Bay entered Virginia history. By 1907 the Cleveland Bay stud showed over 2000 such animals in

America. Now, as need for horses of this type has been decimated by the internal combustion engine the breed has become rare. Charley estimates:

> *"There are perhaps 40 mares in the US, maybe 200 in England. There are a few in Canada, Australia, New Zealand. And the Emperor of Japan has some. ...We give them a little work when they're three – they're not through growing until they're six or seven. They all hunt – they're more valuable as hunters. Driving people will pay a lot for equipment, but hardly anything for a horse. And foxhunting is relatively easy on a horse compared to pounding on hard roads. ...Taking them out four at a time is a nice way to exercise them, but its a lot of work for the grooms."*

Now we come to the horses. Two ladies, his niece Maryalice Matheson and Darby Smith (later succeeded by Anna de Roo), bring them out for inspection. Charley describes one of them:

> *"She's Renown's Springer, 18 years old, half Thoroughbred, by Rambler's Renown, out of Bewitching Deb, a stakes winning Thoroughbred. She drives as a near side leader in the four horse team. She's coming in heat. We may flush her and try an embryo transplant. Crossing the Cleveland Bay with the Thoroughbred means crossing two well-established breeds, and so leads to a fairly predictable result."*

The ladies bring out Tarzan, almost 17 hands, by the Oldenburg stallion, Hall of Fame, out of Winnie.

> *"Crossbred makes the best sport horse. If you want to add quality, you have to add Thoroughbred blood – get more speed and heart. Tarzan's my hunter, best horse I've ever owned, best horse I've ever ridden. He could be a Point-to-Point horse, we're thinking of running him. A half bred mare (Cleveland Bay sire and Thoroughbred mare) bred back to a Thoroughbred stallion is the perfect combination, Thoroughbred on both bottom and top. Jimmy Wofford won everything with his Galloway Bay. He has a picture of the horse jumping 7'6"."*

Next comes Bonnie Brae's Bydand (called Andy), by the Cleveland Bay sire Poseidon, out of an Andalusian mare, Guapita. Like a Cleveland Bay, he has...

> *"...a thick, curly tail, and picks up his front feet like an Andalusian stylist."*

Our conversation turns to Charley's operation at Montpelier, Statesman's Ridge, a breeding facility on the grounds of President Madison's former estate. Here he stands two Cleveland Bay stallions, Forbes Native Statesman and Penrhyn Bayswater. He suggests that I...

> *"Go see Bayswater, a beautifully balanced horse. Take a mare down there*

*and they'll A.I. her with fresh semen."*

Charley has also leased Cleveland Bay mares in England, bred them, and brought the weanlings to Virginia. His purpose is twofold – to preserve the purebred Cleveland Bay and to make Cleveland Bay sires available for cross breeding. He concludes:

*"Breeding fascinates me. I enjoy young horses, making them into something useful, and then being able to use it. It teaches you a certain degree of tolerance. You have to react to the horse's personality. Beating them won't work. You have to get them to do what horses do.*

*"It's a matter of trust. If you believe he can do it, he does."*

We visit Heathfield again a few months later. The wreath on the door, woven around a horse collar, confirms the season, the master's avocation and his "eye" for the uniquely beautiful. In response to our comment Charley says:

PHOTO BY THE AUTHOR

*The Matheson's wreath*

*"We've done it that way for 20 years."*

Then we proceed to the barn. As she had planned (see chapter on Eventing), Darby Smith has left Heathfield to return to Vermont. Her replacement in charge of Charley's barn is Anna De Roo, a native of Holland, a graduate of VPI here in Virginia, and a devotee of horses, driving and hunting. Anna later describes her situation:

*"I came over from Holland to work with horses. After a bit I started thinking 'what if I'm in an accident, what can I do? I need something to fall back on.' So I went to college, got my degree, and worked at something else for a year. But I missed the horses, had to get back to them. They're like my babies, [she breaks into a big grin]… I just love them."*

Anna adds that she has a green card and expects soon to become a US citizen.

Today we plan a drive behind a pair of Cleveland Bays, and Charley and Anna set about putting Winnie and Poseidon to a carriage. Aware of the deleterious effects of an amateur helping to rig a racing boat, I remain quietly on the sidelines as the process is quickly completed.

We climb aboard, a tricky maneuver since it calls for using a spoke of the wheel as a step. Charley assures me the brake is on, and indeed the spoke does not turn under my weight. Once seated, Anna tucks a wool robe over my lap and knees, saying *"It can get cold,"* and I begin to appreciate the amenities of service enjoyed by nineteenth century aristocrats. As the drive proceeds a cold rain begins, causing would-be aristocrats to miss the comforts of twenty-first century car heaters and windshields. Nevertheless the quiet presence of the horses and the gentle motion of the carriage is pleasantly soothing.

Once out of the driveway and on Milestone Road, which is paved, a modern hazard to driving is in evidence – fast-moving cars. From the rear seat Anna keeps up a running report to Charley on approaching traffic. Unfortunately, most cars do not slow down as they pass us, despite Anna's vigorous motions to them to do so. Irritated, I suggest that the drivers' parents were unmarried. Charley drives on unfazed, confident in his horses. I wonder if the gentle motion of the carriage and the two-way communication with the horses – hand to rein to mouth and return – has lulled him into silent contemplation that excludes noisome intrusion by modern externalities.

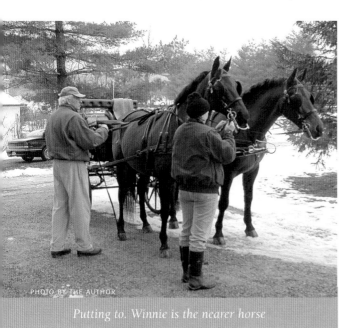

PHOTO BY THE AUTHOR

*Putting to. Winnie is the nearer horse*

Turning onto an unpaved side road the scene changes. There are fewer cars, and those that come by slow down, and wave – a totally different attitude than the auto-egotism of the paved road set. We hear the crunching of wheels on gravel, feel damp air on our faces, and observe and reflect on the stone walls and the winter-brown fields by which we are passing. Back safely at Heathfield, I go to the barn to thank Anna, who is putting the horses in their stalls. *"I can't believe those \*&%#$@' s who wouldn't slow down!"* She says:

> *"Yes, once I tried to slow a pick-up truck coming rapidly from the rear, and as he zipped past I could see him giving me* [she describes a rude gesture] *through his rear window. I drive solo quite a lot, though, and these horses are unflappable, so we've not had any real problems, even though a lot of drivers don't slow down."*

Unfortunately, here is more evidence of a clash of cultures between our resident horse lovers and the rising tide of uninformed urbanites spreading disrespectfully into horse country, one of the issues a subsequent volume will address.

---

Marged Harris has volunteered to educate us in the intricacies of "putting to," and for that purpose has brought her associate Mike Zaetta and her renovated stock trailer, complete with two Hackney horses, an 1880 Dog Cart, and tack to Trappe Hill. First she gives a brief seminar on local driving organizations:

*"There are three driving clubs around here, each with a slightly different flavor. Our Potomac River Driving Association is a teaching club. We bring new drivers on, have clinics. And we have a show in the spring. The Piedmont Driving Club has picnic drives, often visiting the stately homes of Virginia, with a picnic afterwards. It's great fun. They tend to be active when the hunting season isn't – say April to October, and their big show is at Foxcroft in September. The Blue Ridge Driving Society is brand new. It's for people already into driving – intermediate and advanced drivers. Their focus is outreach to save the countryside."*

Marged is an attorney at the Environmental Protection Agency in Washington, and her work interferes with her love of horse sports. She notes:

*"Driving is the fastest growing equestrian sport in America. You don't have to have the athleticism needed for foxhunting. I used to hunt, but with a job in Washington I couldn't stay in shape. So I got some ponies and they taught me to drive. Now we have five Hackneys. Driving a pair is easier than a single – they give each other confidence."*

During this conversation she and Mike have unloaded the horses – a mother

PHOTO BY THE AUTHOR

*Unloading Marged's carriage*

and daughter named Florence and Preference, the carriage and a mountain of tack. Putting to begins, and Edie comments:

*"And I think it takes me a long time to get ready for foxhunting! Look at all this stuff here."*

Marged adds, *"It takes me about a half hour to get ready."* She scolds Mike for doing a casual job of dusting off the carriage. His reply:

*"You're not going to see dust on a black carriage. I'm a young single man and you should see my apartment."*

[Marged]: *"Mike, that's a very bad attitude. Jack wouldn't approve. [then, to me] …This is like the Wooden Boat Club."*

The Wooden Boat Club is an association of yachtsmen who own, maintain and and love antique wooden craft. Curious, I ask Marged, *"How do you know about the Wooden Boat Club?"*

*"I grew up sailing. Driving is so much like sailing it's ridiculous."*

Then, forgetting sailing, she adds:

*"You can do anything you want to, and still do it with horses."*

With that we have a lesson in the steps involved in putting to. Marged begins to explain:

*"The harness goes on in a precise order – established over time, based on safety…*

*First, the collar. I use full collars because they give the horse's shoulder more range of motion than a breast plate harness.*

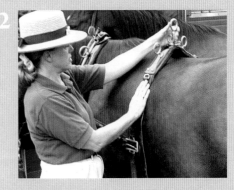

*Next, the saddle – girth looser than a riding saddle – fasten the hames (brass ribs around the collar) tugs to the saddle.*

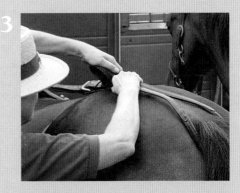

*The crupper and back strap then go on. These keep the saddle from sliding forward when going down hill.*

The traces attach harness and horse to the carriage. Reins then run from bit back through terrets and are placed under the back strap.

The bridle, with blinkers to keep the horse focused forward, carries a Liverpool bit, a traditional driving bit with five different settings for adjustments that can be done on the road.

The horses are then walked to their position on the pole.

The reins (coupled here because we have two horses) are first fastened to the bits, then pole straps…

…then traces — outside first (this order ensures maximum control, e.g. safety, while hooking up) — are attached to the single tree.

*"…Then the whip [driver] checks the rigging\*, gathers the reins, and climbs aboard."*

We go on a short drive from our mare barn to the lawn up hill from the house. There the carriage arouses the curiosity of the mountain field horses, who peer over the fence at the strange contraption that seems to be chasing members

---

\* *"I couldn't resist using sailing terminology!"*

*Mountain field horses peering over the fence*

of their own species, perhaps a predator intent on killing and eating them. Regardless, the mountain field horses show no fear of being eaten, but they do want to know more about the strange new thing in their back yard.

## – Competitive Driving –

The combination of Marged Harris, Candy Smith and Wendy Ying – enthusiasts extraordinaire – has steered me into the world of competitive driving. Loosely speaking, this activity can be subdivided into a number of parts, formally identified by letters in major combined driving events, closely following the three-day event pattern.

- **A 1**. Exhibiting horse(s), vehicle, driver and staff in a show ring, loosely equivalent to an appointments class at a horse show. Considers fit of harness, correctness of vehicle, spares, etc.

- **A 2**. Dressage – but with a vehicle attached

- **B.** A demanding cross-country "Marathon" phase, its segments to be accomplished at varying speeds including difficult obstacles, to create an up to 27 kilometer driving equivalent of the three-day eventing cross-country element.

- **C.** Cones – the process of driving a narrow and tortuous course between cones that if dislodged result in penalty points – analogous to show jumping.

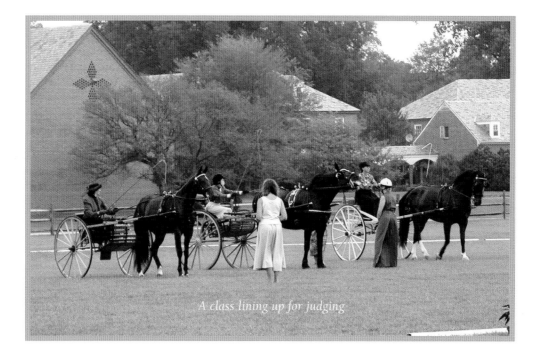

A class lining up for judging

## – Piedmont Driving Club Show –

If Charley hasn't convinced you that *"Coaching exhibitions are heavily about presentation"* you need only to go to the two day Piedmont event at Foxcroft. Here there are 29 classes in the main ring and 19 in the cones ring, supplemented by five in a "Marathon," a drive of three and a half miles. But the heart of this show is the main ring, and the winning formula there is presentation.

PHOTO BY THE AUTHOR

Ladies' hats count!

PHOTO BY THE AUTHOR

Candy Smith driving a Bird in Hand Eagle, with son Ken.

*Ayrshire coach and team*

Queen of the Show is the Ayrshire Park Drag with its team of four gray Shires, staffed by a crew of five – driver, footmen, and grooms – with five attendants on the ground to keep horse, tack and vehicle shiny at all times.

Typical exhibitors, however, drive smaller two- or four-wheeled vehicles with a crew of whip and groom.

Not all classes are deadly serious. Betsy Smith drives mules. In this show Apple Jack won the class with carriage dog(s), dressed as you can see in a farm outfit, obviously appropriate for his class of equines.

*Betsy Smith and Apple Jack*

Wendy Ying has invited me to attend her clinic, with Stirling Graburn as clinician, to be followed by a combined driving marathon practice over the new course behind her barn. It is Sunday in early October, and the weather is gorgeous – a Kodachrome day, if the digital camera has not yet made that expression obsolete.

The schedule includes a seminar on the fine points of driving – for example the technique for switching the horse(s) from one rein to the other while navigating tight turns – much more complex than just twisting the steering wheel.

Next comes the practical phase of the event, runs by about a dozen "competitors" to inaugurate Wendy's new course. But first some background on its owner.

Wendy Ying – make that Dr. Wendy Ying – is a graduate of the School of Veterinary Medicine at North Carolina State University. After introducing me to her guest, Mickie Bowen (a driving judge from Pennsylvania) Wendy explains how she got into driving:

> *"While at NC State I did some foxhunting. A neighbor down the road, Dede Bushneck, offered a driving lesson at a hunt ball auction, and I bought it.*
>
> *"Then I realized how much fun it was – you could wear fabulous hats. And I never met such marvelous people as in driving. They want to do well in competition, but they don't want you to fail, either. They don't want to win that way.*
>
> *"In driving, all breeds and sizes of ponies and horses can win, and people with disabilities can compete. Most of us weren't brought up with driving, but people love it, moving from singles to pairs to four-in-hands.*
>
> *"When I moved to Virginia I had to pick and choose what to do with horses. Now my veterinary practice specializes in equine dentistry. As a side line I breed and show Irish Draught horses. Mine are the only ones in driving competition in the US. There are about 75 Irish Draught mares in the country, but most are strictly broodmares. I also hunt mine and lend them to Pony Club kids to go Beagling "*

I ask, *"But how does this explain the new combined driving course?"*

> *"While in North Carolina I participated in one day events – driving trials – in Southern Pines. I saw the need for something like them here so people could school green horses and get the confidence to move up to bigger*

*shows. No one would make their first hunter show the regular working hunter classes at Devon.*

*"Then for a time I taught at Morven Park. I wondered why we didn't have more schooling opportunities before beginning combined driving competition. That inspired me to build this course and have a clinic. Now we hope to have four such events a year. And in the winter we use the indoor space for arena trials."*

*"Don't some events put tennis balls on top of the cones to show when they've been nudged,"* I ask.

*"Yes, but we can't do that here. My Labradors make off with the tennis balls!"*

SPECIAL CARRIAGES

Higher levels of combined driving require special carriages to be competitive.

Of particular interest in Wendy's carriage shed is her high tech modern competition vehicle, carefully engineered for light weight, stability, driver and navigator security, turning ability, braking and all the other qualifications needed to help your horses or ponies get you around the marathon course safely and quickly. Contact the European Carriage Company and order its "Batmobile" model.

PHOTO BY THE AUTHOR

*Wendy Ying and her Batmobile*

PHOTO BY THE AUTHOR

*Sybil Humphrey's Kuhnle K-140 competition carriage*

Or, if you wish a less Americanized model name, consider this – the K-140 from Kuhnle in Germany. Competition carriages must conform to minimum width and weight specifications, avoiding instability and light-weighting that might compromise safety. "K-140" of course, comes from the vehicle's weight – 140 kilograms.

Out on the course the practical driving event is under way, judges posted – actually, sitting in camp chairs – at strategic points from which to watch each obstacle. These include a forest of vertical posts, arranged as a maze through which horse and carriage must twist and turn in and out of them along a prescribed path; a steep double bank, also with posts; and a water hazard which one must enter and emerge from in three different ways.

After each obstacle the practice course makes a loop into the surrounding countryside to put a distance of at least one kilometer between obstacles, as prescribed by competition standards. Wendy later explains:

> *"If you put the obstacles in a concentrated space you can erect a grandstand where trainers and spectators can see all the action and not have to station themselves by a single hazard."*

While you can see them all from a central spot you are not close enough to photograph them, so I select the water hazard to photograph. The judge across the way is Wayne Porter. Next to the water is a gate through which contestants pass and turn left or right into the woods. Passing through the gate one pair hesitates, not knowing which way to go.

PHOTO BY THE AUTHOR

*Dana Bright driving a pair of green Welsh ponies*

They look at me and I say, pointing to the right, *"The previous ones went that way."* From the reaction of Wayne I fear I have made an error, so I explain, *"…in the military we were encouraged to get help from friendly natives."* He replies that this isn't the military, and that outside help is verboten. But his final comment is consoling:

*"Don't worry, this isn't for big bucks."*

Besides, time is of the essence in combined driving and this entry is slow enough to lose on time faults.

Various entries navigate the water successfully, some cautiously, others with

PHOTOS BY THE AUTHOR

*Through the water, Sue and Dan Wierback…*

*…brought their own Weyerbacher beer to the party*

panache. Only a green pair of Fjords have trouble – this is their first such event. These stylish horses seem top drawer until confronted with getting their feet wet. Perhaps they remember that in their country of origin – Norway – the fjords for which they are named are cold and precipitously deep. They halt at water's edge, looking at it suspiciously. The driver flicks a whip over the near horse's back, imploring, *"Come on, Tobin."* Tobin and his harness mate advance six inches. Again, more

PHOTO BY THE AUTHOR

*Fjords approach the water*

*Fjords hesitate at the water...*

*Fjords drink the water. Navigator on the ground...*

PHOTOS BY THE AUTHOR

*Fjords finally enter the water.*

sternly, *"Come on. Tobin."* There is a lot of one way talk in driving. Tobin lowers his head to inspect the muddy water.

Apparently he's thinking *"Do they want me to drink this stuff?"* The groom gets off and moves to Tobin's head. (Wayne Porter tells me later that putting the groom – actually, in combined driving the non-driver is called "navigator" – on the ground costs 20 fault points.) With human encouragement the Fjords enter the water – *"Goood boy, Tobin,"* – and cautiously complete the test. And they still look very stylish.

The Fjords are the last entry on the course, and Wayne Porter and I walk up to the indoor arena together. He comments:

*"The purpose of combined driving is to show how versatile the horse is – not just to reward the survivors."* *

Then we part, he to his horses – he will have a lesson from Stirling Graburn this afternoon – and I to the car and a three mile drive home for lunch. It is still a Kodachrome day, but this afternoon we must plant bulbs to ensure a colorful spring garden next year.

---

* Wendy later expands on this thought: *"Dressage shows the horse's suppleness, gaits, and athleticism, and the driver's ability. Marathon tests endurance and strength. Cones test ability to be supple after a demanding endurance day."*

## – The Doyenne –

*doy-enne* ( dwa'yan'; Eng. doi'en') n. [Fr.] feminine of doyen (the dean or senior member of a group)
    —Webster's New World Dictionary

During my random walk through coaching and driving circles one name kept coming up with regularity, usually mentioned with a certain sense of awe. From that indirect exposure I unconsciously formed a mental picture of Muffy Seaton. In this image she was a lady in her sixties, graying hair, carefully coifed and dressed, quite formal in manner, and often away from home on pressing commitments. Such a lady was likely to be stand-offish with strangers, especially those who might pry into her life's corners, as journalists and book writers are prone to do. Secure in my preconceptions, but aware that this story required her presence, I picked up the telephone nervously one day, hoping that my new acquaintances among her junior colleagues and the proximity of our farms would push the door ajar.

PHOTO BY THE AUTHOR

*The "real" Muffy Seaton in her element*

On the first call her answering machine failed to evoke a response from its mistress. On the second, a week or more later, a polite voice – I had visions of a uniformed maid – told me Muffy *"has been detained, but will be back by this time tomorrow."*

At *"this time tomorrow"* the Seaton line was busy, but ten minutes later Muffy herself answered my next call. She apologized for not calling me back days ago, and we made a date for 5:00 p.m. a few days hence.

At 4:55 of the scheduled November afternoon I pull into her driveway, meeting two riders coming towards me in the twilight. I roll down the car window, but before I can say anything the lead rider exclaims:

*"Oh. I'm supposed to see you now, aren't I. I forgot."*

Then, despite my protestations they turn around and I follow them back to the barn, sorry to be the cause of aborting their evening ride.

In the barn the overhead light bulb discloses an entirely different person than I expected. The "real" Muffy Seaton is rather tall, athletically robust, and brimming with energy. Nor is she reserved, as I am soon to learn.

She untacks her horse while I stroke him, thinking "quarter horse." I ask, *"What kind of a horse is he?"* …Mistake number one!…

> *"SHE is a Rocky Mountain Horse; she's gaited, very comfortable to ride."*

Soon Rocky Mountain is untacked, and Muffy leads her out to her well worn paddock, where she runs off, kicking and squealing with her mates. She obviously needed the ride she didn't get. Back in the barn I admire a series of ponies. Muffy enlightens me:

> *"Those two are champions. That dun over there is a young Connemara stallion."*

Then she adds other details which, as I type this a day later, have escaped me. (Perhaps they explain why she has a Connemara stallion and Dartmoor mares.)

Outside the barn but under roof I have noticed five driving vehicles, and in a tee-shaped appendage to the barn there are three more. The feeling is of comfortable, happy animals, moderate effort at organization, no time wasted on spit and polish – just about like Trappe Hill. Barn chores over, Muffy says:

> *"Let's go to the house,* [which is perhaps 100 yards away] *and please excuse the mess, we have painters."*

I offer her a lift…

> *"No, you drive over, I'll walk with the dogs."*

And she does, briskly, accompanied by two Border Collies. The house, set against the edge of a grove of trees, feels comfortable but not large. I am quickly introduced to her husband Doug, who is at work in the sink of the kitchen that ells off of a living room with a big stone fireplace, over which a mounted Canada Goose is flying. The uniformed maid of my imagination is nowhere in sight, nor is the household order that her presence would have ensured. It is a home well lived in. We settle into deep leather chairs, warmed by glasses of wine. I ask, *"Driving is growing rapidly. Why?"*

> *"Well, you don't have to be as physically fit, or as brave, as for foxhunting, so it appeals to older people."*

Muffy seems neither old, nor unfit, nor timid, so I ask, *"Why did you get into it?"*

> *"I was a big foxhunter, rode with Piedmont for 13 years, Blue Ridge for*

*seven or eight. And I worked with Hap Puelicher on polo ponies. Then Nancy Bedford and I went to Holland in 1980 for the World Games in combined driving. I'd never heard of the sport. I was amazed what the horses there could do.*

*"I like ponies, but I'm too big to ride them. I had my sister's hunter pony and I got him a little carriage. Then I bought a Welsh pony from Nancy, and got a pair of Dartmoors from Farnley."*

This led her into serious combined driving. From 1998-2001 she was US National Champion with her pair of Dartmoor ponies, and went to Windsor for a meet whose entries were limited to national champions. *"How did you do?"*

*"I was third, which was a thrill. At Windsor they invite teams – a single, a pair, and a team of four. We didn't have a US team so I went with my pair as an individual. There were 10 countries represented."*

*"Was the Queen there?"*

*"Yes. The Duke of Edinburgh was driving, but in another Division. He drives four-in-hand, Fell ponies. My Dartmoors are a British breed – the Brits were pleased to see how well they looked. I guess they expected them to be different because they were from America."*

*"What gives you the biggest kick in driving?"*

*"The gameness of my ponies, their sheer determination. I love their minds. They're so up for this."*

At about this point one of the dogs crowds between me and the coffee table, tail wagging, an action which converts my glass of wine into shards and a red stain on the floor. Muffy apologizes and explains:

PHOTO BY ALF BAKER PHOTOS

*Muffy Seaton competing in England*

443

*"He's new, we just got him from the shelter."*

The mess is quickly cleaned up and the glass replaced and refilled. Sipping it, I ask, *"How about future international competition?"* Muffy is ready…

*"The World Games will be in Austria in August, 2003. I'd have to make the team to go. There are a bunch of selection trials and you have to send a full team. We need to get the funding. It costs about $150K per team, because you have to ship the horses and carriages.*

*"Ever since I got into this I've been promoting driving ponies. They're not just for kids, so the number of ponies has steadily increased – maybe only 200 in combined driving, but God knows how many back yard ponies there are."*

*"How about breeding? How many foals a year?"*

*"We have two or three a year here. Dartmoors are an endangered species, only 12 stallions in the country. Farnley Farm [located in Clarke County, VA.] is the Dartmoor reserve for domestic stock. All my stock came from England, and they have great bloodlines. We sell the foals to little old ladies, to breeders, and to kids – they make wonderful children's ponies. People buy the foals within two weeks of when they are born – of course they stay with mother until they're weaned – and typically we get about $3K each for them."*

*"How do you equate the various elements of what you do? Which do you like best?"*

*"Competition is an addiction. I'd feel lost without it.*

*Muffy Seaton driving a four-pony team in competition at Gladstone, N.J.*

*And I love to teach — that's why I'm so hard to find. It's an addiction, too."*

Muffy is in great demand as a coach, and as a conductor of clinics on driving, and now goes regularly to Oregon for that purpose.

*"And breeding — I love having the babies and promoting the Dartmoor breed. They make people smile. That's the joy of them, to have more of that is great. And the babies are really cute."*

*"But what don't you like?"* Muffy is slow in answering. Then, finally:

*"Okra! It's like eating slugs! Ugh!"*

*"What else do you want to do with your career?"* In view of her schedule it seems — in retrospect — like a stupid question.

*"Well, we have sheep, and a great Border Collie, so I'm trying to get into Sheep Dog Trials."*

On that cue the dogs start barking, the door opens, a young woman enters and I'm introduced to Erin O'Brien. I ask, *"Are you a relative?"*

*"No, but I'm a relative-for-hire. I live here and work with the horses."*

Muffy continues, referring to our community:

*"You can do anything you want with a horse here, for example team penning, and no one looks down their nose at you. They don't question my Rocky Mountain horse because she isn't a Thoroughbred, they want to know more about her. And it's absolutely gorgeous here. Every time I come back home it's with a sigh of relief.*

*"As for driving, you can take your friends along. Doug is my 'back step guy.' It either will ruin a marriage or make you much closer. He's not allowed to bail out unless I tell him to."*

Doug is tactfully silent, but Erin adds:

*"…That's why he's tied in, with duct tape over his mouth."*

I ask Erin why she is here.

*"I got a job offer and came down. I'd be hard pressed to leave. It's the most*

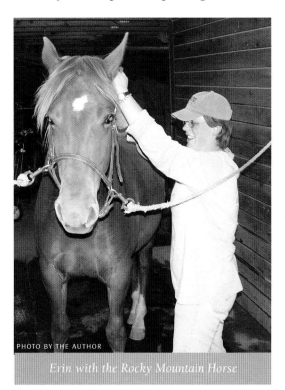

PHOTO BY THE AUTHOR

*Erin with the Rocky Mountain Horse*

*incredible horse country I've ever seen – anywhere in the world. I can trail ride my horse for two hours looking at pretty scenery."*

[Muffy interjects]: *"I hope we never lose it."*

[Erin]: *"In other countries they have control of it. I grew up in Connecticut – you can't do that kind of trail riding there now – and I've been to Europe and Australia on horse related stuff. This country here is the best."*

The reasons Muffy is so highly regarded by her colleagues are now fully unveiled: energy, enthusiasm, focus, lofty goals, persistence and the ability to implant those same qualities in teammates, whether human or equine. In short, they are the ingredients for leadership in any human endeavor. But it is time for me to go.

As I leave I notice three wall-mounted fans of wild turkey tail feathers, and learn that Doug's passion (when 'back step' duty permits) is turkey hunting. There's some of that around the Blue Ridge, too. It isn't just all horses.

### – Seymour Hall –

One of the pleasures of assembling a book such as this is the way in which contact with one fascinating horse person leads to meeting another.

A year or two ago I was going over an inventory of pictures with photographer Janet Hitchen. One literally jumped out at me - two heavy draft grays pulling a carriage and two people across a hilly meadow. Janet told me the owner and driver was Seymour Hall, and that she wouldn't want me to use the picture without his permission. She would check.

Indirect contact thus established, I bumped into Seymour in person, standing along the paddock fence at the Middleburg Spring Races. We fell to talking about horses, and driving, and he invited me to

*"come down to Rappahannock County some time and I'll show you my place."*

"Sometime" turned out to be a few months later. As many readers know, Rappahannock County is a land of rugged wooded hills, tight valleys and old farms where settlers earned a living farming its difficult terrain. It is now also home to the Rappahannock and Old Dominion hunts and to a growing population of wild turkeys and black bears.

Seymour Hall is a native of New Jersey, and once owned a Vermont farm, but now he's retired and, after seeing much of the world, he has chosen Rappahannock County as his home. We are sitting on the second story porch of the old house he is restoring, looking out over beautiful farm land backed by mountains.  I ask him why he came to Virginia. The answer? Horses. Seymour enumerates his own animals: the two gray Percherons, five retired driving horses, and a chestnut for riding. Then he says *"I love to drive, always did"*

The conversation turns to the care of horses, and we find ourselves in full agreement on the folly of pushing two year olds too fast, and the abusive use of drugs on horses. Then, as we start a farm tour, Seymour adds:

*Rappahannock landscape*

PHOTO BY THE AUTHOR

*"I've got tons of bears here that can scare the horses to death. I love birds, but we take in the bird feeders at night so as not to attract bears. Those big grays are sweethearts, most fabulous things I've had. But I don't take them to the top of the mountain for fear we'll meet a bear."*

PHOTO BY THE AUTHOR

*Seymour Hall and his horses*

447

*Harness for a team of four*

In the stable we examine an early combined driving carriage that Seymour designed years ago, made of steel and with special brakes.

*"It's the only carriage I have left, got rid of the others and most of the harness."*

Then, opening a door into a tiny tack room, he says, almost apologetically, as he puts his hand on the lovely harness for a team of four,

*"I shouldn't show you this, there's so little left. I'll never have a four-in-hand again. I probably should sell it."*

The expression on his face says he is not likely to do so; the harness holds too many happy memories. Seymour is no longer married, and lives alone except for a housekeeper. But, with his horses, his rehab project, his farm, his driving and his memories, his days are full and he seems content.

## EPILOGUE

I awoke early this morning, thinking back on my introduction to driving, and wondering what I had learned about it, what it is that so charms its devotees. Obviously it is partly the relationship with horses, and perhaps also the collector's mania for possessing and caressing beautiful relics of the past. But it is also more.

In an automobile, a capsule of steel and glass that encloses you in soft seating and a controlled climate, surrounded by engine hum and stereophonic radio, the driver must still be constantly alert to the hazards of his mode of travel. For most motorists the destination is the objective, to be reached as quickly and comfortably as possible. The surroundings through which one must pass to get there are irrelevant, and often annoying or unattractive as well. Most car drivers are happy to be isolated from them.

In contrast, carriage driving is slow, relaxed and peaceful, providing thinking time. One feels and smells the real weather, hears the sound of the horses and the birds and the wind in the trees. One is not insulated from the surroundings, but a part of them. There is time to notice the details of the roadside – the shine of sun on the water in the road's puddles, the new spring grass or the fall goldenrod in the adjacent field. And one is never lonely – the horse is an ever-present and usually undemanding companion. The destination is unimportant, and there is no hurry to reach it.

In driving, as in a happy life, it is the quality of the journey that counts.

*Seymour Hall and grays going cross country*

# XVII REFLECTIONS

*"The blood runs hot in the Thoroughbred and the courage runs deep. In the best of them, pride is limitless. This is their heritage and they carry it like a banner. What they have, they use."*

—C. W. Anderson

We planned this volume as an exploration of the partnership between humans and horses, the ways in which that relationship has developed, and the human to human connections that have been built upon it. Our story has been told wherever possible by the horses and people who make up our community of the horse. Now we have reached the final pages.

I had wondered as the book unfolded how to end it, how to draw conclusions from the matrix of love, beauty, compassion, danger, striving and ego that humans and horses share with each other. Early in these pages veterinarian Tim Weed said of horses:

> *"I like them because they are aesthetically pleasing, with a fragile athletic beauty. They are complex animals that have evolved to a point where their desire to perform can be detrimental to their health, a potentially tragic consequence."*

By changing Tim's word "perform" to "compete" one might arrive at a similar description for homo sapiens.

One Saturday in May we drove to Pennsylvania to spend the night with sister Katy Place and her husband Bassett, the visit also to include another sister, Nora Wetherill, and an old friend, Nancy Cooke. The next day we would all go to the Radnor Hunt race meet to see Devil's Reach run in the hurdle stakes.

That evening, while the ladies caught up on each other's families – collectively they have 19 children and numerous grands – Bassett and I shared our horror at the current ethics of many now active in our shared profession of business management. Bassett:

> *"Greed, pure greed."*

To which I added, *"They don't manage in the interests of shareholders, employees, and society at large, only for their own enrichment."*

Having agreed on a subject with which we had career-long experience, we turned to the complexities of the Middle East. As the evening wore on we discovered that we knew just how to handle that matter as well, though we were uncertain whether President Bush would call us for our insights.

---

451

Meanwhile, as a lovely wine inspired creative international thought, a predicted rain started to fall outside. Jimmy Day and I had agreed that Devil's Reach badly needed a race – we had scratched him at Middleburg because of deep, wet ground – and that unless the Radnor course was dangerously soft he should go on Saturday though he ran better on a hard, dry surface.

We now move fast forward to the Radnor races, skipping over the difficulty caused by a major traffic pileup on Route I-95 that delayed the arrival of horse, trainer and jockey Robert Massey. Jimmy had brought his 12 year-old son Ian along as company, and the two of them joined us briefly at lunch in the club's dining room. Then it was post time for the first race. Jimmy and I had both checked the course, and separately concluded it was a bit soft, but safe. Both the first and second races went off without incident, and soon it was time for the third – ours.

Devil's was first to the paddock, led by a smiling Isaac Barahona. The white saddle cloth sporting a large black number "2" set off the shiny walnut-brown color of the horse's flanks, projecting a picture of fitness and health. As Edie and I watched, Jimmy said:

*"He's a happy horse. He's quiet, but he's eager for this race."*

Then Robert appeared and it was "riders up." Jimmy gave some last minute tactical advice, I wished Robert *"safe trip, no fouls,"* and they were off toward the start. We decided to go up in the tower to the platform provided for owners, trainers and assorted gate-crashers to watch the race. The Radnor course is not fully visible from any one point, but a television monitor on the platform supplements what you can see directly.

As the flag dropped Al Skywalker, last year's winner, grabbed a quick lead, typical of his front-running style. The first circuit of the course was uneventful. Devil's was jumping well, having no trouble with the ground, and was firmly established in second place behind the leader. As he watched, Jimmy repeated his prior comment, *"He's a happy horse."*

The field of horses moved quickly by us toward the back side on their last lap, and as they slipped from view we picked up their progress on the monitor. Suddenly, at the next fence, there was a confused tumble of yellow silks and brown horse, and Devil's was down. As Jimmy, Ian, and I hurried down the steps of the tower the loudspeaker paged Dr. Leslie. At the far side of the paddock area a man and woman were jumping into an SUV, headed for the far jump. *"We're the owner and trainer, can we ride with you?"*

*"Yes, hop in."* And we did, I in the back seat, crowded by an accumulation of tack and other paraphernalia, and the doctor, the lady, Jimmy and Ian

scrunched in the front seat. Introductions were exchanged. *"Are you a medical doctor or a vet?"* I asked.

*"A vet."*

So we knew it was Devil's, not Rob, that was hurt. As we approached we could see the horse stretched out on the ground beyond the fence, breathing heavily.

*"I hope to God he's just had the wind knocked out."*

Jimmy's voice was prayerful, but his hope was not to be realized. Two men were holding the horse down, restraining him from trying to get up despite a smashed shoulder. A long furrow in the soft ground showed where he had skidded down the sloping incline on which the jump was sited. Clearly he had landed with all his weight on a leg that had buckled, allowing his shoulder to be driven into the ground by the full weight and momentum of his body.

Now he lay on the damp grass, screened from the distant crowd by the yellow curtains used in such cases to spare the spectators.

Dr. Leslie made a quick inspection. It was clear the horse's racing days were finished.

*"Could he be fixed well enough to live out his life in a paddock?"*

The answer was immediate:

*"No."*

A hypodermic was produced, and Devil's days were painlessly over.

Jimmy, Ian and I walked back silently along the track, deep in our own thoughts, as the loud speaker announced Al Skywalker's win. At the paddock I found Edie, quietly watching the next race's entries get saddled. As she looked at me I extended both hands, thumbs down. Neither of us needed to speak, but after she choked back the tears she said quietly:

*"When I saw the curtains on the TV I knew it was bad news. He was a wonderful horse, we were lucky to have him."*

Edie's life has been no stranger to tragedy, and here suddenly was another. Rob was there at the paddock too, now dressed in someone else's silks, mentally trying to prepare himself for the next race by pushing the last to the back of his mind. Quietly he said:

*"I'm so sorry. He was a fine horse."*

Only the grass stains on his white pants gave evidence of his own near miss with serious injury. A day later he told us:

*"He was jumping beautifully. I had him right where we wanted to be, he just landed wrong."*

We stayed that night with the Place family to give our emotions time to settle, and then stopped on Sunday on the way home to see the two year olds assembled at Timonium for Monday's auction. Somehow it was comforting to be in the presence of all those beautiful young animals, to admire and pet them and feel the warmth and life in them. By that evening several of Devil's fans had heard, and as soon as we were home the condolences began. Wayne and Jimmy said it well. Wayne:

*"It's always the good ones that it happens to, because they try the hardest."*

[Jimmy]: *"Devil's had a big heart, he wasn't going to let those horses behind him pass. It was his heart that killed him. [Later he added] …he jumped the best of any horse I ever trained."*

Monday morning I went over the mountain to Jimmy's barn. It seemed necessary to share the beautiful rain-washed morning with that crew. I do not believe they were surprised to see me – it was clear they all shared the loss, for he was a stable favorite. But it was also time to get on with the future. Devil's name was already erased from the blackboard, his stall taken by Flasher. I joined in the routine of bringing horses in from the paddocks, and we watched Seek work. Plans were discussed for each of our horses, and Jimmy will come and look at our two year old Gentlemen colt. He likes his breeding, and his opinion can be helpful in deciding whether we sell him or not.

In all the spare moments since Devil's fall I have been reflecting on his life and death, what meaning is in them, and in our close relationship with these noble animals.

Surely there is tragedy. Animal rights advocates might say needless tragedy, to be blamed on humans pushing animals to unsafe extremes to satisfy some personal ego. That argument may have some validity, though I doubt Devil's and his competitors would agree. One has only to watch them in their work-outs, anticipating the race as they are saddled in the paddock, then sailing over fences together to know that this is what they live for. And those horses that don't love it soon find employment in some quieter haven of equinedom.

There are of course easier ways to enjoy horses than partnering with them in racing, eventing, grand prix jumping, foxhunting, roping, endurance riding or polo. Those sports entail risk for both horse and rider, and horsemen have a responsibility to see that every element of avoidable risk is removed from them, particularly for the horse, a matter hammered home to us by Devil's accident. We plan to address this subject further in a sequel to this volume.

———

But these sports also call for the greatest amount of training, endurance, mental discipline, courage and skill on both sides of the partnership. It is in them that the horseman learns not only about his equine friend, but also about himself. Without them the Thoroughbred and the Quarter Horse would soon recede to the status of breeds whose role in human life has disappeared. Their gene pool would be kept alive, if at all, by a small number of hobby breeders, as relics of a vanished world. There are better fates for Devil's lineage than that.

Now, on the positive side, what are Devil's legacies? He provided years of enjoyment to his riders, trainers, owners, horse care people and his fans. In every race he gave all he had, win or lose, and set an example for all of what one means by "heart." He was a principal in two of the most thrilling races at Glenwood Park in recent years – the Paul Mellon memorial steeplechase, beaten a whisker for third when the first five horses finished within a length and a half of each other, and the 2001 Temple Gwathmey stakes where Devil's beat Rowdy Irishman by a neck, only to be set down for presumed interference on the final turn.

The widely perceived injustice of that call enlarged his fan base tremendously, as well as giving his connections a needed lesson in humility. In short, he loved what he did, and in doing it to the fullest he passed on lessons in living to those who knew and loved him. It was our privilege to share in that circle. Most particularly we are grateful for the friendships he created for us with the Days and the Mackay-Smiths, with his riders and care-givers, and with his many fans.

Finally, what does this say about the horse-human relationship, and our community of the horse?

One of Devil's exercise riders put it well in a note to us:

> *"Words cannot express my sorrow over the loss of your great and much loved Devil. I know what he meant to me… He had a heart as big as a house and a determination to match. I truly would have trusted him with my life. I thank God for the privilege of riding him for two years. Please know he was a great favorite of all who love the sport…*
>
> Tina M. Smith   20 May 2002"

Surely it says, as so many told us at the beginning of the book, that the horse is an equal partner in our equine pursuits. We react to each other, support each other, train each other, love each other to the betterment of both species. Our human community is stronger, our affection and respect for each other greater, our understanding of life deeper because we experience a common bond through our horses.

When I started this book I sensed that this was so. In researching and writing it I have become convinced. Today we enjoy a heritage passed down to us through several millennia. It is a relationship to be built on, preserved, improved where necessary, so that our children – and our horses' children – may continue to benefit each other as, in our time, we and ours have done so fully.

## DEVIL'S REACH

### APRIL 27, 1994 – MAY 18, 2002

PHOTO BY SARA GREENHALGH

*Devil's Reach, winning at Orange County – Danielle Hodsdon up –*
*and jumping into our hearts and our memories forever*

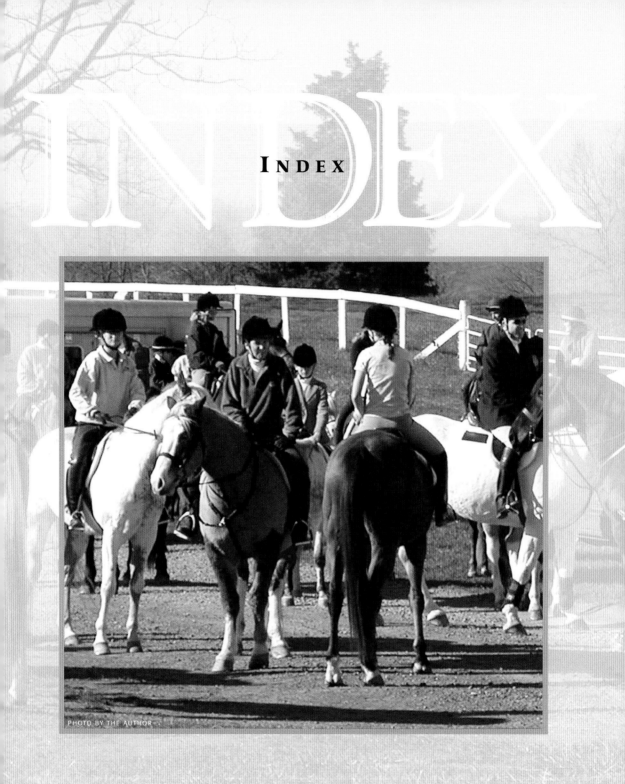

# INDEX

**INDEX**

PHOTO BY THE AUTHOR

─────

## – A Word on Illustrations –

The horse is a beautiful animal, and descriptions of him and his activities are much enhanced by visual images. The author is most grateful to those photographers, artists, collectors and instititions who have made their works available to illustrate this book. These contributors include:

Ron Aira
Daphne Alcock
Howard Allen
Anita Baarns
Carey Beer and Adrienne Hewitt
Alf Baker
Terry Branham
Leonard "Sonny" Brown
Paul Brown Studios
The William Buseman Family
Dasher Chagna
The Chilcote Family
Anna de Roo
Foxcroft School
Juliet Graham
Sarah Greenhalgh
Marshall Hawkins –
     *courtesy of McClannahan Camera*
The Hermitage (Andrew Jackson's home)
Tanja Hess and the M.A.R.E. Center
Flora Hillman
Janet Hitchen
Lesley Howells
Harry Huberth
Kimberly Hurst
Mrs. Walter M. Jeffords
The Jockey Club
Kassie Kingsley
Matthew Klein

Raleigh Kraft
Caroline Leake
Karl Leck
Nancy Lee
Douglas Lees
Sandy Lerner
Sebastian Lezica
Lift Me Up!
The MacKay-Smith Family
Pat MacVeagh
Dan Marzani
Susan McHugh
Kelly Meister
Mischka Farm
Nat and Sherry Morison
National Sporting Library
Kitty Newman
Betsy Parker
"Boots" Parker
Donna Rogers
Dr. Garfield Royer
David L. Sally
Muffy Seaton
M.E. Smith
*Steeplechase Times* and Sean Clancy
Genie Stewart-Spears
Trinity Church
The Virginia Historical Society
Virginia Trails Association

To each of you, and to your subjects, many thanks.

*Bruce Smart*
*Fall, 2003*